ESSENTIAL ELEMENTS
OF PUBLIC SPEAKING

ESSENTIAL ELEMENTS OF PUBLIC SPEAKING

Sixth Edition

Joseph A. DeVito
Hunter College of the City University of New York

Portfolio Manager: Karon Bowers
Content Producer: Barbara Cappuccio
Content Developer: Angela Kao
Portfolio Manager Assistant: Dea Barbieri
Product Marketer: Christopher Brown
Field Marketer: Kelly Ross
Content Producer Manager: Melissa Feimer
Content Development Manager: Sharon Geary
Content Developer, Learning Tools: Amy Wetzel
Art/Designer: Blair Brown
Digital Producer: Amanda Smith
Full-Service Project Manager: Integra Software Services, Inc.
Compositor: Integra Software Services, Inc.
Printer/Binder: LSC Communications/Harrisonburg
Cover Printer: LSC Communications/Harrisonburg
Cover Design: Lumina Datamatics, Inc.
Cover Credit: © ansonsaw/Getty Images description: pebbles in water

Acknowledgments of third party content appear on pages 309–311, which constitutes an extension of this copyright page.

Library of Congress Cataloging-in-Publication Data
Names: DeVito, Joseph A. author.
Title: Essential elements of public speaking/Joseph A. DeVito.
Description: 6th edition. | Hoboken, NJ : Pearson Higher Education, 2016.
Identifiers: LCCN 2016036643| ISBN 9780134402864 | ISBN 0134402863
Subjects: LCSH: Public speaking.
Classification: LCC PN4129.15 .D48 2016 | DDC 808.5/1—dc23 LC record
  available at https://lccn.loc.gov/2016036643

3   17

 Pearson

Student Edition
ISBN-10:   0-13-440286-3
ISBN-13: 978-0-13-440286-4

Books a la Carte
ISBN-10:   0-13-430149-8
ISBN-13: 978-0-13-430149-5

Brief Contents

Contents

11   Speaking on Special Occasions   223

12   Speaking in Groups   239

Specialized Contents

Welcome to *Essential Elements of Public Speaking,* Sixth Edition

It's an enormous pleasure to write an introduction to this sixth edition of *Essential Elements of Public Speaking.* This book and this course will guide you through one of the most important courses you'll take in your entire college career. I know you've heard that before, but this time it's true. Public speaking is a course that will prove exciting, challenging, and immensely practical. It is also a course that is likely to create some anxiety and apprehension; this is normal. Fortunately, the anxiety and apprehension can be managed, and we'll deal with that challenge right at the beginning (in Chapter 1).

This text and this course will help you master the skills you'll need to give effective informative, persuasive, and special occasion speeches and to speak more effectively in and for a group. It will also teach you to listen more critically to the speeches of others and to offer constructive criticism. It will help you increase your personal and professional communication abilities and will enhance a wide variety of academic and career skills such as organization, research, and language usage.

This book is purposely short but not simplified or "dumbed down." An "essentials" book is not an elementary book; it's an *efficient* book. And that's what this book aims to be—an efficient tool that will help you learn the essential skills for preparing and presenting effective informative, persuasive, and special occasion speeches to an audience and to apply these skills in small group settings.

What's New in the Sixth Edition
Revel™
Educational technology designed for the way today's students **read, think,** and **learn**

When students are engaged deeply, they learn more effectively and perform better in their courses. This simple fact inspired the creation of Revel: an immersive learning experience designed for the way today's students read, think, and learn. Built in collaboration with educators and students nationwide, Revel is the newest, fully digital way to deliver respected Pearson content.

Revel enlivens course content with media interactives and assessments—integrated directly within the authors' narrative—that provide opportunities for students to read about and practice course material in tandem. This immersive educational technology boosts student engagement, which leads to better understanding of concepts and improved performance throughout the course.

Learn more about Revel
http://www.pearsonhighered.com/revel/

Rather than simply offering opportunities to read about and study communication, Revel facilitates deep, engaging interactions with the concepts that matter most. For example, when learning about public speaking, students are presented with a Personal Report of Public Speaking Anxiety (PRPSA). The results of the assessment prompt students to examine their level of apprehension and consider how they could reduce their nervousness in public speaking situations. By providing opportunities to read about and practice communication in tandem, Revel engages students directly and immediately, which leads to a greater mastery of course material.

A wealth of student and instructor resources and interactive materials can be found within Revel, such as:

- **Audio Speech Examples and Annotations** In-line audio examples of effective and ineffective speaking approaches are enhanced with audio demonstrations, adding dimension and reinforcing learning in a way that a printed text cannot. In the Public Speaking Sample Assistants, outlines and full speeches are annotated by the author to highlight how the concepts in the text have been effectively applied.

Public Speaking Sample Assistant

Preparation Outline with Annotations (Topical Organization)

Self-Disclosure

General purpose:	To inform Annotation 🔊
Specific purpose:	To inform my audience of the advantages and disadvantages of self-disclosing
Thesis:	Self-disclosure has advantages and disadvantages. Annotation 🔊

Introduction

I. We've all heard them: Annotation 🔊

   A. I'm in love with my nephew.

   B. My husband is not my baby's father.

   C. I'm really a woman.

II. We've all disclosed. Annotation 🔊

   A. Sometimes it was positive, sometimes negative, but always significant.

   B. Knowing the potential consequences will help us make better decisions.

III. We look at this important form of communication in three parts: Annotation 🔊

   A. First, we look at the nature of self-disclosure.

- **Videos and Video Quizzes** A variety of videos are interspersed throughout the narrative. Sketchnote videos walk students through important core concepts, while clips of expert advice and speech examples boost mastery of those concepts. Many videos are bundled with correlating self-checks, enabling students to test their knowledge. In the Appendix, three of the five full-length speeches are available with accompanying video.

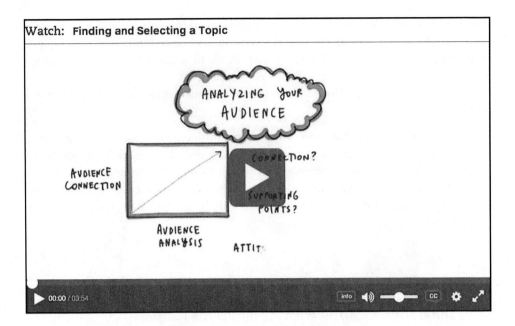

■ **New and Interactive Figures** Interactive figures (such as Figure 1.1: A Model of the Essential Elements of Public Speaking and Figure 1.2: The Steps in Public Speaking Preparation and Delivery) give students a hands-on experience, increasing their ability to grasp difficult concepts. By allowing students to examine specific parts of a model and offering accompanying real-life examples, broad and theoretical concepts suddenly become easier to understand.

Figure 1.1 A Model of the Essential Elements of Public Speaking

Click " Next" to re-create the figure. Use the +/- buttons to manipulate the size of the image, and use your cursor or finger to move the figure around the screen.

Contexts

Audiences

Speaker   Noise

Messages

Channels

Reset   Previous   Next

■ **Integrated Writing Opportunities** To help students connect chapter content with their own personal and social lives, each chapter offers two varieties of writing prompts: Journal: Public Speaking Choice Point questions provide opportunities for free-form, topic-specific responses (one per module) while the Shared Writing prompt at the end of every chapter offers an opportunity for focused, brief responses that students can share with each other.

JOURNAL 2.1 PUBLIC SPEAKING CHOICE POINT

Self-Identification

Claire is planning to give a speech in favor of gay marriage. Claire herself is heterosexual, and she wonders if she should identify her affectional orientation in the speech. *If Claire were giving her speech to your class, what would you see as the advantages and disadvantages of including reference to her own affectional orientation? Would the advantages and disadvantages you identified be different if Claire were a lesbian? What would you advise Claire to do to help her keep her audience listening openly and fairly?*

To access your own Revel account and get more information about the tools and resources in Revel, go to www.pearsonhighered.com/revel.

This new sixth edition of *Essential Elements of Public Speaking* also contains major structural and content changes. All of these changes were made to make the text narrative flow more freely and to give greater emphasis where needed. These changes should make the book easier to read, more easily adaptable to different teaching/learning styles, and more in line with today's public speaking.

Structural Change

There are two major structural changes in this edition.

- The previous edition's Chapter 3 (Preparing and Presenting a Public Speech: Steps 1–10, in Brief) has been condensed and made a part of Chapter 1. This was done to avoid redundancy and to position this brief guide where it will do the most good—right at the beginning of the text in Chapter 1. Another reason for this move was to enable you to see the entire process before going into the individual parts in detail.

- The material from the previous edition's Chapter 6 (Collect Supporting Materials and Presentation Aids) has been expanded and divided into two chapters: Chapter 5 now deals with supporting materials, and Chapter 6 focuses on presentation aids. This was done to give greater coverage to both of these topics.

Updated Coverage

Among the major content changes are these:

- **Chapter 1** (Introducing Public Speaking) contains a new model of public speaking, the 10 steps in public speaking in brief, and a discussion of power priming. Speaker apprehension continues to be included in this first chapter and now includes the complete 34-item Personal Report of Public Speaking Anxiety with scoring instructions.

- **Chapter 2** (Listening and Criticism) has been reorganized, contains a new figure that summarizes the characteristics of effective criticism (Figure 2.3), and a new section on listening critically.

- **Chapter 3** (Select Your Topic, Purposes, and Thesis [Step 1]) now contains coverage on starting early and a new discussion of limiting the topic by subdivision.

- **Chapter 4** (Analyze Your Audience and Research Your Speech [Steps 2 and 3]) contains a revised audience questionnaire, updated examples, and a new exercise on research.

- **Chapter 5** (Collect Supporting Materials [Step 4]) is now devoted entirely to supporting materials (examples, analogies, definitions, testimony, and numerical data as well as quotations, comparison and contrast, series of facts, and repetition and restatement). This change allowed for an expansion of the existing topics, especially numerical data, and more examples.

- **Chapter 6** (Using Presentation Aids [Step 4]) is now entirely devoted to the selection, preparation, and use of presentation aids of all sorts. This change was made in response to the technological advancements in presenting audio and visual materials that are now an essential part of today's public speaking.

- **Chapter 7** (Organize Your Speech [Steps 5, 6, and 7]) now contains all 12 patterns of organization in the text narrative—in previous editions, some organizational patterns appeared in a table. The discussion of the motivated sequence has been moved to Chapter 10 (Persuading Your Audience).

- **Chapter 8** (Word, Rehearse, and Present Your Speech [Steps 8, 9, and 10]) now includes a substantial discussion of cultural sensitivity in language.

- **Chapter 9** (Informing Your Audience) contains a variety of new examples and a new excellent informative speech in the Appendix.

- **Chapter 10** (Persuading Your Audience) now contains the full discussion of the motivated sequence and two new excellent persuasive speeches in the Appendix. The chapter has been streamlined into three major parts: Principles of Persuasive Speaking," "Three Persuasive Proofs," and "Persuasive Speeches of Fact, Value, and Policy."

- **Chapter 11** (Speaking on Special Occasions) contains four new speeches: speeches of apology, dedication, farewell, and a eulogy to provide students with a more diverse range of examples. The classic speeches by Lou Gehrig and Nikki Giovanni remain.

- **Chapter 12** (Speaking in Groups) has been refocused to concentrate on two group speaking tasks: speaking **in** the group and speaking **for** the group.

Text Features

In addition to the interactive enhancements of Revel, this new edition fully integrates the latest research as well as updated examples and photos to keep the text current and pedagogically effective. Throughout the book, readers will find the following features.

- *Ten Steps to Public Speaking* **guide you in the preparation and presentation of a public speech.** The 10-step system makes the preparation and presentation of a public speech more efficient by breaking the process into discrete, manageable steps that are addressed in detail throughout the book. A major section of Chapter 1 presents the 10 steps in brief. Here you'll learn to accomplish everything from selecting a topic to organizing your materials, rehearsing, and presenting your speech. The remaining chapters parallel the steps outlined in this section and elaborate on each step—helping you to gradually refine and perfect your public speaking skills.

- **Learning Objectives** Learning objectives appear at the beginning of the chapter, at the beginning of each major section or module, and in the summary at the end of the chapter. These objectives highlight the major concepts of the chapter and identify what the student should be able to do after reading the text.

- **Ethics** Because public speaking is a powerful medium that can have enormous consequences, it has important ethical or moral implications. In this book, ethics is introduced in Chapter 1 as an essential element of public speaking; in addition, each chapter contains an **Ethical Choice Point** box describing a situation that raises an ethical issue and asks you to identify the choices you have available and what you would do. By the end of the text, you should have formulated a clear and defensible ethical standard to govern your own public speaking.

- **Culture** The effectiveness of public speaking principles varies from one culture to another. Depending on cultural factors, different audiences may respond to speakers in different ways. For example, in some cultures an audience will respond positively to a speaker who appears modest and unassuming; in other cultures, the audience may see this speaker as weak and lacking in confidence. A direct style will prove clear and persuasive in some cultures but may appear invasive and inappropriate in others.

  As a result of the tremendous cultural variations in the ways in which people respond to speakers and speeches and the fact that we are all now living in a multicultural world, cultural insights are integrated into each of the 12 chapters. Among the issues discussed are how members of different cultures give and respond to public criticism (Chapter 2), the cultural factors a speaker should consider when analyzing different audiences (Chapter 4), and the cultural differences in audience responses to emotional and credibility appeals (Chapter 10).

- *The Appendix of Sample Speeches* **provides models that show the public speaking concepts in action.** Five annotated speeches are provided to illustrate the various elements and strategies of public speaking. Two speeches (an informative speech on biases and a persuasive speech on prenups) were purposely written to illustrate what *not* to do. These speeches include annotations that focus on the common problems students may encounter as well as suggested correctives to improve the speeches. All of the other speeches and outlines are models of effectiveness and will show you what good speeches look like. In Revel, the three positive speeches are accompanied by videos of their student authors presenting their work. The annotations will help further guide you through the essential steps of public speaking.

- **Public Speaking Exercises** appear at the end of every chapter and ask students to work actively with the concepts discussed in the text and cover a wide variety of essential communication skills. Completing these experiences will help readers apply the material in the chapter to specific situations and thereby increase and perfect their own communication skills. In Revel, the Experiences are often interactive or short-answer writing opportunities.

- **New summary tables and bulleted lists** throughout the text summarize major sections, making it easier for students to review section content and fix it more firmly in memory. In Revel, the summaries are often interactive drag-and-drop quizzing features.

- **Photo captions,** called **Viewpoints,** ask readers to consider a variety of public speaking issues, many of which are research based and/or focus on the themes of social media, the workplace, and culture.

Instructor and Student Resources

Key instructor resources include an Instructor's Manual (ISBN 0-13-440675-3), TestBank, (ISBN 0-13-430152-8), and PowerPoint Presentation Package (ISBN 0-13-430151-X). These supplements are available at www.pearsonhighered.com/irc (instructor login required). MyTest online test-generating software (ISBN 0-13-440676-1) is available at www.pearsonmytest.com (instructor login required). For a complete list of the instructor and student resources available with the text, please visit the Pearson Communication catalog, at www.pearsonhighered.com/communication.

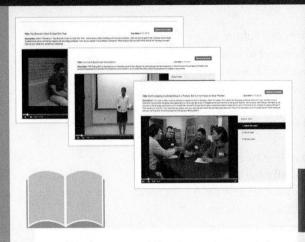

MediaShare is a learning application for sharing, discussing, and assessing multimedia. Instructors easily can assign instructional videos to students, create quiz questions, and ask students to comment and reflect on the videos to facilitate collaborative discussion. MediaShare also allows students to record or upload their own videos and other multimedia projects, which they can submit to an instructor and peers for both evaluation via rubrics and review via comments at time-stamped intervals. Additionally, MediaShare allows students working in a group to submit a single artifact for evaluation on behalf of the group.

← MediaShare offers a robust library of pre-created assignments, all of which can be customized, to give instructors flexibility.

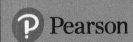 Pearson

→ Record video directly from a tablet, phone, or other webcam (including a batch upload option for instructors) and tag submissions to a specific student or assignment.

- Assess students using customizable, Pearson-provided rubrics or create your own around classroom goals, learning outcomes, or department initiatives.
- Grade in real time during in-class presentations or review recordings and assess later.
- Set up learning objectives tied to specific assignments, rubrics, or quiz questions to track student progress.
- Sync slides to media submissions for more robust presentation options.

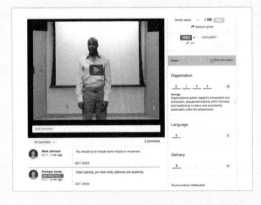

- Set up assignments for students with options for full-class viewing and commenting, private comments between you and the student, peer groups for reviewing, or as collaborative group assignments.
- Use MediaShare to assign or view speeches, outlines, presentation aids, video-based assignments, role plays, group projects, and more in a variety of formats including video, Word, PowerPoint, and Excel.

← Time-stamped comments provide contextualized feedback that is easy to consume and learn from.

→ Create quiz questions for video assignments to ensure students master concepts and interact and engage with the media.

- Embed video from YouTube via assignments to incorporate current events into the classroom experience.
- Ensure a secure learning environment for instructors and students through robust privacy settings.
- Upload videos, comment on submissions, and grade directly from our MediaShare app, available free from the iTunes store and GooglePlay. To download, search for "Pearson MediaShare."

Acknowledgments

I want to thank those who reviewed the text at the various stages of revision; they gave generously of their time and expertise and I am, as always, in their debt.

Rebekah Bell, El Paso Community College

Tracey Holley, Tarleton State University

Pamela Kaylor, Ohio University Lancaster

Gilberto Martinez, Texas A & M International University

Kekeli Nuviadenu, Bethune Cookman College

Albert Pearsall, III, University of the District of Columbia College

Barbara Yancy-Tooks, El Paso Community College, Northwest Campus

I also want to thank the many people who worked so hard to turn a manuscript into this book. I'm especially grateful to the people at Pearson who make revisions so enjoyable, especially communication editor Karon Bowers for her wise counsel and patience; Angela Kao and Elizabeth Rice for their developmental work and for turning printed material into interactive content in Revel; Diana Murphy for managing the book's assessment questions; Barbara Cappuccio, content producer; Dea Barbieri, editorial assistant; Blair Tuckman, senior field manager; Becky Rowland, product marketing manager; Ron Watson, Integra–Chicago project editor; and Liz Kincaid, the rights and permissions editor at SPi-Global.

Joseph A. DeVito
jadevito@earthlink.net
tcbdevito.blogspot.com

INTRODUCING PUBLIC SPEAKING

The first step may be difficult,
but it's the only way to get to the top.

CHAPTER TOPICS

The Benefits of Studying Public Speaking

The Essential Elements of Public Speaking

Managing Your Communication Apprehension

Preparing and Presenting a Speech: The 10 Steps in Brief

LEARNING OBJECTIVES

1.1 Identify three benefits of studying public speaking.

1.2 Define *public speaking* and its essential elements.

1.3 Explain the nature of communication apprehension and suggest ways of managing your fear of public speaking.

1.4 Identify the 10 steps necessary for preparing and presenting a public speech.

public speaking
Communication in which a speaker presents a relatively continuous message to a relatively large audience in a unique context.

Public speaking—presenting a prepared speech to an audience—is one of the essential skills you'll need to function effectively in today's society. The higher up you go in the world's hierarchy—say, from intern, to junior analyst, to manager, to CEO—the more important public speaking becomes. This text explains the essential skills and strategies that you'll need to prepare and present effective public speeches. And, as you'll see throughout this text, these skills will also prove useful to you in a variety of other communication situations as well.

Although public speaking principles were probably developed soon after our species began to talk, it was in ancient Greece and Rome that our tradition of public speaking got its start. This Greco–Roman tradition has been enriched by the experiments, surveys, field studies, and historical studies that have been done since classical times and that continue to be done today.

Contemporary public speaking—the kind discussed in this text—builds on this classical heritage with its emphasis on substance, ethical responsibilities of the speaker, and strategies of organization but also incorporates insights from the humanities, the social and behavioral sciences, and computer science and information technology. Likewise, perspectives from different cultures are being integrated into our present study of public speaking.

This introductory chapter discusses the benefits you'll derive from studying public speaking, the essential elements of every speech, how to manage the very normal fear of speaking in public, and the 10 steps involved in preparing and presenting a speech.

The Benefits of Studying Public Speaking

1.1 Identify three benefits of studying public speaking.

Fair questions to ask of any course or textbook are "What will I get out of this?" and "How will the effort and time I put into this class and this textbook benefit me?" Here are just three of the benefits you'll derive from this text and from your course work in public speaking.

Public Speaking Abilities

At the most obvious level, you'll become a more accomplished and more effective public speaker. Speakers aren't born; they're made. Through instruction, exposure to different speeches, experience with diverse audiences, feedback on your own speeches, and individual learning experiences, you can and will become a more effective speaker. Regardless of your present level of competence, you'll improve your effectiveness in preparing and presenting public speeches through proper training—hence, this course and this book.

At the end of this course you'll be a more competent, confident, and effective public speaker. You'll also be a more effective listener—more open yet more critical; more empathic yet more discriminating. And you'll emerge a more competent and discerning critic of public communication. You'll learn to organize and explain complex concepts and processes clearly and effectively to a wide variety of listeners. You'll learn to support arguments with all the available means of persuasion and to present persuasive appeals to audiences of varied types.

As a leader (and in many ways you can look at this course as training in leadership skills), you'll need the skills of effective communication to help preserve a free and open society. As a speaker who wants your message understood and accepted, as a listener who needs to evaluate and critically analyze ideas and arguments before making decisions, and as a critic who needs to evaluate and judge the thousands of public communications you hear every day, you will draw on the skills you'll learn in this course.

Personal and Social Competencies

In your study of public speaking you'll also learn a variety of personal and social competencies. Perhaps one of the most important is to manage your fear of communication situations in general and of public speaking in particular. You may not eliminate your fear entirely, but you'll be able to manage it so it works for you rather than against you.

You'll also develop greater self-confidence in presenting yourself and your ideas to others—competencies that are consistently ranked high in lists of what employers look for in hiring and promoting (Morealle & Pearson, 2008).

As you master the skills of public speaking, you'll grow in power; you'll become more effective in influencing the thinking and behavior of others. At the same time, power enables you to empower others, whether as organizational manager, political leader, blogger, older sibling, or member of any of hundreds of groups.

Academic and Career Skills

As you learn public speaking, you'll also learn a wide variety of academic and career skills, many of which are largely communication skills (as you can tell from reading the employment ads, especially for middle-management positions in just about any field you can name). For example, you will learn to:

- develop an effective and comfortable communication style (whether for conversation or for that important job interview)
- use verbal and nonverbal messages with greater clarity and persuasiveness
- conduct research efficiently and effectively, using the latest and the best techniques available
- critically analyze and evaluate arguments and evidence from any and all sources
- understand human motivation and make effective use of your insights in persuasive encounters
- communicate your competence, character, and charisma so as to make yourself believable
- give and respond appropriately to criticism, increase your insight into your own strengths and weaknesses, and provide useful and constructive feedback to others

VIEWPOINTS

Career Applications

How might the skills of public speaking benefit you in your own professional life?

Given that these benefits will permeate all aspects of your personal and professional lives, make a commitment to put a major effort into this course. This public speaking course is quite different from all your other courses—it aims to provide you not only with knowledge and understanding of the topics of public speaking (ethics, persuasion, strategic argument, critical analysis, and more) but also with the skills for success that will make a difference every day of your life.

Here are a few suggestions for getting the most out of this unique experience. Although each class has somewhat different norms for what is, and what is not, appropriate or polite, there are certain rules that are a customary part of the public speaking course experience. Add to these those that are specific to your particular class.

- **Give your speeches as assigned,** whether face to face or online. Lateness puts added pressure on the instructor, other students, and the class as a whole, often necessitating a rearrangement of the schedule—something no one enjoys. So, do whatever is within your power to follow the schedule.

- **Respect time limits.** Most public speaking syllabi are tight—speeches are scheduled so that everyone gets the same opportunities. But that's only possible if everyone respects the time limits. So, when you rehearse your speech, give attention to time and, when necessary, revise the speech so it fits into the time allotted.

- **Listen supportively to others.** Getting up and giving a speech to a class or sending a video or podcast online are not easy tasks. But in a face-to-face class, if the audience acts positively toward the speaker, it can help put the speaker at ease. Supportiveness in an online environment will make it easier for the speaker's next efforts.

- **Give listening cues.** Make eye contact with the speaker and allow your positive feelings to be expressed in your facial expressions, posture, and head movements. Let the speaker see that you're listening. This too will help the speaker feel comfortable. In an online environment, participate as appropriate to the norms established for the class.

- **Avoid entering the room during a student presentation.** This is likely to increase the nervousness of the speaker. It also takes attention away from the speaker.

- **Give your full attention to the speaker.** Avoid playing games on your smartphone, texting, or surfing online during class and especially during a student's speech. Turn off your cell phone, or at least put it on vibrate.

- **Offer constructive criticism.** The norm of most public speaking classrooms (whether on- or offline) is that criticism is expected; it's a useful learning device for the speaker, the critic, and, in fact, for everyone in the course.

- **Come to class regularly.** Although class attendance is important in all courses, it's doubly important in the public speaking course. The reason is simply that speakers need audiences, audience feedback and criticism, and the interaction that an audience can best provide. In addition, you'll learn a great deal from observing the efforts of others.

JOURNAL 1.1 PUBLIC SPEAKING CHOICE POINT

The Importance of Public Speaking

Robert is teaching a course in public speaking and wants to explain the importance of public speaking. *Assuming he was teaching your specific class, what are some of the things Robert might say to convince your class of the significance and value of public speaking skills?*

The Essential Elements of Public Speaking

1.2 Define *public speaking* and its essential elements.

Figure 1.1 presents a model of public speaking to illustrate some of the important concepts and processes.

Speaker

In public speaking, the **speaker** delivers a talk and usually is not interrupted, unlike conversation, in which the speaking turns are short and there are frequent interruptions. As the public speaker, you're the center of the transaction: You and your speech are the reason for the gathering. But notice that you, as the speaker, are still receiving messages—from hearing or reading your own material as well as from the audience's reactions. Consequently, Figure 1.1 uses a two-headed arrow to illustrate that messages go both ways.

In this course, your role as speaker is a bit different than it will be later in life. Here you're in a learning environment where you're expected to make mistakes as well as to profit from feedback from others (and to give constructive feedback to others). Outside of the classroom, your role as public speaker will be largely to inform others about something (as a teacher, a health-care provider, or an engineer, for example) and to influence others (as a lawyer arguing for a client, as a parent addressing the PTA, or as a sales representative closing the deal, for example).

speaker
The one who presents the speech.

Audiences

An **audience** is a group of people listening to or reading a message or speech. The audience in public speaking is relatively large, ranging from groups of perhaps 10 or 12 to hundreds of thousands, even millions.

As illustrated in Figure 1.1, the audience is represented as a gradient of color to illustrate that there are a variety of audiences. There is the **immediate audience** who, say, hear the speech in a face-to-face setting. But there is also an audience we might call the **remote audience** that hears the speech from other sources. Perhaps these audience members read about it on a blog, see it on television, or get opinions from Twitter or Facebook. The audience is also illustrated as a parabola to represent the fact that the audience is potentially infinite.

audience
A group of people listening to or reading a speech.

immediate audience
The audience that hears the speech as it is presented.

remote audience
The audience that receives the speech from those who heard/read it or heard/read about it.

Figure 1.1 A Model of the Essential Elements of Public Speaking

Contexts

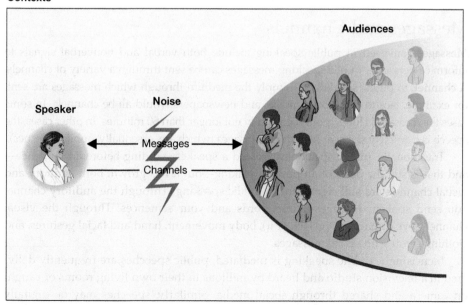

Recognizing that both immediate and remote audiences exist is crucial to understanding the influence of public speaking throughout history as well as in any specific public speaking situation you might name. Abraham Lincoln's Gettysburg Address was presented to a relatively small audience, but it had influence far beyond that audience and that specific time. Martin Luther King Jr.'s "I Have a Dream" speech was presented to thousands but influenced millions. The same is true, though on a smaller scale, with all speeches, including those you'll present in this class. When you address 20 or 30 students in class, that's 20 or 30 people who might relay your message or arguments to others, and these people may continue the process. With social media, remote audiences are becoming significantly larger and more important. As you grow in influence and in public speaking competence, so will your influence on both immediate and remote audiences.

It's important to note that as a message passes from one audience member to another, it becomes more distorted, more unlike what the speaker intended. This is well illustrated in the game of "telephone" where a message is spoken to one person who then relays it to another and that person relays it to another, and so on. With each relay, the message becomes more and more distorted. By the time the message is repeated for the sixth or seventh time, it hardly resembles the original.

Public speaking also incorporates active involvement by the listeners. Listeners/readers are speakers (senders of messages) in the same way that the public speaker is also in part an audience member. In some public speaking situations, during the speech, listeners will tweet comments to which the speaker may want to respond. Similarly, audience members see these messages and may offer additional comments to the speaker and to each other. In other situations, listeners send messages back to the speaker through their nonverbal behavior indicating rapt attention, boredom, or agreement, for example. In online situations, the reactions may be immediate or delayed, sent privately or publicly.

JOURNAL 1.2 PUBLIC SPEAKING CHOICE POINT

Cultural Insensitivity

Ted is giving a speech critical of bullfighting, something he sees as animal cruelty. A significant number of audience members, however, celebrate this as a part of their culture. *What options does Ted have for remaining true to his convictions and yet not insulting audience members?*

Messages and Channels

message

Any signal or combination of signals transmitted to a receiver.

channel

The vehicle or medium through which signals are sent.

Messages conveyed in public speaking include both verbal and nonverbal signals to inform or persuade. Public speaking messages can be sent through a variety of channels. A **channel**, in public speaking, is simply the medium through which messages are sent; for example, face to face, social media, and newspapers would all be channels. In some cases the message is long, though generally not longer than 60 minutes. In other cases, the speech is extremely short, as in Twitter messages (which are, essentially, public speeches).

Traditionally, public speaking involved a speaker standing before an audience—and that is still the basis of all public speaking—but it has grown. Both auditory and visual channels are still significant in public speaking. Through the auditory channel you send spoken messages—your words and your sentences. Through the visual channel—eye contact (or the lack of it), body movement, hand and facial gestures, and clothing—you send visual messages.

Increasingly, public speaking is mediated; public speeches are frequently delivered in a television studio and heard by millions in their own living rooms or caught on camera and shared through social media. Similarly, speeches may be digitally recorded and made available day and night to millions of Internet users. Politicians and business leaders currently post their speeches on websites, blogs, and newsgroups. As video and sound capabilities become more universal, the use of mediated channels is sure to increase in frequency. Advances in technology seem to move computer-mediated communication in the direction of duplicating as many of the elements of face-to-face interaction as possible.

Noise

Noise is anything that distorts the message and prevents the listeners from receiving your message as you intended it to be received. Noise may be physical (others talking loudly, cars honking, illegible handwriting, "restricted access" to an article), physiological (hearing or visual impairment, articulation disorders), psychological (preconceived ideas, wandering thoughts), or semantic (misunderstood meanings, ambiguous language).

Public speaking involves visual as well as spoken messages, so it's important to realize that noise also may be visual. Sunglasses that conceal the nonverbal messages from your eyes would be considered noise, as would dark print on a dark background in your PowerPoint or Prezi slides.

All public speaking situations involve noise. You won't be able to totally eliminate noise, but you can try to reduce its effects. Making your language more precise, organizing your thoughts more logically, and reinforcing your ideas with presentation aids are some ways to combat the influence of noise.

noise
Anything that interferes with a person receiving a message as the source intended the message to be received. Noise is present in a communication system to the extent that the message received is not the message sent.

Contexts

As illustrated in Figure 1.1, the public speaker and the audiences operate in a **context**—a physical, socio-psychological, temporal, and cultural context. The context will influence the speaker, and it will also influence the audience.

context
The physical, social-psychological, temporal, and cultural setting in which communication takes place.

- The **physical context** is the actual place in which you give your speech (the room, hallway, park, or auditorium and whether face to face or computer mediated). A presentation in a small intimate room needs to be very different from an address in a sports arena.

physical context
The tangible environment in which communication takes place.

VIEWPOINTS
Classroom Contexts
How would you describe your class in terms of the four dimensions of context discussed here?

social-psychological context

The status relationships among speakers, the formality of the situation, the norms of a group or organization; you don't talk the same way in the cafeteria as you would at a formal dinner at your boss's house.

temporal context

A message's position within a sequence of events; the time in history in which the communication takes place.

cultural context

The cultural beliefs and customs of those communicating.

ethics

The rightness or wrongness of actions; the branch of philosophy that studies moral values.

- The **socio-psychological context** includes, for example, the relationship between speaker and audience: Is a supervisor speaking to workers or a worker speaking to supervisors? Is a principal addressing teachers, or is a parent addressing a principal? This socio-psychological context also includes the audience's attitudes toward and knowledge of you and your subject.

- The **temporal context** includes factors such as the time of day and where your speech fits into the sequence of events. For example, does your speech follow another presentation that has taken an opposing position? Is your speech the sixth in a series exploring the same topic?

- The **cultural context** has to do with the beliefs, lifestyles, values, and behaviors that the speaker and audience members bring with them and that bear on the topic and purpose of the speech. Gender can be considered a cultural variable—largely because cultures teach boys and girls different attitudes, beliefs, values, and ways of communicating and relating to one another.

Ethics

Because your speech will have an effect on your audience, you have an obligation to consider **ethics**—issues of right and wrong, or the moral implication of your message. When you develop your topic, present your research, create persuasive appeals, and do any of the other tasks related to public speaking, there are ethical issues to be considered (Bok, 1978; Jaksa & Pritchard, 1994; Johannesen, 1996; Neher & Sandin, 2007; Tompkins, 2011).

In thinking about the ethics of public speaking and about the many ethical issues raised throughout this text, you can take the position that ethics is objective or that it's subjective. In an objective view you'd claim that the morality of an act—say, a communication message—is absolute and exists apart from the values or beliefs of any individual or culture. This objective view holds that there are standards that apply to all people in all situations at all times. If lying, advertising falsely, using illegally obtained evidence, and revealing secrets, for example, are considered unethical, then they'll be considered unethical regardless of the circumstances surrounding them or of the values and beliefs of the culture in which they occur.

In a subjective view you'd claim that the morality of an act depends on the culture's values and beliefs as well as on the particular circumstances. Thus, from a subjective position you would claim that the end might justify the means—a good result can justify the use of unethical means to achieve that result. For example, you might argue that lying is wrong to win votes or sell cigarettes but that lying can be ethical if the end result is positive (such as trying to make someone who is unattractive feel better by telling them they look great or telling critically ill patients that they'll feel better soon).

Because of the central importance of ethics in public speaking, each chapter contains an Ethical Choice Point box in which a brief scenario of an ethical dilemma is presented and you're asked to consider your ethical options. In addition, a survey of ethical beliefs appears at the end of this chapter.

ETHICAL CHOICE POINT

Speaking of Religion

A member of your class is going to give a speech on religious beliefs that many members of the class vehemently oppose and plan to boycott the speech. A representative of this group approaches you and asks your support for the boycott. You too oppose these beliefs and yet you strongly believe in free speech. *What are some of your options in this case for being true to both your religious and your free speech beliefs?*

Managing Your Communication Apprehension

1.3 Explain the nature of communication apprehension and suggest ways of managing your fear of public speaking.

Most people would agree that public speaking can be a scary experience. After all, you're the center of attention of 20 or 30 people and you're being evaluated. Your fear is normal. Fortunately, this fear is also something that can be managed and made to work for you rather than against you. So, let's deal with this fear of public speaking, what is called **communication apprehension**, and explain what it is and how you can manage it.

communication apprehension
Fear or anxiety over communicating.

The Nature of Communication Apprehension

Communication apprehension can exist as a trait or a state and can vary from mild to severe. Let's look at each of these characteristics.

TRAIT AND STATE APPREHENSION

Some people have a general communication apprehension that shows itself in all communication situations. These people suffer from **trait apprehension**—a general fear of communication, regardless of the specific situation. Their fear appears in conversations, small group settings, and public speaking situations. Not surprisingly, if you have high trait apprehension, you're also more likely to experience embarrassment in a variety of social situations (Withers & Vernon, 2006). Similarly, high apprehensives are likely to have problems in the work environment; for example, they may perform badly in employment interviews and may contribute fewer ideas in group meetings (Butler, 2005).

trait apprehension
A general fear of communication, regardless of the specific situation. Opposed to *state apprehension.*

Other people experience communication apprehension in only certain communication situations. These people suffer from **state apprehension**—a fear that is specific to a given communication situation. For example, a speaker may fear public speaking but have no difficulty in talking with two or three other people. Or a speaker may fear job interviews but have no fear of public speaking. State apprehension is extremely common. Most people experience it for some situations; not surprisingly, it is public speaking that most people fear.

state apprehension
A fear that is specific to a given communication situation. Opposed to *trait apprehension.*

APPREHENSION EXISTS ON A CONTINUUM

Communication apprehension can vary from mild to severe; it exists on a continuum. Some people are so apprehensive that they're unable to function effectively in any communication situation and will try to avoid communication as much as possible. Other people are so mildly apprehensive that they appear to experience no fear at all; they're the ones who actively seek out communication opportunities. Most of us are between these extremes.

Contrary to popular belief, apprehension is not necessarily harmful. In fact, apprehension can work for you. Fear can energize you. It may motivate you to work a little harder—to produce a speech that will be better than it might have been had you not been fearful. Further, the audience cannot see the apprehension that you may be experiencing. Even though you may think that audience members can hear your heart beat faster, they can't. They can't see your knees tremble. They can't sense your dry throat—at least not most of the time. And there is some evidence to shows that nervousness in public speaking is not necessarily evaluated negatively by the audience (Cuddy, 2015).

You may wish to pause here and consider your own apprehension about speaking in public by taking the accompanying test (McCroskey, 1970).

Personal Report of Public Speaking Anxiety (PRPSA)

Directions: Below are 34 statements that people sometimes make about themselves. Please indicate whether you believe each statement applies to you by marking whether you:

Strongly Disagree = 1; Disagree = 2; Neutral = 3; Agree = 4; Strongly Agree = 5.

1. _____ While preparing for giving a speech, I feel tense and nervous.
2. _____ I feel tense when I see the words speech and public speech on a course outline when studying.
3. _____ My thoughts become confused and jumbled when I am giving a speech.
4. _____ Right after giving a speech I feel that I have had a pleasant experience.
5. _____ I get anxious when I think about a speech coming up.
6. _____ I have no fear of giving a speech.
7. _____ Although I am nervous just before starting a speech, I soon settle down after starting and feel calm and comfortable.
8. _____ I look forward to giving a speech.
9. _____ When the instructor announces a speaking assignment in class, I can feel myself getting tense.
10. _____ My hands tremble when I am giving a speech.
11. _____ I feel relaxed while giving a speech.
12. _____ I enjoy preparing for a speech.
13. _____ I am in constant fear of forgetting what I prepared to say.
14. _____ I get anxious if someone asks me something about my topic that I don't know.
15. _____ I face the prospect of giving a speech with confidence.
16. _____ I feel that I am in complete possession of myself while giving a speech.
17. _____ My mind is clear when giving a speech.
18. _____ I do not dread giving a speech.
19. _____ I perspire just before starting a speech.
20. _____ My heart beats very fast just as I start a speech.
21. _____ I experience considerable anxiety while sitting in the room just before my speech starts.
22. _____ Certain parts of my body feel very tense and rigid while giving a speech.
23. _____ Realizing that only a little time remains in a speech makes me very tense and anxious.
24. _____ While giving a speech, I know I can control my feelings of tension and stress.
25. _____ I breathe faster just before starting a speech.
26. _____ I feel comfortable and relaxed in the hour or so just before giving a speech.
27. _____ I do poorer on speeches because I am anxious.
28. _____ I feel anxious when the teacher announces the date of a speaking assignment.
29. _____ When I make a mistake while giving a speech, I find it hard to concentrate on the parts that follow.
30. _____ During an important speech I experience a feeling of helplessness building up inside me.
31. _____ I have trouble falling asleep the night before a speech.
32. _____ My heart beats very fast while I present a speech.
33. _____ I feel anxious while waiting to give my speech.
34. _____ While giving a speech, I get so nervous I forget facts I really know.

Scoring: To determine your score on the PRPSA, complete the following steps:

Step 1. Add scores for items 1, 2, 3, 5, 9, 10, 13, 14, 19, 20, 21, 22, 23, 25, 27, 28, 29, 30, 31, 32, 33, and 34

Step 2. Add the scores for items 4, 6, 7, 8, 11, 12, 15, 16, 17, 18, 24, and 26

Step 3. Complete the following formula:

PRPSA = 72 - Total from Step 2 + Total from Step 1

If you scored 131 or higher, you would be considered to have high communication apprehension. If you scored between 98 to 130, you'd be considered to have moderate apprehension. A score lower than 98 would indicate you have very little apprehension. ▧

Assuming you're like most people and your score is higher than 98, don't despair. There are lots of ways you can deal with and manage your public speaking apprehension. Here we discuss four of the most important: (1) reverse the factors that cause apprehension, (2) restructure your thinking, (3) practice performance visualization, and (4) desensitize yourself (Bodie, 2010; Richmond & McCroskey, 1998). These same techniques will also help you manage apprehensiveness in most social and work situations.

Reverse the Factors that Cause Apprehension

If you can reverse or at least lessen the factors that cause apprehension, you'll be able to reduce your apprehension significantly. The following suggestions are based on research identifying the major factors contributing to your fear in public speaking (Beatty, 1988; Bodie, 2010; Richmond & McCroskey, 1998).

VIEWPOINTS

Manage Your Apprehension

In light of your score on the Personal Report of Public Speaking Apprehension, what (if anything) are you planning to do?

- **Reduce the newness of public speaking by gaining experience.** New and different situations such as public speaking are likely to make anyone anxious, so try to reduce their newness and differentness. One way to do this is to get as much public speaking experience as you can. Experience will show you that the feelings of accomplishment you gain from public speaking are rewarding and will outweigh any initial anxiety. Try also to familiarize yourself with the public speaking context. For example, try to rehearse in the room in which you'll give your speech.

- **Reduce your self-focus by visualizing public speaking as conversation.** When you're the center of attention, as you are in public speaking, you may feel especially conspicuous, and this often increases anxiety. It may help, therefore, to think of public speaking as another type of conversation (some theorists call it "enlarged conversation"). Or if you're comfortable talking in groups, visualize your audience as a small group.

- **Reduce your perceived differences from the audience by stressing similarity.** When you feel similar to (rather than different from) your audience, your anxiety should lessen. This is especially important when your audience consists of people from cultures different from your own (Stephan & Stephan, 1992): In such cases you're likely to feel fewer similarities with your listeners and experience greater anxiety (Gudykunst & Nishida, 1984; Gudykunst, Yang, & Nishida, 1985). So, with all audiences, but especially with multicultural groups, stress similarities such as shared attitudes, values, or beliefs. This tactic will make you feel more at one with your listeners and therefore more confident as a speaker.

- **Reduce your fear of failure by thoroughly preparing and practicing.** Much of the fear you experience is a fear of failure. Adequate and even extra preparation will lessen the possibility of failure and the accompanying apprehension (Smith & Frymier, 2006). Because apprehension is greatest during the beginning of the speech, try memorizing the first few sentences of your speech. If there are complicated facts or figures, be sure to write them out and plan to read them. This way you won't have to worry about forgetting them completely.

- **Reduce your anxiety by moving about and breathing deeply.** Physical activity—including movements of the whole body as well as small movements of the hands, face, and head—lessens apprehension. Using a presentation aid, for example, will temporarily divert attention from you and will allow you to get rid of your excess energy as you move to display it. Also, try breathing deeply a few times before getting up to speak. You'll feel your body relax, and this will help you overcome your initial fear of walking to the front of the room.

- **Avoid chemicals as tension relievers.** Unless prescribed by a physician, avoid any chemical means for reducing apprehension. Tranquilizers, marijuana, or artificial stimulants are likely to create problems rather than reduce them. And, of course, alcohol does nothing to reduce public speaking apprehension (Himle, Abelson, & Haghightgou, 1999). These chemicals can impair your ability to remember the parts of your speech, to accurately read audience feedback, and to regulate the timing of your speech. Instead, research would advise you to consider the value of exercise and diet. For example, moderate exercise and fermented foods such as sauerkraut decrease stress and anxiety, which should in turn reduce some of your speaking apprehension (Davidson, 2014).

Restructure Your Thinking

cognitive restructuring

A theory for substituting logical and realistic beliefs for unrealistic ones; used in reducing communication apprehension and in raising self-esteem.

Cognitive restructuring is a proven technique for reducing a great number of fears and stresses (Beck, 1988; Ellis, 1988; Nordahl & Wells, 2007). The general idea behind this technique is that the way you think about a situation influences the way you react to the situation. If you can change the way you think about a situation (reframe it, restructure it, reappraise it), you'll be able to change your reactions to the situation. So, if you think that public speaking will produce stress (fear, apprehension, anxiety), then reappraising it as less threatening will reduce the stress, fear, apprehension, and anxiety.

JOURNAL 1.3 PUBLIC SPEAKING CHOICE POINT

Dealing with Apprehension

This is Harry's first experience with public speaking, and he's very nervous. He's afraid he'll forget his speech or stumble somehow, so he's wondering if it would be a good idea to alert the audience to his nervousness. *What are Harry's options in this situation? What would you advise Harry to do if his audience were your public speaking class?*

Much public speaking apprehension is based on unrealistic thinking, on thinking that is self-defeating. For example, you may think that you're a poor speaker or that you're boring or that the audience won't like you or that you have to be perfect. Instead of thinking in terms of these unrealistic and self-defeating assumptions, substitute realistic ones, especially when tackling new things like public speaking.

Positive and supportive thoughts will help you restructure your thinking. Remind yourself of your successes, strengths, and virtues. Concentrate on your potential, not on your limitations. Use **self-affirmations** such as "I'm friendly and can communicate this in my speeches," "I can learn the techniques for controlling my fear," "I'm a competent person and have the potential to be an effective speaker," and "I can make mistakes and can learn from them."

self-affirmation
A positive statement about oneself.

Practice Performance Visualization

A variation of cognitive restructuring is **performance visualization**, a technique designed specifically to reduce the outward signs of apprehension and also to reduce the negative thinking that often creates anxiety (Ayres, 2005).

performance visualization
A method for reducing communication apprehension in which you visualize yourself performing effectively and confidently.

First, develop a positive attitude and a positive self-perception. Visualize yourself in the role of an effective public speaker. Visualize yourself walking to the front of the room—fully and totally confident, fully in control of the situation. The audience is in rapt attention and, as you finish, bursts into wild applause. Throughout this visualization avoid all negative thoughts. As you visualize yourself as this effective speaker, take note of how you walk, look at your listeners, handle your notes, and respond to questions; also, think about how you feel about the public speaking experience.

Another way to do this is to use **power priming**, a technique designed to give you confidence and a sense of power (Cuddy 2015; Galinsky & Kilduff, 2013). You can power prime before giving your speech by, for example, recalling a time when you had power over others, assuming a power position (in which you strike a powerful pose and hold it for a minute or two), or even reading about powerful people or just reading powerful words.

power priming
Verbal and nonverbal movements that make one feel powerful.

Second, model your performance on that of an especially effective speaker. View a particularly competent public speaker on video; YouTube and other online video services make these easy to access and enjoyable to watch. As you view the video, gradually shift yourself into the role of speaker; become this speaker you admire.

Desensitize Yourself

Systematic desensitization is a technique for dealing with a variety of fears, including those involved in public speaking (Dwyer, 2005; Richmond & McCroskey, 1998; Wolpe, 1957). The general idea is to create a hierarchy of behaviors leading up to the desired but feared behavior (say, speaking before an audience). One specific hierarchy might look like this:

systematic desensitization
A theory and technique for dealing with fears (such as *communication apprehension*) in which you gradually expose yourself to and develop a comfort level with the fear-causing stimulus.

    5. Giving a speech in class

   4. Introducing another speaker to the class

  3. Speaking in a group in front of the class

 2. Answering a question in class

1. Asking a question in class

The main objective of this experience is to learn to relax, beginning with relatively easy tasks and progressing to the behavior you're apprehensive about—in this case giving a speech in class. You begin at the bottom of the hierarchy and rehearse the first behavior mentally over a period of days until you can clearly visualize asking a question in class without any uncomfortable anxiety. Once you can accomplish this, move to the second level. Here you visualize a somewhat more threatening behavior—say, answering a question. Once you can do this, move to the third level, and so on, until you get to the desired behavior.

In creating your hierarchy, use small steps to help you get from one step to the next more easily. Each success will make the next step easier. You might then go on to engage in the actual behaviors after you have comfortably visualized them: ask a question, answer a question, and so on.

Preparing and Presenting a Speech: The 10 Steps in Brief

1.4 Identify the 10 steps necessary for preparing and presenting a public speech.

With the nature of public speaking and its benefits in mind and with an understanding of communication apprehension, and some ways for managing it, we can look at the essential steps for preparing an effective public speech (Figure 1.2): (1) Select your topic, purposes, and thesis; (2) analyze your audience; (3) research your topic; (4) collect supporting materials; (5) develop your main points; (6) organize your speech materials; (7) construct your introduction, conclusion, and transitions and outline your speech; (8) word your speech; (9) rehearse your speech; and (10) present your speech.

Step 1: Select Your Topic, Purposes, and Thesis

Your first step is to select your topic, your general and specific purposes, and your thesis (or main idea).

Select a **topic** that is *appropriate* both to you as the speaker and to your audience, *culturally sensitive, and limited in scope.*

Select your **general purpose**. In an *informative speech* you would seek to define a term or theory, describe how something works, or demonstrate how to do something. In a *persuasive speech* you would seek to influence your audience's attitudes or behaviors: to strengthen, weaken, or change them or to move the audience to action. In the special *occasion speech,* which contains elements of both information and persuasion, you would seek to introduce another speaker, present a tribute, secure the goodwill of the listeners, entertain the audience, or serve a variety of other ceremonial functions.

Select your **specific purpose**. For example, specific informative purposes might be to inform the audience about a proposed education budget or to describe the way a television pilot is audience tested. Specific persuasive purposes might be to

topic
The subject matter of the speech.

general purpose
The major aim or objective of a public speech; usually identified as to inform and to persuade.

specific purpose
The information you want to communicate (in an informative speech) or the attitude or behavior you want to change (in a persuasive speech).

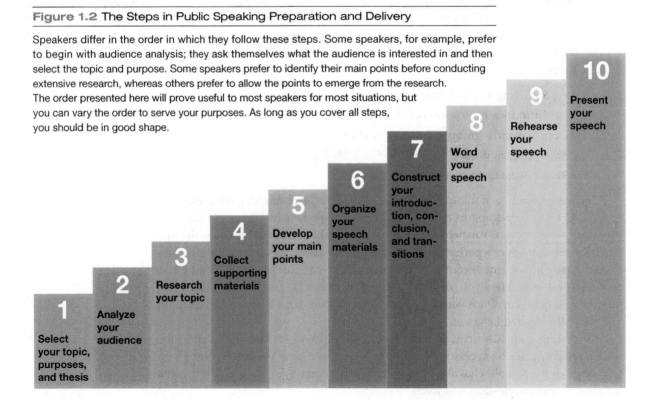

Figure 1.2 The Steps in Public Speaking Preparation and Delivery

Speakers differ in the order in which they follow these steps. Some speakers, for example, prefer to begin with audience analysis; they ask themselves what the audience is interested in and then select the topic and purpose. Some speakers prefer to identify their main points before conducting extensive research, whereas others prefer to allow the points to emerge from the research. The order presented here will prove useful to most speakers for most situations, but you can vary the order to serve your purposes. As long as you cover all steps, you should be in good shape.

1 Select your topic, purposes, and thesis

2 Analyze your audience

3 Research your topic

4 Collect supporting materials

5 Develop your main points

6 Organize your speech materials

7 Construct your introduction, conclusion, and transitions

8 Word your speech

9 Rehearse your speech

10 Present your speech

persuade audience members to support a proposed budget or to influence them to vote for Smith. Specific purposes for special occasion speeches might include introducing a guest speaker to a class, celebrating a holiday, or giving a toast at a friend's wedding.

Formulate your **thesis** or central idea in one sentence. This is the essence of your speech, the one thing you want your audience to remember. If your speech is informative, then your thesis is the main idea that you want your audience to understand. For example: A newspaper company has three divisions. If your speech is persuasive, then your thesis is the central idea that you want your audience to accept or believe. For example: We should adopt the new e-mail system.

thesis
The main assertion of a message, the central idea—for example, the theme of a public speech.

Step 2: Analyze Your Audience

In public speaking your audience is central to your topic and purpose. Your success in informing or persuading an audience rests largely on **audience analysis**—the extent to which you know your listeners and the extent to which you've adapted your speech to them.

audience analysis
The process of analyzing a speaker's intended listeners.

For example, ask yourself:

- Need you adapt your speech on the basis of the audience's age or sex or culture?
- Need you adapt your speech to their knowledge or lack of knowledge of your topic? If they're knowledgeable, then your speech needs to build on what they already know; if unknowledgeable, then you'll need to start with the basics.
- Need you adapt your speech on the basis of their attitudes, beliefs, and opinions?

Step 3: Research Your Topic

If your speech is to be worthwhile and if both you and your audience are to profit from it, you'll need to **research** your topic—to conduct a systematic search for relevant information. The most obvious value to doing research is that it is through research that you'll find examples, illustrations, and definitions to help you inform your listeners; testimony, statistics, and arguments to support your major ideas; personal anecdotes, quotations, and stories to help you bring your topics to life.

research
The systematic search for information; an investigation of the relevant information on a topic; an inquiry into what is known or thought about a subject.

VIEWPOINTS
Analyzing an Audience

Sophia wants to give her speech on the values of atheism. *If this speech were to be given to your class, what are some of the things Sophia would need to know about her audience?*

Research will also help you establish your credibility—your competence, your mastery over the material. If audience members see you as credible—as having done your research—the more likely are they to believe in you—even apart from any specific argument you might make.

As you would in a term paper, cite the research—briefly and simply—in what is called an **oral citation**. For example: *In my explanation of xyz, I'm following the ideas of ABC in the ABC Guide to Corporations* or *as stated in the last issue of* The Washington Post or *the Federal Bureau of Statistics notes that…*

oral citation
The source citation in the speech itself.

Step 4: Collect Supporting Materials

Once you've identified your thesis, know something about your audience, and have begun to do your research, turn your attention to supporting each point. Tell the audience what it needs to know about the newspaper divisions. Convince the audience that the new e-mail system is better than the present one.

In the informative speech your **supporting materials**—for example, definitions, statistics, examples, illustrations, and visual and audio aids—will enable you to define, describe, or demonstrate what you want. In a persuasive speech your support is—in addition to the supporting materials already noted—**proof**, material that offers evidence, argument, and motivational appeal and establishes your credibility.

supporting materials
Usually used in reference to public speaking; enlarging a concept or principle through the use of examples, illustrations, narratives, testimony, definitions, statistics, and visual aids.

proof
Evidence for a proposition.

JOURNAL 1.4 PUBLIC SPEAKING CHOICE POINT

Finding the Right Supporting Material

Assuming you were giving a speech on the development of popular icons, what options would you have for supporting materials?

Step 5: Develop Your Main Points

Once you have worded your thesis, identify the main ideas you want to use to clarify or support your thesis. We'll call these the **main points** of the speech. You can identify these main points by asking strategic questions of your thesis. For informative speeches the most helpful questions are "What?" and "How?" For example, for the thesis "A newspaper company has three divisions," you'd ask, "What are the divisions?" Your answers might yield something like the following in outline form:

main points
The major assertions or propositions of a speech.

> Thesis: "A newspaper company has three divisions." (What are the divisions?)
>
> > I. The publishing division makes major decisions for the entire paper.
> >
> > II. The editorial division produces news and features.
> >
> > III. The business division sells advertising and prints the paper.

For a persuasive speech the question you'd ask of your thesis is often "Why?" For example, if your thesis is "We should adopt the new e-mail system," then the inevitable question is "Why should we adopt the new system?" Your answers to this question will identify the major parts of the speech, which might look like this:

> Thesis: "We should adopt the new e-mail system." (Why should we adopt the new e-mail system?)
>
> > I. The new system is easier to operate.
> >
> > II. The new system has a better spell checker.
> >
> > III. The new system provides more options for organizing messages.

Step 6: Organize Your Speech Materials

The appropriate **organization** of your materials will help your audience understand and retain what you say. It will help your audience follow your train of thought. In fact, you might want to tell your audience something about the organization you'll use—for example, *I'm going to follow a chronological pattern in describing the events leading up to the riots* or *I'm going to first present the problems that the current system creates and then the solutions that will eliminate these problems.*

organization

In public speaking, the pattern of the speech.

Step 7: Construct Your Introduction, Conclusion, and Transitions

In your introduction, try to accomplish these three goals.

- **First, gain your listeners' attention.** A provocative statistic, a little-known fact, an interesting story, or a statement explaining the topic's significance will help secure this initial attention.
- **Second, establish connections among yourself, the topic, and the audience.** To establish such connections, you might tell audience members why you're speaking on this topic, why you're concerned with the topic, and why you're competent to address them.
- **Third, orient your audience;** tell them what you're going to talk about.

In your conclusion, you can do three things (though not all conclusions need all three).

- **First, summarize your ideas.** For example, you might restate your main points, summing up what you've told the audience.
- **Second, motivate the audience.** For example, you might ask for a specific response (for instance, to volunteer at the local hospital), restate the importance of the issue for the audience, or suggest future actions your listeners might take (this function is most appropriate for persuasive speeches).
- **Third, wrap up your speech.** Develop a crisp ending that makes it clear to your audience that your speech is at an end.

Transitions connect the parts of your speech and will help the audience follow you. Use transitions: (1) between your introduction and your first major proposition, for example, *Let's now look at the first of these three elements*; (2) between each of your main points, for example, *But not only is cigarette smoking dangerous to the smoker, it's also dangerous to the nonsmoker*; (3) between your last main point and your conclusion, for example, *As we saw, there were three sources of evidence against the butler: motive, means, and opportunity.*

transitions

Words or statements that connect what was said to what will be said.

Step 8: Word Your Speech

Because your audience will hear your speech only once, make what you say instantly intelligible. Don't talk down to your audience, but do make your ideas, even complex ones, easy to understand in one hearing. Use words that are simple rather than complex, concrete rather than abstract. Use personal and informal rather than impersonal and formal language.

Step 9: Rehearse Your Speech

You've prepared your speech to deliver it to an audience, so your next step is **rehearsal**. Practice your speech, from start to finish, out loud, at least four times before presenting it in class. During these rehearsals, time your speech to make sure that you stay within the specified time limits. Include in your outline any notes that you want

rehearsal

The process of practicing the delivery of your public speech.

to remember during the actual speech—notes to remind you to use a presentation aid, for example, or to read a quotation.

Speak extemporaneously, a method in which you rehearse your speech thoroughly but you avoid memorizing it. You may, however, wish to memorize your main points and their order and perhaps your introduction and conclusion.

Step 10: Present Your Speech

In your actual presentation, use your voice and bodily action to reinforce your message. Make it easy for your listeners to understand your speech. Any vocal or body movements that draw attention to themselves (and away from what you're saying) should be avoided. Here are a few guidelines that will prove helpful.

- When called on to speak, approach the front of the room with enthusiasm; even if, like most speakers, you feel nervous, show your desire to speak with your listeners.
- When at the front of the room, don't begin immediately; instead, pause, engage your audience eye to eye for a brief moment, and then begin to talk directly to the audience.
- Throughout your speech, maintain eye contact with your entire audience; avoid concentrating on only a few members or looking out of the window or at the floor.

SUMMARY: INTRODUCING PUBLIC SPEAKING

This first chapter looked at the benefits of public speaking, its essential elements, and probably the most important obstacle to public speaking—namely, communication apprehension. In addition, the 10 steps for preparing and presenting a public speech were identified and discussed briefly.

The Benefits of Studying Public Speaking

1.1 Identify three benefits of studying public speaking.

1. Among the benefits of studying public speaking are:
   - Improved public speaking abilities—as speaker, as listener, and as critic—which result in personal benefits as well as benefits to society.
   - Increased personal and social abilities.
   - Improved academic and career skills in organization, research, style, and the like.

The Essential Elements of Public Speaking

1.2 Define *public speaking* and its essential elements.

2. Public speaking is a transactional process in which (1) a speaker (2) addresses (3) a relatively large audience with (4) a relatively continuous message.

3. The essential elements of public speaking are:
   - Speaker, the one who presents the speech.
   - Audiences, the intended receivers of the speech; may be immediate or remote.
   - Messages, the verbal and nonverbal signals.
   - Noise, the interference that distorts messages.
   - Contexts, the physical space, the socio-psychological atmosphere, the time, and the culture in which the speech is presented and of the audience.
   - Channels, the medium through which the signals pass from speaker to listener.
   - Ethics, the moral dimension of communication.

Managing Your Communication Apprehension

1.3 Explain the nature of communication apprehension and suggest ways of managing your fear of public speaking.

4. Communication apprehension, the fear of speaking, is often especially high in public speaking. In managing your fear of public speaking, try to:

- Reverse the factors that contribute to apprehension by reducing newness, self-focus, perceived differentness with the audience, and fear of failure by thoroughly preparing and practicing, and move about to eliminate some excess energy.
- Restructure your thinking.
- Practice performance visualization.
- Desensitize yourself.

Preparing and Presenting a Speech: The 10 Steps in Brief

1.4 Identify the 10 steps necessary for preparing and presenting a public speech.

5. An effective speech generally entails these 10 steps.
   - Select your topic, general and specific purposes, and thesis (Step 1).
   - Analyze your audience: Seek to discover what is unique about your listeners and how you might adapt your speech to them (Step 2).
   - Research your topic so you know as much as you possibly can, within your time limit (Step 3).
   - Collect your supporting materials (Step 4).
   - Develop your main points (Step 5).
   - Organize your speech materials into an easily comprehended pattern (Step 6).
   - Construct your introduction (to gain attention, establish a speaker–audience–topic connection, and orient the audience), conclusion (to summarize, motivate, and close), and transitions (to hold the parts together and make going from one part to another clear to your audience) (Step 7).
   - Word your speech, focusing on being as clear as possible (Step 8).
   - Rehearse your speech until you feel confident and comfortable with the material and with your audience interaction (Step 9).
   - Present your speech to your intended audience (Step 10).

KEY TERMS: INTRODUCING PUBLIC SPEAKING

audience	noise	socio-psychological context
audience analysis	oral citation	speaker
channel	organization	specific purpose
cognitive restructuring	performance visualization	state apprehension
communication apprehension	physical context	supporting materials
context	power priming	systematic desensitization
cultural context	proof	temporal context
ethics	public speaking	thesis
general purpose	rehearsal	topic
immediate audience	remote audience	trait apprehension
main points	research	transitions
message	self-affirmation	

PUBLIC SPEAKING EXERCISES

These exercises, presented at the end of each chapter, are designed to stimulate you to think more actively about the concepts and skills covered in the chapter and to help you practice your developing public speaking skills.

1.1 A Model of Public Speaking

Construct your own model of public speaking and indicate how it differs from various other forms of communication, such as face-to-face conversation, e-mail, blogging, interviewing, and small group communication.

1.2 Cultural Beliefs and Your Audience

Evaluate each of the cultural beliefs listed below in terms of how effective each would be if used as a basic assumption by a speaker addressing your public speaking class. Use the following scale: *A* = the audience would accept this assumption and welcome a speaker with this point of view; *B* = some members would listen open-mindedly and others wouldn't; or *C* = the audience would reject this assumption and would not welcome a speaker with this point of view. What guidelines for speeches to be given to this class audience does this analysis suggest?

1. _____ A return to religious values is the best hope for the world.
2. _____ Embryonic stem cell research should be encouraged.
3. _____ The invasion of Iraq was morally unjustified.
4. _____ Winning is all-important; it's not how you play the game, it's whether you win that matters.
5. _____ Keeping the United States militarily superior is the best way to preserve world peace.
6. _____ Immigration to the United States should be significantly reduced.
7. _____ Gay and lesbian relationships are equal in all ways to heterosexual relationships.
8. _____ The strong and the rich are responsible for taking care of the weak and the poor.
9. _____ Getting to heaven should be life's major goal.
10. _____ Money is a positive good; the quest for financial success is a perfectly respectable (even a noble) goal.

1.3 What Do You Believe Is Ethical?

For each of the following statements, place a *T* (for true) if you feel the statement accurately explains what ethical behavior is and an *F* (for false) if you feel the statement does not accurately explain what ethical behavior is.

1. _____ My behavior is ethical when I feel (in my heart) that I'm doing the right thing.
2. _____ My behavior is ethical when it is consistent with my religious beliefs.
3. _____ My behavior is ethical when it is legal.
4. _____ My behavior is ethical when the majority of reasonable people would consider it ethical.
5. _____ My behavior is ethical when it benefits more people than it harms.

These statements are based on responses given to the question "What does ethics mean to you?" that appeared on the Santa Clara University website on ethical decision making.[1] All five of these statements are false; none of

_____

[1] www.scu.edu/ethics/practicing/decision/whatisethics.html, accessed March 20, 2009.

them states a useful explanation of what is and what is not ethical. In connection with the explanations below, you may find it interesting to read the comments of others on this little test—see "ABCD: Ethics" at http://tcbdevito .blogspot.com.

1. Statement 1 is false simply because people often do unethical things they feel are morally justified. Jack the Ripper killing prostitutes is a good historical example, but there are many current ones such as stalking (*I'm so in love I need to be with this person*) or insurance scams (*My family needs the money more than the insurance company*). Even though Jack, the stalker, and the scam artist may feel justified in their own minds, it doesn't make their behavior moral or ethical.

2. Statement 2 must be false when you realize that different religions advocate very different kinds of behavior, often behaviors that contradict one another. Examples abound in almost every issue of a daily newspaper.

3. Statement 3 must be false when you realize so much discrimination against certain people is perfectly legal in many parts of the world, and, in many countries, war (even preemptive war) is legal.

4. Statement 4 is false because the thinking of the majority changes with the times and has often proven to be extremely immoral. The burning of people supposed to be witches or of those who spoke out against majority opinion (as in the Inquisition) are good examples.

5. Statement 5 is also false. Realize that the burning of innocent people who were labeled "witches," for example, was in the interest of the majority as were slavery and discrimination against gay men and lesbians, certain religions, or different races. But, despite this majority interest, we'd readily recognize these actions as immoral.

So, how would you complete the statement: *My behavior is ethical when…*?

CHAPTER 2

LISTENING AND CRITICISM

Listening is crucial in all forms of communication and a skill worth cultivating.

CHAPTER TOPICS

Listening in Public Speaking

Guidelines for Listening

Criticism in Public Speaking

Listening, Criticism, and Culture

LEARNING OBJECTIVES

2.1 Define *listening,* explain its five stages, and identify the suggestions for improvement at each stage.

2.2 Identify the guidelines to improve your own listening.

2.3 Define *criticism* and its role in public speaking and identify the guidelines for giving and receiving criticism.

2.4 Identify some of the ways in which culture influences listening and criticism.

Listening in Public Speaking

2.1 Define *listening*, explain its five stages, and identify the suggestions for improvement at each stage.

In light of Facebook, Twitter, wikis, and blogs, we need to expand the traditional definition of listening as the receiving and processing of *auditory* signals. If posting messages on social media sites is part of human communication (which it surely is), then reading these messages must also be part of human communication and most logically a part of listening. **Listening**, then, may be defined as *the process of receiving, understanding, remembering, evaluating, and responding to verbal and/or nonverbal messages.*

Effective listening will help you increase the amount of information you learn and will decrease the time you need to learn it. It will help you distinguish logical from illogical appeals and thus decrease your chances of getting duped. And effective listening will help you become a better public speaker. When you listen effectively to other speakers, you'll see more clearly what works and what doesn't work (and why); this will help you identify the principles of public speaking to follow along with the pitfalls to avoid.

Speakers also have a responsibility to help the audience listen, to make it as easy and as comfortable for them to do so. As you'll see throughout this text, the best way for speakers to help listeners is to follow the principles of public speaking. For example, giving audience members a preview of what you're going to talk about will help them focus more clearly. Using a logical and clear organization will help your listeners follow your train of thought. Wording your speech in clear and simple language and with appropriate repetition and restatement will help listeners understand more easily.

According to our contemporary definition, then, listening is a collection of skills involving attention and concentration *(receiving)*, learning *(understanding)*, memory *(remembering)*, critical thinking *(evaluation)*, and feedback *(responding)*. You can enhance your listening ability by strengthening these skills, which make up the five steps of the listening process (Figure 2.1).

Receiving

Hearing and listening are two distinctly different processes. Hearing begins and ends with the first stage of **receiving**, and it is something that just happens when you get within earshot of some auditory stimulus. Listening, on the other hand, is quite

listening
The process of receiving, understanding, remembering, evaluating, and responding to verbal and/or nonverbal messages.

receiving
In receiving messages, focus your attention on both the verbal and the nonverbal messages because both communicate meaning.

Figure 2.1 The Process of Listening

This five-step model draws on a variety of models that listening researchers have developed (Alessandra, 1986; Barker, 1990; Brownell, 2015).

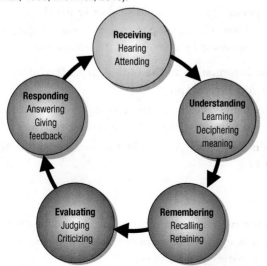

JOURNAL 2.1 PUBLIC SPEAKING CHOICE POINT

Self-Identification

Claire is planning to give a speech in favor of gay marriage. Claire herself is heterosexual, and she wonders if she should identify her affectional orientation in the speech. *If Claire were giving her speech to your class, what would you see as the advantages and disadvantages of including reference to her own affectional orientation? Would the advantages and disadvantages you identified be different if Claire were a lesbian? What would you advise Claire to do to help her keep her audience listening openly and fairly?*

different; it begins (but does not end) with receiving a speaker's messages. The messages a listener receives are both verbal and nonverbal; they consist of words as well as gestures, facial expressions, variations in volume and rate, and lots more, as we will see throughout this book.

At this stage of listening you recognize not only what is said but also what is not said. For example, you receive both the politician's summary of accomplishments in education as well as his or her omission of failed promises to improve health-care programs.

Receiving messages is a highly selective process. You don't listen to all the available auditory stimuli. Rather, you selectively tune in to certain messages and tune out others. Generally, you listen most carefully to messages that you feel will prove of value to you or that you find particularly interesting. At the same time, you give less attention to messages that have less value or interest. Thus, you may listen carefully when your instructor tells you what will appear on the examination but may listen less carefully to an extended story or to routine announcements. To improve your receiving skills:

- **Keep your eyes on the speaker.** Make your mind follow your body and focus attention on the person speaking.
- **Be mindful of verbal and nonverbal messages.** Listen to the speaker's verbal and nonverbal messages, on what is said and on what isn't said.
- **Focus your attention on the information.** Consider what the speaker is saying rather than on any questions or objections you may have to what the speaker is saying.
- **Ignore distractions.** Avoid attending to light or noise distractions in the environment.

Understanding

understanding

A stage in the listening process in which you decode the speaker's signals and grasp their meaning.

Understanding a speaker means grasping not only the thoughts that are expressed but also the emotional tone that accompanies these thoughts; for example, the urgency or the joy or sorrow expressed in the message. To enhance understanding:

- **Relate the new information to the old.** Connect the information the speaker is giving to what you already know.
- **See the speaker's messages from the speaker's point of view.** Avoid judging the message until you fully understand it as the speaker intended.
- **Rephrase the information.** As you listen, paraphrase the speaker's ideas into your own words.

Remembering

remembering

To enhance your ability to remember messages, identify the central ideas, summarize the message in an easy-to-retain form, and repeat (aloud or to yourself) key terms and names.

Messages that you receive and understand need to be retained for at least some period of time. In public speaking situations you can enhance the process of **remembering** by taking notes or by recording the messages.

What you remember is actually not what was said but what you think (or remember) was said. Memory for speech isn't reproductive; you don't simply reproduce in your memory what the speaker said. Rather, memory is reconstructive; you actually reconstruct the messages you hear into a system that seems to make sense to you.

- **Identify the thesis and the main points.** Knowing the central idea and main points will help you reconstruct the rest of the speech.
- **Repeat names and key concepts to yourself.** Fill in the crucial details or important qualifications that support the thesis and main points.
- **Identify the organizational pattern.** Knowing the organizational pattern will help you visualize and follow what the speaker is saying.
- **Summarize the message in note form.** Take notes in a retainable form that makes sense to you.

Evaluating

Evaluating consists of judging the message and the speaker's credibility, truthfulness, or usefulness in some way. At this stage your own biases and prejudices become especially influential. They will affect what you single out for evaluation and what you'll just let pass. They will influence what you judge to be good and what you judge to be bad. In some situations, evaluation is more in the nature of critical analysis—a topic explored in detail later in this chapter.

evaluating
A stage in the listening process in which you judge the messages you hear.

- **Resist evaluating the speech until you understand the message.** Wait until you feel you understand (at least reasonably well) the speaker's point of view.
- **Distinguish facts from inferences.** Make sure you can tell the facts from the opinions or personal interpretations that you're making as well as those made by the speaker.
- **Identify any speaker biases.** These include any self-interests or prejudices that may lead the speaker to slant unfairly what he or she is presenting.
- **Identify any of your own biases.** Your own biases may lead you to remember what supports your attitudes and beliefs and to forget what contradicts them.

Responding

Responding occurs in two phases: (1) nonverbal (and occasionally verbal) responses you make while the speaker is talking and (2) responses you make after the speaker has stopped talking. Responses made while the speaker is talking should support the speaker and show that you're listening. These include what nonverbal researchers call **backchanneling cues**—gestures that let the speaker know that you're listening, such as nodding your head, smiling, and leaning forward (Burgoon, Guerrero, & Floyd, 2010).

responding
A stage in the listening process in which you react to the messages.

backchanneling cues
Verbal and nonverbal signals that tell the speaker you're listening.

Responses you make to the speaker after he or she has stopped talking are generally more elaborate and might include questions of clarification ("I wasn't sure what you meant by reclassification"), expressions of agreement ("You're absolutely right on this, and I'll support your proposal when it comes up for a vote"), and expressions of disagreement ("I disagree that Japanese products are superior to those produced in the United States").

- **Backchannel.** Use a variety of supportive backchanneling cues. Using only one cue—for example, nodding constantly—will make it appear that you're not listening but are on automatic pilot.
- **Support the speaker.** Say something positive in your final responses.
- **Own your own responses.** State your thoughts and feelings as your own, and use I-messages. For example, say, "I think the new proposal will entail greater expense than you outlined" rather than "Everyone will object to the plan because it will cost too much."

Guidelines for Listening

2.2 Identify the guidelines to improve your own listening.

The skills of listening in public speaking are important for at least two reasons. First, listening (to your teacher or friends or public figures in real life or on television and the Internet) occupies a good part of your communication day, every day. And so it would seem logical to learn to use that time effectively and efficiently. A second reason is that you need to listen carefully and critically lest you be persuaded of things that are not beneficial or productive. These same public speaking listening skills will also prove applicable in your personal and professional life. Listening is consistently ranked among the most important skills that both relationship partners and employers look for (Allen, 1997; Brownell, 2013; Salopek, 1999; Worthington & Fitch-Hauser, 2012). To make your public speaking listening more effective, consider using these few guidelines.

Listen Actively

The first step in listening improvement is to recognize that it isn't a passive activity. You cannot listen without effort. Listening is a difficult process. In many ways it's more demanding than speaking. In speaking you control the situation; you can talk about what you like in the way you like. In listening, however, you have to follow the pace, the content, and the language of the speaker.

active listening
A process of putting together into some meaningful whole the listener's understanding of the speaker's total message—the verbal and the nonverbal, the content and the feelings.

The best preparation for **active listening** is to act like an active listener: to focus your complete attention on the speaker (Perkins & Fogarty, 2006). Recall, for example, how your body almost automatically reacts to important news. You sit up straighter, cock your head toward the speaker, and remain relatively still and quiet. You do this almost reflexively because this is how you listen most effectively. This isn't to say that you should be tense and uncomfortable, but only that your body should reflect your active mind.

- **Use your listening time wisely.** Think about what the speaker is saying, summarize the speaker's thoughts, formulate questions, and draw connections between what the speaker says and what you already know. At the same time, avoid focusing on external issues—with what you did last Saturday or your plans for this evening.

VIEWPOINTS
Wanting to Listen

What makes you want to listen to a classroom speech? What makes you want to go to sleep?

- **Work at listening.** Listening is hard, so be prepared to participate actively. Avoid "the entertainment syndrome," the expectation that you'll be amused and entertained by a speaker (Floyd, 1985). Set aside distractions (cell phones, laptops, and headphones) so that your listening task will have less competition.
- **Assume there's value in what the speaker is saying.** Resist assuming that what you have to say is more valuable than the speaker's remarks.
- **Take notes if appropriate.** Taking notes may be helpful if you want to ask a question about a specific item of information or if you want to include a specific statement in your critical evaluation.

Listen Politely

Politeness is often thought of as the exclusive function of the speaker, as solely an encoding or sending function. But politeness (or impoliteness) may also be signaled through listening (Fukushima, 2000). Here are a few suggestions for demonstrating that you are in fact listening politely.

- **Give supportive listening cues.** These might include nodding your head, smiling, or positioning yourself to listen more closely. Listen in a way that demonstrates that what the speaker is saying is important. In some cultures, polite listening cues must be cues of agreement (Japanese culture is often used as an example); in other cultures, polite listening cues are attentiveness and support rather than cues of agreement (as in much of United States, for example).
- **Maintain eye contact.** In much of the United States this is perhaps the single most important rule. If you don't maintain eye contact when someone is giving a speech, then you'll appear not to be listening—and definitely not listening politely.
- **Give positive feedback.** Throughout the listening encounter, though perhaps especially after the speaker has finished, positive feedback will be seen as polite and negative feedback as impolite. If you must give negative feedback, then do so in a way that does not attack the person. For example, first mention areas of agreement and what you liked about what the person said and stress your good intentions.

Listen for Total Meaning

The meaning of a message isn't only in what the speaker says; it's also in what the speaker doesn't say. The speaker on contemporary social problems who omits references to homeless people or to drug abuse communicates important messages by these very omissions. For example, listeners may infer that the speaker is poorly prepared, that the speaker's research was inadequate, or that the speaker is trying to fool the audience by not mentioning these issues. As a listener, therefore, be particularly sensitive to the meanings that significant omissions may communicate. As a speaker, recognize that most inferences that audiences draw from omissions are negative and will reflect negatively on your credibility and on the total impact of your speech.

Meaning is also communicated by the speaker's nonverbal movements and gestures, by facial expressions, and by vocal volume and rate.

- **Focus on both verbal and nonverbal messages.** Recognize both consistent and inconsistent "packages" of messages, and take these cues as guides for drawing inferences about the meaning the speaker is trying to communicate. Ask questions when in doubt.
- **See the forest, then the trees.** Connect the specifics to the speaker's general theme rather than merely remembering isolated facts and figures.

JOURNAL 2.2 PUBLIC SPEAKING CHOICE POINT

Active Listening

Alex is taking a public speaking class that meets at four o'clock, and he realizes that it will take some extra effort to encourage the class to listen to his speech. *What are some of the things Alex can do to encourage the class to listen?*

■ **Balance your attention between the surface and the underlying meanings.** Don't disregard the literal (surface) meaning of the speech in your attempt to uncover the more hidden (deeper) meanings.

■ **Resist the temptation to filter out difficult or unpleasant messages.** You don't want to hear that something you believe is untrue or to be told that people you respect are behaving unethically, yet these are the very messages you need to listen to with great care. If you filter out this kind of information, you risk failing to correct misinformation. You risk losing new and important insights.

Listen with Empathy

empathy
The feeling of another person's feeling; feeling or perceiving something as another person does.

The word **empathy** refers to the process by which you are able to feel what others are feeling, to see the world as they see it, to walk in their shoes (Eisenberg & Strayer, 1987). Of course, you can never feel exactly what the speaker is feeling, but you can attempt to feel something of what he or she is feeling, to listen to the feelings as well as the thoughts.

Empathic listening is best viewed in two stages. First, there is the empathy that you feel for the speaker, which enables you to understand better the speaker's thoughts and feelings. Second, there are the empathic responses that you communicate back to the speaker to let the speaker know that you do indeed understand what he or she means and feels. Let's start with a few suggestions for feeling empathy for the speaker.

■ **See the speaker's point of view.** Before you can understand what the speaker is saying, you have to see the message from the speaker's vantage point. Try putting yourself in the role of the speaker and looking at the topic from his or her perspective.

■ **Understand the speaker's thoughts and feelings.** Don't consider your listening task complete until you've understood what the speaker is feeling as well as thinking.

■ **Avoid "offensive listening."** Offensive listening is the tendency to listen to bits and pieces of information that will enable you to attack the speaker or to find fault with something the speaker has said.

■ **Don't distort messages because of the "friend-or-foe" factor.** In other words, avoid listening for positive statements about friends and negative statements about enemies. For example, if you dislike Fred, make the added effort to listen objectively to Fred's speeches or to make comments that might reflect positively on Fred.

The second part of empathy—expressing your empathy back to the speaker—can best be accomplished in two steps corresponding to the two parts in true empathy: thinking empathy and feeling empathy (Bellafiore, 2005). In *thinking empathy* you express an understanding of what the person means. For example, when you paraphrase someone's comment—as part of your criticism, for example—showing that you understand the meaning the person is trying to communicate, you're communicating *thinking empathy*. When you nod your head in approval of a speaker's argument, you're communicating *thinking empathy*. In communicating *feeling empathy*, you express your feeling of what the other person is feeling. When your facial expressions are appropriate to the tone of the speaker's talk, you're communicating *feeling empathy*. Often you'll respond with both thinking and feeling empathy in the same brief response; for example, *I can understand what it must be like living with a partner who is always depressed [thinking empathy]; you must get depressed yourself [feeling empathy]*.

Listen with an Open Mind

Listening with an open mind is difficult. It isn't easy to listen to arguments attacking your cherished beliefs. Listening often stops when such remarks are made. Yet in these situations it's particularly important to continue listening openly and fairly. To listen with an open mind, try to avoid prejudging, filtering, and **assimilation** and recognize your own **biases** and **prejudices**.

- **Avoid prejudging.** Delay both positive and negative evaluation until you've fully understood the intention and the content of the message being communicated. Also avoid prejudging the speech as irrelevant or uninteresting. Give the speaker a chance.

- **Avoid filtering out difficult, unpleasant, or undesirable messages.** Avoid distorting messages through oversimplification or leveling—the tendency to eliminate details and to simplify complex messages to make them easier to remember.

- **Avoid assimilation.** The tendency to reconstruct messages so they reflect your own attitudes, prejudices, needs, and values is known as *assimilation*. It is the tendency to hear relatively neutral messages ("Management plans to institute drastic changes in scheduling") as supporting your own attitudes and beliefs ("Management is going to screw up our schedules again").

- **Recognize your own biases.** A *bias* or *prejudice* may interfere with accurate listening and cause you to distort message reception to fit your own prejudices. Biases may also lead to sharpening—an effect in which an item of information takes on increased importance because it seems to confirm your stereotypes or prejudices.

assimilation
A process of message distortion in which messages are reworked to conform to our own attitudes, prejudices, needs, and values.

bias
Preconceived ideas that predispose you to interpret meaning on the basis of these ideas rather than on the basis of the evidence and argument.

prejudice
Preconceived and unreasonable negative evaluations, usually used in reference to race.

Listen Critically

In many public speaking situations, you'll need to exercise critical evaluation or judgment. In **critical listening**, you think logically and dispassionately about what the speaker is saying. Listening with an open mind will help you understand the messages better; listening with a critical mind will help you analyze and evaluate the messages. In listening critically, focus on the following guidelines:

critical listening
A style of listening that includes analyzing and evaluating the message rather than simply receiving it.

- **Avoid filtering out or oversimplifying complex messages.** Similarly, avoid filtering out undesirable messages. Clearly, you don't want to hear that something you believe is untrue, that people you care for are unkind, or that ideals you hold are self-destructive. Yet it's important that you reexamine your beliefs by listening to these messages.

- **Combat the tendency to sharpen**—to highlight, emphasize, and perhaps embellish one or two aspects of a message. Often the concepts that we tend to *sharpen* are incidental remarks that somehow stand out from the rest of the message. Be careful, therefore, about sharpening your blind date's "Thank you, I had a nice time" and assuming that the date was a big success—while ignoring the signs that it was just so-so, such as the lack of eye contact, the awkward silences, and the cell phone interruptions.

- **Watch out for language fallacies,** language used to serve less-than-noble purposes, to convince or persuade you without giving you any reasons, and sometimes to fool you.

Listen Ethically

As a listener you share not only in the success or failure of any communication but also in the moral implications of the communication exchange. Consequently, bear ethical issues in mind when listening as well as when speaking. Two major principles govern ethical listening:

- **Give the speaker an honest hearing.** You don't have to agree with the speaker, but try to understand emotionally as well as intellectually what he or she means. Then accept or reject the speaker's ideas on the basis of the information offered—not on the basis of some bias or prejudice or incomplete understanding.

- **Give the speaker honest responses and feedback.** In a learning environment such as a public speaking class, listening ethically means giving frank and constructive criticism to help the speaker improve. It also means reflecting honestly on the questions speakers raise. Much as the listener has a right to expect an active speaker, the speaker has the right to expect a listener who will actively deal with, rather than just passively hear, the message of a speech.

In addition to these guidelines, consider the specific situation of listening in the classroom. After all, if you're going to spend the time, you might as well spend it efficiently and effectively. Table 2.1 provides a few useful strategies.

TABLE 2.1 Listening in the Classroom

Oliver Wendell Holmes once said, "It is the privilege of wisdom to listen." Nowhere is that more true than in the classroom where a large part of your listening takes place. As you read these, consider any additional suggestions that you might offer.

General Guides	Specific Strategies
Prepare yourself to listen.	■ Sit up front where you can see your instructor and any visual aids clearly and comfortably. ■ Remember that you listen with your eyes as well as your ears.
Avoid distractions.	■ Avoid mental daydreaming as well as physical distractions like your laptop, smartphone, or newspaper.
Pay special attention to the introduction; this will often contain a preview and will help you outline the lecture.	■ Listen for orienting remarks and for key words and phrases such as *another reason, three major causes,* and *first*. ■ Use these cues to help you outline the lecture.
Take notes in outline form.	■ Listen for headings and then use these as major headings in your outline. When the instructor says, for example, "there are four kinds of noise," you have your heading and you will have a numbered list of four items.
Assume that what is said is relevant.	■ It may eventually prove irrelevant (unfortunately), but if you listen with the assumption of irrelevancy, you'll never hear anything relevant.
Listen for understanding.	■ Avoid taking issue with what is said until you understand fully and then, of course, take issue if you wish. When you take issue before understanding, you run the risk of missing additional explanation or qualification.

Criticism in Public Speaking

2.3 Define *criticism* and its role in public speaking and identify the guidelines for giving and receiving criticism.

Critics and criticism are essential parts of any art. The word **criticism** comes into English from the Latin *criticus,* which means "able to discern," "able to judge." Speech criticism, therefore, is the process of evaluating a speech, of rendering a judgment of its value. Note that there is nothing inherently negative about criticism; criticism may be negative, but it also may be positive.

Perhaps the major value of criticism in the classroom is that it helps you improve your public speaking skills. Through the constructive criticism of others, you'll learn the principles of public speaking more effectively. You'll be shown what you do well; what you could improve; and, ideally, how to improve. As a listener–critic you'll also learn the principles of public speaking through assessing the speeches of others. Just as you learn when you teach, you also learn when you criticize.

When you give criticism—as you do in a public speaking class—you're telling the speaker that you've listened carefully and that you care enough about the speech and the speaker to offer suggestions for improvement.

Of course, criticism can be difficult—for the critic (whether student or instructor) as well as for the person criticized. As a critic, you may feel embarrassed or uncomfortable about offering evaluation. After all, you may think, "Who am I to criticize another person's speech? My own speech won't be any better." Or you may be reluctant to offend, fearing that your criticism may make the speaker feel uncomfortable. Or you may view criticism as a confrontation that will do more harm than good.

But consider this alternative view: By offering criticism you're helping the speaker; you're giving the speaker another perspective that should prove useful in future speeches. When you offer criticism, you're not claiming to be a better speaker; you're simply offering another point of view. It's true that by offering criticism you're stating a position with which others may disagree. That's one of the things that will make this class and the study of public speaking exciting and challenging.

Criticism is also difficult to receive. After working on a speech for a week or two and dealing with the normal anxiety that comes with giving a speech, the last thing you want is to stand in front of the class and hear others say what you did wrong. Public speaking is ego-involving, and it's normal to take criticism personally. But if you learn how to give and how to receive criticism, it will help you improve your public speaking skills.

A useful standard to use in evaluating a classroom speech is the speech's degree of conformity to the principles of the art. Using this standard, you'll evaluate a speech positively when it follows the principles of public speaking established by the critics, theorists, and practitioners of public speaking (as described throughout this text) and evaluate it negatively if it deviates from these principles. These principles include speaking on a subject that is worthwhile, relevant, and interesting to listeners;

criticism
The reasoned judgment of some work; although often equated with faultfinding, criticism can involve both positive and negative evaluations.

JOURNAL 2.3 PUBLIC SPEAKING CHOICE POINT

Ethical Listening

Simone is teaching a class in public speaking, and one of her students, a sincere and devou Iranian Muslim, gives a speech on "why women should be subservient to men." After the first 2 minutes of the speech, half the class walks out, returning 10 minutes later, after the speech is over. Simone decides to address this incident. *What would you advise Simone to say?*

designing a speech for a specific audience; and constructing a speech that is based on sound research. A critical checklist for analyzing public speeches that is based on these principles is presented on the inside front cover of this book.

Before reading the specific suggestions for making critical evaluations a more effective part of the total learning process and avoiding some of the potentially negative aspects of criticism, consider the following critical statements and try to identify what's wrong with each of them (assume, for the purposes of this exercise, that each of the following 10 comments represents the critic's complete criticism):

1. The speech didn't do anything for me.
2. I loved the speech. It was great. Really great.
3. The speech was weak.
4. Your position was unfair to those of us on athletic scholarships; we earned those scholarships.
5. I liked the speech; we need more police on campus.
6. The introduction didn't gain my attention.
7. I found four things wrong with your speech. First,...
8. You needed better research.
9. Nobody was able to understand you.
10. We couldn't hear you clearly.

Giving Criticism

Criticism in the public speaking classroom can be viewed as a three-part process:

1. You say something positive.
2. You identify something that was not effective (to you).
3. You suggest some way to improve what you suggested was not effective.

Figure 2.2 presents an example of a brief critical comment that follows the suggestions noted in this section:

Figure 2.2 A Sample Criticism

Notice the frequent use of "I" and the total absence of "*should.*" The critic is speaking for the critic and not for the other members of the audience. The critic is giving a personal perception and is not telling the speaker what to do or not to do but what the critic thinks would have worked better.

Here the critic identifies something that could be improved (Step 2).

This comment is clearly owned by the critic; note the frequent use of "*I.*"

Here the critic explained what the speaker might have done to improve the speech (Step 3). The critic's comment is constructive.

I got really interested in your speech when you told the story about the wrongly imprisoned shopkeeper. I had trouble relating to the other examples; I didn't feel they were real. I would have preferred fewer examples but told in more detail. Then I think I would have been able to feel what it's like to be wrongly imprisoned.

Here the critic begins with something positive (Step 1).

This criticism is phrased in an indirect style; some critics might prefer a more direct approach and say, for example, *I thought your examples were too many and too brief to be of any value.* This type of criticism, however, is likely to be seen as insensitive and overly negative.

Notice that the critic focused solely on the speech and in no way attacked the speaker. The comments are also pretty specific, which will help the speaker more than would overly general ones.

In offering criticism keep the following principles in mind. They will explain why the 10 critical comments above are not effective as well as the ways in which you can more effectively phrase your critical comments.

STRESS THE POSITIVE

Egos are fragile, and public speaking is extremely personal. Part of your function as a critic is to strengthen the already-positive aspects of someone's public speaking performance. Positive criticism is particularly important in itself, but it's almost essential as a preface to negative comments. There are always positive characteristics about any speech, and it's more productive to concentrate on these first. Thus, instead of saying (as in the above example), "The speech didn't do anything for me," tell the speaker what you liked first, then bring up a weak point and suggest how it might be improved.

When criticizing a person's second or third speech, it's especially helpful if you can point out specific improvements ("You really held my attention in this speech," "I felt you were much more in control of the topic today than in your first speech").

Remember, too, that communication is irreversible. Once you say something, you can't take it back. Remember this when offering criticism—especially criticism that may be negative. If in doubt, err on the side of gentleness.

BE SPECIFIC

Criticism is most effective when it's specific. General statements such as "I thought your delivery was bad," "I thought your examples were good," or, as in the above list, "I loved the speech…Really great" and "The speech was weak" are poorly expressed criticisms. These statements don't specify what the speaker might do to improve delivery or to capitalize on the examples used. When commenting on delivery, refer to such specifics as eye contact, vocal volume, or whatever else is of consequence. When commenting on the examples, tell the speaker why they were good. Were they realistic? Were they especially interesting? Were they presented dramatically?

When giving negative criticism, specify and justify—to the extent that you can—positive alternatives. Here's an example.

> I thought the way you introduced your statistics was vague. I wasn't sure where the statistics came from or how recent or reliable they were. It might have been useful to say something like "The U.S. Census figures for 2010 show…" In that way I would know that the statistics were as recent as possible and the most reliable available.

BE OBJECTIVE

When criticizing a speech, transcend your own biases as best you can, unlike the above example ("Your position was unfair…; we earned those scholarships"). See the speech as objectively as possible. Assume, for example, that you're strongly for a woman's right to an abortion and you encounter a speech diametrically opposed to your position. In this situation you'll need to take special care not to dismiss the speech because of your own biases. Examine the speech from the point of view of a detached critic. Evaluate, for example, the validity of the arguments and their suitability to the audience, the language, and the supporting materials. Conversely, take special care not to evaluate a speech positively because it presents a position you agree with, as in "I liked the speech; we need more police on campus."

BE CONSTRUCTIVE

Your primary goal in this learning laboratory class should be to provide the speaker with insight that will prove useful in future public speaking transactions. For example, saying that "The introduction didn't gain my attention" doesn't tell the speaker how he or she might have gained your attention. Instead, you might say, "The example about the computer crash would have more effectively gained my attention in the introduction."

Another way you can be constructive is to limit your criticism. Cataloging a speaker's weak points, as in "I found four things wrong with your speech," will overwhelm, not help, the speaker. If you're the sole critic, your criticism naturally will need to be more extensive. If you're one of many critics, limit your criticism to one or perhaps two points. In all cases, your guide should be the value your comments will have for the speaker.

FOCUS ON BEHAVIOR

Focus criticism on what the speaker said and did during the actual speech. Try to avoid the very natural tendency to read the mind of the speaker—to assume that you know why the speaker did one thing rather than another. Compare the critical comments presented in Table 2.2. Note that those in the first column, "Criticism as Attack," try to identify the reasons the speaker did as he or she did; they try to read the speaker's mind. At the same time, they blame the speaker for what happened. Those in the second column, "Criticism as Support," focus on the specific behavior. Note, too, that those in the first column are likely to encourage defensiveness; you can almost hear the speaker saying, "I was *so* interested in the topic." Those in the second column are less likely to create defensiveness and are more likely to be appreciated as honest reflections of how the critic perceived the speech.

OWN YOUR CRITICISM

I-messages
A type of message in which the speaker takes responsibility for the message.

you-messages
A type of message in which the speaker avoids personal responsibility for the message and blames the other person.

owning criticism
Taking responsibility for your comments and evaluations.

When giving criticism, own your comments; take responsibility for them. The best way to express this ownership is to use **I-messages** rather than **you-messages**. That is, instead of saying, "You needed better research," say, "I would have been more persuaded if you had used more recent research."

Owning criticism also means avoiding attributing what you found wrong to others. Instead of saying, "Nobody was able to understand you," say, "I had difficulty understanding you. It would have helped me if you had spoken more slowly." Remember that your criticism is important precisely because it's your perception of what the speaker did and what the speaker could have done more effectively. Speaking for the entire audience ("We couldn't hear you clearly" or "No one was convinced by your arguments") will not help the speaker, and it's likely to prove demoralizing.

Employing I-messages also will prevent you from using "should messages," a type of expression that almost invariably creates defensiveness and resentment. When you say, "You should have done this" or "You shouldn't have done that," you assume a superior position and imply that what you're saying is correct and that what the speaker did was incorrect. On the other hand, when you own your evaluations and use I-messages, you're giving your perceptions; it's then up to the speaker to accept or reject them.

TABLE 2.2 Criticism as Attack and as Support

Criticism as Attack	Criticism as Support
"You weren't interested in your topic."	"I would have liked to see greater variety in your delivery. It would have made me feel that you were more interested."
"You should have put more time into the speech."	"I think it would have been more effective if you had looked at your notes less."
"You didn't care about your audience."	"I would have liked it if you had looked more directly at me while speaking."
"You didn't know your topic enough."	"I would have liked you to tell us more about your research on the topic and your experiences with this issue."

Figure 2.3 The Characteristics of Effective Speech Criticism

Can you identify additional characteristics that might be added to these seven?

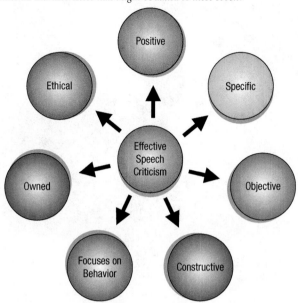

RECOGNIZE YOUR ETHICAL OBLIGATIONS

Just as the speaker and listener have ethical obligations, so does the critic. Here are a few guidelines. First, the ethical critic *separates personal feelings about the speaker* from his or her evaluation of the speech. A liking for the speaker shouldn't lead you to give positive evaluations of the speech, nor should disliking the speaker lead you to give negative evaluations of the speech.

Second, the ethical critic *separates personal feelings about the issues* from an evaluation of the validity of the arguments. The ethical critic recognizes the validity of an argument even if it contradicts a deeply held belief; similarly, he or she recognizes the fallaciousness of an argument even if it supports a deeply held belief.

Third, the ethical critic *is culturally sensitive,* is aware of his or her own ethnocentrism, and doesn't negatively evaluate customs and forms of speech simply because they deviate from her or his own. Similarly, the ethical critic does not positively evaluate a speech just because it supports her or his own cultural beliefs and values. The ethical critic does not discriminate against or favor speakers simply because they're of a particular sex, race, nationality, religion, age group, or affectional orientation.

Figure 2.3 summarizes the characteristics of effective criticism.

Responding to Criticism

At the same time that you need to express your criticism effectively, you'll also want to listen to criticism effectively. Here are some suggestions for making listening to

ETHICAL CHOICE POINT

Open Listening

You're listening to a speech advocating a position with which you strongly disagree. Your first impulse is to stop listening, lest your faith in your current beliefs gets shattered. At the same time, however, you want to give the speaker a fair and honest hearing; after all, you're in college and you should be able to listen logically to all opinions—not just to those with which you agree. *What are some of the things you can do to remain true to your own beliefs but also to follow the ethical principle of giving the speaker a fair hearing?*

VIEWPOINTS

Open-Mindedness

Are you less open-minded when listening to things you disagree with than you are when listening to those things with which you do agree? What are some of the consequences of this way of thinking and listening?

criticism a less difficult and more productive experience. The following suggestions are appropriate in a learning environment such as a public speaking class, where criticism is used as a learning tool. In business and professional public speaking, in contrast, listeners don't offer suggestions for improvement; rather, they focus on the issues you raised.

ACCEPT THE CRITIC'S VIEWPOINT

Criticism reflects the listener's perception. Because of this the critic is always right. If the critic says that he or she wasn't convinced by your evidence, it won't help to identify the 10 or 12 research sources that you used in your speech; this critic was simply not convinced. Instead, consider why your evidence was not convincing. Perhaps you didn't make clear how the evidence was connected to your thesis or perhaps you raced through it too quickly. If you hear yourself saying, "But I did…," then consider the possibility that you're not accepting the critic's point of view.

LISTEN TO THE CRITIC WITH AN OPEN MIND

If you've already given your first speech, you know that public speaking is highly ego-involving. Because of this it may be tempting to block out criticism. After all, it's not easy to listen to criticism, especially in a fairly public place like a classroom filled with your peers. But if you do block out such criticism, you'll likely lose out on some useful suggestions for improvement. Realize too that you're in a learning environment—a kind of public speaking laboratory—and you're expected to make mistakes. And if this is your first exposure to public speaking, there's likely to be much room for improvement. So listen to criticism with an open mind, and let the critics know that you're really paying attention to what they have to say. In this way you'll encourage critics to share their perceptions more freely; in the process you'll gain greater insight into how you come across to an audience.

SEPARATE SPEECH CRITICISM FROM PERSONAL CRITICISM

Some speakers personalize the criticism to the point where they perceive a suggestion for improvement as a personal attack. Even when this perception is not conscious, it seems to influence the way in which criticism is taken. So recognize that when some aspect of your speech is criticized, your personality or your worth as an individual isn't being criticized or attacked. Listen to speech criticism with the same detachment that you'd use in listening to a biology instructor help you adjust the lens on the microscope or a computer expert tell you how to import photos into your blog.

SEEK CLARIFICATION

If you don't understand the criticism, ask for clarification. For example, if you're told that your specific purpose was too broad but it's unclear to you how you might narrow it, ask the critic to explain—being careful not to appear defensive or confrontational. Even when the criticism is favorable, if you don't understand it or it's not specific enough, ask for clarification. If a critic says, "Your introduction was great," you might want to say something like "Did it grab your attention?" or "Was it clear what I was going to cover in the speech?" In this way you encourage the critic to elaborate.

EVALUATE THE CRITICISM

The suggestion to listen open-mindedly to criticism does not mean that you should do as critics say. Instead, evaluate what the critics suggest; perhaps even try out the suggestions (in your next rehearsal or in the actual speech); but then make your own decisions as to what criticisms you'll follow totally, what you'll modify and adapt, and what you'll reject.

Listening, Criticism, and Culture

2.4 Identify some of the ways in which culture influences listening and criticism.

Culture influences all aspects of public speaking, and listening and criticism are no exceptions. Here are some ways in which culture exerts this influence.

Listening and Culture

Listening is difficult, partly because of the inevitable differences between the communication systems of speaker and listener. Because each person has had a unique set of experiences, each person's communication and meaning system is going to be different from the next person's system. When speaker and listener come from different cultures the differences and their effects are naturally much greater. Here are just a few areas where misunderstandings can occur.

LANGUAGE AND SPEECH

Even when speaker and listener speak the same language, they speak it with different meanings and different accents. No two speakers speak exactly the same language. Every speaker speaks an idiolect—a unique variation of the language. Speakers of the same language will sometimes have different meanings for the same terms because they have had different experiences.

Speakers and listeners who have different native languages and who may have learned English as a second language will have even greater differences in meaning. Translations are never precise and never fully capture the meaning in the other language. If your meaning for *house* was learned in a culture in which everyone lived in their own house with lots of land around it, then communicating your meaning for *house* with someone whose meaning was learned in a neighborhood of high-rise tenements is going to be difficult. Although you'll each hear the same word, the meanings you'll each construct from this "same" word will be drastically different. In adjusting your listening—especially when in an intercultural setting—understand that the speaker's meanings may be very different from yours even though you each know and speak the same language.

Another aspect of speech is the speaker's accent. From a linguistic point of view, everyone speaks with an accent. But we only notice accents that are different from ours; we don't notice accents that are similar to our own. When accents differ widely from our own, our attention may be momentarily taken away from what the speaker is saying to the speaker's accent. In many classrooms throughout the United States, there will be a wide range of accents, both regional and foreign. People whose native language is tonal such as Chinese (in which differences in pitch signal important meaning differences) may speak English with variations in pitch that may seem unnatural to others. Those whose native language is Japanese may have trouble distinguishing *l* from *r*, as Japanese does not make this distinction. Regional accent differences may make it difficult for people from Mississippi and Maine, for example, to understand each other without focusing some attention on accent. With increased exposure to a wide variety of linguistic differences, this focus on accents will lessen.

NONVERBAL DIFFERENCES

As you listen to other people, you also "listen" to their nonverbal communication. If their nonverbal messages are drastically different from what you expect on the basis of the verbal message, the nonverbals may be seen as a kind of noise or interference or they may be seen as contradictory messages.

Additionally, speakers from different cultures have different display rules—cultural rules that govern which nonverbal behaviors are appropriate and which are inappropriate in a public setting. Also, different cultures may give very different meanings to the same nonverbal gesture. For example, Americans consider direct eye contact an expression of honesty and forthrightness, but the Japanese often view this as a lack of respect. The Japanese will glance at the other person's face rarely and then only for very short periods (Axtell, 1990; Matsumoto, 2006). Among some Latin Americans and Native Americans, direct eye contact between, say, a teacher and a student is considered inappropriate, perhaps aggressive; appropriate student behavior is to avoid eye contact with the teacher.

ETHNOCENTRISM

How do you feel about your own culture versus those of others? For example, do you believe that other cultures are backward when compared to yours? Do you believe that other cultures would do well to become more like your culture? Do you believe that people would be happier if they lived in your culture than they would in another? Do you believe that people from other cultures are less trustworthy than people from your own (Neuliep, Chaudoir, & McCroskey, 2001)?

If you answer *yes* to these and similar questions, it's likely that you're ethnocentric in your thinking. **Ethnocentrism** is the tendency to evaluate the values, beliefs, and behaviors of your own culture as being more positive, logical, and natural than those of other cultures. The nonethnocentric, on the other hand, would see himself or herself and others as different but equal, with neither being inferior nor superior.

Recognizing the tendency toward ethnocentrism is the first step in combating any excesses. In addition, try following the suggestions for effective listening offered throughout this chapter—especially when you're in an intercultural public speaking situation. Expose yourself to culturally different experiences, but resist the temptation to evaluate these through your own cultural filters.

LISTENING AND GENDER

According to Deborah Tannen (1990) in her best-selling *You Just Don't Understand: Women and Men in Conversation*, women seek to build rapport and establish a closer

ethnocentrism
The tendency to see others and their behaviors through our own cultural filters, often as distortions of our own behaviors; the tendency to evaluate the values and beliefs of our own culture more positively than those of another culture.

relationship and so use listening to achieve these ends. Men, on the other hand, tend to play up their expertise, emphasize it, and use it to dominate the interaction. Women are apt to play down their expertise and are more interested in communicating supportiveness. Tannen argues that the goal of a man in conversation is to be accorded respect, so he seeks to show his knowledge and expertise. A woman, on the other hand, seeks to be liked, so she expresses agreement.

Men and women also show that they're listening in different ways (Hall, 2006). Women are more apt to give lots of listening cues, such as interjecting *yeah* or *uh-huh*, nodding in agreement, and smiling. A man is more likely to listen quietly without giving a lot of listening cues as feedback. Tannen (1990) argues, however, that men do listen less to women than women listen to men. The reason, says Tannen, is that listening places a person in an inferior position, whereas speaking places the speaker in a superior role.

As a result of these differences men may seem to assume a more combative posture while listening, as if getting ready to argue. They also may appear to ask questions that are more argumentative or that are designed to puncture holes in your position as a way to play up their own expertise. Women are more likely to ask supportive questions and perhaps to offer more positive criticism than men. Women also use more cues in listening in a public speaking context. They let the speaker see that they're listening. Men, on the other hand, seem to use fewer listening cues in a public speaking situation.

Men and women act this way to both men and women; their customary ways of communicating don't seem to change depending on whether they are addressing a male or a female speaker. There's no evidence to show that these differences represent any negative motives or any conscious attempt on the part of men to prove themselves superior or of women to ingratiate themselves. Rather, these differences in listening are largely the result of the ways in which men and women have been socialized.

Criticism and Culture

There are vast cultural differences in what is considered proper when it comes to public speaking criticism. For example, criticism will be viewed very differently depending on whether members come from an **individualist culture** (which

individualist culture

A culture in which the individual's rather than the group's goals and preferences are given primary importance. Opposed to *collectivist culture*.

collectivist culture

A culture in which the group's goals rather than the individual's goals are given primary importance and where, for example, benevolence, tradition, and conformity are given special emphasis. Opposed to *individualist culture*.

emphasizes the individual and places primary value on the individual's goals) or a **collectivist culture** (which emphasizes the group and places primary value on the group's goals).

Those who come from cultures that are highly individualist and competitive (the United States, Germany, and Sweden are examples) may find public criticism a normal part of the learning process. Those who come from cultures that are more collectivist and therefore emphasize the group rather than the individual (Japan, Mexico, and Korea are examples) are likely to find giving and receiving public criticism uncomfortable. Cultural rules that maintain peaceful relations among the Japanese (Hendry, 1995; Midooka, 1990; Watts, 2004) and norms of politeness among many Asian cultures (Fraser, 1990) may conflict with the classroom cultural norm calling for listeners to express criticism openly.

Collectivist cultures place a heavy emphasis on face-saving—on always allowing people to appear in a positive light (Hofstede, Hofstede, & Minkov, 2010). In these cultures people may prefer not to say anything negative in public. In fact, they may even be reluctant to say anything positive, lest any omission be construed as negative. In cultures in which face-saving is especially important, communication rules such as the following tend to prevail:

- Don't express negative evaluation in public; instead, compliment the person.
- Don't prove someone wrong—especially in public; express agreement even if you know the person is wrong.
- Don't correct someone's errors; don't even acknowledge them.
- Don't ask difficult questions lest the person not know the answer and lose face or be embarrassed; generally, avoid asking any questions that may potentially embarrass the other person.

The difficulties that these differences may cause can be lessened if they're discussed openly. Some people may become comfortable with public criticism once it's explained that the cultural norms of most public speaking classrooms include public criticism just as they incorporate informative and persuasive speaking and written outlines. Others may feel more comfortable offering written criticism as a substitute for oral and public criticism. Or perhaps private consultations can be arranged.

JOURNAL 2.4 PUBLIC SPEAKING CHOICE POINT

Culture Clash

Lucy just doesn't feel comfortable criticizing her classmates speeches, yet it's part of the course and grade. *What are some of the things Lucy can do to function effectively in the classroom and yet not betray her cultural beliefs and values?*

SUMMARY: LISTENING AND CRITICISM

This chapter looked at listening and criticism and offered suggestions for making your listening and your criticism more effective.

Listening in Public Speaking

2.1 Define *listening*, explain its five stages, and identify the suggestions for improvement at each stage.

1. Listening is a five-stage process: (1) receiving the speaker's verbal and nonverbal messages, (2) understanding the speaker's thoughts and emotions, (3) remembering and retaining the messages, (4) evaluating or judging the messages, and (5) responding or reacting to the messages.

Guidelines for Listening

2.2 Identify the guidelines to improve your own listening.

2. Among the principles for effective listening are these:
   - Listen actively.
   - Listen politely.
   - Listen for total meaning.
   - Listen with empathy.
   - Listen with an open mind.
   - Listen ethically.

Criticism in Public Speaking

2.3 Define *criticism* and its role in public speaking and identify the guidelines for giving and receiving criticism.

3. Criticism is a process of judging and evaluating a work. Criticism can (1) identify strengths and weaknesses and thereby help you improve as a public speaker, (2) identify standards for evaluating all sorts of public speeches, and (3) show that the audience is listening and is concerned about the speaker's progress.

4. Among the principles for giving effective criticism are these:
   - Stress the positive.
   - Be specific.
   - Be objective.
   - Be constructive.
   - Focus on behavior.
   - Own your criticism.
   - Recognize your ethical obligations.

5. In listening to criticism:
   - Accept the critic's viewpoint.
   - Listen with an open mind.
   - Separate speech criticism from personal criticism.
   - Seek clarification.
   - Evaluate the criticism.

Listening, Criticism, and Culture

2.4 Identify some of the ways in which culture influences listening and criticism.

6. Cultural differences in language and speech, nonverbal behavioral differences, ethnocentrism, and gender differences can create listening difficulties.

7. Cultural differences in criticism need to be considered. Cultures differ in their views of criticism and in the rules considered appropriate. For example, members of individualist cultures may find public criticism easier and more acceptable than people from collectivist cultures.

KEY TERMS: LISTENING AND CRITICISM

active listening
assimilation
backchanneling cues
bias
collectivist culture
criticism
critical listening

empathy
ethnocentrism
evaluating
I-messages
individualist culture
listening
owning criticism

prejudice
receiving
remembering
responding
understanding
you-messages

PUBLIC SPEAKING EXERCISES

2.1 Do You Really Remember What You Hear?

When you remember a message, do you remember what was said, or do you remember what you think you heard? The common-sense response, of course, would be that you remember what was said. But before accepting this simple explanation, try to memorize the list of 12 words presented, modeled on an idea from a research study (Glucksberg & Danks, 1975). Don't worry about the order of the words; only the number of words remembered counts. Take about 20 seconds to memorize as many words as possible. Then hide the list, and write down as many words as you can remember.

dining	table	milk
cafeteria	shopping	hungry
green beans	steak	having lunch
satisfied	knife	menu

Don't read any further until you've tried to memorize and reproduce the list of words.

If you're like most people, you not only remembered a good number of the words on the list but also "remembered" related words that weren't on the list, perhaps *eating, food,* or *meal.* What happens is that in remembering you don't simply reproduce the list; you reconstruct it. In this case you gave the list meaning, and part of that meaning included the word *eating* or some related word. In remembering speech, then, you reconstruct the messages you hear into a system that makes sense to you—but, in the process, often remember distorted versions of what was said.

2.2 Listening to New Ideas

Ideally, speeches communicate information that is new and potentially useful to you as a listener. A useful technique in listening to new ideas is PIP'N, a technique that derives from the insights of Carl Rogers (1970) on paraphrase as a means for ensuring understanding and from Edward deBono's (1976) PMI (plus, minus, interesting) technique for critical thinking. In analyzing new ideas with the PIP'N technique, you follow four steps:

> **P = Paraphrase.** State in your own words what you think the other person is saying. Paraphrasing will help you understand and remember the idea.
>
> **I = Interesting.** Consider why the idea is interesting.
>
> **P = Positive.** Think about what's good about the idea; for example, might it solve a problem or improve a situation?
>
> **N = Negative.** Think about any negatives that the idea might entail; for example, might it be expensive or difficult to implement?

Consider how you might use PIP'N to gain insight—into, say, the cultural emphasis you find in your college textbooks or in a particular required course or into the PIP'N technique itself.

2.3 Writing a Critical Review

Online reviews of restaurants, movies, television shows, home products, and services, for example, are now commonplace. The Yelp website, perhaps the largest review site, notes that in April, May, and June of 2015 it had 83 million unique visitors per month, so clearly these reviews seem helpful to people searching for a suitable place to eat. Write a review of a place, product, or service using the principles of criticism discussed in this chapter. In your review identify the principles of criticism you are following in Word Tracking or in some similar system that enables you to coordinate what you say with the specific principle for expressing criticism. Post your review if you wish.

SELECT YOUR TOPIC, PURPOSES, AND THESIS (STEP 1)

Finding speech topics can be as exciting as you make it.

CHAPTER TOPICS

Your Topic

Your Purposes

Your Thesis

LEARNING OBJECTIVES

3.1 Paraphrase the qualities of a good speech topic and describe the ways to find and limit your topic.

3.2 Explain the nature of and how to phrase a general and a specific speech purpose.

3.3 Define *thesis,* explain how purpose and thesis differ, and identify the suggestions for wording your thesis for greatest effectiveness.

Now that you understand the basic steps in public speaking preparation, the fundamentals of controlling apprehension, and the basics of listening and criticizing, you can now focus on the first step in the public speaking process—selecting a topic (and narrowing it down so you can cover it in the allotted time), selecting a purpose, and framing your central idea or thesis.

One important piece of advice as you tackle the first step is to start early. A common problem in public speaking is the tendency to delay the preparation of the speech. Substitute this unproductive tendency to procrastinate with a start-early ethic. Starting early provides you with the time to overcome the inevitable unanticipated roadblocks— a website that you thought would be helpful is now dead, the person you wanted to interview isn't available, or your neighbor's parties make the weekends useless for working on your speech. Starting early will also give you the time to rehearse your speech to ensure that your delivery will be effective and to help reduce any fear of public speaking you might have. Starting early may even enable you to avoid health problems often associated with procrastination—college students who procrastinate experience more colds and flu, more gastrointestinal problems, and more insomnia (Marano, 2003).

Here are several suggestions for overcoming the tendency to delay certain tasks.

- **Think mindfully about the task.** Be mindful of the fact that delaying your preparation will only make it harder and is likely to increase your natural fear of public speaking. Make a commitment to starting early. Create a computer file for your speech, and collect information and file it for easy retrieval.

- **Don't lie to yourself.** One popular lie is that you do better under pressure. With very few possible exceptions, this is simply not true (Marano, 2003). You do more poorly under pressure.

- **Avoid distractions.** Distractions are all around us, so beware of your tendency to seek these out. You don't need to update your Facebook status or clean your room before you can begin preparing your speech, for example. When you get the urge to do something else, become mindful of what you're really doing—making an excuse to delay the task at hand.

- **Work in small units.** Fortunately, as already mentioned, this aid to overcoming procrastination is built into the 10-step public speaking system used here; each step is already a relatively small unit. Set aside 20 or 30 minutes (it's often best to start with small units of time) and see what you can do with Step 1. Then when you're farther along in the process, increase the time you spend on each step.

Your Topic

3.1 Paraphrase the qualities of a good speech topic and describe the ways to find and limit your topic.

As you begin to think about public speaking (and especially about your own future speeches) perhaps the first question you have is "What do I speak about?" The answer to this question will change as your life situation changes. In the years ahead you'll most likely speak on topics that grow out of your job or your social or political activities. In the classroom, however, where your objective is to learn the skills of public speaking, there are literally thousands of subjects to talk about. Some topics, of course, are better than others. What distinguishes a good from a poor speech topic is that a good topic deals with matters of substance, is appropriate to you and the audience, and is culturally sensitive. These three characteristics suggest some guidelines for selecting a good topic, so let's consider each briefly.

- **Substantive.** The most important criterion of a good topic is that it should *deal with matters of substance*. So select a topic that is important enough to merit the time and attention of a group of intelligent people. Ask yourself: Would this topic engage

VIEWPOINTS

Topics

Each person has his or her own ideas as to what constitutes a topic that will engage the attention of a group of college students. *How would you describe such a topic?*

the attention of my classmates? Would a reputable newspaper cover such a topic? Would students find this topic relevant to their social or professional lives?

- **Appropriate to You as Speaker.** Select a topic that is *appropriate to you as the speaker.* The best way to look at this criterion is to ask if—given what the audience already knows about you and what you'll tell them during your speech—your listeners will see you as a knowledgeable and believable spokesperson on this topic. If the answer is yes, then you have a topic appropriate to you as a speaker. If the answer is no, then it will probably be useful to continue your search for an appropriate topic.

- **Appropriate to Your Audience.** Also, select a topic that is *appropriate to members of your audience in terms of their interests and needs.* Always look to the members of your audience when thinking about a topic, and try to gauge their reaction to it. After all, audience members are giving you their time and attention; selecting a topic that is responsive to their needs and interests seems only fair.

- **Culturally Sensitive.** A good topic is *culturally sensitive.* Select a topic that will not offend members of other cultures. At the same time, demonstrating **cultural sensitivity** will likely enhance your own image in the minds of the audience. Perhaps the most general suggestion would be to avoid stereotyping; avoid assuming or implying that all members of a group are the same. But there are many specific suggestions that can be offered for achieving cultural sensitivity. For example, in many Arab, Asian, and African cultures, discussing sex in an audience of both men and women would be considered obscene and offensive. In Scandinavian cultures, on the other hand, sex is discussed openly and without embarrassment or discomfort. Listed below are some taboos that intercultural experts recommend that Americans avoid when traveling abroad. These **taboo topics** change with the times, however, so what is true today may not be true tomorrow (Allan & Burridge, 2007; Axtell, 2007):

  - In Spain avoid discussing family, religion, or jobs or making negative comments on bullfighting.

  - In the Caribbean avoid discussing race, local politics, or religion.

  - In Brazil avoid discussing politics or religion and avoid telling ethnic jokes.

  - In Japan avoid discussing World War II or making bodily contact (patting someone on the back or putting your arm around someone's shoulders).

cultural sensitivity

An awareness of and responsiveness to the rules for communicating in varied cultural settings.

taboo topics

Subjects that violate a culture's principles of appropriateness and that are best avoided in public speeches.

- In Mexico avoid talking about the Mexican–American War, illicit drugs, or illegal aliens.
- In many Muslim countries avoid talking about religion, politics, and sexuality and avoid any references that can be interpreted as profane.

Finding Topics

Here are five ways to find topics: yourself, brainstorming, surveys, news items, and topic lists.

YOURSELF

Perhaps your first step in thinking about appropriate speech topics is to look at your interests. What are you interested in? What engages your time? If you were surfing the Web (say, a news site), what topics would encourage you to go to the actual site? What headlines would interest you enough that you would access the article? What do you want to learn more about? In short, start by thinking about your own interests; they may be similar to your audience's. If you plan a speech on a topic that you're interested in and want to learn more about, you'll enjoy and profit from the entire experience a great deal more. The research that you do for your speech will be more meaningful; the facts you uncover will be more interesting. At the same time, your enthusiasm for your topic is likely to make your delivery more exciting, less anxiety-provoking, and more engaging to the audience. All around, you win by selecting a topic in which you're especially interested or to which you have a special connection.

At the same time that you consider your interests, consider your experiences. Have you been a part of well-known events or lived in different places? Do you have special talents? Are you knowledgeable about odd or different topics? What are your hobbies? If you're a philatelist, a speech on unique stamps or the value of some stamps or the way in which stamps are printed might prove interesting. If you're a spelunker, perhaps a speech on caves, how they form, and what they mean to the ecology of the area might prove interesting.

BRAINSTORMING

brainstorming

A technique for generating ideas either alone or, more usually, in a small group.

Another useful method for finding a topic is **brainstorming**, a technique designed to enable you to generate lots of topics in a relatively short time (DeVito, 1996; Osborn, 1957). You begin with your "problem," which in this case is "What will I talk about?" You then record any and all ideas that occur to you. Allow your mind to free-associate. Don't censor yourself; instead, allow your ideas to flow as freely as possible. Record all your thoughts, regardless of how silly or inappropriate they may seem. Write them down or record them. Try to generate as many ideas as possible. The more ideas you think of, the better your chances of finding a suitable topic in your list. After you've generated a sizable list—it should take you no longer than 5 minutes—read over the list or replay the recording. Do any of the topics on your list suggest other topics? If so, write these down as well. Can you combine or extend your ideas? Which ideas seem workable?

SURVEYS

Look at some of the national and regional issues that are identified by polls or research organizations. For example, one political website, On the Issues, identifies such issues as abortion, budget and economy, civil rights, crime, drugs, education, families and children, gun control, homeland security, immigration, and infrastructure. The Rand Corporation's website reports such issues as Obama's health-care reform bill, intellectual property rights, air pollution, drug use, employment among military spouses, risk management, health-care quality, and patient protection. And the website for Issues in Science and Technology identifies such major topics as climate, competitiveness, education, energy, environment, foreign policy, national security, public health, and transportation.

Survey data are now easier than ever to obtain because many of the larger poll results are available on the Internet. For example, the Gallup Organization maintains a website that includes national and international surveys on political, social, consumer, and other issues speakers often talk about. The Polling Report website also will prove useful; it provides a wealth of polling data on issues in fields such as political science, business, journalism, health, and social science. One of the best and most accessible is the Pew Research Center, whose major topics are politics media, social trends, religion, Internet and technology, Hispanics, and global issues. Many search engines and browsers provide lists of "hot topics," which are often useful starting points. These are exactly the topics that people are talking about and therefore often make excellent subjects for speeches.

Or you can conduct a survey yourself. Roam through the nonfiction section of your bookstore (online, if you prefer—for example, Amazon or Barnes & Noble), and you'll quickly develop a list of the topics book buyers consider important. A glance at online best-seller lists will give you an even quicker overview.

NEWS ITEMS

The easiest way to find news items is simply to go to the news or top stories pages of Google, Bing, Yahoo!, *The Huffington Post*, or any newspaper or magazine of your choice. Here you'll find a lot more than you'll be able to use, but you're likely to find several items that will interest you and that would make suitable speech topics.

Depending on your own interests, check out the more specific websites, magazines, and newspapers; for example, those that deal with financial matters or social media or politics. Editorials and letters to the editor also are useful indicators of what people are concerned about.

While online, don't ignore the international publications. These publications will often give a different perspective on the news. Web translators make these formerly unusable sources of information easily accessible.

TOPIC LISTS

One of the easiest ways of examining and selecting a potential topic is to look at some of the topic lists that are available. A variety of educational and commercial websites contain **topic generators**, where you can repeatedly press a button and view a wide variety of topics. For example, WritingFix helps you with topics for writing (which can often, though not always, be adapted for public speaking). And McMaster eBusiness Research Center maintains a topic generator for business topics. There are also useful topic lists that have been compiled by various communication and English instructors. For example, the University of Hawaii maintains a website, Topic Selection Helper, which lists hundreds of topics. Similarly, Cincinnati State Technical and Community College has lists for both informative and persuasive speeches.

topic generators
Computer programs that generate a variety of subject matter topics, often useful for finding ideas for speeches and compositions.

There is another class of websites that will sell you speeches and term papers for a fee. When searching for topics you're likely to run across these sites. Avoid these websites. Many colleges now have software to identify plagiarism, so it's easy to get caught; considering that the consequences are often severe, it's not worth going that route. Another reason for not using these sites and services is that by letting others do your work for you, you'll never learn the very skills that you'll need later in life.

Limiting Topics

Probably the major error beginning speakers make is to try to cover a huge topic in too short a period of time. The inevitable result is a very superficial speech, a speech without any depth. To be suitable for a public speech, a topic must be limited in scope; it must be narrowed down to fit the time restrictions and yet permit some depth of coverage.

Another reason to narrow your topic is that it will help you focus your collection of research materials. If your topic is too broad, you'll be forced to review a lot more research material than you're going to need. On the other hand, if you narrow your topic, you can search for information more efficiently. Here are two methods for narrowing and limiting your topic: topoi and tree diagrams.

JOURNAL 3.1 PUBLIC SPEAKING CHOICE POINT

Limiting A Topic

Richard wants to give a speech on women's rights, but he can't seem to narrow the topic down to manageable proportions. Everything he comes across seems important and cries out for inclusion. *What options does Richard have for limiting his topic? What would make a good topic?*

topoi

A system for analyzing a topic according to a preestablished set of categories.

TOPOI, THE SYSTEM OF TOPICS

Topoi, the system of topics, is a technique that comes from the classical rhetorics of ancient Greece and Rome but today is used more widely as a stimulus to creative thinking (DeVito, 1996). When using the method of topoi, you ask yourself a series of questions about your general subject. The process will help you see divisions of your general topic on which you might want to focus. Table 3.1 provides an example; the column on the left contains seven general questions (Who? What? Why? When? Where? How? and So?) and a series of subquestions (which vary depending on your topic). The right column illustrates how some of the questions on the left might suggest specific aspects of the general subject of "homelessness."

SUBDIVISION

Dividing a topic into its component parts is another way of limiting your topic. All topics can be broken down into subtopics and the subtopics can be further broken down into additional subtopics. The idea here is to start with a general topic in which you're interested and divide it into its natural parts. Of course, the way in which they're broken down into their component parts varies with the topic. Here are a few examples:

- **Time.** Historical topics and events can generally be divided by time periods. From the very general space exploration, for example, you might divide the topic into

TABLE 3.1   Topoi, the System of Topics: Homelessness

These questions should enable you to use general topics to generate more specific ideas for your speeches. You'll be amazed at how many topics you'll be able to find with this simple and ancient technique.

General Questions	Subject-Specific Questions
Who? Who is he or she, or who are they? Who is responsible? To whom was it done?	Who are the homeless? Who is the typical homeless person? Who is responsible for the increase in homelessness? Who cares for the homeless?
What? What is it? What effects does it have? What is it like? What is it different from? What are some examples?	What does it mean to be homeless? What does homelessness do to the people themselves? What does homelessness do to the society in general? What does homelessness mean to you and me?
Why? Why does it happen? Why does it not happen?	Why is there homelessness? Why are there so many homeless people? Why did this happen? Why does it happen in the larger cities more than in smaller towns? Why is it more prevalent in some countries than in others?
When? When did it happen? When will it occur? When will it end?	When did homelessness become so prevalent? When does it occur in the life of a person?
Where? Where did it come from? Where is it going? Where is it now?	Where is homelessness most prevalent? Where is there an absence of homelessness?
How? How does it work? How is it used? How do you do it? How do you operate it? How is it organized?	How does someone become homeless? How can we help the homeless? How can we prevent others from becoming homeless?
So? What does it mean? What is important about it? Why should I be concerned with this? Who cares?	Why is homelessness such an important social problem? Why must we be concerned with homelessness? How does all this affect me?

fantasy exploration or sci-fi, early Russian exploration, or recent U.S. missions to Mars. Whereas space exploration is much too general to cover in a speech, these divisions look a lot more promising.

- **Space.** Most physical things can be conveniently divided by space or geographical area. So, for example, if your topic is home decoration—too broad—you might take one room—decorating your kitchen or organizing your study. If your topic is landscaping, you might divide it into walkway, garden, driveway, or special features.

- **Types.** A variety of topics are easily divisible into types. Let's say you want to talk about television—limiting by types seems natural: comedies, dramas, talk shows, game shows, reality TV, or sports. The general topic of foods can easily be divided in a number of ways: healthy and unhealthy; protein, fat, fiber; prepared and fresh. And you can always subdivide one of the categories. For example, healthy food can be divided into vegetarian or vegan, organic or nonorganic, or so-called "super foods."

- **People.** Another useful category is to narrow the topic by narrowing the people involved. So, if you wanted to talk about the civil rights movement—clearly too broad a topic—you might narrow it by specific people and devote your speech to the contributions of one particular civil rights worker or a group of civil rights workers such as Thurgood Marshall and the NAACP.

Your Purposes

3.2 Explain the nature of and how to phrase a general and a specific speech purpose.

The overall purpose of your speech is the goal you want to achieve; it identifies the effect that you want your speech to have on your audience. In constructing your speech you'll first identify your **general purpose** and then your **specific purpose**.

General Purpose

Because you're now in a course learning about public speaking skills, your general purpose will likely be chosen for you. And in this way the classroom is very like the real world. The situation, the audience you'll address, and the nature of your job will dictate whether your speech is to be informative or persuasive. If you're a lawyer giving a closing at a trial, your speech must be persuasive. If you're an engineer explaining new blueprints, your speech must be informative. If you're a college professor, your speeches will be largely informative; if a politician, they will be mostly persuasive.

There are three major types of speeches: the **informative speech**, the **persuasive speech**, and the **special occasion speech**.

- In the *informative speech* you seek to create understanding: to clarify, to enlighten, to correct misunderstandings, to demonstrate how something works. In this type of speech you'll rely most heavily on materials that amplify—examples, illustrations, definitions, testimony, visual aids, and the like.

- In the *persuasive speech* you try to influence attitudes or behaviors; you seek to strengthen or change existing attitudes or get the audience to take some action. In this type of speech you'll rely heavily on materials that offer proof—on evidence, argument, and psychological appeals, for example.

- In the *special occasion speech*, which contains elements of information and persuasion, you might, for example, introduce another speaker or a group of speakers, present a tribute, try to secure the goodwill of the listeners, toast your friends' anniversary, or "just" entertain your listeners.

general purpose
The overall aim of your speech, for example, to inform or to persuade.

specific purpose
The aim of your speech put in concrete, specific terms, for example, to inform my audience of the dangers of not having children vaccinated.

informative speech
A speech designed to communicate information to an audience rather than to persuade.

persuasive speech
A speech designed to strengthen or change the attitudes or beliefs of audience members or to move them to take some kind of action.

special occasion speech
A speech designed for and presented at some specific occasion such as a commencement speech at a graduation or a toast at a wedding.

Specific Purpose

Once you have chosen your general purpose, develop your specific purpose by identifying more precisely what you aim to accomplish. For example, in an informative speech, your specific purpose will identify the information you want to convey to your audience. Here are a few possible specific purposes for a speech on the topic of stem cell research:

General purpose:	To inform.
Specific purposes:	To inform my audience of the differences between embryonic and adult stem cell research.
	To inform my audience about two areas of stem cell research progress.
	To inform my audience of the current federal regulations on funding stem cell research.

You may find it helpful to view your specific informative purpose in behavioral terms: identifying how you want audience members to demonstrate what they've learned from your speech. Here are a few examples:

- After listening to my speech, audience members should be able to describe the procedures for systematic desensitization.
- After listening to my speech, audience members should be able to define the three major differences between communism and capitalism.
- After listening to my speech, audience members should be able to demonstrate the three techniques of active listening.

In a persuasive speech, your specific purpose identifies what you want your audience to believe, to think, or perhaps to do. Here are a few examples:

General purpose:	To persuade.
Specific purposes:	To persuade listeners to use systematic desensitization to reduce their apprehension.
	To persuade listeners to believe that capitalism is superior to communism.
	To persuade listeners to use active listening more often.

As you formulate your specific purpose, follow these five guidelines: Use an infinitive phrase, focus the purpose in terms of its impact on your audience, limit it to one idea, limit it to what you can reasonably expect to achieve, and use specific terms.

USE AN INFINITIVE PHRASE

Begin the statement of each specific purpose with your general purpose (to inform, to persuade) and elaborate on your general purpose. For example:

> To inform my audience of the new registration procedures.

> To persuade my audience to contribute a book for the library fundraiser.

> To introduce the main speaker of the day to my audience.

FOCUS ON THE AUDIENCE

Right now your audience is your public speaking class. It may at first seem unnecessary to include reference to the audience in each specific purpose (as was done in the previous examples). Actually, referring to the audience is crucial because it keeps you focused on the people you want to inform or persuade; it's a reminder that everything you do in your speech needs to be directed by the purpose you want to achieve with this specific audience. In your life and career, you'll probably address a variety of different audiences, and you need to keep each unique and distinct audience clearly in focus.

LIMIT YOUR SPECIFIC PURPOSE TO ONE IDEA

Most public speaking textbooks urge you to avoid the common pitfall of trying to accomplish too much in too short a time. Often, however, it's necessary to inform before you persuade. So, for example, if your speech purpose is to persuade your audience to avoid websites that offer to write your speech or essay, you might have to first explain the nature and function of these websites before going on to identify the reasons why these sites should be avoided.

Nevertheless, the advice to limit your specific purpose to one idea is most often useful, especially in your beginning efforts. Try to avoid specific purposes that contain the word *and*; it's often a sign that you have more than one purpose. Here are the kinds of specific purpose statements to avoid:

> To inform audience members of the history of gun control laws *and* the changes proposed by the administration *and* why these changes are worthless.

> To persuade audience members of the prevalence of date rape in our community *and* throughout the country *and* that they should attend the dating seminars offered on campus.

LIMIT YOUR SPECIFIC PURPOSE TO WHAT IS REASONABLE

Limit your specific purpose to what you can reasonably develop and achieve in the allotted time. Specific purposes that are too broad are useless. Note how broad and overly general are such purposes as:

> To inform my audience about clothing design.

> To persuade audience members to improve their health.

JOURNAL 3.2 PUBLIC SPEAKING CHOICE POINT

Specific Purposes

Harry is interested in the importance of recycling. *What are some specific purposes that Harry might use for a 10-minute information speech?*

You couldn't hope to cover such topics in one speech. It would be much more reasonable to have such purposes as:

To inform my audience of the importance of color in clothing design.

To persuade audience members to exercise three times a week.

USE SPECIFIC TERMS

Phrase your specific purpose with specific terms. The more precise your specific purpose, the more effectively it will guide you in the remaining steps of preparing your speech. Notice that the purposes used as examples of covering too much are also overly general and very unspecific (*clothing design* can mean hundreds of things as can *improve your health*). Instead of the overly general: "To persuade my audience to help the homeless," consider the more specific: "To persuade my audience to donate a few hours a month to make phone calls for the Homeless Coalition."

Generally, the purpose of your speech is not stated explicitly in your speech, but there are occasions when you want to be very specific about what you're trying to achieve. Here, for example, in a speech arguing against allowing people to opt their children out of life-saving vaccines, Kate Ryland (2012) of Louisiana State University, Shreveport, states her purpose clearly and early in the speech:

Today, I'm here to convince you to help me stop these exemptions before they take more Abigail Petersons from us.

Your Thesis

3.3 Define *thesis*, explain how purpose and thesis differ, and identify the suggestions for wording your thesis for greatest effectiveness.

thesis

The main assertion of a message—for example, the theme or central idea of a public speech.

Like your specific purpose, your **thesis** needs to be given special attention. This section defines the thesis and explains how you should word your thesis and use it in your preparation and in your actual speech.

The Nature of the Public Speaking Thesis

Your thesis is your central idea; it's the theme, the essence of your speech. It's your point of view; it's what you want the audience to get out of your speech. The thesis of Lincoln's Second Inaugural Address was that Northerners and Southerners should work together for the entire nation's welfare, the thesis of Martin Luther King Jr.'s "I have a dream" speech was that true equality is a right of African Americans and all people, and the thesis of political campaign speeches is generally something like "Vote for me" or "I'm the better candidate" or "My opponent is the wrong choice."

In an informative speech your thesis states what you want your audience to learn. For example, a suitable thesis for an informative speech on jealousy might be "There are two main theories of jealousy." Notice that here, as in all informative speeches, the thesis is relatively neutral and objective. As a result, many public speaking instructors prefer the term *central idea* instead of *thesis* for information speeches.

In a persuasive speech your thesis states what you want your audience to believe or accept; it summarizes the claim you're making, the position you're taking. For example, let's say that you're planning to present a speech against using animals for experimentation. Your thesis statement might be something like "Animal experimentation should be banned." Here are a few additional examples of persuasive speech theses:

- We should all contribute to the Homeless Shelter Project.
- Everyone over 40 should get tested for colon cancer.
- Condoms should be distributed free of charge.

As you can see, these thesis statements identify what you want audience members to believe or do as a result of your speech—you want them to contribute to the homeless shelter, to believe that everyone over 40 should be tested for colon cancer, and to be convinced that condoms should be distributed without charge. Notice that in persuasive speeches the thesis statement puts forth a point of view, an opinion. The thesis is arguable; it's debatable.

Differences Between Theses and Purposes

The thesis and the specific purpose are similar in that they are both guides to help you select and organize your speech materials. Because they both serve these similar goals, they are often confused. They differ in three major ways.

■ **Thesis and purpose differ in their form of expression.** The specific purpose is worded as an infinitive phrase; for example, "To inform my audience of the provisions of the new education budget" or "To persuade my audience to vote in favor of the new education budget." The thesis, on the other hand, is phrased as a complete declarative sentence; for example, "The education budget must be increased."

■ **Thesis and purpose differ in their focus.** The specific purpose is audience-focused; it identifies the change you hope to achieve in your audience. For example, your specific purpose may be for the audience to gain information, to believe something, or to act in a certain way. The thesis, on the other hand, is message-focused. It identifies the main idea of your speech; it summarizes—it epitomizes—the content of your speech. It's the one idea that you want audience members to remember even if they forget everything else.

VIEWPOINTS
One versus Two

Public speaking textbooks are virtually unanimous in advising students to limit their speeches to one specific purpose and one specific thesis. Yet many contemporary speeches have more than one purpose and thesis— often an informative thesis to explain some proposal and a persuasive one to influence you to support this proposal. *Do you see an advantage to limiting your speech purpose and thesis to one (at least while in a learning environment)? Are there disadvantages?*

■ **Thesis and purpose differ in their concern for practical limitations.** No matter how sweeping or ambitious the thesis, the specific purpose must take into consideration the time you have to speak and the attitudes of the audience toward you and your topic. The specific purpose, therefore, needs to be phrased with these practical limitations in mind. For example, the thesis might be that "Colleges are not educating students for today's world." The speech, however, might have any one of several different specific purposes: for example, (1) to persuade my audience that colleges must change to keep pace with today's world, (2) to persuade my audience to adapt the Illinois Educational Proposal, or (3) to persuade my audience to quit college. The thesis epitomizes the speech without regard to practical limitations of, say, time or current audience attitudes.

Here is an example to clarify further the difference between purpose and thesis:

General purpose: To inform.
Specific purpose: To inform audience members of three ways to save on their phone bills.
Thesis: You can reduce your phone bills.

Especially in your early stages of mastering public speaking, formulate both the specific purpose and the thesis statement. With both of these as guides, you'll be able to construct a more coherent and more understandable speech.

Wording and Using Your Thesis

Here are a few suggestions on how to word and use your thesis.

LIMIT YOUR THESIS TO ONE CENTRAL IDEA

Be sure to limit your thesis statement to one and only one central idea. A statement such as "Animal experimentation should be banned, and companies engaging in it should be prosecuted" contains not one but two basic ideas. Whenever you see an *and* or a semicolon (;) in a thesis statement, it probably contains more than one idea.

STATE YOUR THESIS AS A COMPLETE DECLARATIVE SENTENCE

In phrasing your thesis, word it as a complete declarative sentence; for example:

> Hate speech corrupts.

> Speak out against hate speech.

> Support the college's new hate speech code.

This will help you focus your thinking, your collection of materials, and your organizational pattern. Avoid stating your thesis as a question or a sentence fragment; these will not provide the clear and specific focus you need to use the thesis effectively.

USE YOUR THESIS TO FOCUS AUDIENCE ATTENTION

Because the thesis sentence focuses the audience's attention on your central idea and reveals what you hope to achieve in your speech, you'll want to consider the options you have for stating your thesis. Here, for example, is how one student, Kevin King, expressed his thesis in a persuasive speech on the need to fund research on Alzheimer's disease (King, 2015):

> We have to end our collective silence about this disease and make Alzheimer's research a financial priority—before it's too late.

USE YOUR THESIS STATEMENT TO GENERATE MAIN POINTS

Within each thesis there is an essential question that allows you to explore and subdivide the thesis. Your objective here is to find this question and use it to help you discover the major ideas or assertions or propositions that will support this thesis. For example, let's take a hypothetical proposed bill—call it the Hart Bill—and let's say your thesis is "The Hart Bill provides needed services for senior citizens." When the thesis is stated in this form, the obvious question suggested is "What are the needed services?" The answer to this question suggests the main parts of your speech, let's say health, food, shelter, and recreational services. These four areas then become the four main points of your speech.

Some public speaking instructors and trainers advise speakers to include their main points in the statement of the thesis. If you did this, your thesis for the above speech would be "The Hart Bill provides needed health, food, shelter, and recreational services for senior citizens." You may find it helpful to use the briefer thesis statement for some speech topics and purposes and the more expanded thesis statement for others.

General purpose:	To inform.
Specific purpose:	To inform my audience of the provisions of the Hart Bill.
Thesis:	The Hart Bill provides needed services for senior citizens.

Or, if you were using an expanded thesis, it might be stated like this:

> The Hart Bill provides needed health, food, shelter, and recreational services for senior citizens.

Regardless of whether you use the brief or the expanded thesis, an outline of the main points would look like this:

> I. The Hart Bill provides needed health services.
>
> II. The Hart Bill provides needed food services.
>
> III. The Hart Bill provides needed shelter services.
>
> IV. The Hart Bill provides needed recreational services.

The remainder of the speech would then be filled in with supporting materials. Under main point I, for example, you might identify several health services and

ETHICAL CHOICE POINT

Thesis Appropriateness

Visualize yourself as a public speaking instructor. Your students are getting ready to deliver their first round of speeches. You've asked them to submit their choice of informative or persuasive speech topics to you so that you can make sure they're on the right track and offer whatever help may be needed. Among the theses you receive are the following:

1. You can create computer viruses in three easy steps.
2. Terrorism can be justified.
3. You can make fake IDs for fun and profit.
4. States should be able to fly the Confederate flag.
5. All religions are destructive.

You believe that in a democracy, speakers should be free to speak on any side of an issue, and so your first impulse is to approve all these theses. At the same time, you don't want to create problems in the classroom (and possibly beyond) and divert attention from the purpose of the course—to teach the skills of public speaking. *What ethical choices do you have for dealing with these seemingly contradictory goals?*

explain how the Hart Bill would provide them. In outline form, this first main point of your speech might look something like this:

    I. The Hart Bill provides needed health services.

        A. Neighborhood clinics will be established.

        B. Medical hotlines will be established.

In the completed speech, this first main point and its two subordinate statements might be spoken like this:

> The Hart Bill provides senior citizens with the health services they need so badly. Let me give you some examples of these necessary health services. One of the most important services will be the establishment of neighborhood health clinics. These clinics will help senior citizens get needed health advice and medical care right in their own neighborhoods.
>
> A second important health service will be the health hotlines. These phone numbers will be for the exclusive use of senior citizens. These hotlines will connect seniors with trained medical personnel who will be able to give advice and send emergency medical services to seniors as needed.

USE YOUR THESIS TO SUGGEST ORGANIZATIONAL PATTERNS

Your thesis will provide you with useful guidelines in selecting the organization for your main points. For example, let's suppose your thesis is "We can improve our own college education." Your answer to the inherent question "What can we do?" will suggest a possible organizational pattern. If, for example, you identify the remedies in the

JOURNAL 3.3 PUBLIC SPEAKING CHOICE POINT

Statement of Thesis

Miranda wants to give her speech in favor of allowing singles to adopt children. *What choices does Miranda have for presenting her thesis? What advice would you give Miranda about presenting her thesis if she were facing an audience opposed to her position? What advice would you give if the audience was in favor of her position and she wanted to strengthen it? What advice would you give Miranda if she were addressing your class in public speaking?*

order in which they should be taken, then a time-order pattern will be appropriate. If you itemize a number of possible solutions, all of which are of about equal importance, then a topical pattern will be appropriate. If your thesis is "The proposed fringe benefits package has both advantages and disadvantages," then your speech might logically be organized into two parts: advantages and disadvantages. These and other patterns are explained in detail in Chapter 7.

USE YOUR THESIS TO FOCUS AUDIENCE ATTENTION

Because the thesis sentence focuses the audience's attention on your central idea and reveals what you hope to achieve in your speech, you'll want to consider the options you have for stating your thesis. Here are a few guidelines that will help you make a strategically effective decision about how and when to present your thesis to your audience.

- **In an informative speech, state your thesis early, clearly, and directly:**
  Immigration patterns are predicted to change drastically over the next 50 years.
  Carpal tunnel syndrome can be corrected with surgery.
  A smartphone can organize your life.

- **In a persuasive speech addressed to an audience already in agreement with you,** state your thesis explicitly and early in your speech:
  Immigration laws should be changed.
  You can avoid carpal tunnel syndrome with rest and exercise.
  Organize your life electronically.

- **In a persuasive speech addressed to an audience opposed to your position,** give your evidence and arguments first and gradually move the audience into a more positive frame of mind before stating your thesis explicitly.

- **When you are speaking to a relatively uneducated or uninformed audience, it is probably best to state your thesis explicitly.** If the thesis is not explicit, the listeners may fail to grasp what your thesis is and therefore may be less likely to change their attitudes or behaviors.

- **Recognize, too, that there are cultural differences in the way a thesis should be stated.** In some Asian cultures, for example, making a point too directly or asking directly for audience compliance may be considered rude or insulting.

SUMMARY: SELECT YOUR TOPIC, PURPOSES, AND THESIS (STEP 1)

In this chapter we considered the speech topic and ways to find and limit it, general and specific speech purposes and how to phrase them, and speech theses and how to word and use them to their best effect.

Your Topic

3.1 Paraphrase the qualities of a good speech topic and describe the ways to find and limit your topic.

1. Suitable speech topics are topics that are substantive, appropriate to you and your audience, and culturally sensitive.

2. Topics may be found through:
   - Yourself.
   - Brainstorming.
   - Surveys.
   - News items.
   - Topic lists.

3. Speech topics may be limited by:
   - Topoi, the system of topics.
   - Subdivision.

Your Purposes

3.2 Explain the nature of and how to phrase a general and a specific speech purpose.

4. Speech purposes are both general (for example, to inform or to persuade) and specific (for example,

to inform an audience of new health plan options). A specific purpose should be:
   - Worded as an infinitive phrase.
   - Focused on the audience.
   - Limited to one idea.
   - Limited to what you can reasonably accomplish.
   - Phrased with precise terms.

Your Thesis

3.3 Define *thesis*, explain how purpose and thesis differ, and identify the suggestions for wording your thesis for greatest effectiveness.

5. The speech thesis is your central idea, the theme, the essence of your speech.

6. In wording and using your thesis:
   - Limit your thesis to one central idea.
   - State your thesis as a complete declarative sentence.
   - Use your thesis statement to generate main ideas.
   - Use your thesis to suggest organizational patterns.
   - Use your thesis to focus audience attention.

KEY TERMS: SELECT YOUR TOPIC, PURPOSE, AND THESIS (STEP 1)

brainstorming	persuasive speech	thesis
cultural sensitivity	special occasion speech	topic generators
general purpose	specific purpose	topoi
informative speech	taboo topics	

PUBLIC SPEAKING EXERCISES

3.1 Brainstorming for Topics

With a small group of students or with the entire class sitting in a circle, brainstorm for suitable speech topics. Be sure to appoint someone to write down all the contributions or use a recorder.

After this brainstorming session, consider:

1. Did any members give negative criticism (even nonverbally)?
2. Did any members hesitate to contribute really wild ideas? Why?
3. Was it necessary to restimulate the group members at any point? Did this help?
4. Did some useful speech topics emerge in the brainstorming session?

3.2 Limiting Topics

Listed below are a few overly general topics. Using one of the methods discussed in this chapter (or any other method you're familiar with), limit each topic to a subject that would be reasonable for a 5- to 10-minute speech.

1. Bullying
2. Children
3. Civil disobedience
4. Comic books
5. Drug laws
6. Fitness
7. Fraternities and sororities
8. Male–female relationships
9. MOOCs (Massive Open Online Courses)
10. Morality
11. Nutrition
12. Parole
13. Plastic surgery
14. Political corruption
15. Self-driving cars
16. Sports
17. Student problems
18. Surveillance on the Internet
19. Tattoos
20. Violence

ANALYZE YOUR AUDIENCE AND RESEARCH YOUR SPEECH (STEPS 2 AND 3)

→ Research will always be a part of your life.

CHAPTER TOPICS

Approaching Audience Analysis and Adaptation (Step 2)

Analyzing Audience Sociology and Psychology

Researching: Finding and Evaluating Information (Step 3)

Plagiarism

LEARNING OBJECTIVES

4.1 Identify the two principles of audience analysis and the ways in which you might learn about your audience.

4.2 Identify the sociological and psychological characteristics that are important to consider in audience analysis and some of the ways in which you might adapt to specific types of audiences.

4.3 Identify the major sources of information, the criteria to use in evaluating research, and some of the guidelines for integrating research into your speech.

4.4 Define *plagiarism,* the reasons plagiarism is unacceptable, and the suggestions for avoiding plagiarism.

You can inform or persuade an audience only if you know who its members are, what they know, and what they believe. Once you have this information you can begin to tailor your speech to these specific listeners. In this chapter we look at the nature of today's audiences, ways to analyze the sociology and psychology of the audience, and some suggestions for adapting to the audience during the actual speech.

Approaching Audience Analysis and Adaptation (Step 2)

4.1 Identify the two principles of audience analysis and the ways in which you might learn about your audience.

The public speaking audience is best defined as a group of people with the common purpose of listening and responding to a speech. An audience can be of almost any size—five people listening to a street orator, 20 students in a classroom, thousands at a stadium listening to a political or religious speaker. Audience analysis is the process of discovering useful information about these listeners so as to tailor a speech to them.

Two Principles of Audience Analysis

Among all the qualities that might be said to characterize today's audiences, two stand out: uniqueness (no audience is like any other audience) and diversity (audiences are never truly homogeneous). Let's look at each of these briefly.

- **All audiences are unique.** Each public speaking audience you address is unique. Audiences are unique because people are different and unique as individuals; but even when you address the same persons repeatedly (as you will in this course and in various business and other situations), the individuals are not necessarily the same as they were the last time you addressed them. For example, audiences on September 10 and on September 12, 2001, may have been composed of the same people, but probably very few audience members were the same in attitudes and beliefs on those two different dates. Not only world events but also personal experiences (new relationships, children, graduation, new jobs) change us all to some extent and in some way.

- **All audiences are diverse.** As important as uniqueness is the contemporary audience's diversity—in age, race, gender, religion, affectional orientation, nationality, economic situation, relationship status, occupation, political affiliation, attitudes, values, beliefs, and hundreds of other ways. If you're in a typical college classroom in the United States, your classroom audience represents a diverse group of people. Further, each subgroup within this diverse group is itself diverse. People of the same age will differ in race, gender, and religion; those of the same religion will differ from one another in age, nationality, and politics. As you prepare to learn about your audience, keep this notion of diversity in mind. It will help you focus on your audience as a mix of unique individuals rather than a blend.

Learning About Your Audience

You can seek out audience information in four general ways: observation, data collection, interviewing, and inference (Sprague & Stuart, 2008). Let's explore each.

OBSERVE

Think about your audience based on the way members present themselves physically. What can you infer about their economic status from their clothing and jewelry,

ETHICAL CHOICE POINT

Audience Interests

You've just been hired by an advertising agency to design a campaign to promote a cereal that's extremely high in sugar and trans fat—both of which you know are not healthy. The job, however, is a particularly good one, and should you succeed on this account, your future in advertising would be assured. Your problem is relatively simple: you don't want to promote unhealthy foods and yet you want the job, and these goals are incompatible. *What are some of your ethical choices for dealing with this dilemma? What would you do?*

for example? Might their clothing reveal any conservative or liberal leanings? Might clothing provide clues to attitudes on economics or politics? What do they do in their free time? Where do they live? What do they talk about? Are different cultures represented? Do your observations give you any clue as to what audience members' interests or concerns might be?

COLLECT DATA SYSTEMATICALLY

Two major ways to collect data are polling sites and questionnaires. Polling sites enable you to discover what a wide range of people think about varied topics, whereas questionnaires reveal what your specific audience (in this case, your class) thinks.

Polling Sites.   A good place to start with understanding what people think is to visit some of the numerous polling sites on the Internet. Here you'll find a variety of information on all sorts of attitudes and opinions on economics, business, politics, lifestyles, buying habits, and more; search for "opinion poll." One of the most extensive polling websites is the well-known Gallup Organization. Many newspapers maintain polls, one of the best of which is maintained by *The Washington Post*. Another useful source is the Polling Report, which tracks trends in American public opinion.

Many universities conduct polls and make the results available on their websites. Some of the best include the Cornell Institute for Social and Economic Research's website, with links to a wide variety of polls and surveys; Marist College's Institute for Public Opinion; Quinnipiac University's Polling Institute; and Fairleigh Dickenson University's Public Opinion Research Center.

Audience Questionnaires.   Another useful way to secure information about your audience is to use a questionnaire. Let's say you've taken a course in Web design and are thinking about giving an informative speech on ways to design effective Web pages. One thing you'll need to know is how much your audience already knows about design principles. A questionnaire asking audience members about their experience with design can help you judge the level at which to approach the topic, the information that you can assume the audience already has, or the terms you need to define. You might also want to find out how much experience audience members have had with HTML coding.

To help you answer these and other relevant questions, you might compose a questionnaire. If your class is set up as a listserv, if members can communicate through some Web group (like Blackboard or WebCT), or if you all follow each other on Twitter, these questionnaires will be extremely easy to distribute. You can do it with one e-mail questionnaire sent to the listserv or one tweet. Online survey sites like SurveyMonkey and Doodle Poll can also help you distribute questionnaires. If your class is not electronically connected, you can distribute printed questionnaires before class begins or as students are leaving.

Audience questionnaires are even more useful as background for persuasive speeches. Let's say you plan to give a speech in favor of allowing single people to adopt children. To develop an effective speech, you need to know audience members' attitudes toward single-parent adoption. Are they in favor of this idea? Opposed to it? Do they have reservations? If so, what are they? Are audience members undecided? To answer such questions, you might use a questionnaire such as that presented in Figure 4.1.

Figure 4.1 A Sample Audience Questionnaire

This sample questionnaire is built around the four audience factors considered later in this chapter and illustrates the different types of questions you might ask.

A clear title focuses the respondent's attention on your topic. Note too that this doesn't reveal the speaker's purpose or thesis. This helps ensure that the respondents feel comfortable agreeing or disagreeing and will likely be more honest and open.

SINGLE-PARENT ADOPTION QUESTIONNAIRE

Hello classmates: I'm planning a speech on single-parent adoption and would appreciate learning something about your feelings on this topic.

This brief introduction identifies the purpose of the questionnaire.

1. Do you favor single-parent adoption?

- Yes
- No
- Not sure

This type of question—often without the "not sure" option—forces the respondent to take a stand on one side or the other and can give you a general idea of their favorableness to your thesis.

2. How important is this issue to you?

- Very important
- Important
- Neither important nor unimportant
- Unimportant
- Very unimportant

This type of question will enable you to get a general idea of your audience's willingness to listen to your topic and speech. This type of question allows for more variation in response than question 1. You can also combine the responses to the first two categories and the last two categories to get a clearer picture.

3. How knowledgeable do you feel you are about single-parent adoption? On a 10-point scale (with 10 indicating very knowledgeable and 1 indicating very unknowledgeable), how would you rate your knowledge?

This question will give you an indication of what the audience members feel they know about the topic and uses the ubiquitous 10-point scale, which respondents seem to like.

(very unknowledgeable) 1 2 3 4 5 6 7 8 9 10 (very knowledgeable)

4. What to you is the most important issue in single-parent adoption?

_____

_____

_____

This open-ended question will give you a good idea of what the audience feels is important. Other open-ended questions that might be asked might include: "If you are against single-parent adoption, what is your main argument against it? If you are in favor of single-parent adoption, what is your main argument for it?" This question would give you a good idea of what you'd need to cover if you're going to influence your audience. Open-ended questions like these can often provide you with interesting examples to use in your speech.

A simple thank you is an expected politeness.

Thank you. I appreciate your time.

JOURNAL 4.1 PUBLIC SPEAKING CHOICE POINT

Analyzing an Audience

Shirley, a professor of engineering, has been asked to speak about the engineering program in her college to a group of freshman who are undecided about their majors. *What are some of the things Shirley would need to know about her audience? What are her options for learning this needed information?*

In constructing your questionnaire, keep it brief, express thanks to responders for filling it out, and include whatever background information the responders will need to fill out the form (for example, definitions of technical terms). Generally, it's best not to reveal your thesis in the questionnaire—after all, you're going to use this information to help formulate your thesis; besides, you may not want audience members to know your thesis before you give them some evidence and specific examples that support your position.

INTERVIEW MEMBERS OF YOUR AUDIENCE

In a classroom situation you can easily take the time to interview members of your audience in order to find out more about them. But if you're to speak to an audience you'll not meet prior to your speech, you might interview those who know the audience members better than you do. For example, you might talk with the person who invited you to speak and inquire about the audience's culture, age, gender, knowledge and educational levels, or religious background.

USE INFERENCE AND EMPATHY

Use your knowledge of human behavior and human motivation, and try to adopt the perspective of the audience. Intelligent inference and empathy will help you estimate your listeners' attitudes, beliefs, values, and even their thoughts and emotions on your topic (Sprague & Stuart, 2008). For example, let's say you're addressing your class on the need to eliminate (or expand) affirmative action. What might you infer about your audience—are members likely to be in favor of affirmative action or opposed to it? Can they be easily classified in terms of their liberal or conservative leanings? How informed are they likely to be about the topic and about the advantages and disadvantages of affirmative action? What feelings might they have about affirmative action?

Let's turn now to some of the ways in which audiences differ—sociologically and psychologically—and consider how you might analyze and adapt to the unique and diverse audiences you'll face.

Analyzing Audience Sociology and Psychology

4.2 Identify the sociological and psychological characteristics that are important to consider in audience analysis and some of the ways in which you might adapt to specific types of audiences.

In analyzing your audience, consider both the sociological (or demographics) and the psychological dimensions such as audience members' willingness to listen, the degree to which they are in favor of or in opposition to your thesis, and their knowledge of your topic.

Audience Sociology and Adaptation

Sociological audience analysis includes consideration of six major sociological or demographic variables of audiences: (1) age, (2) gender, (3) affectional orientation, (4) educational levels, (5) religion and religiousness, and (6) cultural factors.

AGE

Different age groups have different attitudes and beliefs largely because they have had different experiences in different contexts and they have different futures. To complicate matters further, recognize that culture will also influence attitudes toward age. Among some Native Americans and Chinese, for example, there is great respect for the aged and elders are frequently asked for advice and guidance by the young. Among some groups in the United States—though certainly not all or even necessarily a majority—the aged are often ignored and devalued. In thinking about your next speech, consider how the age of your listeners might influence the topics you speak on and the way you develop, support, and word what you say.

Different age groups vary in their goals, interests, and day-to-day concerns that may be related to your topic and purpose. Consider, for example, how your class would respond to such topics as the following:

1. Achieving corporate success
2. Raising a family
3. Successful job interviewing

If your class is typical (say, with most members from 18 to 24 or so) they are likely to react somewhat like this:

1. Corporate success would be nice, but I'm not at that point yet—I need to get my foot in the door first;
2. Raising a family is important, but that's not on my mind and won't be for a few years at least;
3. Job interviewing is something relevant to me now and might help me achieve my immediate goals, like getting a job.

At the same time, recognize that topic 1 might be highly relevant to middle-management people, topic 2 might be interesting to new mothers and fathers, and topic 3 might be irrelevant and uninteresting to a group of people in their 80s.

Very often, the age of your audience members will give you clues as to what they may and may not be interested in, what their goals are, what they feel they need and want. Show your audience members how they can more effectively achieve their goals, and you'll have an interested and attentive group of listeners.

Different age groups will also differ in their knowledge of the topics and supporting materials you might discuss. For example, if you are using examples of musicians, people like Dizzy Gillespie or Hoagy Carmichael will have little meaning to people in their 20s but much meaning for those in their 70s or 80s, while their knowledge of Lady Gaga and Jay Z will likely be reversed. Similarly, events that happened 10 or so years ago will mean a great deal to people in their 30s and older but a great deal less to those in their 20s.

The most important implication here is that you need to adjust your speech to the age of the audience. Adjust your speech to appeal to your audience's current concerns, and use supporting materials members can easily relate to from recent experience.

GENDER

Gender is one of the most difficult audience variables to analyze. The rapid social changes taking place today make it difficult to pin down the effects of gender. At one time researchers focused primarily on biological sex differences. Now, however, many researchers are focusing on psychological sex roles. When we focus on a psychological sex role, we consider a person feminine if that person has internalized those traits (attitudes and behaviors) that society considers feminine and rejected those traits society considers masculine. We consider a person masculine if that person has internalized those traits society considers masculine and rejected those traits society considers feminine. Thus, a biological woman may display masculine sex-role traits and behaviors, and a biological man may display feminine sex-role traits and behaviors (Pearson, West, & Turner, 1995).

Because of society's training, biological males generally internalize masculine traits and biological females generally internalize feminine traits. So there's probably great overlap between biological sex roles and psychological sex roles, even though they're not equivalent.

Although it's not possible to make generalizations about all men or all women, you may be able to make some assumptions about the men and women in your specific audience. At the same time that you want to take gender differences into consideration, realize the dangers of stereotyping.

Men and women often differ in the values they consider important and that are related to your topic and purpose. For example, research shows that men consider power, stimulation, achievement, self-direction, and hedonism more important than do women (Schwartz & Rubel, 2005). Traditionally, men have been found to place greater importance on theoretical, economic, and political values. Women have traditionally been found to place greater importance on aesthetic, social, and religious values. Of course, you're unlikely ever to find yourself speaking to an audience of all "traditional" men and "traditional" women. Rather, your audience is likely to be composed of men and women whose values overlap. Be careful not to assume that the women in your audience are religious simply because they're women and that the men, because they're men, are not or that the men are interested in sports and the stock market but that the women are not.

Men and women may see your topic differently. Although both men and women may find the topic important, they may nevertheless view it from different perspectives. For example, men and women don't view such topics as abortion, date rape, performance anxiety, anorexia, equal pay for equal work, or exercise in the same way. So if you're giving a speech on date rape on campus, you need to make a special effort to relate the topic and your purpose to the attitudes, knowledge, and feelings that the men and the women in your audience bring with them.

AFFECTIONAL ORIENTATION

The issue of affectional orientation has received enormous media attention within the past decade or so—especially when you compare today's coverage to the way the subject was treated 40 or 50 years ago. *The New York Times*, for example, now regularly features same-sex unions along with those of opposite-sex couples in its Sunday Styles section, and gay and lesbian celebrities and fictional characters are common in the media. Despite these changes, because of the social climate, much of the gay and lesbian experience remains unreported and unknown. Yet you can be reasonably sure that in all your public speaking experiences, you will never address an audience that is totally heterosexual.

The affectional orientation of your audience members may influence the way they see your topic—especially if your topic is politics, the military's current policies on gay men and lesbians, taxes, marriage, or any of a host of other topics. Polls and frequent news items consistently report on attitudes among gay men and lesbians that differ from those of heterosexuals in significant ways. But don't assume that heterosexuals and homosexuals necessarily see things differently on every topic. There are differences, but there are also many similarities.

Be especially careful that you don't come across stereotyping people according to their affectional orientation. While it's true that the media are portraying more gay and lesbian characters, most of them are stereotypical and these ultimately prove

insulting to everyone. Be especially careful that you avoid stereotypical portrayals in your examples (the heterosexual male as boorish, the gay male as compulsively neat) or language that is not as inclusive as it might be. Especially with an educated audience, stereotypes are likely to destroy your credibility.

EDUCATIONAL LEVELS

The interests and concerns of audience members may differ on the basis of their educational level. Generally, educated people are more concerned with issues outside their immediate field of operation. They're concerned with international affairs, economic issues, and the broader philosophical and sociological issues confronting the nation and the world. Educated groups recognize that these issues affect them in many ways. Uneducated people often don't see the connection. Therefore, when speaking to a less-educated audience, draw connections explicitly to relate such topics to their more immediate concerns.

The educational level of your listeners may also influence how critical the audience will be of your evidence and argument. More educated audiences will probably be less swayed by appeals to emotion and to authority (see Chapter 11). They'll be more skeptical of generalizations (as you should be of the generalizations put forth in this chapter). They'll question the validity of statistics and frequently will demand better substantiation of your propositions. Therefore, pay special attention to the logic of your evidence and arguments in addressing an educated audience.

Also consider the educational background of your listeners when you word your speech. While clear and forthright language works for audiences of all educational levels, depending on your topic, you may need to define more terms. Specialized references to literary theory, scientific formulas, or the mechanics of a combustion engine may need to be limited or explained to those without knowledge of the topic.

In all your adjustments on the basis of education and intelligence, be especially careful not to talk down to your listeners.

RELIGION AND RELIGIOUSNESS

Today there's great diversity among the religious backgrounds of audiences. And the attitudes of religions vary widely on numerous issues: abortion, same-sex marriage, women's rights, immigration, divorce, capital punishment, and war, for example. Attitudes also vary within religions; almost invariably there are conservative, liberal, and middle-of-the-road groups within each.

According to a 2006 Pew Research Center study, the clergy have addressed such issues as the following from the pulpit: hunger and poverty, abortion, the situation in Iraq, laws regarding homosexuals, the environment, evolution, the death penalty, stem cell research, and immigration (The Pew Research Center for the People & the Press, 2006). A more recent study identifies such topics as same-sex marriage, suicide, and abortion as the major social issues on which different religions are divided (YouGov, 2013). There seem to be few topics that religion does not address—despite the fact that almost half the population (46 percent) believes that religion should stay out of politics.

Consider if members of your audience will see your topic and your thesis from the point of view of their religion. On a most obvious level, we know that views on such issues as birth control, abortion, and divorce are closely connected to religious affiliation. Similarly, attitudes about premarital sex, marriage, child rearing, money, cohabitation, responsibilities toward parents, and thousands of other issues are clearly influenced by religion. Religion is also important, however, in areas where its connection isn't so obvious. For example, religion influences people's ideas concerning such topics as obedience to authority; responsibility to government; and the usefulness of such qualities as honesty, guilt, and happiness.

Be especially careful of appearing insensitive to the religious beliefs of any segment of your audience. Even people who claim total alienation from the religion in which they were raised may still have strong emotional (though perhaps unconscious) ties to that religion that may influence attitudes and beliefs. When dealing with any religious beliefs (and particularly when disagreeing with them), recognize that you're likely to meet stiff opposition. Proceed slowly and inductively. Present your evidence and argument before expressing your disagreement.

Realize also that members of any religion may deviate from many of the official teachings of their religion. Don't assume that the rank-and-file members of a faith necessarily accept religious leaders' opinions or pronouncements. Official statements by religious leaders often take more conservative positions than those of laypeople.

CULTURAL FACTORS

Nationality, race, and cultural identity are crucial in audience analysis. Largely because of different training and experiences, members of different cultures develop different interests, values, and goals.

The use of cultural information about your audience to help you select the right motivational appeals may be effective only in certain situations. For example, researchers have found that appeals to self-interest have greater influence on audiences from individualist cultures (the United States, Australia, Canada, Denmark, and Sweden, for example) than on audiences from collectivist cultures (Guatemala, Venezuela, Indonesia, Pakistan, and China, for example). And appeals to other-interests are more influential on audiences of collectivist cultures than on people from individualist cultures (Dillard & Marshall, 2003; Han & Shavitt, 1994). Thus, using an audience's cultural information to select appeals works best when you speak to audiences that are almost exclusively from one cultural orientation and when all or almost all members of that audience subscribe to the specific values you are addressing.

Consider if the attitudes and beliefs held by different cultures are relevant to your topic and purpose. Find out what these are. For example, the degree to which listeners are loyal to family members, feel responsibility for the aged, and believe in the value of education will vary from one culture to another. Build your appeals around your audience's attitudes and beliefs.

Consider too if the cultures differ in their expectations of the speaker. Members of some cultures—for example, many Asian cultures—expect speakers to be humble and to avoid self-praise and self-commendation. With these groups, if you appear too confident or mention your accomplishments and credits too directly or too often,

VIEWPOINTS
Class Demographics

How would you describe the sociology or demographics of your public speaking class?

you run the risk of appearing forward, arrogant, or pushy. On the other hand, if you are addressing an American audience, the humbleness and avoidance of self-praise may work against you, and you'll be perceived as less competent than you otherwise might be.

Speakers who fail to demonstrate an understanding of cultural differences will be distrusted. For example, speakers, especially those who are seen to be outsiders, who imply that all African Americans are athletic and all lesbians are masculine will quickly lose credibility. Avoid any implication that you're stereotyping audience members (or the groups to which they belong). It's sure to work against achieving your purpose.

OTHER AUDIENCE FACTORS

No list of audience characteristics can possibly be complete, and the list presented here is no exception. You'll need another category—"other factors"—to identify any additional characteristics that might be significant to your particular audience. Here are a few categories and questions you might want to ask.

- **Occupation and income.** Is your audience's level of job security and occupational pride related to your topic, purpose, or examples? Will people from different economic levels have different preferences for immediate or long-range goals?
- **Relational status.** Will singles be interested in hearing about the problems of selecting preschools? Will those in long-term relationships be interested in the depression many people who are not in close relationships experience during the holidays?
- **Special interests.** What special interests do audience members have? What occupies their leisure time? How can you integrate these interests into your examples and illustrations or use them as you select quotations?
- **Political beliefs.** Will audience members' political affiliations influence how they view your topic or purpose? Are they politically liberal? Conservative? Might this influence how you develop your speech?
- **Organizational memberships.** Might audience members' affiliations give you clues as to their other beliefs and values? Might you use references to these organizations in your speech, perhaps as examples or illustrations?

CONTEXT CHARACTERISTICS

In addition to analyzing specific listeners, think about **context factors**—aspects of the specific context in which you'll speak. In this class, the context will likely remain the same for all your speeches. Yet outside of this learning laboratory, the context will exert significant influence and needs to be considered.

- **Number of listeners.** Generally, the larger the audience, the more formal the speech presentation should be. With a small audience, you may be more casual and informal. In a large audience you'll have a wider variety of religions, a greater range of occupations and income levels, and so on. All the variables noted earlier will be intensified in a large audience. Therefore, you'll need supporting materials that will appeal to all members.

- **Physical environment.** Consider the physical environment—indoors or outdoors, room or auditorium, sitting or standing audience—which will obviously influence your speech presentation. Also, consider the equipment that is available. Is there a whiteboard, flip chart, or transparency projector? Is there a slide projector and screen? Is there a computer with a projector for showing PowerPoint slides? Are markers available? If at all possible, rehearse in the room you'll be speaking in with the same equipment that you'll have when you deliver your speech.

- **Occasion.** Consider the occasion for your speech. When you give a speech as a class assignment, for example, you'll probably be operating under a number of restrictions—time limitations, the type of general purpose you can use, the types of supporting materials, and various other matters. The same will be true of your speeches outside the classroom; you'll be operating under various requirements and expectations. If you're invited to speak to a group, find out what the group expects of you, how long you'd be expected to speak, how many will be in the audience, or if there'll be a question-and-answer session.

- **Time of day.** Consider the time of your speech. If your speech is to be given in an early morning class, say around 8 A.M., then take into consideration that some of your listeners will still be half asleep. Express your appreciation for their attendance; compliment their attention. If necessary, wake them up with your voice, gestures, attention-gaining materials, visual aids, and the like. If your speech is in the evening, when most of your listeners are anxious to get home, recognize this fact as well.

Audience Psychology and Adaptation

Psychological audience analysis considers audience members along such dimensions as willing-to-unwilling, favorable-to-unfavorable, and knowledgeable-to-unknowledgeable.

HOW WILLING IS YOUR AUDIENCE?

Audiences gather with varying degrees of willingness to hear a speaker. Some are anxious to hear the speaker and may even have paid a substantial admission price. The "lecture circuit," for example, is a most lucrative aspect of public life. But whereas some audiences are willing to pay to hear a speaker, others don't seem to care one way or the other. Some audiences need to be persuaded to listen (or at least to sit still during the speech). Still other audiences gather because they have to. For example, negotiations on a union contract may require members to attend meetings where officers give speeches, just as students are required to attend class.

Your immediate concern, of course, is with the willingness of your fellow students to listen to your speeches. How willing are they? If they're a willing group, then you have few problems. If they're an unwilling group, all is not lost; you just have to work a little harder in adapting your speech. Here are a few suggestions to help change your listeners from unwilling to willing.

context factors

Those characteristics of the place in which the speech will be given, for example, the physical environment in which the speech will be presented.

psychological audience analysis

An analysis of such audience characteristics as the willingness to listen and the degree to which audience members favor your position.

- **Get their interest and attention as early in your speech as possible.** Then maintain this attention throughout your speech by using little-known facts, humor, quotations, startling statistics, examples, narratives, audiovisual aids, and the like.

- **Reward audience members for their attendance and attention.** Do this in advance of your main arguments. Let audience members know you're aware they're making a sacrifice in coming to hear you speak. Tell them you appreciate it. One student, giving a speech close to midterm time, said simply:

  > I know how easy it is to cut classes during midterm time to finish the unread chapters and do everything else you have to do. So I especially appreciate your being here this morning. What I have to say, however, will interest you...

- **Relate your topic and supporting materials directly to your audience's needs and wants.** Show audience members how they can save time, make more money, solve their problems, or become more popular. If you fail to address your listeners' needs and wants, then your audience has good reason for not listening.

HOW FAVORABLE IS YOUR AUDIENCE?

Audiences vary in the degree to which they're favorable or unfavorable toward your thesis or point of view. And even within the same audience, of course, you're likely to have some who agree with you, others who disagree, and perhaps still others who are undecided. If you hope to change audience members' attitudes, beliefs, or values and ultimately their behaviors, you must understand their current attitudes, beliefs, and values and how these might influence the way they view your speech and especially your thesis. In estimating this possible influence, you'll find it helpful to ask some of the following questions about their attitudes, beliefs, and values.

attitude

A predisposition to respond for or against an object, person, or position.

What **attitudes** (tendencies to respond for or against an object, person, or position) do your listeners have that might influence their response to your thesis? If your audience members have a favorable attitude toward conservation, then they'll likely be more favorable toward speeches on the need to reduce pollution, to drive smaller cars, and to recycle. On the other hand, they might not favor proposals for reducing fines for companies guilty of pollution or a speech on the benefits of owning larger SUVs. How might you use the listeners' current attitudes to adapt your speech to them? For example, if you know their attitudes and your thesis is consistent with them, you might mention your attitudinal similarity.

belief

Confidence in the existence or truth of something; conviction.

What **beliefs** (convictions in the existence or truth of something) do your listeners have that will have an impact on your speech? If they believe in a specific religion, then they will likely respond well to religious examples, will respect testimony from religious leaders, and will likely believe what the religion teaches. At the same time, they're likely to resist ideas that go against their religious beliefs. Capital punishment, abortion, and same-sex marriage are just some of the topics about which the listeners' religious beliefs will influence their responses. How can you use the beliefs of the audience in adapting your speech to them?

JOURNAL 4.2 PUBLIC SPEAKING CHOICE POINT

Unwilling Audience

Ted is scheduled to give a speech on careers in computer technology to a group of high school students who have been forced to attend on a Saturday. The audience definitely qualifies as unwilling. *What are some of Ted's options in dealing with this type of audience?*

What **values** (the worth a person puts on something or some action) does your audience have, and how might these have an impact on your topic? For example, if your listeners value equality and cultural diversity, they're likely to favor interracial adoption and fewer restrictions on immigration than would those who do not value cultural diversity. How can you use the values of your listeners to adapt your speech to them? For example, if people value financial success, they'll likely be interested in hearing speeches on the stock market, foreign currency, and the stories of successful entrepreneurs. Further, audiences respond favorably to topics that promise financial rewards or that teach skills that will prove financially beneficial.

Of course, when you face audience members whose attitudes, beliefs, and values are consistent with your thesis, your adaptation task is going to be relatively easy. But when you face audience members whose attitudes, beliefs, and values are contrary to your thesis, adapting your speech becomes much more difficult. Here are a few suggestions for dealing with the unfavorably disposed audience.

- **Clear up any possible misapprehensions.** Often disagreement is caused by a lack of understanding. If you feel this is the case, then your first task is to clear this up. For example, if audience members are hostile to the new team approach you are advocating because they wrongly think it will result in a reduction in their autonomy, then explain it to them very directly, saying something like:

    > I realize that many people oppose this new team approach because they feel it will reduce their own autonomy and control. Well, it won't; as a matter of fact, with this approach, each person will actually gain greater control, greater power, greater autonomy.

- **Build on commonalities.** Emphasize not the differences between you and your listeners but the similarities. Stress what you and audience members share as people, as interested citizens, as fellow students. Theorist and critic Kenneth Burke (1950) argued that we achieve persuasion through identification with the audience. Identification involves emphasizing similarities between speaker and audience. When audience members see common ground between themselves and you, they become more favorable both to you and to your speech.

    For example, a former student who returns to her high school to speak about the importance of preparing early for college might identify with her audience by saying something like this:

    > It wasn't very long ago that I sat in this auditorium and had to listen to speakers talk about college. And I remember wanting to be somewhere else, anywhere else. But I'm glad I listened because it helped me tremendously, and I hope I'll be able to help you in the same way I was helped.

- **Organize your speech inductively.** Try to build your speech from areas of agreement, through areas of slight disagreement, up to the point where major differences exist between the audience's attitudes and your own position. Let's say, for example, that you represent management and you wish to persuade employees to accept a particular wage offer. You might begin with such areas of agreement as the mutual desire for improved working conditions or for long-term economic growth. Once areas of agreement are established, it's easier to bring up differences such as, perhaps, the need to delay salary increases until next year. In any disagreement or conflict, there are still areas of agreement; emphasize these before considering areas of disagreement.

- **Strive for small gains.** Don't use a 5-minute speech to try to convince a pro-life group to contribute money for the new abortion clinic or a pro-choice group to vote against liberalizing abortion laws. Be content to get your listeners to see some validity in your position and to listen fairly. About-face changes take a long time to achieve. Attempting to exert too much persuasion or asking for too much change can result only in failure or resentment.

value

Relative worth of an object; a quality that makes something desirable or undesirable; ideals or customs about which we have emotional responses, whether positive or negative.

- **Acknowledge the differences explicitly.** If it's clear to the audience that they and you are at opposite ends of the issue, it may be helpful to acknowledge this very directly. Show audience members that you understand and respect their position but that you'd like them to consider a different way of looking at things. Say something like:

> I know you don't all agree that elementary school teachers should have to take tests every several years to maintain their certification. Some teachers are going to lose their certification, and that isn't pleasant. And we all feel sorry that this will happen. What isn't widely known, however, is that the vast majority of teachers will actually benefit from this proposal. And I'd like an opportunity to sketch out the benefits that many of us will enjoy as a result of this new testing procedure.

HOW KNOWLEDGEABLE IS YOUR AUDIENCE?

Listeners differ greatly in the knowledge they have. Some listeners will be quite knowledgeable about your topic; others will be almost totally ignorant. Mixed audiences are the most difficult ones.

If you're unaware of the audience's knowledge level, you won't know what to assume and what to explain. You won't know how much information will overload the channels or how much will bore audience members to sleep. Perhaps you want to show that their previous knowledge is now inadequate. Perhaps you want to demonstrate a new slant to old issues. Or perhaps you want to show that what you have to say will not repeat but instead will build on the already-extensive knowledge of the audience. However you accomplish this, you need to make audience members see that what you have to say is new. Make them realize that you won't simply repeat what they already know.

Treat audiences that lack knowledge of the topic very carefully. Never confuse a lack of knowledge with a lack of ability to understand.

- **Don't talk down to your audience.** This is perhaps the greatest communication error that teachers make. Having taught a subject for years, they face, semester after semester, students who have no knowledge of the topic. As a result, many teachers tend to talk down to the students and, in the process, lose their audience.
- **Don't confuse a lack of knowledge with a lack of intelligence.** An audience may have no knowledge of your topic but be quite capable of following a clearly presented, logically developed argument. Try especially hard to use concrete

VIEWPOINTS

Class Psychology

How would you describe the psychology of your public speaking class for listening to a speech advocating the right for students and faculty to carry concealed weapons on campus?

examples, audiovisual aids, and simple language. Fill in background details as required. Avoid jargon and specialized terms that may not be clear to someone new to the subject. In sum, never overestimate your audience members' knowledge, but never underestimate their intelligence.

■ **Let your listeners know that you're aware of their knowledge and expertise.** Try to do this as early in the speech as possible. Emphasize that what you have to say will not be redundant. Tell them that you'll be presenting recent developments or new approaches. In short, let them know that they won't be wasting their time listening to your speech.

■ **Emphasize your credibility, especially your competence in this general subject area** (see Chapter 11). Let your listeners know that you have earned the right to speak. Let them know that what you have to say is based on a firm grasp of the material.

Here, for example, Senator Christopher Dodd (2007) of Connecticut, addressing the Jesse Jackson Wall Street Summit, establishes his credibility:

> When Dr. King and President Kennedy asked young Americans to serve the cause of freedom and justice, I was among those who answered in the affirmative. I joined the Peace Corps as a young man. I lived and worked in a small village in the Dominican Republic. I worked side by side with people who had a different ethnic heritage, a different nationality, and a different language than me. I was very much in the minority. Yet, I was accepted into the community. We all brought different abilities and experiences to our common work. And together, we achieved significant things. We built a road, a school, and several homes.

Analyzing and Adapting During the Speech

In addition to analyzing your audience and making adaptations in your speech before delivering it, devote attention to analysis and adaptation during the speech. This during-the-speech analysis is especially important when you know little about your audience or find yourself facing an audience very different from the one you expected. Here are a few suggestions.

FOCUS ON LISTENERS AS MESSAGE SENDERS

As you're speaking, look at your audience. Remember that just as you're sending messages to your listeners, they're also sending messages to you. Pay attention to these messages; on the basis of what they tell you, make the necessary adjustments.

Remember that members of different cultures operate with different **display rules**, cultural rules that state what types of expressions are appropriate to reveal— and what expressions are inappropriate to reveal and should be kept hidden. Some display rules call for open and free expression of feelings and responses; these listeners will be easy to read. Other display rules call for little expression, and these listeners will be difficult to read.

display rules
Cultural norms for what is and what is not appropriate to display in public.

You can make a wide variety of adjustments to each type of audience response. For example, if audience members show signs of boredom, increase your volume, move closer to them, or tell them that what you're going to say will be of value to them. If audience members show signs of disagreement or hostility, stress a similarity you have with them. If audience members look puzzled or confused, pause for a moment and rephrase your ideas, provide necessary definitions, or insert an internal summary. If audience members seem impatient, say, for example, "my last argument…" instead of your originally planned "my third argument…."

USE ANSWERS TO YOUR "WHAT IF" QUESTIONS

The more preparation you put into your speech, the better prepared you'll be to make on-the-spot adjustments and adaptations. For example, let's say you have been told that you're to explain the opportunities available to the nontraditional student at your college. You've been told that your audience will consist mainly of working women in their 30s and 40s who are just beginning college. As you prepare your speech with this audience in mind, ask yourself **"what if" questions**. For example:

"what if" questions
Questions of anticipation, useful in considering and preparing for the unexpected.

- What if the audience has a large number of men?
- What if the audience consists of women much older than 40?
- What if the audience members also come with their spouses or their children?

Keeping such questions in mind will force you to consider possible answers as you prepare your speech. Use these answers to make on-the-spot adjustments.

ADDRESS AUDIENCE RESPONSES DIRECTLY

Another way of dealing with audience responses is to confront them directly. To people who are reacting negatively to your message, for example, you might say:

> Regardless of your present position, hear me out and see if this new way of doing things will not simplify your accounting procedures.

Or, to those who seem puzzled, you might say:

> This plan may seem confusing, but bear with me; it will become clear in a moment.

Or, to those who seem impatient, you might respond:

> I know this has been a long day, but give me just a few more minutes and you'll be able to save hours recording your accounts.

By responding to your listeners' reactions and feedback, you acknowledge their needs. You let them know that you hear them, that you're with them, and that you're responding to their very real concerns.

Researching: Finding and Evaluating Information (Step 3)

4.3 Identify the major sources of information, the criteria to use in evaluating research, and some of the guidelines for integrating research into your speech.

Throughout the process of preparing your public speeches, you'll need to find information to use as source material in your speech. This means doing **research**, a systematic search for information. Through research you'll find examples, illustrations, and definitions to help you inform your listeners; testimony, statistics, and arguments to support your major ideas; personal anecdotes, quotations, and stories to help you bring your topics to life.

research
A systematic search for information; an investigation of the relevant information on a topic; an inquiry into what is known or thought about a subject.

Research, however, also serves another important function: It helps you persuade your listeners because it makes you appear more believable. For example, if your listeners feel you've examined lots of research, they'll be more apt to see you as competent and knowledgeable and therefore more apt to believe what you say. And, of course, presenting the research is itself convincing. When you present research to your listeners, you give them the very reasons they need to draw conclusions or decide on a course of action.

Research is a systematic search for information; it's an investigation of the relevant information on a topic and an inquiry into what is known or thought about a subject. According to the University of Idaho's literacy website, research is undertaken, almost always, to discover an answer to one of several types of questions.

- **Research for specifics.** Research is a search for specific facts, examples, illustrations, statistics, or definitions. Here your question is simple: "How is socialism defined?" "What is the population of Japan?" "What is the average salary for accountants?" You'll make use of this type of research in all your speeches as you search for supporting materials.

- **Research to discover what is known.** Here your question is "How?" "How might you describe some person or object," or "How you can describe an event or process?" Or you might want to discover how a term or theory is defined and the differences and similarities among terms and systems. Or you might want to discover how to do something or how something operates. These types of research are at the heart of informative speech making.

- **Research to support a position.** Here your questions can revolve around a variety of issues. For example, you might conduct research to discover which explanation or position is the closest to being true: "Are the parents guilty of child negligence?" "Do gay men and women make effective military personnel?" Another type of question focuses on what is just or moral: "Can bullfighting ever be morally justified?" "What procedures will be most humane?" Still another type of question focuses on the policies that should or should not be adopted: "Should medical marijuana be made legal?" "What should the government's policy be on immigration?" These types of research questions are at the heart of persuasive speech making.

Of course, your time is limited and you cannot research all that has been written and said about a topic. But you can learn to use your research time more effectively and more efficiently. Table 4.1 identifies some principles of **time management**.

time management
The efficient use of the available time.

Sources of Information

There are so many sources of information that we can only skim the surface. Here we discuss libraries, general reference works, government publications, and the Web. In using these sources, keep in mind the distinction among primary, second, and tertiary sources and between scholarly and popular journals. Let's look at the last two items first.

TABLE 4.1   Principles of Time Management

Generally	Specifically
Understand your use of time.	Take a look at what takes up most of your time. Once you know how you spend your time, you'll be able to see what can be and should be cut back.
Attack your time wasters.	Identify your time wasters and get rid of the one time waster that you can most easily do without. Then tackle the next.
Avoid procrastination.	Avoid the tendency to delay things to the last minute, another strategy that college students often use in the mistaken belief that they work better under pressure.
Use tools.	Whether you use the low-tech schedule book or Google Calendar or Rescue Time's app on your smartphone, use a tool.
Prioritize.	Make lists of items you need to accomplish, and classify them in terms of importance. Lists help you put order into your work life.
Break up large tasks.	Divide large tasks into units or steps (as we do here in preparing and presenting a public speech); the steps will seem more manageable and not as daunting.
Set realistic time limits.	When the task is large, it often helps to set time limits; in this way the task will not seem oppressive or overly difficult.
Reward yourself.	Reward yourself after completing a unit of work, but keep the reward in proportion. Don't reward yourself with unhealthy food or overly long "breaks."
Do things once rather than twice.	Try to look only once at a piece of paper or electronic message, act on it, and then file or get rid of it.

PRIMARY, SECONDARY, AND TERTIARY SOURCES

As you collect information keep in mind the important distinctions among primary, secondary, and tertiary source material.

primary sources

Firsthand, contemporary accounts written or spoken by someone who has had direct experience with or witnessed a particular event. Distinguished from *secondary sources* and *tertiary sources.*

secondary sources

Materials that interpret, comment on, analyze, or summarize primary source material. Distinguished from *primary sources* and *tertiary sources.*

tertiary sources

A combination of primary and secondary source materials. Distinguished from *primary sources* and *secondary sources.*

Primary sources are firsthand, contemporary accounts written or spoken by someone who has had direct experience with or witnessed a particular event. Also considered primary sources are reports of original research by the researcher himself or herself. Primary sources include, for example, an original research study reported in an academic journal, a corporation's annual report, and an eyewitness report of an accident. With primary sources there is nothing (or very little) standing between the event (say, an accident) and the reporting of it (the eyewitness testimony).

Secondary sources are those that interpret, comment on, analyze, or summarize primary source material. Secondary sources include, for example, a summary of research appearing in a popular magazine, a television news report on a corporation's earnings, and a report by someone who talked to someone who witnessed an accident. With secondary sources someone stands between the actual event and the report; for example, a science reporter reads the scientist's monograph (primary source), then writes up a summary for the popular press (secondary source).

Tertiary sources are a combination of primary and secondary sources. Tertiary source material would include articles in encyclopedias, almanacs, handbooks, and guidebooks. Also considered tertiary are statistical compilations such as movie attendance figures or Nielsen figures. Your textbooks are in part secondary source material (they interpret and summarize the primary source material that appears in scholarly journals) and in part tertiary source material (they also make use of summaries of research and theories, i.e., secondary source material).

As a listener and speaker you'll hear and use all three types of source material. Yet there are important differences that you should keep in mind. Secondary source material is usually less reliable than primary source material because it's a step removed from the actual facts or events. The writer of secondary material may have forgotten important parts, may be biased, or may have misunderstood the data. On the other hand, the writer may have been able to express complicated data in simple language—often making it easier for a nonexpert to understand than the original report. Tertiary material (say, an encyclopedia article) is usually an excellent starting place, but your research needs to go beyond that and include secondary and perhaps primary source materials.

SCHOLARLY AND POPULAR JOURNALS

Throughout your research, you'll use both scholarly journals and popular magazines, each for different purposes. If you want scientifically reliable information, then the scholarly journals are what you need to look at, though they'll prove difficult to read—especially if they're outside your area of expertise. If you want more popular material in easy-to-understand language, then you should consult popular magazines. The type of information you seek will determine which types of publications you'll need to consult. If you want to read the original research studies on, say, emotional contagion, then you'll consult scholarly journals; if you want to get a broad and general overview of the nature of emotional contagion, then an article written in a popular magazine might prove more useful. If you want information on Madonna's latest concert, then a popular magazine would likely have what you need. If you want information on Madonna and feminist theory, then a scholarly journal might be more helpful.

Some publications are not so easy to classify. For example, *Psychology Today* would normally be considered a popular magazine, and yet it often contains scholarly articles by academic researchers. *National Geographic* is both a scholarly publication and a popular magazine. With this caveat in mind, Table 4.2 presents a chart comparing these two types of publications.

TABLE 4.2   A Comparison of Scholarly Journals and Popular Magazines

	Scholarly Journals	Popular Magazines
Purpose	To advance research, to stimulate research and theory building; to communicate specialized knowledge, research findings	To entertain and inform people about general issues and concerns; to communicate general interest knowledge, to summarize and popularize more specialized knowledge
Types of Articles	Original scientific research studies; critical analyses; usually written in the jargon of the particular field, making it difficult for outsiders to understand	Personality profiles; news summaries; usually written in easy-to-understand, fast-paced prose
Article Authors	Professors, researchers, scientists, graduate students	Professional writers, journalists, and some academics
Hardcopy and Online Accessibility	Available by subscription, usually fairly expensive; online access available for a fee that libraries, publishers, or individuals purchase	Available by subscription, usually fairly inexpensive, and at newsstands and bookstores; online copies are often free
Review Process	Often blind review by peers (ideally the reviewers do not know the author when they review the article)	Varies greatly from a review board to a general editor
Reliability	Probably the most reliable types of articles available	Varies greatly depending on the magazine, though reliability for most mass market magazines is generally quite high
Readers	Academics, scientists, researchers, undergraduate and graduate students	The general reading public or those interested in specific areas, for example, photography, finance, or sports
Design and Appearance	Scholarly looking, one color, little variation in typeface, seldom containing photos (with obvious exceptions as in art and architecture journals); few advertisements, perhaps of other scholarly journals or books	Glossy, colorful, varied fonts, lots of photos, advertisements for various products
Examples of Journals and Magazines	*Communication Monographs, Journal of Personality and Social Psychology, New England Journal of Medicine*	*People, Fast Company, Reader's Digest, Time, Businessweek, Forbes, Wired, Rachael Ray Everyday*
Examples of Articles	■ *Interpersonal Surveillance over Social Network Sites* ■ *The Mathematics of Sexual Attraction* ■ *Early vs. Late Parenteral Nutrition in Children*	■ *Airbnb Wants to Share Your Bed. Are You In?* ■ *The Worst Party Ever* ■ *Ben Affleck vs. Henry Cavill*
Publication Schedule	Usually quarterly; articles are often published 9–24 months after they are submitted. As a result, most articles do not address immediate concerns or very recent issues.	Usually weekly or monthly; articles are likely to be published within days of the happenings they report

LIBRARIES

Libraries, the major depositories of stored information, have evolved from a concentration on print sources to their current focus on computerized databases. Starting your research at the library (and with the librarian's assistance) is probably a wise move.

Here are a few online libraries that you'll find especially helpful.

■ Quick Study, the University of Minnesota's Library Research Guide, will help you learn how to find the materials you need and will answer lots of questions you have about research.

■ The largest library in the United States is the Library of Congress, which houses millions of books, maps, multimedia, and manuscripts.

■ Maintained by the National Archives and Records Administration, the presidential libraries may also prove of considerable value.

■ The Virtual Library is a collection of links to 14 subject areas; for example, agriculture, business and economics, computing, communication and media, and education.

■ If you're not satisfied with your own college library, visit the libraries of some of the large state universities, such as the University of Pennsylvania or the University of Illinois.

Of course, you'll also need to go to a brick-and-mortar library because it houses materials that are not on the Web and/or that you want to access in print. Because each library functions somewhat differently, your best bet in learning about a specific library—such as your own college library—is to talk with your librarian about what the library has available, what kinds of training or tours it offers, and how materials are most easily accessed.

GENERAL REFERENCE WORKS

General reference works are tertiary sources and are excellent starting points for researching your topic.

Encyclopedias One of the best general reference works is the standard encyclopedia. Any good encyclopedia will give you a general overview of your subject and suggestions for additional reading. Perhaps the most widely known online encyclopedia, and one that you'll find extremely useful, is Wikipedia. The articles in Wikipedia—some brief and some extremely long and detailed—are written by people who are not necessarily experts. Many of the articles are reviewed, updated, and corrected periodically. But because this work is an open and collaborative effort by unknown users, you'll need to check the facts and statistics—most of which you'll find easy to do because of the extensive hot links written into each article and the list of additional sources provided for most articles. Different instructors have different views on the usefulness of Wikipedia, so check the research guidelines of your specific class.

Almanacs Another excellent general reference work is the almanac, in print or online. Start with Infoplease, which contains a wide variety of hot links to almanacs and similar works covering such categories as the world, U.S. history and government, biography, sports, business, society and culture, health and science, and arts and entertainment.

Biographical Materials As a speaker you'll often need information about particular individuals. For example, in using expert testimony, it's helpful to stress your experts' qualifications, which you can easily learn about from even brief biographies. Knowing something about your sources enables you to more effectively evaluate their competence, convey their credibility to the audience, and answer audience questions about them. Some excellent general resources include the Biography Almanac available at Infoplease, the University of Michigan's Internet Public Library, and Biographical Dictionary.

Statistical Information A variety of organizations collect statistics but none as thoroughly as the government and its various agencies. Each government department publishes statistics, and you can go to the website of the specific department (for example, the Department of the Treasury) to access relevant statistics. An even easier way is to log on to FedStats. Here you'll find statistics from more than 100 U.S. federal agencies, including statistical profiles of each state, country, and city as well as statistics on crime, population, economics, mortality, and energy, along with comparisons with other countries.

News Sources Often you'll want to read reports on scientific breakthroughs, political speeches, congressional actions, obituaries, financial news, international developments, UN actions, or any of a host of other topics. Or you may wish to locate the date of a particular event and learn something about what else was going on in the world at that particular time. For this type of information, you may want to consult one or more of the many news sources available. Especially relevant are newspaper and newsmagazine websites, new wire services, and online news networks.

- **Newspaper and newsmagazine websites.** Most newspapers and magazines maintain their own websites from which you can access current and past issues. Among the most respected newspaper websites are those of the *Los Angeles Times, USA Today, The Wall Street Journal, The New York Times*, and *The Washington Post*.

- **News wire services.** Four wire services should prove helpful: the Associated Press, Reuters, United Press International, and PR Newswire.

- **Online news networks.** All of the television news stations maintain extremely useful websites. Among those most useful are CNN, ESPN, ABC News, CBS News, and NBC News.

As you read content available through these news sources, you'll find it helpful to compare the news available on one of the major newspapers' websites (for example, *The Washington Post* site or *The New York Times* site) with the news presented by a wire service such as the Associated Press or Reuters. Which seems the more reliable? The more complete? The more impartial?

THE GOVERNMENT

The various governments throughout the United States (federal, state, and municipal) publish an enormous amount of information that you're sure to find useful in speeches on almost any topic. One excellent starting point is Google's government search. This engine covers all websites in the *.gov* domain. The amount of information you'll find, however, may at first be daunting. For example, if you searched for "publications," you'd find more than 27 million websites, 94 million for "education," and 125 million for "health." You'll definitely need to narrow your search. One way to do this is of course to include additional terms (for example, health + drugs + teenagers) or use phrases in quotations ("teenage drug use"). Another useful way to learn about these sites is to take any of the many tutorials that are readily available online. The U.S. government websites contain a variety of tutorials that will help you research your topic more efficiently.

Another way is to visit one or more of the 13 relevant departments of the federal government (these are the Departments of Agriculture, Commerce, Defense, Education, Energy, Health and Human Services, Housing and Urban Development, Interior, Justice, Labor, State, Treasury, and Transportation). All publish reports, pamphlets, books, and assorted documents dealing with their various concerns. Here are a few of the topics on which some of the departments have information that you'll find useful as you research your speeches.

- **Department of the Treasury:** taxes, property auctions, savings, economy, financial markets, international business, and money management.

- **Department of Housing and Urban Development:** home buying, selling, renting, and owning; fair housing, foreclosures, consumer information, FHA refunds, homelessness; and information for tenants, landlords, farm workers, senior citizens, and victims of discrimination.

- **Department of Defense:** news releases, speech texts, military pay/benefits, casualty reports.

- **Department of Justice:** drugs and drug enforcement; Patriot Act information; trafficking in persons; inmate locator; Americans with Disabilities Act; sentencing statistics; and information from the Bureau of Alcohol, Tobacco, Firearms, and Explosives.

- **Department of Health and Human Services:** aging, AIDS, disease, safety issues, food and drug information, disaster and emergency protection, families and children, disabilities, homelessness, and immigration.

- **Department of Education:** teaching resources in science, math, history, and language arts; innovations in education; reports on performance and accountability; "no child left behind" reports; at-risk and gifted students; Pell grant program; religious expression in schools.

- **Department of Labor:** pensions, unemployment, wages, insurance, and just about any topic even remotely related to labor.
- **Department of Energy:** materials on science and technology, energy efficiency, national security, and health and safety; issues currently in the news such as oil spills and ways to save money on energy.
- **Department of the Interior:** managing and sustaining America's water, wildlife, lands, and energy; other topics including those relating to Native Americans.

Other departments are equally prolific in their publishing of a wide range of information and are worth visiting. All of these departments can be followed on a variety of networks including Facebook and Twitter.

THE WEB

It's convenient to think of the Web as a three-part system consisting of the open, the deep, and the social Web.

The open Web (or visible or surface) consists of those materials that you'd be able to access with a simple search from most of your favorite search engines or directories. When you do a simple Google search, for example, you'd be accessing the open Web.

The deep Web (or invisible or hidden or deepnet)—estimated to be perhaps 50 times the size of the open Web—contains that collection of documents that are not accessible through simple searches on general search engines or directions. These include databases of scholarly articles and academic research journals that are available only for a fee that your college library or the publisher of your textbook pays. It also includes all those websites you need a password to enter. Many image and video files also reside on the deep Web.

The social Web is actually a part of the deep Web, but because it deals with a unique type of material, it's helpful to consider it as a separate category. The social Web consists of the millions of blogs, Facebook and Google+ pages, tweets, newsgroups, and listservs. Blogs are now extremely popular and often contain information that may be useful in public speaking. But don't assume that anything on a blog is necessarily reliable and accurate; check first.

Be aware that search engines yield an enormous number of websites but do not distinguish between reliable and unreliable information. A high school student's term paper may well be listed next to that of a world-famous scientist with no distinction between them.

You can also search the Web by setting up alerts. For example, you can go to Google, Bing, or Yahoo! and enter your speech topic, the kind of search you want (whether news, Web, news and Web, or groups), and how often you want to receive alerts (daily, weekly, or as-it-happens). You'll then receive in your e-mail alerts with links to sites that include your speech topic. More easily, these search engines prompt you at the very end of your search results page with an invitation to establish an alert.

JOURNAL 4.3 PUBLIC SPEAKING CHOICE POINT

Research Sources

If you were preparing a speech on the state of current immigration laws, what resources would you go to? What sources would you go to if your speech was on the need to change our immigration laws?

Evaluating Internet Resources

As you research your topic, keep in mind that anyone can "publish" on the Internet, making it essential that you subject everything you find on the Web to critical analysis. An article on the Internet can be written by world-renowned scientists or by elementary school students; by fair and objective reporters or by people who would spin the issues to serve their own purposes. It's not always easy to tell which is which. Table 4.3 presents the five criteria to use in evaluating research—built around the acronym FACQS (**F**airness, **A**ccuracy, **C**urrency, **Q**ualifications, and **S**ufficiency) to help you remember the questions you'd want to ask about these criteria and the precautions to take. Of course, these criteria and questions are relevant for evaluating research of all kinds (including information you receive from print media, from interpersonal interaction, from film and television, and from social media) but for Internet research in particular, the questions you'd want to ask, and the precautions that are helpful to take.

Integrating and Citing Research

Even the best and most extensive research would count for little if you didn't integrate it into your speech. Hence the need for the **oral citation**, the citation of research in your speech. By integrating and acknowledging your sources of information in your speech, you'll give fair credit to those whose ideas and research findings you're using, and you'll lessen the risk that anything you say can be interpreted as plagiarism, discussed below. At the same time you'll help establish your own reputation as a responsible researcher and thus increase your own credibility. Here are a few suggestions for integrating your research into your speech.

oral citation

The reference to the sources used woven into the speech.

CITE THE SOURCES IN YOUR SPEECH

Cite the author or the organization; if appropriate, cite the publication and the date. Check out some of the speeches reprinted in this book and on any of the many Internet sites, and note how the speakers have integrated their sources in the speech.

TABLE 4.3 Evaluating Internet Research

Criteria	Questions To Ask	Precautions To Take
Fairness	Does the author of the material present the information fairly and objectively, or is there a bias favoring one position? Some websites, although objective on the surface, are actually arms of some political, religious, or social organization.	It's often useful to go to the home page and look for information on the nature of the organization sponsoring the website. Reviewing a range of research on the subject will help you see how other experts view the issue.
Accuracy	Is the presented information accurate? (The more you learn about your topic, the more able you'll be to judge accuracy.) Is the information primary or secondary? If it's secondary information, try to locate the primary source material (often a link in the Internet article or a reference at the end).	Check to see whether the information is consistent with information found in other sources and whether the recognized authorities in the field accept this information.
Currency	When was the information published? When were the sources that are cited in the article written?	To ensure currency check important figures in a recent almanac, in a newspaper, or at a frequently updated source such as provided at the FedStats website.
Qualifications	Does the author have the necessary credentials? For example, does the author have enough of a background in science or medicine to write authoritatively on health issues?	Do an Internet search to check on the writer's expertise and credentials.
Sufficiency	Is the presented information sufficient to establish the claim or conclusion? The opinion of one dietitian is insufficient to support the usefulness of a particular diet; statistics on tuition increases at five elite private colleges are insufficient to illustrate national trends in tuition costs.	The broader your conclusion, the more information you'll need to meet the requirements for sufficiency. If you claim the usefulness of a diet for all people, then you're going to need a great deal of information from different populations—men and women, old and young, healthy and sickly, for example.

Here is an example of how you might cite your source:

> My discussion of the causes of dizziness is based on the report published on the Mayo Clinic website and written by the Mayo Clinic Staff that I accessed on July 1 of this year. In this discussion five major causes of dizziness are identified. It's these causes that I want to cover in this talk.

Although it's possible to overdo oral source citations—to give more information than listeners really need—there are even greater dangers in leaving out potentially useful source information. Because your speeches in this course are learning experiences, it will be better to err on the side of being more rather than less complete.

INTEGRATE THE CITATION SMOOTHLY

Avoid lead-in expressions such as "I have a quote here" or "I want to quote an example." Let the audience know that you're quoting by pausing before the quote, taking a step forward, or—to read an extended quotation—referring to your notes. If you want to state more directly that this is a quotation, you might do it this way:

> Recently, Senator Quakenbush put this in perspective when she said: [pause] "Men and women are different, but their capacity for leadership is not."

INCLUDE WRITTEN CITATIONS IN OUTLINE

In addition to the oral citation, you'll most likely want to include a listing of your references in your preparation outline. In citing references, first find out what style manual is used in your class or at your school. Generally, it will be a style manual developed by the American Psychological Association (APA), the Modern Language Association (MLA), or the University of Chicago (*The Chicago Manual of Style*). Different colleges and even different departments within a given school often rely on different formats for citing research, which, quite frankly, makes a tedious process even worse.

Fortunately, a variety of websites provide guides to the information you'll need to cite any reference in your speech. A good starting point is Purdue University's research handouts. Both cover APA and MLA style formats and provide examples for citing books, articles, newspaper articles, websites, e-mail, online postings, electronic databases, and more.

Additional suggestions for citing sources in your speech as well as in your written outline are provided in Table 4.4. The written citations would be included at the end of your speech in a list of references. The American Psychological Association (APA) style is used here. Numerous websites are available that will convert your sources into the desired style.

VIEWPOINTS

The Oral Citation

As an audience member, what do you want to know about the research cited in a speech? Put differently, what information should the speaker include in the oral citation so that it's sufficient but not boring or excessive?

TABLE 4.4 The Oral Citation

Source and Written Citation	Oral Citation	Research and Presentation Notes
Book Danna, Sammy R. (2015). *Lydia Pinkham: The face that launched a thousand ads.* London: Rowman & Littlefield.	Sammy Danna, an authority on the history of advertising and pop culture and the author of *Lydia Pinkham: The Face That Launched a Thousand Ads,* notes that advertising…	Try to establish the importance of the author to add weight to your argument.
Magazine Article Webber, R. (2016, February). Odd emotions. *Psychology Today, 49,* 42–51, 77.	A recent article in *Psychology Today* magazine identifies some of the strategies for dealing with unnamed feelings.	If the magazine is well known, as is *Psychology Today,* it's sufficient to name the magazine. If it were less well known, then you might establish its credibility for your listeners by noting, for example, its reputation for fairness, its longevity, or its well-known authors.
Newspaper Article Bulos, N., Hennigan, W. J., & Bennett, B. (2016, March 27). In Syria, militias armed by the Pentagon fight those armed by the CIA. *Los Angeles Times.* Retrieved from http://www.latimes.com/. If a letter to the editor or an editorial, then insert [Letter to the Editor] or [Editorial] after the article title.	An article in the online *Los Angeles Times,* one of the world's most influential newspapers, on March 27, 2016 reported that…	It sometimes helps to establish the credibility of the newspaper—some are more reputable than others. And always include reference to the date of the article. You should also indicate whether it was a regular news item or a letter to the editor or editorial.
Encyclopedia article Bondarenko, P. (2016, March 27). 5 of the world's most-devastating financial crises. *Encyclopaedia Britannica.* Retrieved from http://www.britannica.com/list/5-of-the-worlds-most-devastating-financial-crises	The online version of the *Encyclopaedia Britannica,* accessed March 27, 2016, identifies five particularly significant financial crises.	It isn't necessary to say www.britannica.com. Your audience will know how to access the encyclopedia.
Research Study Tokunaga, R. S. (2016, March). Interpersonal surveillance over social network sites. *Journal of Social and Personal Relationships, 33,* 171–190.	In the March 2016 issue of the *Journal of Social and Personal Relationships,* one of the leading journals on relationships, online surveillance…	In citing a research study, make it clear that what you're reporting is from the primary source and not a secondary source such as a magazine's summary of the research.
Blog Campbell, A. (2016, March 27). Thousands petition to allow guns at Republican convention for "safety" [Web log post]. Retrieved from http://www.huffingtonpost.com/entry/republican-convention-guns-petition_us_56f70018e4b014d3fe234d28	Just this week, *The Huffington Post,* perhaps the most widely read of all blogs, posted an article on guns that's relevant here.	Anyone can maintain a blog. If the blog is used for more than examples or illustrations, you need to establish the authority of the blog or blogger and the currency of the post.
Television Show McCreary, Lori and James Younger (Producers). (2016, April 3). *Beyond death: How Hindus honor the dead and usher in the next life* [Television broadcast]. Washington, D.C.: National Geographic Channel.	*National Geographic* covered this religious practice earlier this week.	It's helpful to name the network as well as the specific show. If the program is an interview, then identify the person being interviewed and perhaps the interviewer.
Personal Interview Because this is not retrievable, this is not included in the reference list.	In an e-mail interview I conducted with Margaret Wilder, the sheriff of Forest County, in September of this year, Wilder wrote that…	State how the interview was conducted—in person, by telephone, or through e-mail—and establish the currency of the interview.
Classroom Lecture Brommel, B. (2016, April 7). Communication at Hunter College in New York City.	In a lecture last week in "Communication in the Family," Professor Bernard Brommel noted that…	Citations of classroom lectures should include the professor's name, the course, and the approximate date the comment was made.
Statistics Centers for Disease Control and Prevention. (2016, March 27). Asthma surveillance data. Retrieved from http://www.cdc.gov/asthma/asthmadata.htm	The Centers for Disease Control and Prevention website, which I accessed earlier this week, provides sobering statistics on the numbers of people with asthma.	It's important with most statistics to stress the authority of the source that collected the statistics (.gov sites are more reliable than .com sites) and the recency of the statistics. Providing information on the date of the page and when you accessed the website will further establish the currency of the statistics.

Plagiarism

4.4 Define *plagiarism*, the reasons plagiarism is unacceptable, and the suggestions for avoiding plagiarism.

One of the most difficult tasks in a public speaking course—and, actually, in every course—is that of plagiarism. Very often plagiarism is committed because of a lack of understanding of how to cite properly. This section aims to clarify what plagiarism is, why it's unacceptable, and how you can avoid even the suggestion of plagiarism.

The Nature of Plagiarism

plagiarism

The act or process of passing off the work (ideas, words, illustrations) of others as your own.

The word **plagiarism** refers to the process of passing off the work (ideas, words, illustrations) of others as your own. Understand that plagiarism is not the act of using another's ideas—we all do that. It is using another's ideas without acknowledging that they are the ideas of this other person; it is passing off the ideas as if they were yours.

Several types of plagiarism may be identified:

- Taking another's work word for word without acknowledging the source, often referred to as global or direct plagiarism

- Paraphrasing another's work without citation

- Paying for a person or some service to write your speech or term paper (or even part of it) without acknowledging this

- Using selected phrases or tracking the structure of another's work without acknowledgment

- Using your own previous work as new and original—as might be the case in using the same paper for two different courses without acknowledgment, often referred to as self-plagiarism

As you can see from the types just described, plagiarism exists on a continuum, ranging from representing as your own an entire term paper or speech written by someone else (the global or direct plagiarism) to using a quotation or research finding without properly citing the author (this is often called "misattribution plagiarism").

A related issue is "fair use," which, according to the Stanford University Libraries, grants permission to use copyright material for purposes of review, criticism, or commenting. Unfortunately, "fair use" has not been defined in specific terms; it merely says that the material used must in some way be of value to those reading or listening to it and that there is a limit on the amount of copyrighted information you can present under your name even if you acknowledge your source. It would be unethical under the "fair use standard" to deliver a speech in which you took three-quarters from another source even if you credit the person, especially when it's an ambiguous credit line like "some of this material I got from Professor Smith's lecture." The best guide in public speaking seems to be to make it very clear to your audience not only your sources but exactly what you are using from others, for example, "This first argument was originally presented by . . ."

In some cultures—especially collectivist cultures (cultures that emphasize the group and mutual cooperation, such as Korea, Japan, and China)—teamwork is strongly encouraged. Students are encouraged to help other students with their work. In the United States and in many other individualist cultures (cultures that emphasize individuality and competitiveness), teamwork without acknowledgment is considered plagiarism.

Why Plagiarism is Unacceptable

In U.S. colleges and universities, plagiarism is a serious violation of the rules of academic honesty and can bring serious penalties, sometimes even expulsion. And it's interesting to note that instructors are mobilizing and are educating themselves in techniques for detecting plagiarism. Further, as with all crimes, ignorance of the law is not an acceptable defense against charges of plagiarism. This last point is especially important because many people plagiarize through a lack of information as to what does and what does not constitute plagiarism.

Here are just a few reasons why plagiarism is wrong.

- Plagiarism is a violation of another's intellectual property rights. Much as it would be unfair to take another person's watch without permission, it's unfair to take another person's ideas without acknowledging that you did it.

- You're in college to develop your own ideas and your own ways of expressing them; plagiarism defeats this fundamental purpose.

- Evaluations (everything from grades in school to promotions in the workplace) assume that what you present as your work is in fact your work.

How You Can Avoid Plagiarism

Here are a few guidelines to help you avoid plagiarism.

Let's start with the easy part. You do not have to, and should not, cite sources for common knowledge—information that is readily available in numerous sources and is not likely to be disputed. For example, the population of Thailand, the amendments to the U.S. Constitution, the actions of the United Nations, or the way the heart pumps blood all are widely available knowledge, and you would not cite the almanac or the political science text from which you got this information. On the other hand, if you were talking about the attitudes of people from Thailand or the reasons the constitutional amendments were adopted, then you would need to cite your sources because this information is not common knowledge and may well be disputed.

For information that is not common knowledge, you need to acknowledge your source. Four simple rules will help you avoid even the suggestion of plagiarism:

1. Acknowledge the source of any ideas you present that are not your own. If you learned of an idea in your history course, then cite the history instructor or the textbook. If you read an idea in an article, then cite the article.

2. Acknowledge the words of another. It's obvious what to do when you're quoting another person exactly; then, of course, you need to cite the person you're quoting. You also should cite the person even when you paraphrase his or her

JOURNAL 4.4 PUBLIC SPEAKING CHOICE POINT

Plagiarism

Zoe, an art major, is scheduled to give her first informative speech tomorrow. She has chosen to speak about the ways public art can benefit the entire community. She has collected an array of opinions from experts on the subject and wants to incorporate them into her speech but does not want to plagiarize in the process. *What advice can you give her?*

ETHICAL CHOICE POINT

Plagiarism Detection

You hear a speech in class that you've seen on the Internet—a clear case of plagiarism. The instructor didn't realize it, gave the speech an A, and thereby upset the expectations for all the speeches to be heard in class and screwed up the curve. You don't want to be a rat and get the student in trouble—the consequences of which could range from failing the speech assignment, failing the entire course, or being brought up on charges of plagiarism. At the same time you don't want yourself and the other students to be penalized because your speech and those of the other students are unlikely to be as good as this plagiarized speech. *What are some ethical options you have for dealing with this problem?*

words because you are still using the other person's ideas. It is not always clear when paraphrases need to be credited, so some of the plagiarism websites established by different universities include exercises and extended examples; those of Indiana University and Purdue University will prove especially helpful.

3. Acknowledge help from others. If your roommate gave you examples or ideas or helped you style your speech, acknowledge the help. But you don't need to acknowledge the assistance of, say, a librarian who helped you find a book or website.

4. When in doubt as to whether you should cite a source or how you might best do it, ask your instructor.

SUMMARY: ANALYZE YOUR AUDIENCE AND RESEARCH YOUR SPEECH (STEPS 2 AND 3)

This chapter looked at the audience and particularly at how you can analyze your listeners and adapt your speeches to them.

Approaching Audience Analysis and Adaptation (Step 2)

4.1 Identify the two principles of audience analysis and the ways in which you might learn about your audience.

1. In analyzing any audience, remember that all audiences are unique and all audiences are diverse.

2. In seeking information about your audience, consider the values of observation, collecting data (for example, with audience questionnaires), interviewing members, and using intelligent inference and empathy.

Analyzing Audience Sociology and Psychology

4.2 Identify the sociological and psychological characteristics that are important to consider in audience analysis and some of the ways in which you might adapt to specific types of audiences.

3. In analyzing the sociology or demographics of your audience, consider especially the following characteristics:
   - Age
   - Gender (biological sex role and psychological sex role)
   - Affectional orientation
   - Educational levels
   - Religion and religiousness
   - Cultural factors

4. In addition, look into other relevant audience factors such as audience members' occupation and income status, relational status, special interests, and political attitudes and beliefs.

5. Consider the context factors such as the physical space, the number of listeners, and the format expected for the speech.

6. In analyzing audience psychology consider your listeners' willingness, degree of favorableness toward your ideas, knowledge level, and degree of homogeneity.

7. In adapting to an unwilling audience:
   - Secure listeners' attention as early as possible.
   - Reward audience members for their attendance and attention.
   - Relate your topic and supporting materials to audience members' needs and interests.

8. In adapting to an unfavorable audience:
   - Clear up any possible misunderstandings.
   - Build on the similarities you have with the audience.
   - Build your speech from areas of agreement up to the major areas of difference.
   - Strive for small gains.

9. In adapting to an unknowledgeable audience:
   - Avoid talking down to your listeners (or to any audience).
   - Avoid confusing a lack of knowledge with a lack of intelligence.

10. In adapting to a knowledgeable audience:
   - Let your listeners know that you're aware of their expertise.
   - Establish your credibility.

11. To help you adapt your speech during your presentation:
   - Focus on audience members as message senders, not merely as message receivers.
   - Use answers to your "what if" questions for on-the-spot adjustments.
   - Address audience responses directly.

Researching: Finding and Evaluating Information (Step 3)

4.3 Identify the major sources of information, the criteria to use in evaluating research, and some of the guidelines for integrating research into your speech.

12. A multitude of source materials are readily available for research, including libraries, general reference works, government publications, and the Web. In reading these sources keep in mind the differences among primary, secondary, and tertiary materials and between popular and scholarly magazines/journals.

13. In evaluating sources consider their fairness, accuracy, and currency; the qualifications of the author; and the sufficiency of the information presented.

14. Integrate the material into your speech, and cite it as appropriate.

Plagiarism

4.4 Define *plagiarism*, the reasons plagiarism is unacceptable, and the suggestions for avoiding plagiarism.

15. Plagiarism is the process of passing off the work of others as if it's your own. Avoid even the suspicion of plagiarism.

KEY TERMS: ANALYZE YOUR AUDIENCE AND RESEARCH YOUR SPEECH (STEPS 2 AND 3)

attitude
belief
context factors
display rules
oral citation

plagiarism
primary sources
psychological audience analysis
research
secondary sources

sociological audience analysis
tertiary sources
time management
value
"what if" questions

PUBLIC SPEAKING EXERCISES

4.1 How Well Do You Know Your Audience?

Here are some statements of beliefs that members of your class may agree or disagree with—and that you might want to use as basic theses (propositions) in your in-class speeches. Try predicting how favorable or unfavorable you think your class members would be to each of these beliefs. Use a 10-point scale ranging from 1 (extremely unfavorable) through 5 (relatively neutral) to 10 (extremely favorable).

1. _____ The welfare of the family must come first, even before your own.

2. _____ Sex outside of marriage is wrong and sinful.

3. _____ In a heterosexual relationship, a wife should submit graciously to the leadership of her husband.

4. _____ Individual states should be allowed to fly the Confederate flag if they wish.

5. _____ Intercultural relationships are OK in business but should be discouraged when it comes to intimate or romantic relationships; generally, the races should be kept "pure."

6. _____ Money is good; the quest for financial success is a perfectly respectable (even noble) one.

7. _____ Immigration into the United States should be curtailed, at least until current immigrants are assimilated.

8. _____ Parents who prevent their children from receiving the latest scientific cures because of a belief in faith healing should be prosecuted for child abuse.

9. _____ Single people should be allowed to adopt children in the same way that couples do.

10. _____ Recreational marijuana should be readily available in all states.

11. _____ Physician-assisted suicide should be legalized.

12. _____ Male and female prostitution should be legalized and taxed like any other income-producing occupation.

After you've indicated your predictions, discuss these with the class as a whole to get a better idea of how your audience thinks and ultimately how you can adapt your speeches given these attitudes and beliefs of your audience.

4.2 Analyzing an Unknown Audience

This experience should familiarize you with some of the essential steps in analyzing audience members on the basis of relatively little evidence and in predicting their attitudes on the basis of that analysis. The class should be broken up into small groups of five or six members. Each group will be given a different magazine (print or online); its task is to analyze the audience (i.e., the readers or subscribers) of that particular magazine in terms of the characteristics discussed in this chapter. The only information the groups will have about their audience members is that they're avid and typical readers of the given magazine. Pay particular attention to the types of articles published in the magazine, the advertisements, the photographs or illustrations, the editorial statements, the price of the magazine, and so on. Magazines that differ widely from one another are most appropriate for this experience.

After all groups have analyzed their audiences, try to identify at least three favorable and three unfavorable attitudes that each audience probably holds on contemporary issues. On what basis do you make these predictions? If you had to address this audience and advocate a position with which it disagreed, what adaptations would you make? What strategies would you use to prepare and present this persuasive speech?

Each group should share with the rest of the class the results of its efforts, taking special care to point out not only its conclusions but also the evidence and reasoning group members used in arriving at the conclusions.

4.3 Research Effectiveness and Efficiency

This exercise focuses on research effectiveness and efficiency and asks all members of the class to find the answers to the questions presented below (as efficiently as possible, that is, in the shortest amount of time) and then explain their research strategies (those that worked and those that didn't work). In a classroom, this can be set up in a number of different ways. For example, small groups can each be assigned one, two, or three questions and compete with one another in answering the question most efficiently. Or questions can be assigned to the class as a whole and students can each try to answer the question first.

Questions

These questions vary in difficulty. Some are extremely easy and the answers are likely to be found in under a minute. Some are extremely difficult and the answers are likely to take a great deal longer.

1. What is the current population of Missouri?
2. What film grossed the most money (adjusted for inflation)?
3. What is the literacy rate for Cuba versus the United States?
4. What has the last Van Gogh painting sold for at auction?
5. How much does it cost for a full-page advertisement in Sunday's *Washington Post*?
6. What profit did Apple make in the previous year?
7. Who said (and in what work): "It is better to have loved and lost than never to have loved at all?"
8. What researchers developed the concept and measurement of argumentativeness?
9. How many single parents with children under 18 years of age are there in the United States?
10. How much U.S. debt does China hold?
11. What are the lowest and highest points on earth?
12. How many men and how many women are currently in the U.S. Senate?
13. What did the flag of the United States look like in 1840?
14. How much money does the United States give to its three largest beneficiaries (countries)?
15. What was the world's tallest building in 1880? What is the tallest building today?
16. What is the average salary for elementary school teachers in your state?
17. Who is currently the longest serving U.S. Supreme Court Justice?
18. What percentage of children under 16 have ADHD?
19. What are the five most widely spoken languages in the world?
20. What are the major religions of Africa?

COLLECT SUPPORTING MATERIALS (STEP 4)

The well-chosen example often makes for the biggest impact.

CHAPTER TOPICS

Examples, Illustrations, and Narratives

Analogies

Definitions

Testimony

Numerical Data

Additional Forms of Support

LEARNING OBJECTIVES

5.1 Define *examples, illustrations,* and *narratives* and explain the guidelines for using this type of support.

5.2 Define and distinguish between *figurative* and *literal analogies* and identify the guidelines for using analogies.

5.3 Identify the various types of definitions and the guidelines for using them in a public speech.

5.4 Define *testimony* and identify the guidelines for using this form of support.

5.5 Explain the types of numerical data that may be useful in a public speech and the guidelines for using such support.

5.6 Explain the usefulness of quotations, comparisons and contrasts, fact series, and repetition and restatement.

This chapter focuses on Step 4 and examines the various types of supporting materials. Supporting materials are a vital part of an effective public speech; they add concreteness, help maintain interest and attention, and provide vital information and persuasive appeal. Here we cover examples, illustrations, narratives, analogies, definitions, testimony, and numerical data, explain their nature, and spell out the guidelines to follow in using them in public speaking.

Examples, Illustrations, and Narratives

5.1 Define *examples*, *illustrations*, and *narratives* and explain the guidelines for using this type of support.

Examples, illustrations, and narratives are specific instances that are explained in varying degrees of detail and will contribute greatly in helping the audience understand and remember your speech. Examples are useful for reinforcing ideas, providing memorable reminders, and making general ideas more specific and more closely related to the audience's experiences and knowledge.

Types of Examples, Illustrations, and Narratives

Generally, a relatively brief specific instance is referred to as an **example**, a longer and more detailed example is referred to as an **illustration**, and an example told in story-like form is referred to as a **narrative**. Examples (the shorthand *examples* will be used to refer to all three of these forms of support) may be distinguished on the basis of their being real or hypothetical.

The main value of examples is that they allow you to bring an abstract concept down to specifics. For example, to clarify what you mean by determination, you might provide a brief example, give an illustration from history, or narrate the story of any of the numerous great people who rose to prominence against the odds. In the following excerpt the speaker, Thomas Hill (2015) of the University of Texas at Austin, used a specific example to illustrate the abuses that a law can create:

> Jennifer Boatright had been saving up to buy a new car for years. When the Houston waitress finally amassed enough tips to make the purchase, she set out with her $6,000 in savings and two sons on a road trip to buy the new vehicle. But outside Tenaha, Texas, Jennifer was pulled over and an officer asked to search her car. Nothing harmful was found, but a few hours later, a number of loopholes later, and a drug trafficking accusation later, the district attorney told her she had two options: face felony charges of money laundering and lose custody of her kids, or sign over the $6,000 in cash to the police.

In a speech on the abuses suffered by poultry workers, Neil Decenteceo (2015) used a specific example:

> Beatriz Nevado was a processing line worker at the Wayne Farms poultry factory in Enterprise, Alabama. One day, while working, she felt a sharp pain in her chest; it was a heart attack. However, after informing the factory's nurse about her potentially fatal situation, the nurse dismissed her claim, refused to call an ambulance, and offered her aspirin. After both Beatriz and her daughter left their shift early to go the hospital, the factory superiors then proceeded to add penalty points to their employee records, which, if enough accrue, can result in job termination. Such is the life of tens of thousands of modern-day poultry factory workers.

In a speech on unfair sentencing practices, student Jillian Collum (2008) provided an illustration to reinforce her thesis. After stating that a man was sentenced to 55 years

example

A form of supporting material in which a specific instance is used to explain a concept.

illustration

A specific instance drawn in greater detail than a brief example.

narrative

An illustration told in story form.

in prison under the federal mandatory minimum sentencing laws for selling marijuana, she said:

> The sentencing brief noted that if Angelos had provided weapons to a terrorist organization, hijacked an aircraft, committed second-degree murder, and raped a 10-year-old child he would have received a lower combined sentence than he got for selling about $1,000 worth of marijuana.

Here's another example of the effectiveness of an illustration, from a speech by Kyle Akerman, a student from the University of Texas at Austin (2010):

> Initially, a Human Rights Watch report on March 19, 2009 substantiates that there are reports of detainees being shackled, and denied basic medical procedures. The January 9, 2010 *New York Times* tells the story of Nery Romero, a 22-year-old detainee who repeatedly begged for treatment of unbearable pain, and was repeatedly denied. The Office of Professional Responsibility discovered falsified documents saying that Romero received medication. Falsification was easy to detect...because [he] died days before he supposedly received his last treatment. This article notes that there have been 107 deaths of this type since October of 2003.

Guidelines for Using Examples, Illustrations, and Narratives

LIMIT THE LENGTH

Keep in mind that the function of examples is to make your ideas vivid and easily understood; they are not ends in themselves. Make your examples only as long as necessary to ensure that your purpose is achieved.

STRESS RELEVANCY

Make sure your example is directly relevant to the proposition you want it to support, and make its relationship with your assertion explicit. Remember that although this relationship is clear to you (because you've constructed the speech), the audience is going to hear your speech only once. Show the audience exactly how your example relates to the assertion or concept you're explaining. Here for example, then–New York Mayor Rudolph Giuliani, in his address to the United Nations after the World Trade Center attack of September 11, 2001, gave relevant examples to support his proposition that we are a land of immigrants and must continue to be so (Guiliani, 2001):

> New York City was built by immigrants and it will remain the greatest city in the world so long as we continue to renew ourselves with and benefit from the energizing spirit from new people coming here to create a better future for themselves and their families. Come to Flushing, Queens, where immigrants from many lands have created a vibrant, vital commercial and residential community. Their

ETHICAL CHOICE POINT

Misleading Your Audience

For a speech on false arrests, you develop a hypothetical story about a college student who gets arrested and is held unlawfully in custody for several days. As you rehearse this story, you realize it would be a lot more convincing if the audience were allowed to think that the story was true and that the person was you. Actually, you wouldn't be saying that it was you or that it wasn't you; you'd just be allowing the audience to infer this from what you say. *What are your ethical choices to be both truthful and effective?*

children challenge and astonish us in our public school classrooms every day. Similarly, you can see growing and dynamic immigrant communities in every borough of our city: Russians in Brighton Beach, West Indians in Crown Heights, Dominicans in Washington Heights, the new wave of Irish in the Bronx, and Koreans in Willow Brook on Staten Island.

DISTINGUISH BETWEEN REAL AND HYPOTHETICAL EXAMPLES

Don't try to foist a hypothetical example on audience members as a real one. If they recognize the deception, they'll resent your attempt to fool them. Let the audience know when you're using a real example and when you're using a hypothetical example.

Real examples

- A situation such as this occurred recently; it involved...
- I have a friend who...
- An actual example of this was reported in the...

Hypothetical examples

- We could easily imagine a situation such as...
- I think an ideal friend would be someone who...
- A hypothetical example of this type of friendship would be like...

USE EXAMPLES TO EMPHASIZE THE WIDESPREAD NATURE OR SIGNIFICANCE OF AN ISSUE OR PROBLEM.

Here, for example, President Obama (NPR, 2015) uses specific examples to make the point that racism is still with us.

> I always tell young people in particular:"Do not say that nothing's changed when it comes to race in America—unless you've lived through being a black man in the 1950s, or '60s, or '70s. It is incontrovertible that race relations have improved significantly during my lifetime and yours, and that opportunities have opened up, and that attitudes have changed. That is a fact. What is also true is that the legacy of slavery, Jim Crow, discrimination in almost every institution of our lives—you know, that casts a long shadow. And that's still part of our DNA that's passed on. We're not cured of it.

In another example, New York Governor Andrew Cuomo (Associated Press, 2013) uses two recent examples to make the point that we need greater gun control:

> The tragic events of just the last few weeks in Newtown, Conn., and West Webster, N.Y., have indelibly taught us guns can cut down small children, firefighters and policemen in a moment.

USE EXAMPLES THAT ARE REPRESENTATIVE OR OUTSTANDING

Generally, use an example that is representative of the class of objects about which you're speaking. For example, colleges and universities frequently show a successful graduate in their advertisements because they want their audience to see this individual as representative of its population. In some cases, representativeness isn't desired by the advertiser.

VIEWPOINTS

The Power of Examples

What do you see as the greatest value of examples, illustrations, and narratives?

JOURNAL 5.1 PUBLIC SPEAKING CHOICE POINT

The Effective Example

Mike wants to use an example from television or film to illustrate the difficulties of finding true love. *What might be some choices that you could suggest?*

Although representativeness is the usual goal, there may be times when you wish to draw an example that is purposefully farfetched. Perhaps you wish to poke fun at a particular proposal or show the inadequacies of an alternative point of view. The important point is that everyone involved sees the example in the same way.

USE EXAMPLES THAT ARE RELEVANT

Use examples that relate directly to the proposition you wish to explain. Leave out irrelevant examples, however interesting or entertaining. Be certain that the audience see the relevance.

Analogies

5.2 Define and distinguish between *figurative* and *literal analogies* and identify the guidelines for using analogies.

Analogies are comparisons that are often extremely useful in making your ideas clear and vivid to your audience.

Types of Analogies

Analogies may be of two types: figurative and literal. **Figurative analogies** compare items from different classes—for example, the flexibility afforded by a car with the freedom of a bird, a college degree with a passport to success, playing baseball with running a corporation. Figurative analogies are useful for illustrating possible similarities and provide vivid examples that are easily remembered.

Literal analogies compare items from the same class, such as two cars or two cities. For example, in a literal analogy you might argue (1) that two companies are similar—both are multinational, multibillion-dollar pharmaceutical companies, and both have advertising budgets in the hundreds of millions of dollars; and (2) therefore the advertising techniques that worked for one company will work for the other.

Guidelines in Using Analogies

Analogies do not constitute evidence of the truth or falsity of an assertion. Avoid presenting analogies as proof and beware of speakers who do this; they may be doing this because there is no real evidence.

Use comparable cases. When using literal analogies, make sure that the cases compared are alike in essential respects. For example, if you were comparing two schools' graduation rates, the schools would have to be similar in, say, admission standards and student services. It would be unfair to draw an analogy between an open-enrollment college and an Ivy League school.

Place differences in context. When using an analogy to support a key idea, point out the varying level of significance your analogy illustrates. For example, if you're

analogy
Comparison of two things; analogies may be literal (in which items from the same class are compared) or figurative (in which items from different classes are compared).

figurative analogy
An expressed comparison of two items of different types.

literal analogy
An expressed comparison of two items from the same class or type.

JOURNAL 5.2 PUBLIC SPEAKING CHOICE POINT

Selling Analogies

Tanya is a car salesperson trying to persuade her customer to buy the car she's showing instead of the buyer's other choice. *What are some of the Tanya's possible choices for using analogies in her persuasive attempts?*

comparing the salaries of entry-level accountants across the country, point out that the cost of living is typically higher in the city than in rural areas. So an entry-level accountant in Chicago with a higher salary compared to one in Lubbock, Texas, is not really earning more after living expenses have been accounted for.

Definitions

5.3 Identify the various types of definitions and the guidelines for using them in a public speech.

A **definition** is a statement explaining the meaning of a term or concept; it explains what something is.

definition
A statement explaining the meaning of a term, phrase, or concept.

Types of Definitions

Some of the most important ways in which you can define a term are etymology, authority, negation, and specific examples.

DEFINITION BY ETYMOLOGY

One way to define a term is to trace its historical or linguistic development. In defining the word *communication*, for example, you might note that it comes from the Latin *communis*, meaning "common"; in "communicating" you seek to establish a commonness, a sharing, a similarity with another individual. And *woman* comes from the Anglo-Saxon *wifman*, which meant literally a "wife man," where the word *man* was applied to both sexes. Through phonetic change *wifman* became *woman*. Most larger dictionaries and, of course, etymological dictionaries will help you find useful etymological definitions.

Or you might define a term by noting not its linguistic etymology but how it came to mean what it now means. For example, you might note that *spam*, meaning unwanted e-mail, comes from a Monty Python television skit in which every item on a menu contained the product Spam. And much as the diner was forced to get Spam, so the e-mail user gets spam, even when he or she wants something else.

definition by etymology
A type of definition that refers to the origin and development of the word's meaning.

DEFINITION BY AUTHORITY

You can often clarify a term by explaining how a particular authority views it. You might, for example, define lateral thinking by authority and say that Edward deBono, who developed lateral thinking in 1966, has noted that "lateral thinking involves moving sideways to look at things in a different way. Instead of fixing on one particular approach and then working forward from that, the lateral thinker tries to find other approaches." Or you might use the authority of cynic and satirist Ambrose Bierce and define love as nothing but "a temporary insanity curable by marriage" and friendship as "a ship big enough to carry two in fair weather, but only one in foul."

definition by authority
A type of definition advanced by an expert.

DEFINITION BY NEGATION

You also might define a term by noting what the term is not; that is, define it by negation. "A wife," you might say, "isn't a cook, a cleaning person, a babysitter, a seamstress, a sex partner. A wife is…" or "A teacher isn't someone who tells you what you should know but rather one who…."

definition by negation
A type of definition in which a word is defined by what it's not.

DEFINITION BY SPECIFIC EXAMPLES

An example is not a definition, but it can serve defining functions; it can help clarify terms or phrases. Here, for example, Ohio Congressman Dennis Kucinich (2007) uses

definition by specific example
A type of definition in which the word's meaning is suggested by examples.

a series of specific examples to clarify what he means by "human rights" in a speech presented to the Wall Street Project Conference on January 8, 2007:

> We have a right to a job.
> We have a right to a living wage.
> We have a right to an education.
> We have a right to health care.
> We have a right to decent and affordable housing.
> We have a right to a secure pension.
> We have a right to air fit to breathe.
> We have a right to water fit to drink.
> We have a right to be free of the paralyzing fear of crime.

Guidelines in Using Definitions

Use definitions when you wish to explain difficult or unfamiliar concepts or when you wish to make a concept more vivid or forceful. If the purpose of the definition is to clarify, then it must do just that. This would be too obvious to mention except for the fact that so many speakers, perhaps for want of something to say, define terms that don't need extended definitions. Some speakers use definitions that don't clarify and sometimes even complicate an already-complex concept. Make sure your definitions define only what needs defining.

Here, for example, in a speech advocating against panhandling bans, Greta Wolking (2015) of James Madison University needed to define *panhandling*, a term that most people have an idea about but of which they may not have a detailed understanding:

> Panhandling is defined as begging, or attempting to solicit money from another person. Panhandling can be done verbally, by asking, or nonverbally, like using a sign or playing an instrument for tips.

Here is another example where it was necessary for the audience to have a clear definition of the term *redlining*, which would be used throughout this speech by Branden DaVon Lindsay (2015) of William Carey University:

According to the magazine *Inc.* September 2, 2014 redlining is defined as the practice of arbitrarily denying or limiting financial services to specific neighborhoods, generally because its residents are people of color or poor and dates back to the 1920s.

As you think of terms to define or after you've selected a term, take a look at the One Look Dictionary Search website. This website will enable you to search a wide variety of dictionaries at the same time. There are, of course, many other useful online dictionaries; search for "dictionary," "definitions," or "thesaurus," and you'll find a wealth of material for speeches of definition. Once you have the definition, make sure that you pronounce it correctly; defining a word you mispronounce is likely to severely damage your credibility. Fortunately, many online dictionaries include audio of the correct pronunciation.

JOURNAL 5.3 PUBLIC SPEAKING CHOICE POINT

Using Definitions

Marco is giving a speech on some of the cultural differences in the treatment of time. *What are some of the definitions that might be used in such a speech?*

Testimony

5.4 Define *testimony* and identify the guidelines for using this form of support.

Testimony is often a useful form of support and involves using the opinions of others to clarify or support your assertions.

testimony
A form of supporting material consisting of the opinions or eyewitness report of another person.

Types of Testimony

Testimony is of two basic types: expert and eyewitness. In **expert testimony**, the speaker cites the opinions, beliefs, predictions, or values of some authority or expert. For example, you might want to state an economist's predictions concerning inflation and depression, or you might want to support your analysis by citing an art critic's evaluation of a painting or art movement. The faculty of your college or university is one of the best, if rarely used, sources of expert information for almost any speech topic. Regardless of what your topic is, a faculty member of some department likely knows a great deal about the subject. At the very least, faculty members will be able to direct you to appropriate sources. Experts in the community can serve similar functions. Local politicians, religious leaders, doctors, lawyers, museum directors, and the like, often are suitable sources of information.

expert testimony
The testimony of an authority.

Beyond your college or university lies a world of experts—religious and business leaders, politicians, educators at other colleges and research institutes, medical personnel, and researchers in almost any field imaginable. Ask yourself if your speech and your audience could profit from the insights of experts. If your answer is *yes*— and few topics could not so profit—then consider the steps suggested in the previous chapter for interviewing such experts. Interviews can take place in person, by telephone, or over the Internet, especially via e-mail or Skype.

Of course, if 500 public speaking students all descend on the faculty or on the community, chaos can easily result. So going to these experts is often discouraged as a class assignment. But it's often a useful practice for speeches you'll give later in life.

The second type is **eyewitness testimony**. Here you'd cite the testimony of someone who saw or heard some event or situation. For example, you might cite the

eyewitness testimony
The testimony of someone who has witnessed an event.

testimony of someone who saw an accident, of a person who spent two years in a maximum-security prison, or of a person who had a particular kind of operation.

Here, for example, John Groves (2014) of the University of Texas at Austin used expert testimony to support his thesis that we fail to give those accused of crimes proper defense:

> Of 146.5 billion dollars of public money spent annually on criminal proceedings, 98% funds police forces and prosecution, whereas indigent defense systems struggle to function with the remaining 2%. American Bar Association President James Silkenat laments that while the Constitution provides effective counsel, we continue to empower and promote a system that fails in giving the accused a fair fight.

Interviews

In securing testimony, you may wish to interview an expert or an eyewitness. For example, you might want to interview a veterinarian for information on proper nutrition for household pets; an eyewitness for information on living through a hurricane; or average people for information on their opinions on politics, religion, or any of a wide variety of topics. A great part of your effectiveness in securing this information will hinge on your ability to listen actively, for total meaning, with empathy, with an open mind, and ethically. Here are 10 additional suggestions to help you use interviewing to secure the needed testimony (DeVito, 2010).

1. **Select the person you wish to interview.** You might, for example, look through your college catalog for an instructor teaching a course that involves your topic or visit blogs and look for people who have posted articles on your topic. If you want to contact a book author, you can always write to the author in care of the publisher or editor (listed on the copyright page), though many authors are now including their e-mail address. Blog, newsgroup, and listserv writers are relatively easy to contact because their e-mail addresses are included with their posts.

2. **Secure an appointment.** Phone the person or send an e-mail requesting an interview. State the purpose of your request and say that you hope to conduct a brief interview by phone or that you'd like to send this person a series of questions by e-mail.

VIEWPOINTS

Negative Testimony

In what ways might testimony backfire and actually damage the speaker's persuasiveness?

3. **Select your topic areas.** Depending on the topic of your speech, the time you have available, and the areas of expertise that your interviewee has, you'll need to select the areas you want to talk about. Generally, it will be best to limit these to perhaps two or three.

4. **Create a cheat sheet.** A *cheat sheet* is a list of what you want to say during the interview. If this is a phone interview, you can keep the cheat sheet in front of you; if it is a face-to-face interview, review the cheat sheet immediately before the interview. On this cheat sheet write all the questions you want to ask in the order you want to ask them along with notes to yourself to thank the interviewer at the beginning and again at the end of the interview.

5. **Establish rapport with the interviewee.** Open the in-person, telephone, e-mail, or chat-group interview by thanking the person for making the time available and again stating your purpose. You might say something like "I really appreciate your making time for this interview. As I mentioned, I'm preparing a speech on XYZ, and your experience in this area will help a great deal."

6. **Ask open-ended questions.** Generally, ask questions that provide the interviewee with room to discuss the issues you want to raise. Thus, asking, "Do you have formal training in the area of family therapy?" may elicit a simple yes or no. On the other hand, "Can you tell me something of your background in this field?" is open-ended, allowing the interviewee to talk in some detail.

7. **Display effective interpersonal communication.** Generally, it will help to be open, positive, and flexible. Be open to the interviewee's ideas. Avoid challenging the person; after all, your aim is to get this person's perspective. Be positive about the interview and the interviewee. Be flexible and be ready to adjust your interview on the basis of the ongoing interaction.

8. **Ask for permission to record or print the interview.** It's a good idea to keep an accurate record of the interview, so ask permission to record the interview if it's in person or by telephone. Recording will eliminate your worry about taking notes and having to ask the interviewee to slow down or repeat. It will also provide you with a much more accurate record of the interview than will handwritten notes. Also, if the interview is by e-mail or via Skype and you want to quote the interviewee's responses, ask permission first.

9. **Close with an expression of appreciation.** Of course, you'll want to thank the person for the interview. In your expression of appreciation be specific and try to refer back to the conversation, for example, "I want to thank you for making time for me and for sharing those great stories about how you started your business; they will make wonderful examples in my speech."

10. **Follow up with a thank-you note.** Even though you thank the person at the end of the interview, it's especially polite to follow up with a thank-you note later that day or the next day. Or perhaps you might send the person you interviewed a copy of your speech (e-mail would work well here) with a note of thanks.

JOURNAL 5.4 PUBLIC SPEAKING CHOICE POINT

The Ideal Interviewees

With your next speech in mind, imagine that you had unlimited resources and unlimited access to anyone in the world. *What one, two, or three people would you choose to interview? Why?*

Guidelines in Using Testimony

Whether you use the testimony of a world-famous authority or draw on an eyewitness account, you need to establish your source's credibility—to demonstrate to the audience that your expert is in fact an authority or that your eyewitness is believable.

STRESS THE COMPETENCE OF THE PERSON

Whether the person is an expert or a witness, make sure the audience sees this person as competent. To cite the predictions of a world-famous economist of whom your audience has never heard will mean little, so first explain the person's competence. To prepare the audience to accept what this person says, you might introduce the testimony by saying, for example:

> This prediction comes from the world's leading economist, who has successfully predicted all major financial trends over the past 20 years.

Here, for example, is how student Ashley Hatcher established the credibility of her testimony:

> As the 2005 book *The Structure of the Innate Mind* states, the answer may lie in Homicide Adaptation Theory, the conclusion of an unprecedented six-year study conducted by leading evolutionary psychologists David Buss and Joshua Duntley from the University of Texas.

STRESS THE UNBIASED NATURE OF THE TESTIMONY

If listeners perceive the testimony to be biased—whether or not it really is—it will have little effect. You want to check out the biases of a witness so you may present accurate information. But you also want to make the audience see that the testimony is in fact unbiased. You might say something like this:

> Researchers and testers at *Consumer Reports*, none of whom has any vested interest in the products examined, found wide differences in car safety. Let's look at some of these findings. In the October 2013 issue, for example,...

STRESS THE RECENCY OF THE TESTIMONY

When you say, for example, "General Bailey, who was interviewed last week in *The Washington Post*, noted that the United States has twice the military power of any other world power," you show your audience that your information is recent and up to date.

Numerical Data

5.5 Explain the types of numerical data that may be useful in a public speech and the guidelines for using such support.

Numerical data are often essential and will help to support what you mean by, say, high tuition, reasonable wage, or appropriate executive compensation.

Types of Numerical Data

raw numbers

Numbers that have not be subjected to manipulation.

Numerical data are of two basic types: raw numbers and statistics. **Raw numbers** are simply figures unmodified by any mathematical operation. For example, if you want to show that significant numbers of people now get their news from the Internet, you could give the total number of online users for each of the past 10 years and compare those numbers with the numbers of newspaper readers and television news viewers in those same years. These data would then allow you to show that the number of people who get their news the Internet is increasing, while the number of those getting the news from papers and television is declining.

statistics

Summary numbers such as the mean (or average) or the mode (or most common score).

Statistics, on the other hand, are summary figures that help you communicate the important characteristic of a complex set of numbers. Among the most important for public speakers are measures of central tendency, measures of correlation, measures of difference, and percentages.

- **Measures of central tendency** tell you the general pattern in a group of numbers.
  - The **mean** is the arithmetic average of a set of numbers. For example, if the mean grade on an examination was 88, it means that if you added up all the scores and divided by the number of students taking the exam, the result would be 88.
  - The **median** is the middle score; 50 percent of the scores are higher and 50 percent of the scores are lower. For example, if the media score on an examination was 83, it means that 50 percent of the students scored above 83 and 50 percent scored below.
  - The **mode** is the most frequently occurring score. It's the single score that most people received. If the mode of the examination was 81, it means that more students received a score of 81 than any other single score.

- **Measures of correlation** tell you how closely two or more things are related. For example, there's a high **positive correlation** between smoking and lung cancer; smokers have a greater incidence of lung cancer than nonsmokers and heavy smokers have a greater incidence than light smokers. As your smoking increases, so does the likelihood of lung cancer. Correlations can also be negative. For example, there's a high **negative correlation** between the amount of money you have and the likelihood that you'll be convicted of a crime. As the amount of money increases, the likelihood of criminal conviction decreases; as the amount of money decreases, the likelihood of conviction increases. Recognize that high correlations (whether positive or negative) do not mean causation. The fact that two things vary together (that is, are highly correlated) does not mean that one causes the other. They may each be caused by some third factor. So, in the example of money and criminal conviction, the correlation simply tells you that the two items are related.

- **Measures of difference** tell you the extent to which scores differ from the average or from each other. For example, the **range** tells you how far the lowest score is from the highest score. If the lowest score on the exam was 76 and the highest was 99, the range was 23 points. Generally, a high range indicates great diversity, whereas a low range indicates great similarity. The range may be used to show, for example, the discrepancy in income between management and labor or between college and high school graduates.

- **Percentages** allow you to express a score as a portion of 100. So, if 78 percent of the people favored coffee over tea, that would mean that 78 people out of every 100 favored coffee over tea. Percentages are useful if you want to show, say, the growth of cable television over the past 10 years, the amount of the proposed tuition increases, or the divorce rate in different parts of the world. In some cases, you might want to compare percentages. For example, you might compare percentages among the various ways in which people get their news. You might note, for instance, that 75 percent get their news from the Internet while only 25 percent get it from newspapers and television to illustrate the importance and growth of Internet news. To illustrate the growth of the Internet as a new medium, you might note that in 1995 only 4 percent of people got their news from the Internet but in 2018 that number has increased to, say, 75 percent.

In a speech against the anti-homelessness legislation common in many cities, Brianna Mahoney (2015) of the University of Florida used simple percentages to illustrate the increase in the bans and also to identify the types of bans she is arguing against:

> According to a 2014 report from the National Law Center of Homelessness and Poverty, bans on begging are up by 25%, bans against sitting or lying down in public spaces 43%, and bans against sleeping in your own vehicle 119%.

measures of central tendency
Typical values, for example, the mean, median, and mode.

mean
The arithmetic average.

median
The middle score in an array of scores.

mode
The most frequent score in an array.

measures of correlation
A measure of the degree to which two items are related; the extent to which one item can be predicted from the other item.

positive correlation
A relationship in which two items move in the same direction, for example, as one becomes higher so does the other.

negative correlation
A relationship is which two items move in opposite directions, for example, as one becomes higher the other becomes lower.

measures of difference
A measure of disparity or difference, for example, the difference between the highest score and the lowest score.

range
The difference between the highest and the lowest score.

percentages
The portion of a total, expressed as a portion of 100.

JOURNAL 5.5 PUBLIC SPEAKING CHOICE POINT

Supporting Materials

Luanne is planning to give a speech on the lack of research on women's health issues and wants to show that it's a real problem needing a real solution. *What kinds of supporting materials would help Luanne to establish the severity of the problem for, say, an audience of students from your college? How about for an audience consisting of the parents of students in your class?*

In this example, Daniel Hinderliter (2013) of West Chester University, Pennsylvania used percentages to illustrate the tremendous waste of food and then linked the percentages to specific items:

> This food waste becomes mote staggering when considering the nation as a whole: an August 2012 report from the National Resources Defense Council, or NRDC, disclosed that 25% of all household food purchases are wasted. That's four slices in the average loaf of bread, one quart of every gallon of milk, three eggs out of each dozen.

Here is a good example of how President Barack Obama (2006) (then U.S. Senator from Illinois) used statistics in his speech to the 2006 Global Summit on AIDS and the Church:

> You know, AIDS is a story often told by numbers. Forty million infected with HIV. Nearly 4.5 million this year alone. Twelve million orphans in Africa. Eight thousand deaths and 6,000 new infections every single day. In some places, 90 percent of those with HIV do not know they have it. And we just learned that AIDS is set to become the third leading cause of death worldwide in the coming years. These are staggering, these numbers, and they help us understand the magnitude of this pandemic.

In a speech on auto safety, Meagan Hagensick of Wartburg College used numbers effectively to drive home the importance of seat belts (Schnoor, 2008):

> One fatality every 13 minutes. One injury every 10 seconds. One accident every 5 seconds. Six million crashes. 2.8 million injuries. 43,000 people killed each year. These numbers are not spawned from a deadly virus or new strain of bacteria; they are the result of avoidable human error.

Guidelines for Using Numerical Data

Here are a few guidelines to help you use numerical data more effectively in public speeches.

- **Make sure the numbers are clear.** Remember that your audience will hear the figures only once. Round off figures so they're easy to comprehend and retain. If your numbers are difficult to remember, reinforce your oral presentation with some type of presentation aid—perhaps a slide or a chart. Numbers presented without some kind of visual reinforcement are often difficult to grasp and remember.
- **Make explicit the meaning of the numbers you're using.** For example, if you state that the average home health aide makes less than $30,000 a year, you need to compare this figure to the salaries of other workers and to your proposition that salaries need to be increased.
- **Use numbers in moderation.** Most listeners' capacity for numerical data presented in a speech is limited, so use figures sparingly.
- **Use only reliable and current numerical data.** And make sure that your audience is aware of their reliability and currency.

Additional Forms of Support

5.6 Explain the usefulness of quotations, comparisons and contrasts, fact series, and repetition and restatement.

There are a variety of additional forms of support you might use. Here are a few in brief.

Quotations

Quotations are useful for adding spice and wit as well as authority to your speech. Quotations can, however, become cumbersome. Too often they're not related directly to the point you're trying to make, and their relevance gets lost if the quotation is in technical language that listeners may not understand. It then becomes necessary to interject definitions as you go along—not a very good idea. Therefore, unless the quotation is short, easily comprehensible to the audience, and related directly to the point you're making, use your own words; paraphrase the essence of the idea, and credit the person.

Comparison and Contrast

Another useful form of support is comparison and contrast. For example, you might want to compare the Android with the iPhone, living conditions in Norway versus the United States, or introversion and extroversion.

Simple Statement of Facts or Series of Facts

It's often useful to cite facts or a series of facts to explain a statement or position. In a speech on the growing crime rate in your city, you might find it useful to use a series of facts:

- Car thefts have increased 12 percent over last year.
- Burglaries increased 7 percent.
- Property damage increased 22 percent.
- Assaults increased 5 percent.

Such a series of facts clearly makes your point—crime is increasing.

Repetition and Restatement

Repetition involves repeating your idea in the same words at strategic places throughout your speech. Restatement, on the other hand, involves repeating your idea but in different words. Repetition and restatement are especially helpful in public speeches because of the inevitable lapses in audience attention. When you repeat or restate your idea you provide listeners with one more opportunity to grasp what you're saying. Restatement is especially important when addressing members of a culturally diverse audience who may not have learned your language as their first language and consequently may not understand certain idioms and figures of speech. Restating these ideas in different words increases the chances of audience comprehension. Use your judgment as to when to use these strategies, but keep in mind that overusing either one can lead to a monotonous speech.

JOURNAL 5.6 PUBLIC SPEAKING CHOICE POINT

Additional Forms of Support

With your next speech in mind, what are some of the ways you can use these additional forms of support?

SUMMARY: COLLECT SUPPORTING MATERIALS (STEP 4)

This chapter focused on supporting materials, especially examples, analogies, definitions, narration, testimony, and statistics.

Examples, Illustrations, and Narratives

5.1 Define *examples*, *illustrations*, and *narratives* and explain the guidelines for using this type of support.

1. Examples and illustrations are specific instances that are explained in varying degrees of detail.

2. Narratives are stories that illustrate an assertion and are normally longer than examples and illustrations.

3. Examples, illustrations, and narratives work best when limited in length, clearly relevant to the issues, real and hypothetical are distinguished, and they emphasize the significance of an issue.

Analogies

5.2 Define and distinguish between *figurative* and *literal analogies* and identify the guidelines for using analogies.

4. Analogies are comparisons and may be figurative or literal.

5. A figurative analogy is a comparison of items from different classes—men and dogs, children and birds learning to fly, or Cincinnati and France.

6. A literal analogy is a comparison of items from the same class—two breeds of dog, two countries, or two professors.

7. Analogies are most effective when the cases are clearly comparable and when placed in context.

Definitions

5.3 Identify the various types of definitions and the guidelines for using them in a public speech.

8. Definitions are statements of the meaning of a term or concept.

9. Terms may be defined by:
   - Etymology, the origin and development of a word
   - Authority, the meaning and explanation of an expert
   - Negation, explaining what something is not
   - Specific examples of a term's meaning

10. Definitions are most effective when they are clear and simple.

Testimony

5.4 Define *testimony* and identify the guidelines for using this form of support.

11. Testimony is the statement of another person concerning some issue.

12. Testimony can be of an expert's statements (an environmental scientist, a noted historian, or a famous psychologist) or an eyewitness's account.

13. To make testimony effective, stress the competence of the authority, the unbiased nature of the testimony, and the recency of the observation or opinion.

Numerical Data

5.5 Explain the types of numerical data that may be useful in a public speech and the guidelines for using such support.

14. Numerical data involve raw numbers and statistics such as measures of central tendency, percentages, correlations, and measures of difference.

15. Numerical data are especially effective when they are clear, meaningful to the audience, connected to the idea they support, visually and verbally reinforced, and used in moderation.

Additional Forms of Support

5.6 Explain the usefulness of quotations, comparisons and contrasts, fact series, and repetition and restatement.

16. Quotations can add wit and spice.

17. Comparisons and contrast highlight important similarities and differences.

18. Fact series can make an argument memorable.

19. Repetition and restatement help audience understanding and memory.

KEY TERMS: COLLECT SUPPORTING MATERIALS (STEP 4)

analogies

definition

definition by authority

definition by etymology

definition by negation

definition by specific example

example

expert testimony

eyewitness testimony

figurative analogies

illustration

literal analogies

mean

measures of central tendency

measures of correlation

measures of difference

median

mode

narrative

negative correlation

percentages

positive correlation

range

raw numbers

statistics

testimony

PUBLIC SPEAKING EXERCISES

5.1 Supporting Materials

Select one the following overly broad statements, and support it using at least three different types of supporting materials discussed in this chapter. Because the purpose of this exercise is to provide greater insight into supporting materials, you may, for this exercise, invent facts, figures, illustrations, examples, and the like.

1. Significant social contributions have been made by persons over 65.
2. The writer of this article is an authority.
3. Attitudes toward women in the workplace have changed over the past 20 years.
4. This college sounds ideal.
5. The events of September 11, 2001, were world changing and life changing.
6. The athlete enjoyed a lavish lifestyle.

5.2 Evaluating Testimony

If you were presenting someone's testimony on one of the following issues, how would you establish the person's qualifications so that your audience would accept what he or she said?

- Nutritionist, on proper diet
- Real estate agent, on the advantages and disadvantages of condos and co-ops
- Psychiatrist, on the nature of bipolar disorder
- Biologist, on how to feed your pet
- Drama teacher, on how to write a play

USING PRESENTATION AIDS (STEP 4)

→ Presentation aids are an essential part of contemporary public speaking. Learning to use them wisely will greatly increase your effectiveness.

CHAPTER TOPICS

The Importance of Presentation Aids

Types of Presentation Aids

Computer-Assisted Presentation Aids

Guidelines for Creating and Using Presentation Aids

LEARNING OBJECTIVES

6.1 Identify some of the reasons why presentation aids are useful in public speaking.

6.2 Identify the major types of presentation aids.

6.3 Explain the nature of computer-assisted presentation aids.

6.4 Identify the guidelines for creating and using presentation aids.

T his chapter continues Step 4 and focuses on presentation aids, their importance, what choices you have, and how to use them effectively.

The Importance of Presentation Aids

6.1 Identify some of the reasons why presentation aids are useful in public speaking.

presentation aid
A visual or auditory form of supporting material.

As you plan your speech, consider using some kind of **presentation aid**—a visual or auditory means for clarifying ideas. Ask yourself how you can visually present what you want your audience to remember. For example, if you want audience members to see the growing impact of the sales tax, consider showing them a line graph of rising sales tax over the past 10 years. If you want them to see that Brand A is superior to Brand X, consider showing them a bar chart identifying the superiority of Brand A. Presentation aids are not added frills—they are integral parts of your speech. They will enable you to increase your effectiveness considerably. Here are just a few ways presentation aids can help you.

Presentation Aids Help You Gain Attention and Maintain Interest

We live in a multimedia world; we're used to it, and we enjoy it. It's not surprising, then, that we, as members of an audience, appreciate it when a speaker makes use of visuals or audio aids. We perk up when the speaker says, "I want you to look at this chart showing the employment picture for the next five years" or "Listen to the vocal range in this voice." Presentation aids provide variety in what we see and hear—something audiences appreciate and respond to favorably.

Presentation Aids Add Clarity

Let's say you want to illustrate the projected growth in Internet usage. You might note that in 1993 there were approximately 14,000,000 Internet users worldwide, in 2000, 413,000,000, in 2005, 1,000,000,000, in 2010, 2,000,000,000, in 2014, 2,900,000,000, and in 2016, 3,700,000,000. But such recitals get boring pretty fast. Further, the numbers you want the audience to appreciate are difficult to retain in memory, so by the time you get to the current figures, your listeners have already forgotten the previous figures. As a result, the very growth that you want your audience to see is likely to get lost. It would be much easier to communicate this kind of information in a bar graph.

Another way in which presentation aids are helpful is when addressing a culturally diverse audience. Often photos and illustrations are more universal in meaning than certain terms or idioms that might be unknown by non-native speakers.

Presentation Aids Reinforce Your Message

Presentation aids help ensure that your listeners understand and remember what you've said. Presentation aids help you present the same information in two different ways: verbally, as audience members hear you explain the aid, and visually, as they see the chart, map, or model. The same is true with audio aids. For example, you might discuss the range of vocal variety and at the same time provide recorded samples. This kind of one-two punch helps the audience understand your ideas more clearly and remember them more accurately.

Presentation Aids Contribute to Credibility and Confidence

If you use appropriate and professional-looking presentation aids—something that will be covered later in this chapter—your listeners are likely to see you as a credible

VIEWPOINTS
Presentation Aids

What do you see as the greatest advantage of presentation aids?

speaker; as someone who cares enough about both them and the topic to do this "extra" work. When listeners view you as credible and have confidence in you, they're more likely to listen carefully and to believe what you have to say.

Presentation Aids Help to Reduce Apprehension

When you have to concentrate on coordinating your speech with your presentation aids, you're less likely to focus on yourself—and self-focus often increases apprehension. In addition, the movement involved in using presentation aids relaxes many speakers, and with greater relaxation comes greater confidence and less anxiety.

Presentation Aids Can Offer Evidence

Presentation aids can often present evidence in a compelling way and in a way that verbal-only messages cannot. For example, a short video on unsanitary conditions at a restaurant or on the crowdedness of a homeless shelter will help you substantiate your assertions, in many cases, more than words.

JOURNAL 6.1 PUBLIC SPEAKING CHOICE POINT

Presentation Aids

Harry is scheduled to give a speech on the way we think and wonders if presentation aids are necessary or if they'd be helpful. In what ways might presentation aids be of value to Harry?

Types of Presentation Aids

6.2 Identify the major types of presentation aids.

You have lots of choices when it comes to selecting your presentation aid. Most of these—whether charts, photographs, or maps, for example—you'll present through slides that you create in a computer presentation program. But, in many cases, you

chart boards
Large semi-rigid boards that come in a variety of colors and sizes and are useful when you have one or two relatively simple graphs, a few word charts, or diagrams that you want to display during your speech.

flip chart
A presentation aid consisting of sheets of paper for writing key terms or numbers while presenting a speech.

can use low-tech alternatives. For example, the whiteboard may be used to record key terms or names, important numerical data, or even the main points of your speech (in very abbreviated form). **Chart boards**, large semi-rigid boards that come in a variety of colors and sizes, are useful when you have one or two relatively simple graphs, a few tables, or diagrams that you want to display during your speech. **Flip charts**, large pads of paper (usually about 24 × 24 inches) mounted on a stand or easel, can be used to record a variety of information, for example, key concepts or main points. Writing these out before the speech saves you the time of writing them during the speech (as you're forced to do with a whiteboard). All of these are useful in their own way and are often useful as backups should anything go wrong with the technical equipment.

The Object Itself

As a general rule (to which there are many exceptions), the best presentation aid is the object itself. Bring it to your speech if you can. Notice that infomercials sell their products not only by talking about them but by showing them to potential buyers. You see how OxiClean works and what the new slow cooker looks like; you see the jewelry, the clothing, or the new mop from a wide variety of angles and in varied settings.

If you're talking about types of print magazines or the qualities of a good tennis racket, it would be helpful to use these as presentation aids. In a speech on the uses of different types of glues, for example, one student brought in the glues and the pieces of plastic, wood, and metal with which he explained how each glue worked differently on different materials.

Models

models
Replicas of actual objects.

Models—replicas of the actual object—are useful for a variety of purposes. For example, if you want to explain complex structures such as the human auditory or vocal mechanism, the brain, or the structure of DNA, a model will prove useful. You may remember from science classes that these models (and, to a lesser degree, the pictures of them in the textbooks) made a lot more sense than just the verbal explanations. Models help clarify the relative sizes and positions of parts and how each part interacts with each other part.

In a speech on native styles of dress, one student brought in a collection of dolls, each dressed in the style of a different culture. In a speech on stretching exercises, one student used a 14-inch wooden artist's model. In a speech on how to buy a diamond ring, one enterprising student brought in a crystal-looking water faucet knob that enabled her to illustrate the qualities to look for in buying a diamond ring—size, quality, and clarity.

Diagrams

diagrams
Simplified drawings often in outline form that are often useful for explaining complex structures.

flow diagram
Drawings that show a sequence of events or processes.

Diagrams, simplified drawings often in outline form, are often useful for explaining complex structures. Figure 6.1 shows a diagram of the ear that a speaker might use to explain a variety of ear-related topics.

Another type of diagram is the **flow diagram** (or flow chart), which shows a sequence of events or processes. Figure 6.2, for example, presents a flow diagram of the process of emotional contagion, the process by which one person comes to feel the emotions of the other person. This type of diagram helps the audience see how things or events are related and in a particular sequence.

Graphs

graphs
Diagrams showing relationships that are useful for clarifying how a whole is divided into parts, showing differences over time, and comparing different amounts or sizes.

Graphs, diagrams showing relationships, are useful for clarifying how a whole is divided into parts, showing differences over time, and comparing different amounts or sizes. As you know, there are a variety of different types of graphs that you might use; choosing

Figure 6.1 Diagram Example

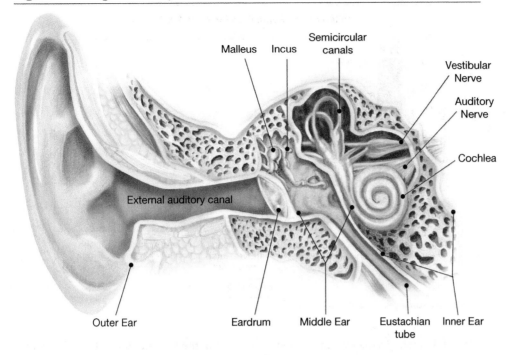

Figure 6.2 Flow Diagram Example

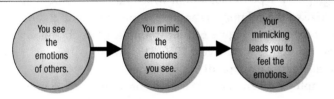

the best one for your data will help you communicate your meaning most clearly. These figures can be drawn freehand or generated with the graphics capabilities of any word-processing or presentation software. Let's look at several of the most popular.

The **pie graph**, a graph in the form of a circle, is useful for showing relative proportions when the totals add up to 100 percent. For example, Figure 6.3 shows the

pie graph
A type of presentation aid that divides a whole into pieces and represents these as pieces of a pie.

Figure 6.3 3-Dimensional Pie Graph Example

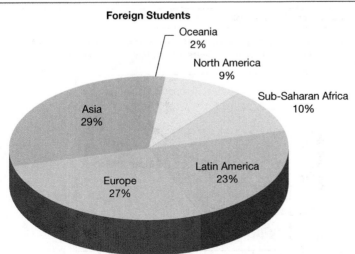

SOURCE: Data from DeSilver, D. (2015) Growth from Asia drives surge in in U.S. foreign students. Pew Research Center, (www.pewresearch.org). Accessed January 9, 2016.

Figure 6.4 Bar Graph Example

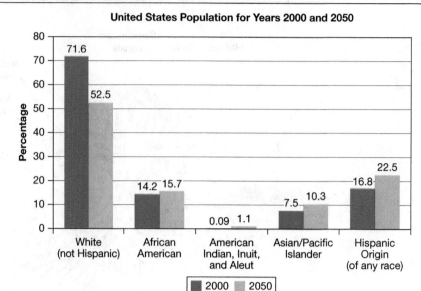

United States Population for Years 2000 and 2050

SOURCE: Data from the U.S. Census Bureau.

bar graph

A type of diagram in which numerical values are represented in the height or size of the column.

line graph

A diagram in which numerical values are connected with lines and that is especially useful for showing changes over a period of time and comparing the relative changes of two or more groups.

picture graphs

Diagrams that use images (icons, symbols, or photos) to represent numerical values.

cultural diversity in the foreign students studying in the United States. This pie graph, as you can see, is particularly helpful for showing relative proportions.

The **bar graph**—a type of diagram in which numerical values are represented in the height or size of the column—is another popular type of graph that enables you to see relative proportions. Figure 6.4, for example, gives the population figures for 2000 and projected figures for the year 2050. This graph enables you to see at a glance demographic changes that are predicted to occur by 2050.

The **line graph**—a diagram in which numerical values are connected with lines—is especially useful for showing changes over a period of time and also enables you to compare the relative changes of two or more groups. Figure 6.5, for example, illustrates the percentages of African Americans and Hispanics for four different periods: the actual percentages as recorded in 1990 and 2000 and the projected percentages for the years 2025 and 2050. Additional groups could have been added, but the graph would become increasingly difficult to read.

Picture graphs—diagrams that use images (icons, symbols, or photos) to represent numerical values—add a bit more interest than word-and-number-only charts. By using

Figure 6.5 Line Graph Example

United States Population of African Americans and People of Hispanic Origin for Years 1990, 2000, 2025, and 2050

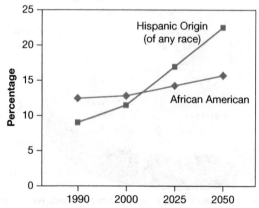

SOURCE: Data from the U.S. Census Bureau.

Figure 6.6 Picture Graph Example

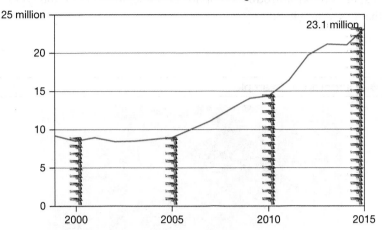

SOURCE: Data from FBI National Instant Criminal Background Check System.

images of the items you're talking about, you will most likely increase audience attention to and retention of your message. Figure 6.6 is a picture graph used to show the increase in guns in the past 15 years; each gun represents 1,000,000 purchases and permits, which the speaker would note during the explanation of the aid and which could also be written into the aid. This picture graph clearly etches the tremendous increase in guns in the minds of the audience much more clearly than simple bars or words.

Tables

Present information in a table when you want to summarize or compare data or ideas. Tables are especially useful for identifying the key points in one of your propositions or in your entire speech—in the order in which you cover them, of course. Another use of tables is to show information you want your audience to write down. Emergency phone numbers, addresses, or titles of recommended books or websites are examples of the type of information that listeners will welcome in written form. Tables often present numbers to offer a visual explanation of a statement with evidence in support of an assertion. Figure 6.7 presents an example. This table clearly illustrates how few vacation days American employees have compared with other countries.

Infographics

With the increased ease and sophistication of various computer programs, **infographics**—visual (often with numbers and words) representations of information—are becoming more and more popular. These are especially helpful

infographic
Visual representation of information.

Figure 6.7 Table Example

Average Number of Paid Vacation Days per Year

Country	Vacation Days
Italy	42
France	37
Brazil	34
United Kingdom	28
Canada	26
Japan	25
USA	13

SOURCE: http://www.infoplease.com/ipa/A0922052.html, accessed 2/29/16

they effectively combine the verbal and the nonverbal and convey a message clearly and concisely. Figure 6.8 presents an infographic of the author's DNA that might be used in a speech of self-introduction or, for example, to illustrate the types of information that DNA can yield.

Figure 6.8 Infographic Example

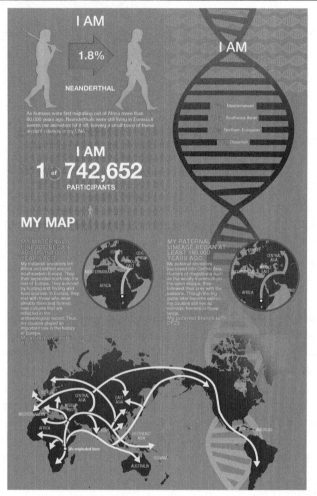

SOURCE: Generated from The National Geographic Genographic Project, https://genographic.nationalgeographic.com/ (using author's information).

JOURNAL 6.2 PUBLIC SPEAKING CHOICE POINT

The Infographic

Gary wants to give a speech on what to expect when you get to college to be presented to junior high school students. *What are some ways Gary might use an infographic? Try creating one for this topic or, better, your next speech.*

ETHICAL CHOICE POINT

Professional Preparation

You're pressed for time and have to give a speech using computer-assisted presentation aids. A number of online companies will prepare professional Prezi or PowerPoint slides for a reasonable fee which you can well afford. *If you do have these slides professionally prepared, would you have an ethical obligation to mention this in your speech?*

Maps

If you want to illustrate the locations of geographic features such as cities, lakes, rivers, or mountain ranges, maps will obviously prove useful as presentation aids. But maps also can be used for illustrating population densities, immigration patterns, world literacy rates, varied economic conditions, the spread of diseases, and hundreds of other issues you may wish to examine in your speeches. For example, in a speech on natural resources, one speaker used a variety of maps to illustrate the location of large reserves of oil, gas, and precious metals. Another speaker used maps to illustrate the concentration of wealth, while another used maps to show differences in the mortality rate throughout the world. A wide variety of maps may be searched for on the Internet and then shown as slides. Chances are you'll find a map on the Internet for exactly the purpose you need. If you do use presentation materials from the internet, be sure to include the source URL and date of access in your list of references.

For example, Figure 6.9 presents a map showing the countries that are highest in "indulgence"—countries that value having fun and enjoying the present and countries that are high in "restraint"—countries that value saving and planning for the future.

Figure 6.9 Map Example

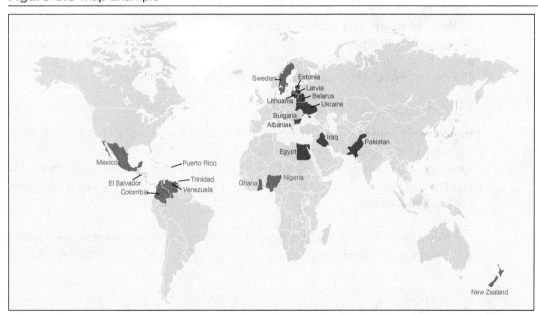

■ Citizens of these countries emphasize gratification of desires and are among the happiest cultures. They see themselves as having control over their lives and ample leisure time. These cultures also stress the importance of friendships and close relationships.

■ Citizens of these countries curb personal gratification and are less happy than indulgent cultures. They see themselves as having little control over their lives and little leisure time. Friendships and close relationships are less important.

People

If you want to demonstrate the muscles of the body or different voice patterns, skin complexions, or hairstyles, consider using people as your aids. Aside from the obvious assistance they provide in demonstrating their muscles or vocal qualities, people help to secure and maintain the attention and interest of the audience.

And don't overlook yourself as a presentation aid. For example, if you're giving a speech on boxing strategies, exercise techniques, or sitting and standing postures that can lead to backaches, you might demonstrate these yourself. As an added plus, going through these demonstrations is likely to reduce your apprehension and make you more relaxed.

Photographs

Types of trees, styles of art, kinds of exercise machines, or the horrors of war—all can be made more meaningful with photographs. Millions of such photographs are readily available on the Internet, and you're sure to find many that will meet your specific needs. You'll also be able to point to specific parts of the photo as you explain the devastation of war or the differences among trees. Passing pictures around the room is generally a bad idea. Listeners will wait for the pictures to circulate to them, will wonder what the pictures contain, and will miss a great deal of your speech in the interim.

Audio Materials

In many speeches it would be helpful to use audio aids. For example, in a speech on accents, differences in male–female voices, or music trends, audio aids would be essential. When using audio materials, it often helps if you preface the audio to place it into the context of the speech and then follow the audio with a brief restatement of its connection with your specific message.

Videos

Basically, you have two options with videos: You can record a scene from a film or television program or pick one up from the Internet and show it at the appropriate time in your speech, or you can create your own video. Videos (and the same goes for audios) add variety to your presentation and will help to maintain audience attention. A wide variety of types of speeches would profit from the use of videos. For example, a speech on culturally different dances, the layout of a museum, or how to put shingles on a roof would be greatly improved with short and relevant videos.

Handouts

handouts
Printed materials distributed to the audience.

Handouts are printed materials that you distribute to the audience. Handouts are especially useful to help explain complex material, provide listeners with a record of your speech or significant data from your speech, and encourage listeners to take notes. As you know, a variety of handouts can be easily prepared with many of the computer presentation packages.

Now that you understand the types of presentation aids you want to use, you can create them or download them into any of the computer-assisted presentation packages.

Computer-Assisted Presentation Aids

6.3 Explain the nature of computer-assisted presentation aids.

A variety of presentation software packages are available, each with its own uniqueness. Most likely you'll be using PowerPoint, Prezi, Keynote, or Google Docs, but depending on your technological sophistication, there are many others with features that you may wish to explore.

VIEWPOINTS

Presentation Packages

With your next speech in mind, which type of presentation software would you be likely to use? Why?

Most presentation software is relatively linear; one slide follows another and another. Prezi is a bit different in that it presents all your slides on one canvas. You then zoom in and out of each slide as you discuss it (see accompanying photo). All enable you to import photos and add text in varied typefaces, colors, and backgrounds.

Computer-assisted presentations possess all of the advantages of aids already noted (for example, maintaining interest and attention, adding clarity, and reinforcing your message). In addition, however, they have advantages all their own. They give your speech a professional, up-to-date look and in the process add to your credibility. They show you're prepared and care about your topic and audience. Along with this chapter, take one of the many tutorials available from Prezi, Keynote, or PowerPoint.

In addition to enabling you to produce and show a variety of slides, computer presentation software also enables you to print out a variety of materials: slides, slides with speaker's notes, and slides with room for listener notes. You can print out your complete set of slides to distribute to your listeners. Or you can print out a select portion of the slides or even slides that you didn't have time to cover in your speech but you'd like your audience to look at later. The most popular options are to print out two, three, or up to six slides per page. The two-slide option provides for easy readability and would be especially useful for slides of tables or graphs that you want to present to your listeners in an easy-to-read size. The three-slide option is probably the most widely used; it prints the three slides down the left side of the page with space for listeners to write notes on the right. This option is useful if you want to interact with audience members and you want them to take notes as you're speaking. You'd most likely distribute this handout during your introduction or, better, at that point when you want your listeners to begin taking notes. A sample three-slide printout with space for notes is provided in Figure 6.10. You can, of course, also print out any selection of slides you wish—perhaps only those slides that contain graphs or only those slides that summarize your talk.

Another useful option is to print out your slides with your speaker's notes. That way you'll have your slides and any notes you may find useful—examples you want to use, statistics that would be difficult to memorize, quotations that you want to read to your audience, delivery notes, or anything that you care to record. The audience will see the slides but not your speaker's notes. It's generally best to record these notes in outline form, with key words rather than complete sentences. This will prevent you from falling into the trap of reading your speech. A sample printout showing a slide plus speaker's notes is provided in Figure 6.11.

Before reading about ways to use presentation aids effectively, see how much you know about designing slides. Respond to the following statements with *true* or *false*:

_____ **1.** A good size font to use is about 16 or 18 points with about 8 or 9 lines per slide.

_____ **2.** Use italics for emphasis.

_____ **3.** Read your slides word for word.

Figure 6.10 Slides with Space for Listeners' Notes

This is an especially popular handout style because it can be easily prepared and because it provides a neat combination of what you said and what listeners might be thinking.

Figure 6.11 Slide and Speaker's Notes

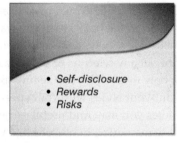

PAUSE!
SCAN AUDIENCE!
Today I'd like to discuss an extremely interesting and significant form of communication. It's called self-disclosure.
S-Disclosure can be greatly rewarding.
You might disclose your secret love and find that you too are your secret lover's secret lover.
S-Disclosure can also be risky.
You might disclose a mental or physical problem to your employer only to find yourself without a job,
Because the rewards and the risks are so high, we need to understand this unique form of communication. Before discussing the rewards and risks, we need to understand a little more about the nature of *S*-D.
PAUSE!

_____ 4. Use lots of color and sound effects; these will keep the audience awake.

_____ 5. Blue and green or red and green are almost always appropriate colors for slides.

_____ 6. Like in the preparation outline, use full sentences for the slides.

_____ 7. Your slides should be your main attraction.

_____ 8. When you have few words on a slide, add a photo or graphic.

_____ 9. A 10-minute informative speech can easily have 30 to 40 slides.

These statements were selected to point out some of the misconceptions people have about computer-assisted presentations; all are false. Briefly, here's why:

1. Font size 16 or 18 is too small; use at least 24-point, though 30-point font would be even better. Four lines is best, though six is generally fine. Any more than this will work against you.

2. Italics are difficult to read and don't give real emphasis.

3. Never.

4. Too much color and too many sounds will be distracting.

5. These colors do not provide sufficient contrast—as would, say, red and black. Also, many people have difficulty distinguishing red and green.

6. Use phrases for the slides; sentences take too much time to read.

7. No, _you_ should be the main attraction. Your slides are simply aids to your presentation.

8. Only add photos or graphics when they are integral to your slide's message.

9. Any more than 10 slides is probably too much.

JOURNAL 6.3 PUBLIC SPEAKING CHOICE POINT

Powerpoint

James is one of the admissions directors at his college and needs to present information to his audience of potential freshmen and their parents about the career paths of recent graduates. There is a lot of information to present, and he thinks a PowerPoint slide show would be helpful, but he wants to avoid boring his audience to death. _What advice can you offer him?_

Guidelines for Creating and Using Presentation Aids

6.4 Identify the guidelines for creating and using presentation aids.

Your presentation aids will be more effective if you follow a few simple guidelines. Here are some guidelines for using and for avoiding misusing presentation aids.

Know Your Aids Intimately

Be sure you know in what order your aids are to be presented and how you plan to introduce them. Know exactly what goes where and when. Do all your rehearsal with your presentation aids so you'll be able to introduce and use them smoothly and effectively. Avoid talking to your aid. Although obviously the wrong thing to do, it's also a very natural tendency but one that needs to be resisted. Instead, talk to your audience at all times. Know your aids so well that you can point to what you want without breaking eye contact with your audience.

Stress Relevance

Always keep in mind that a presentation aid is just that, an aid to help you make your message clearer or more persuasive. Use only those that are relevant and that will add to your message. At the same time, make sure the audience sees the relevance of the aid. It may be very clear to you, but to listeners who see it only once, it may not be clear without more detailed explanation. Use your aid only when it's relevant. Show each aid when you want the audience to concentrate on it and then remove it. If you don't remove it, the audience's attention may remain focused on the visual when you want it focused on what you'll be saying next. At the same, be careful that you don't remove the aid too early. Make sure that you have sufficiently explained and that the audience fully understands the aid before you remove it.

Stress Clarity

Make sure that your aids can be seen easily from all parts of the room. Don't underestimate, for example, how large lettering must be to be read or how large a photo must be to be seen by those in the back of the room.

Rehearse Your Speech with The Presentation Aids Incorporated into The Presentation

Practice your actual movements with the aids you'll use. If you're going to use a chart, how will you use it? Will it stand by itself? Will you ask another student to hold it for you?

Another type of rehearsal is to check out the equipment available in the room you'll speak in and its compatibility with the presentation software you're using. If possible, rehearse with the very equipment you'll have available on the day you're speaking. In this way you can adjust to or remedy any incompatibilities or idiosyncrasies that are identified.

Integrate Presentation Aids into Your Speech Seamlessly

Just as a verbal example should flow naturally into the text and seem an integral part of the speech, so should the presentation aid. It should appear not as an afterthought but as an essential part of the speech.

Use The Templates Provided by The Software

If you're using a computer presentation such as Prezi or PowerPoint, use their templates. Allow the design wizards to help you choose colors and typefaces. The templates are created by professional designers who are experts at blending colors, fonts, and designs into clear and appealing renderings. These templates will also give your aids a professional appearance, which can only add to your credibility.

Use Consistent Typeface, Size, and Color

Give each item in your outline that has the same level head (for example, all your main points) the same typeface, size, and color throughout your presentation. This will help your listeners follow the organization of your speech. Notice your textbooks; all the major headings are in the same font and all photo captions are in the same font, for example. If you're using one of the predesigned templates, this will be done for you.

Be Brief and Simple

Your objective is to provide the audience with key words and ideas that will reinforce what you're saying in your speech; you don't want your audience members to spend their time reading rather than listening. Generally, put one complete thought on a slide and don't try to put too many words on one slide. Aids that are too detailed, too long, or overly complex will work against your goal. Presentation aids should be designed to add clarity to your speech. Consequently, they need to be simple to be understood.

This suggestion to be brief is especially important when using audio and video materials; these should almost always be very brief. In a 6- or 7-minute speech, a 20- to 30-second video is about the maximum.

Use Colors for Contrast

Remember that many people have difficulty distinguishing red from green, so if you want to distinguish ideas, it is probably best to avoid this color pairing. Similarly, if you're going to print out your slides in shades of gray, make sure the tones you choose provide clear contrasts. Also, be careful that you don't choose colors that recall holidays that have nothing to do with your speech—for example, red and green for Christmas or orange and black for Halloween. Remember, too, the cultural attitudes toward different colors; for example, among some Asian cultures, writing a person's name in red means that the person has died.

Use Only The Aids You Really Need

Presentation software packages make inserting visuals so easy that they sometimes encourage the user to include too many visuals. Most presentation packages provide a variety of graphic pictures, animated graphics, photos, and videos that are useful for a wide variety of speeches, or you could create your own. Use visuals only when they are directly related to your speech thesis and purpose. In deciding whether to include a visual, ask yourself if the inclusion of this graph or photo will advance the purpose of your speech. If it does, use it; if it doesn't, don't.

Use Charts and Tables When Appropriate

Charts and tables are useful, as noted above, when you want to communicate complex information that would take too much text for one slide to explain. You have a tremendous variety of chart and graph types (for example, pie, bar, and cumulative charts) and tables to choose from. If you're using presentation software that's part of a suite, then you'll find it especially easy to import files from your word processor or spreadsheet. Also, consider the advantages of chart animation. Just as you can display bullets as you discuss each one, you can display the chart in parts so as to focus the audience's attention on exactly the part of the chart you want.

Anticipate Questions

If there's a question-and-answer period following your speech, consider preparing a few extra slides for responses to questions you anticipate being asked. Then, when someone asks you a predicted question, you can say: "I anticipated that someone might ask that question; it raises an important issue. The data are presented in this chart." You can then show the slide and explain it more fully. This is surely going the extra mile, but it can help make your speech a real standout.

Anticipate Technical Problems

If you're planning to use a slide show, for example, consider what you'd do if the computer malfunctioned or the electricity didn't work. A useful backup procedure is to have handouts ready just in case something goes wrong. Or be prepared to use the whiteboard, chart boards, or a flip chart as your plan B.

Avoid Problems with Handouts

Handouts are often useful, and listeners often appreciate having them, but they can create problems in taking attention away from what you're saying. If you do use handouts, encourage your audience to listen to you when you want them to and to look at the handout when you want them to by simply telling them. If you distribute your handouts at the end of the speech, encourage your audience to read them by including additional material.

JOURNAL 6.4 PUBLIC SPEAKING CHOICE POINT

Presentation Aids

Take a look at any one of the speeches in the Appendix of Speeches. *What choices did the speaker have for using presentation aids?*

CHAPTER 6

SUMMARY: USING PRESENTATION AIDS (STEP 4)

This chapter examined presentation aids, their importance, types of aids, computer-assisted presentations, and it presented guidelines for using all sorts of presentation aids.

The Importance of Presentation Aids

6.1 Identify some of the reasons why presentation aids are useful in public speaking.

1. Presentation aids are useful for
   - Gaining attention and maintaining interest.
   - Adding clarity.
   - Reinforcing your message.
   - Contributing to your credibility and confidence.
   - Reducing apprehension.
   - Offering evidence.

Types of Presentation Aids

6.2 Identify the major types of presentation aids.

2. Common types of presentation aids are:
   - the actual object
   - models
   - diagrams
   - graphs (pie, bar, line, pictorial)
   - tables
   - infographics
   - maps
   - people
   - photographs
   - audio materials
   - videos
   - handouts

Computer-Assisted Presentation Aids

6.3 Explain the nature of computer-assisted presentation aids.

3. Computer-assisted presentation software enables you to incorporate all your presentation aids in a professional-looking format and enables you to print out a variety of materials.

Guidelines for Creating and Using Presentation Aids

6.4 Identify the guidelines for creating and using presentation aids.

4. When using presentation aids:
   - Know your aids intimately.
   - Stress relevance.
   - Stress clarity.
   - Rehearse your speech with the presentation aids incorporated into the presentation.
   - Integrate presentation aids into your speech seamlessly.
   - Use the templates provided by the software.
   - Use consistent typeface, size, and color.
   - Be brief and simple.
   - Use colors for contrast.
   - Use only the aids you really need. Use charts and tables when appropriate.
   - Anticipate questions.
   - Anticipate technical problems.
   - Avoid problems with handouts.

KEY TERMS: USING PRESENTATION AIDS (STEP 4)

bar graph	graphs	picture graphs
chart boards	handouts	pie graph
diagrams	infographic	presentation aid
flip chart	line graph	
flow diagram	models	

PUBLIC SPEAKING EXERCISES

6.1 Galileo and the Ghosts

Galileo and the Ghosts is a technique for seeing a topic or problem through the eyes of a particular group of people and should prove useful at just about any stage of the public speaking preparation process (DeVito, 1996; Higgins, 1994; von Oech, 1990). In "ghost-thinking" (analogous to ghostwriting), you select a team of four to eight "people"—for example, historical figures like Galileo or Aristotle, fictional figures like Wonder Woman or James Bond, or persons from other cultures or of a different gender or affectional orientation. Selecting people who are very different from you and from one another will increase the chances that different perspectives will arise.

You then pose a question or problem ("What presentation aids can I use?" "How can I make this presentation aid more powerful?" "In what ways might I present these statistics?") and ask yourself how each of these ghost-thinkers would answer your question or solve your problem, allowing yourself to listen to what each has to say. Of course, you're really listening to yourself—but to yourself acting in the role of another person. The technique forces you to step outside of your normal role and to consider the perspective of someone totally different from you. Try selecting a ghost-thinking team and asking your "team" for suggestions for finding, evaluating, and fine-tuning your presentation aids (or supporting materials generally) for your next speech.

6.2 Evaluating Presentation Aids

Review the various examples of presentation aids provided in this chapter, selecting one, two, or three of them, and identify (1) what is good about the presentation aid, (2) what is bad about it, and (3) how you might make it better.

ORGANIZE YOUR SPEECH (STEPS 5, 6, AND 7)

A clear organization makes a speech easier to remember for both speaker and audience.

CHAPTER TOPICS

Develop Your Main Points (Step 5)

Organize Your Main Points (Step 6)

Construct Your Introduction, Conclusion, and Transitions (Step 7)

Outline the Speech

LEARNING OBJECTIVES

7.1 Explain how to develop main points that are limited in number, focus on your audience, and are worded effectively.

7.2 Explain the major organizational patterns.

7.3 Explain the characteristics of effective introductions, conclusions, and transitions.

7.4 Explain how to create preparation and delivery outlines.

n this chapter we first look at organizing the body of the speech, in which you set forth your main ideas. Once you've accomplished this, you can move on to develop your introduction, your conclusion, and the transitions that hold the pieces of the speech together. As you are developing these parts of the speech, you'll also be preparing outlines of your speech.

- **Organizing will help guide the speech preparation process.** As you develop your organization, you'll be able to see the speech more clearly and as a whole (even in a preliminary and unfinished form). This will help you to see what needs further development, what needs paring down, or what should be rearranged or repositioned.

- **Organizing will help your audience understand your speech.** Because audience members will hear your speech only once, it must be instantly clear to them. They can't (as when you reread a paragraph you didn't quite understand) rehear what was just said. Whether your aim is to inform or to persuade, your audience will be better able to follow your thinking if you present it in an organized pattern. If your listeners can visualize the pattern or outline you're following, it will be easier for them to understand your speech and to see, for instance, how an example supports a main point or how two arguments are related to your thesis.

- **Organizing will help your audience remember your speech.** People simply remember organized material better than unorganized material. If you want audience members to remember your speech, help them by presenting them with information in an easily identifiable and memorable organizational pattern.

- **Organizing will help establish your credibility.** Everything you do and say reflects on your credibility (the extent to which the audience believes you), and organization is no exception. When you present an effectively organized speech, you say in effect that you put work into this and that you're concerned with the audience understanding and remembering your speech. Your audience is more likely to see you as a competent person and as someone who is truly concerned with achieving your purpose.

Develop Your Main Points (Step 5)

7.1 Explain how to develop main points that are limited in number, focus on your audience, and are worded effectively.

Begin organizing your speech by selecting and wording your main points. Let's look first at how you can select and word your main points and then at how you can logically arrange them.

Select Your Main Points

Chapter 3's discussion of the thesis showed how you can develop your main points or propositions by asking strategic questions. To see how this works in detail, imagine that you're giving a speech to a group of high school students on the values of a college education. Your thesis is: "A college education is valuable." You then ask, "Why is it valuable?" From this question you generate your main points. Your first step may be to brainstorm this question and generate as many answers as possible without evaluating them. You may come up with answers such as the following:

1. It helps you get a good job.

2. It increases your earning potential.

3. It gives you greater job mobility.

4. It helps you secure more creative work.

5. It helps you to appreciate the arts more fully.

6. It helps you to understand an extremely complex world.

7. It helps you understand different cultures.

8. It allows you to avoid taking a regular job for a few years.

9. It helps you meet lots of people and make new friends.

10. It helps you increase your personal effectiveness.

There are, of course, other possibilities, but for purposes of illustration, these 10 potential main points will suffice. But not all 10 are equally valuable or relevant to your audience, so you should look over the list to see how to make it shorter and more meaningful.

JOURNAL 7.1 PUBLIC SPEAKING CHOICE POINT

Generating Main Points

Jan wants to give a speech with the thesis: "Photography [or any skill you'd like to focus on] is a useful skill to learn." *What are some of Jan's options for main points?*

Limit the Number of Main Points

For your class speeches, which will generally range from 5 to 15 minutes, use two, three, or four main points. Too many main points will result in a speech that's confusing, contains too much information, and proves difficult to remember. So we need to pare down the list from 10 to perhaps three.

First, eliminate those points that seem least important to your thesis. On this basis you might want to eliminate number 8, as this seems least consistent with your intended emphasis on the positive values of college.

Second, combine those points that have a common focus. Notice, for example, that the first four points all center on the value of college in terms of jobs. You might, therefore, consider grouping these four items into one proposition:

A college education helps you get a good job.

This point might become a main point, which you could develop by defining what you mean by a "good job." This main point or proposition and its elaboration might look like this:

I. A college education helps you get a good job.

A. College graduates earn higher salaries.

B. College graduates enter more creative jobs.

C. College graduates have greater job mobility.

Note that A, B, and C are all aspects or subdivisions of a "good job."

Focus on your Audience

Select those points that are most relevant or interesting to your audience. On this basis you might eliminate numbers 5 and 7, on the assumption that the audience will not see learning about the arts or different cultures as exciting or valuable at the present time. You also might decide that high school students would be more interested in increasing personal effectiveness, so you might select number 10 for inclusion as a second main point:

A college education increases your personal effectiveness.

Earlier you developed the subordinate points in your first proposition (the A, B, and C of I above) by defining more clearly what you meant by a "good job." Follow the same procedure here by defining what you mean by "personal effectiveness." It might look something like this:

    I. A college education increases your personal effectiveness.

      A. A college education helps you improve your ability to communicate.

      B. A college education helps you acquire the skills for learning how to think.

      C. A college education helps you acquire coping skills.

Follow this same general procedure to develop the subheadings under A, B, and C. For example, point A might be divided into two major subheads:

      A. A college education helps improve your ability to communicate.

        1. College improves your writing skills.

        2. College improves your speaking skills.

Develop points B and C in essentially the same way, defining more clearly in B what you mean by "learning how to think" and in C what you mean by "coping skills."

Word Your Main Points

Develop your main points so they're separate and discrete. Don't allow your main points to overlap each other. Each section labeled with a Roman numeral should be a separate entity.

Not This	**This**
I. Color and style are important in clothing selection.	I. Color is important in clothing selection.
	II. Style is important in clothing selection.

In addition, phrase your main points in parallel style; your main points should be phrased in similar grammatical structure with many of the same words. Julius Caesar's famous "I came, I saw, I conquered" is a good example of parallel style: Each statement is structured the same way, using the pronoun *I* plus a verb in the past tense. Phrase points labeled with Roman numerals in parallel style. Likewise, phrase points labeled with capital letters and subordinate to the same Roman numeral (for example, A, B, and C under point I or A, B, and C under point II) in a similar style. Parallel styling will help the audience follow and remember your speech. Notice in the following that the first outline is more difficult to understand than the second, which is phrased in parallel style.

Not This	**This**
The mass media serve four functions.	The mass media serve four functions.
I. The media entertain.	I. The media entertain.
II. The media function to inform their audiences.	II. The media inform.
III. Creating ties of union is a major media function.	III. The media create ties of union.
IV. The conferral of status is a function of all media.	IV. The media confer status.

Organize Your Main Points (Step 6)

7.2 Explain the major organizational patterns.

Once you've identified the main points you wish to include in your speech, you need to devote attention to how you'll arrange these points in the **body**, or main part, of your speech. Here are 12 organizational patterns that should cover just about any informative or persuasive topic. Another pattern, the motivated sequence, most often associated with persuasive speaking, is covered in Chapter 10.

body
The main part of your speech; the speech minus the introduction and conclusion.

VIEWPOINTS

Organizing a Speech

Sean wants to give a speech on how to be successful in online dating. As you read this section on patterns of organization, keep Sean's speech in mind. *What would be appropriate main points for such a speech? What organizational pattern would be best to use, given the main points you identified?*

Time Pattern

When you organize your topic on the basis of a time, or **temporal pattern**, relationship, you generally divide the speech into two, three, or four major parts. You might begin with the past and work up to the present or future or begin with the present or future and work back to the past. Most historical topics lend themselves to organization by a time pattern. Topics such as events leading to the Civil War, how to plant a vegetable garden, and the history of the Internet are all candidates for temporal patterning. For example, you might organize a speech on children's development of speech and language according to a temporal pattern.

temporal pattern

An organizational scheme, often referred to as chronological, in which the main points of a speech are arranged chronologically, for example, from past to present.

General Purpose:	To inform
Specific Purpose:	To inform my audience of the four stages in the child's acquisition of language
Thesis:	The child goes through four stages in learning language.

   I. Babbling occurs first.
   II. Lallation occurs second.
   III. Echolalia occurs third.
   IV. Communication occurs fourth.

Spatial Pattern

Organizing the main points of a speech on the basis of its **spatial pattern** is similar to temporal patterning. Discussions of most physical objects fit well into spatial patterns. For example, a presentation on the structure of a hospital, a school, a skyscraper, or even a dinosaur might lend itself to this pattern. Here, a speech on places to visit in Central America uses a spatial pattern.

spatial pattern

An organizational scheme in which the main topics of a speech are arranged in spatial terms, for example, high to low or east to west.

General Purpose:	To inform
Specific Purpose:	To inform my audience of a great way to visit Central America
Thesis:	You can have a great visit to Central America by visiting four countries.

   I. First, visit Guatemala.
   II. Second, visit Honduras.
   III. Third, visit Nicaragua.
   IV. Fourth, visit Costa Rica.

Topical Pattern

topical pattern

An organizational pattern in which a topic is divided into its component parts.

The **topical pattern** divides the speech topic into subtopics or component parts. The world's major religions, great works of literature, and the problems facing the college graduate are examples of speech topics that lend themselves to a topical organizational pattern. This pattern is an obvious choice for organizing a speech on a topic such as the branches of government:

General Purpose:	To inform
Specific Purpose:	To inform my audience of the ways the three branches of government work
Thesis:	Three branches govern the United States.

I. The legislative branch is controlled by Congress.
II. The executive branch is controlled by the president.
III. The judicial branch is controlled by the courts.

Problem–Solution Pattern

problem–solution pattern

An organizational structure for a public speech divided into the problem and the solution, a structure that's especially useful in persuasive speeches in which you want to convince the audience that a problem exists and that your solution would solve or lessen the problem.

As its name indicates, the **problem–solution pattern** divides the main ideas into two main parts: problems and solutions. Let's say you're trying to persuade an audience that home health aides should be given higher salaries and increased benefits. In the first part of the speech, you might discuss some of the problems confronting home health aides. In the second part, you would consider the possible solutions to these problems. The speech, in outline form, might look like this:

General Purpose:	To persuade
Specific Purpose:	To persuade my audience of the solutions to the three main problems of the home health care industry
Thesis:	The home health care industry can be improved with three changes.

I. Three major problems confront home health care.
   A. Industry lures away the most qualified graduates.
   B. Numerous excellent health aides leave the field after a few years.
   C. Home health care is currently a low-status occupation.

II. Three major solutions to these problems exist.
   A. Increase salaries for home health aides.
   B. Make benefits for health aides more attractive.
   C. Raise the status of the home health care profession.

In some instances, you may want to use a topical pattern (for the main heads) and a problem–solution pattern (for the subheads). Here, for example, is how Kevin King (2015) used this organizational system in his speech on the need to increase funding for Alzheimer's disease. Stigma, practical challenges, and advocacy are in a topical pattern, but the subpoints for each are presented in a problem–solution pattern.

I. Stigma
   A. Stigma as problem
   B. Stigma solutions

II. Practical challenges [lack of research subjects]
   A. Practical challenges as problem
   B. Practical challenges solutions

III. Advocacy
   A. Lack of advocacy as problem
   B. Lack of advocacy solutions

It's interesting to note that the organizational pattern that is used most often in the award-winning speeches of the Interstate Oratorical Association (Schnoor, 2013, 2014,

2015) is a variation of the problem–solution pattern; instead of dividing the speech into two parts, it's divided into three: causes, effects (of the causes), and solutions. Here, for example, is how one student organized her speech on the need to change the U.S. food aid program (Djietror, 2013). The excerpt is from her introduction.

> To understand why ineffective food aid persists, we must first address the problems, identify its causes, and finally suggest solutions that could fix the ineffective U.S. food aid system.

Here's another example on a speech on spyware stalking (Boyle, 2015). This excerpt is from the speaker's conclusions:

> Today, we discussed the problem of advanced cyber stalking, the causes of its devastating current stage, and offered solutions to protect victims who have endured enough.

Cause–Effect/Effect–Cause Pattern

Similar to the problem–solution pattern of organization is the **cause–effect pattern**, or effect–cause pattern. Using this pattern, you divide the speech into two major sections: (1) causes and (2) effects. Highway accidents, illnesses, or low self-esteem, for example, could be explained using a cause–effect pattern. An outline of the causes and effects of low self-esteem might look something like this:

cause–effect pattern
An organizational system in which the speech is divided into causes and effects.

General Purpose:	To inform
Specific Purpose:	To inform my audience of the causes and effects of low self-esteem
Thesis:	Low self-esteem is caused by a history of criticism and unrealistic goals, which lead to depression and an unwillingness to socialize.

   I. Low self-esteem often has two main causes.
      A. A history of criticism can contribute to low self-esteem.
      B. Unrealistic goals can contribute to low self-esteem.

   II. Low self-esteem often has two main effects.
      A. Depression is one frequent effect.
      B. An unwillingness to socialize with others is another frequent effect.

You can also organize your persuasive speeches around causes and effects. For example, you might organize a persuasive speech around persuading your audience that, say, a history of criticism does in fact contribute to low self-esteem as do unrealistic goals. Here you would have two major points:

   I. A history of criticism leads to low self-esteem.
      A. Double blind studies show...
      B. A recent survey...
      C. Psychologist John Smith of Harvard University has said...

   II. Unrealistic goals lead to low self-esteem.
      A. My own experience illustrates...
      B. A study conducted...
      C. Educational theorists have long...

Structure–Function Pattern

In **structure–function pattern** there are generally two main points, one for structure and one for function. This pattern is useful in informative speeches in which you want to discuss how something is constructed (its structure) and what it does (its function). It might prove useful, for example, in a speech explaining what a business organization is and what it does, identifying the parts of a university and how they operate, or describing the nature of a living organism: its anatomy (its structures) and its physiology (its functions).

structure–function pattern
An organizational pattern in which the speech is divided into two parts, one dealing with structure and one with function.

General Purpose:	To inform
Specific Purpose:	To inform my audience of the structure and function of the brain
Thesis:	To understand the brain you need to understand its structure and its function.

I. The brain consists of two main parts [explanation of structures]
  A. The cerebrum consists of...
  B. The cerebellum consists of...

II. The brain enables us to do a variety of things [explanations of functions]
  A. The cerebrum enables us to...
  B. The cerebellum enables us to...

Comparison and Contrast Pattern

comparison and contrast pattern

A pattern for organizing a speech in which you compare and contrast two different items.

In the **comparison and contrast pattern** your main points might be the main divisions of your topic and you would identify similarities and differences. This pattern is often useful in informative speeches in which you want to analyze two different theories, proposals, departments, or products in terms of their similarities and differences. In this type of speech, you would be concerned not only with explaining each theory or proposal but also with clarifying how they're similar and how they're different.

General Purpose:	To inform
Specific Purpose:	To inform my audience of two main differences between liberal and conservative political philosophies
Thesis:	Liberal and conservative political philosophies differ in important ways.

I. Government regulation...
  A. The liberal attitude is...
  B. The conservative attitude is...

II. Redistribution of income...
  A. Liberals view this...
  B. Conservatives view this...

Pro-and-Con Pattern

pro-and-con pattern

A pattern for organizing a speech in which the arguments for the thesis are advanced and the arguments against the thesis are noted and attacked; also referred to as the advantages–disadvantages pattern or the comparative advantage pattern.

In the **pro-and-con pattern**, sometimes called the *advantages–disadvantages pattern* or the *comparative advantage pattern*, the speech has two main points—the advantages of Plan A and the disadvantages of Plan A (or Plan B). This pattern is useful in informative speeches in which you want to explain objectively the advantages (the pros) and the disadvantages (the cons) of a plan, method, or product. Or you can use this pattern in a persuasive speech in which you want to show the superiority of Plan A (identifying its advantages) over Plan B (identifying its disadvantages). In this example, we'll consider a persuasive speech.

General Purpose:	To persuade
Specific Purpose:	To persuade my audience that Plan A is better than Plan B
Thesis:	The proposals of the two health plans differ in co-payments, hospital benefits, and sick leave.

I. Co-payments...
  A. Plan A provides lower co-payments.
  B. Plan B provides higher co-payments.

II. Hospital benefits...
  A. Plan A provides greater hospital benefits.
  B. Plan B provides fewer hospital benefits.

III. Sick leave…
    A. Plan A provides for more sick days
    B. Plan B provides for fewer sick days.

Claim-and-Proof Pattern

In the **claim-and-proof pattern** your thesis would essentially be your claim, and then each main point would be support for your claim. This pattern is especially useful in a persuasive speech in which you want to prove the truth or usefulness of a particular proposition. It's the pattern that you see frequently in trials, where the claim made by the prosecution is that the defendant is guilty and the proof is the varied evidence designed to show that the defendant had a motive, opportunity, and no alibi.

claim-and-proof pattern
An organizational pattern in which the thesis is the claim and each main point offers proof in support of this claim.

General Purpose:	To persuade
Specific Purpose:	To persuade my audience that the city must actively combat drug addiction
Thesis/Claim:	The city must become proactive in dealing with the drug addicted.

I. Drug usage is increasing. [Proof No. 1]
    A. A particularly vivid example…
    B. Recent statistics…

II. Drug related crimes are increasing. [Proof No. 2]
    A. On-street crimes have increased…
    B. Business break-ins…

Multiple-Definition Pattern

In the **multiple-definition pattern** each of your main points would consist of a different type of definition. This pattern is useful for informative speeches in which you want to explain the nature of a concept.

multiple-definition pattern
An organizational structure for a public speech in which each of your main points consists of a different type of definition.

General Purpose:	To inform
Specific Purpose:	To inform my audience of the meaning of creative thinking
Thesis:	The nature of creative thinking is often misunderstood.

I. Creative thinking is not… [definition by negation]

II. According to Webster's dictionary… [dictionary definition]

III. Edward deBono defines… [a creative thinking theorist's view]

IV. A good example of creative thinking… [definition by example]

Who? What? Why? Where? When? Pattern

In this pattern your main points are explanations of who, what, why, where, and/or when. The **Who? What? Why? Where? When? pattern** traditionally used by journalists is useful when you wish to report on or explain an event; for example, a robbery, political coup, war, or trial. Not all questions need to be addressed in any one speech.

Who? What? Why? Where? When? pattern
An organizational pattern dividing the speech into sections that answer the questions *who, what, why, where,* and *when.*

General Purpose:	To inform
Specific Purpose:	To inform my audience of the nature of the U.S. Constitution as a citizen's responsibility
Thesis:	Understanding the Constitution is a first step toward responsible citizenship.

I. The Constitution is a document that sets forth… [answers the question What is the Constitution?]

II. The Constitution was needed because… [answers the question Why was it written?]

III. The Constitution was written at a time...[answers the question When was it written?]

IV. The Constitution was written by...[answers the question Who wrote it?]

Fiction–Fact Pattern

fiction–fact pattern
An organizational pattern in which the fictions or untruths are identified and disputed by the facts.

In the **fiction–fact pattern** your main points would be the fiction, and under these would be the facts. This pattern may be useful in informative speeches when you wish to clarify misconceptions that people have about various things. In persuasive speeches this pattern might be used to defend or attack, whether a proposal, belief, or person.

General Purpose:	To inform
Specific Purpose:	To inform my audience of the three misconceptions people have about the flu shot
Thesis:	Three main misconceptions exist about the flu shot.

I. The first misconception is that you can get the flu from the flu shot.
    A. Studies show...
    B. The flu shot contains...

II. The second misconception is that antibiotics will help with the flu.
    A. Actually, antibiotics...
    B. Viruses, such as the flu, however,...

III. The third misconception is that older people spread the flu.
    A. Actually, children...
    B. In studies done...

JOURNAL 7.2 PUBLIC SPEAKING CHOICE POINT

Organizational Patterns

Sammy wants to give a speech against legalizing marijuana and is considering the best organizational pattern. *What choices does Sammy have? What choice would you suggest he take?*

Cultural Considerations in Organization

high-context culture
A culture in which much of the information in communication is in the context or in the person rather than explicitly coded in the verbal message. Opposed to *low-context culture.*

low-context culture
A culture in which most of the information in communication is explicitly stated in the verbal messages. Individualist cultures are usually low-context cultures. Opposed to *high-context culture.*

Cultural considerations are as important in organization as they are in all other aspects of public speaking. One factor that's especially important is whether the audience's culture is high-context or low-context (Hall & Hall, 1987). **High-context cultures** (Japanese, Arabic, Latin American, Thai, Korean, Apache, and Mexican are examples) are those in which much of the information in communication is in the context or in the person rather than in the actual spoken message. Both speaker and listener already know the information from, say, previous interactions, assumptions each makes about the other, or shared experiences. **Low-context cultures** (German, Swedish, Norwegian, and American are examples) are those in which most information is explicitly stated in the verbal message. In formal communications, the information would be in written form as well—as it is with mortgages, contracts, prenuptial agreements, or apartment leases.

Extending this distinction to speech organization, we can see that members of high-context cultures will probably prefer an organization in which the supporting materials are offered and audience members are allowed to infer the general principle or proposition themselves. Low-context culture members, on the other hand, will likely prefer an organization in which the proposition is clearly and directly stated and the supporting materials are clearly linked to the proposition.

Persons from the United States speaking in Japan, to take one well-researched example, need to be careful lest they make their point too obvious or too direct and thus

VIEWPOINTS
Audience Culture

How would you describe the cultures of your classmates? In what way, if any, might culture influence the way in which you organize your speech?

inadvertently insult their audience. Speakers in Japan are expected to lead their listeners to the conclusion through example, illustration, and various other indirect means (Lustig & Koester, 2006). Persons from Japan speaking in the United States need to be careful lest their indirectness be perceived as unnecessarily vague, underhanded, or suggestive of an attempt to withhold information.

You might, for example, organize a speech on the need for random drug testing in the workplace somewhat differently depending on whether you are addressing a high-context or a low-context audience.

High-Context Audience	**Low-Context Audience**
Implicitness and indirectness are preferred.	Explicitness and directness are preferred.
The main point is implicitly identified only after the evidence is presented.	The main point is clearly stated at the outset, even before the evidence is presented.
Drugs in the workplace cause accidents. Drugs in the workplace contribute to the national drug problem. Drugs in the workplace increase costs for employers and consumers. These are some factors we need to think about as we consider the proposal to establish random workplace drug testing.	Random drug testing in the workplace is a must. It will reduce accidents. It will reduce the national drug problem. It will reduce costs. Let's examine each of these reasons why random drug testing in the workplace should become standard.

Construct Your Introduction, Conclusion, and Transitions (Step 7)

7.3 Explain the characteristics of effective introductions, conclusions, and transitions.

Now that you have the body of your speech organized, devote your attention to the introduction, conclusion, and transitions that will hold the parts of your speech together.

As you read about introductions, conclusions, and transitions, also visit some websites containing speeches and examine the ways the speakers introduced, concluded, and tied the parts of their speeches together. Start with the websites of such organizations as History and Politics Out Loud, the History Channel, or American Rhetoric. Most of these sites provide both audio and video material.

Introductions

Together with your general appearance and your nonverbal messages, your introduction gives your listeners their first impression of you and your speech. And, as you know, first impressions influence the perception of later events and are very resistant to change. Because of this, the introduction is an especially important part of the speech. It sets the tone for the rest of the speech; it tells your listeners what kind of a speech they'll hear.

Begin collecting suitable material for your introduction as you prepare the entire speech, but wait until all the other parts are completed before you put the pieces together. In this way you'll be better able to determine which elements should be included and which should be eliminated.

Your introduction may serve three functions: gain attention, establish a speaker–audience–topic connection, and orient the audience as to what is to follow. Gaining attention in your introduction is essential, establishing an S–A–T connection is almost always useful, and an orientation in some form is always needed. Let's look at how you can accomplish each of these functions.

FUNCTION 1. GAIN ATTENTION

attention

The process of responding to a stimulus or stimuli; usually some consciousness of responding is implied.

Your introduction should gain the **attention** of your audience and focus it on your speech topic. (And, of course, it should help you maintain that attention throughout your speech.) You can secure attention in numerous ways; here are just a few.

Ask a Question   Questions are effective because they're a change from the more common declarative statements, and listeners automatically pay attention to change. Rhetorical questions—questions to which you don't expect an answer—or polling-type questions that ask the audience for a show of hands are especially helpful in focusing the audience's attention on your subject:

> Do you want to succeed in college?
> Do you want to meet the love of your life?
> How many of you have suffered through a boring lecture?
> How many of you intend to continue school after graduating from college?

Refer to Recent Happenings   Referring to a previous speech, a recent event, or a prominent person currently making news helps gain attention because the audience is familiar with this and will pay attention to see how you're going to connect it to your speech topic.

Here is an especially good example by Caleb Graves (2010) from the University of Texas at Austin:

> On March 14, 2010, an American task force in Afghanistan successfully raided and apprehended a sizeable number of weapons stored by Taliban forces. *USA Today* of the same date reports though this effectively removed weapons from enemy hands, the task force soon realized the weapons should have never been there in the first place, considering they were supplied by the U.S. government. The article further substantiates that from the $330 million Americans spent on transports to Afghanistan in the past year, at least 13,000 weapons and 200,000 rounds of ammunition have gone missing, causing task force member Ken Feiereisen to worry that Americans are being killed by our very own weapons.

Use an Example, Illustration, or Narrative   Much as we are drawn to soap operas, so we are drawn to illustrations and stories about people, especially if they are dramatic or even startling. Here, for example, Tiernan Cahill from Emerson College gains attention with a specific illustration that makes us want to hear more about this individual.

> At the age of 27, Michael Wallerstein is a quarter of a million dollars in debt, with no steady job, no savings and more than a dozen collection agencies on his tail. Now, if he sounds like the victim of a shady investment scheme gone wrong, that's because he is.

Use a Quotation   Quotations are useful because audience members are likely to pay attention to the brief and clever remarks of someone they have heard of or read about. Make sure that the quotation is directly relevant to your topic; if you have to explain its relevance, it probably isn't worth using. Quotations are easy to find; visit some of the many available quotation sites. You also may find it helpful to say something about the author of the quotation by consulting some of the biography sites mentioned in the discussion of research in Chapter 4.

Cite a Little-Known Fact or Statistic   These help pique an audience's attention. Headlines on unemployment statistics, crime in the schools, and political corruption sell newspapers because they gain attention. In a speech on the need for more severe punishments for hate speech, the speaker might cite a specific hate speech incident that the audience hadn't heard of yet or the statistic that violence inspired by hate speech tripled over the past 6 months.

Use Humor   Humor is useful because it relaxes the audience and establishes a quick connection between speaker and listeners. In using humor make sure it's relevant to your topic, brief, tasteful, seemingly spontaneous, and appropriate to you as a speaker and to the audience.

FUNCTION 2. ESTABLISH A SPEAKER–AUDIENCE–TOPIC RELATIONSHIP

In addition to gaining attention, use your introduction to establish a connection among yourself as the speaker, the audience members, and your topic. Try to answer your listeners' inevitable question of why they should listen to you speak on this topic. You can establish an effective speaker–audience–topic (or S–A–T) relationship in any of numerous ways.

Establish Your Credibility   The introduction is a particularly important time to establish your competence, character, and charisma (see Chapter 10). Here, for example, Ohio congressman and 2008 presidential hopeful Dennis Kucinich (2007) establishes his credibility by telling the audience of his background and accomplishments in a speech at the Tenth Annual Wall Street Project Conference on January 8, 2007:

> I am a product of the city. My parents never owned a home. I grew up in 21 different places by the time I was 17, including a few cars. I've learned about opportunities. I've learned that if you believe it you can conceive it.

Refer to Others Present   Referring to others present not only will help you to gain attention; it also will help you to establish an effective speaker–audience–topic relationship. Use this technique sparingly and only when you know it will not embarrass any member to whom you refer. Be especially careful to avoid referring to a small group of friends; it might have the effect of making the others in the audience feel like outsiders. This technique is probably best used when there are several distinguished people in the audience and you want to point to their accomplishments, which, ideally, will be closely related to your thesis.

Express Your Pleasure or Interest in Speaking   In the following example Senator Christopher Dodd (2007) expresses his pleasure at speaking at Reverend Jesse Jackson's Tenth Annual Wall Street Summit:

> It's an honor for me to be invited to speak to you today at this, the 10th Anniversary of the Wall Street Economic Summit. Reverend Jackson, you should take enormous pride in the success of this event, and the growth of the Rainbow Push Wall Street Project. Your efforts over the years have helped millions more Americans achieve their dreams and aspirations.

Compliment the Audience   Complimenting the audience is a commonly used technique to establish an S–A–T connection in much professional public speaking. In the classroom, however, this technique may seem awkward and obvious and so is probably best avoided. But it's important to realize that paying the audience an honest and sincere compliment (never overdoing it) not only will encourage your listeners to give you their attention but will help make them feel a part of your speech. In some cultures—Japan and Korea are good examples—the speaker is expected to compliment the audience, the beauty of the country, or its culture. It's one of the essential parts of the introduction. In this example, musician Billy Joel (1993) compliments his audience, the graduating class of the Berklee College of Music, directly and honestly:

> I am truly pleased that the road has twisted and turned its way up the East Coast to Boston. The Berklee College of Music represents the finest contemporary music school there is, and I am honored to be here with you this morning to celebrate.

Express Similarities with the Audience   By stressing your own similarities with members of the audience, you create a bond with them and become an "insider" instead of an "outsider." Here Lester M. Crawford (2005), Acting Commissioner of Food and Drugs, in a speech before the World Pharma IT Congress, established an S–A–T connection by expressing similarities:

> I think most people would be surprised to find the Commissioner of Food and Drugs at an IT conference. And certainly, I was asking myself just this question during most of this morning's presentations. However, I think it's significant to stress the importance of IT in the health care industry and that's why I'm pleased to be here today.*

FUNCTION 3. ORIENT THE AUDIENCE

The introduction should orient the audience in some way as to what is to follow in the body of the speech. Preview for the audience what you're going to say. The **orientation** may be covered in a variety of ways.

Give a General Idea of Your Subject   Orientation can consist simply of a statement of your topic. For example, you might say, "Tonight I'm going to discuss atomic waste" or "I want to talk with you about the problems our society has created for the aged." In a speech at the groundbreaking ceremony for the Dr. Martin Luther King Jr. National

orientation

In public speaking, a preview of what is to follow in the speech.

---

* Reprinted with permission from Eastman & Eastman, on behalf of the author.

Memorial on November 13, 2006, President Barack Obama (then Senator from Illinois) (2006) gave a general idea of what he'd say in the main part of his speech:

> I have two daughters, ages five and eight. And when I see the plans for this memorial, I think about what it will [be] like when I first bring them here upon the memorial's completion.... And at some point, I know that one of my daughters will ask, perhaps my youngest, will ask, "Daddy, why is this monument here? What did this man do?" How might I answer them?

Identify the Main Points You'll Cover In your orientation you may want to identify very briefly the main points you'll cover. For example, Shannen Walsh (2012), a student from Glendale Community College, did it very simply and effectively:

> There are two major symptoms that highlight the problem with our current pharmaceutical system: inflation of prices and criminalizing patients.

Give a Detailed Preview Or you may wish to give a detailed preview of the main points of your speech. After giving an introduction to the topic of devocalizing animals, Chelsea Anthony (2012), a student from Louisiana State University, Shreveport, oriented her audience in this way:

> First, we need to understand what convenience devocalization is, second, we need to investigate the reasons some people feel this barbaric act is necessary, and then, we will examine what must be done to help give a voice back to those who can't speak, or bark, for themselves.

Identify Your Goal Here former California Governor Arnold Schwarzenegger (2007) oriented the audience by giving a general idea of the goal he hoped to achieve.

> Hello everybody. Thank you for being here. I believe that in Sacramento this year, we are going to make history. Using a comprehensive approach built on shared responsibility where everyone does their part we will fix California's broken health care system and create a model that the rest of the nation can follow. I know everyone has been eager to hear exactly what we are proposing.

In an outline (and in summary of this section), your introduction would look something like this:

Introduction

I. **Attention** (Ask a question; refer to recent events; use an example, illustration, or narrative; use a quotation; mention a little-known fact; and/or use humor.)

II. **S–A–T Connection** (Establish your credibility, refer to others present, express your pleasure or interest in speaking, compliment the audience, and/or mention your similarities to the audience.)

III. **Orientation** (Give a general idea of your subject, identify your main points, and/or identify your goal.)

Here, in Figure 7.1, is a sample introduction to illustrate further its various parts.

JOURNAL 7.3 PUBLIC SPEAKING CHOICE POINT

Formulating an Effective Introduction

Alan plans to give an informative speech outlining the changes that are taking place in health care. He knows that some members of his audience are not interested in the topic, and he fears they may tune him out immediately. *What options does Alan have for introducing his speech and securing the attention and interest of all audience members? What might he say?*

Figure 7.1 A Sample Introduction

> Attention getter, involves the audience and makes them listen.

> Here is a brief orientation in which the speaker explains that the speech will consist of reasons for separating sports and education and also gives you an idea of the first and last point to be made. The speaker could have identified all the reasons in this orientation.

> Here is a very brief S-A-T, a connection among speaker, audience, and topic.

> It will help your listeners if you follow your introduction with a simple transition. As you begin to learn the principles of public speaking, don't be afraid to be "too obvious" and say, as does this speaker, "Let's first look . . . . . ." Your listeners will appreciate your clarity.

How many here played on the varsity baseball, football, or basketball team of your high school? Well, I did—basketball. Since I'm 6' 11" you're probably not surprised it was basketball. But, you probably will be surprised to hear that I regret that experience and feel I wasted a great deal of time. Most people seem to feel that sports and education are so closely related that any suggestion to separate them would be unthinkable. But, there are reasons why we should consider separating them and I'd like to explain some of these reasons which range from draining funds from other activities and programs to setting up unrealistic goals for students.

[Let's first look at how sports programs drain funds from other activities and programs that would benefit students more in the long run.]

Conclusions

Your conclusion is especially important because it's often the part of the speech that the audience remembers most clearly. Your conclusion may serve three major functions: to summarize, motivate, and provide closure. A summary of the speech is useful to the listener in nearly any circumstance. Motivation is appropriate in many persuasive speeches and in some informative speeches. Providing closure in any speech is essential.

FUNCTION 1. SUMMARIZE

You can summarize your speech in a variety of ways.

Restate Your Thesis or Purpose   In the restatement type of summary, you recap the essential thrust of your speech by repeating your thesis or perhaps the goals you hoped to achieve.

Here is how Aviva Pinchas, a student from the University of Texas at Austin, accomplished this:

> In 2008, Congress passed the ADA Amendments Act in the hopes of righting decades of judicial wrongs against disabled employees. While this law has not lived up to its potential, we have the power to ensure that, someday soon, it will. After looking at the causes for the law's failure, the effects of these court rulings, and the ways to combat a biased court system, it is clear that the job of protecting disabled workers lies not in the hands of lawyers or politicians but our own— to stand up and declare that this difficult economic time will not deter us from protecting America's most vulnerable workers.

Restate the Importance of the Topic   Another method for concluding is to tell the audience again why your topic or thesis is so important. In the following example, Linse Christensen of Northern State University, in a speech on automobile safety, restated the importance of the topic by recalling a particularly dramatic example of why precautions need to be taken (Schnoor, 2008, p. 68).

> Andrew Clemens will forever remember the little sister, his best friend, Adrianna, who died as a result of being backed over by their father right in front of his own house.

Restate Your Main Points   In this type of summary you restate your thesis and the main points you used to support it. In her conclusion, Christi Liu restates her main point like this:

> After looking at how wireless electricity works, what devices we no longer need to plug in, and the implications of Witricity, it is clear that our relationship with electricity is about to heat up, and within the next few years we could all be charging our devices with a little bit of magic.

FUNCTION 2. MOTIVATE

A second function of the conclusion—most appropriate in persuasive speeches—is to motivate members of your audience to do what you want them to do. In your conclusion you have the opportunity to give audience members one final push in the direction you wish them to take. Whether it's to buy stock, vote a particular way, or change an attitude, you can use the conclusion for a final motivation, a final appeal. Below are three excellent ways to motivate.

Ask for a Specific Response   Specify what you want the audience to do after listening to your speech.

In a speech on bridge safety, Sarah Hoppes of Ohio University asks for a specific response (Schnoor, 2008, p. 54):

> I have prepared a handout that lists the web addresses for you to research bridge safety in your area. To get you started, and to protect you on the way home, I have included the location of three bridges in the greater Madison area you should avoid at all costs.

Reiterate the Importance of the Issue   In a speech designed to strengthen attitudes, it may prove of value to restate the importance of the issue to the audience and to the community at large. For example, Alberto Mora (2006), in accepting the 2006 John F. Kennedy Profile in Courage Award on May 26, 2006, restates why it's so important to address the issue of cruelty and torture.

> We should care because the issues raised by a policy of cruelty are too fundamental to be left unaddressed, unanswered, or ambiguous. We should care because a tolerance of cruelty will corrode our values and our rights and degrade the world in which we live. It will corrupt our heritage, cheapen the value of the soldiers upon whose past and present sacrifices our freedoms depend, and debase the legacy we will leave to our sons and daughters.*

Provide Directions for Future Action   Another type of motivational conclusion is to spell out the action you wish the audience to take. Here's an example from a speech by Brett Martz (2012) from Ohio University:

> First, I want you to give the clothes off your back, literally. Hold your horses, not right now; you can leave that jacket on. But seriously, we as competitors and coaches are in ready supply of something that so many people need... our dress clothes. Do what I did. I pledged to donate one of my suits at the end of the season. And don't worry what condition it is in, the people at most

---

* *Source*: Alberto Mora/Kennedy Library Foundation.

food pantries will be able to find someone to mend anything. If you go to my Facebook page, "Just Do Something," you will find a link where you can donate your old suits.

FUNCTION 3. PROVIDE CLOSURE

The third function of your conclusion is to provide closure. Often your summary will accomplish this, but in some instances it will prove insufficient. End your speech with a conclusion that is crisp and definite. Make the audience aware that you have definitely and clearly ended. Some kind of wrap-up, some sort of final statement, is helpful in providing this feeling of closure. Here are three ways you can achieve closure.

Refer to Subsequent Events   You can achieve closure by looking ahead to events that will take place either that day or soon afterward. Notice how effectively former U.S. Secretary of State Madeleine K. Albright (1998) used this method in a speech on NATO.

> Our task is to make clear what our alliance will do and what our partnership will mean in a Europe truly whole and free, and in a world that looks to us for principles and purposeful leadership for peace, for prosperity, and for freedom. In this spirit, I look forward to our discussion today and to our work together in the months and years to come.

Refer Back to the Introduction   It's sometimes useful to connect your conclusion with your introduction. One student, David DePino (2012) from North Central College, Illinois, accomplished this neatly. After introducing his speech with a dramatic illustration of the savage beating of Chrissy Lee, a transgendered 22-year-old, he concludes his speech by referring back to this introductory story.

> Unfortunately for Chrissy Lee, change came far too late. As she lay upon the McDonald's bathroom floor convulsing, the police were called but no one arrested and hers became one more story shrouded in silence. I hope that our community, the forensics community will WAKE UP. It is time to hear those stories that haven't been told, because it is those that must come through the loudest.

Rephrase or Repeat Your Thesis   Especially in persuasive speeches, it's often useful to repeat the essence of your thesis in a crisp wrap-up. In a speech on voting disenfranchisement, Michelle Colpean (2012), a student from Ball State University, concluded her speech simply but powerfully:

> Voting lies at the heart of our nation's democracy—we should be building bridges to the polls, not barriers.

Thank the Audience   Speakers frequently conclude their speeches by thanking the audience for their attention or for their invitation to the speaker to address them. In almost all cases, the "thank you" should be brief—a simple "thank you" or "I appreciate your attention" is all that's usually necessary.

In summary and in your outline, your conclusion would look something like this:

Conclusion

I. **Summary** (Restate your thesis or purpose, restate the topic's importance, and/or restate your main points.)

II. **Motivation** (Ask for a specific audience response, reiterate the importance of the issue, and/or provide directions for further action.)

III. **Closure** (Refer to subsequent events, refer back to the introduction, and/or thank the audience.)

Here, in Figure 7.2, is a sample conclusion to illustrate further its varied parts.

Figure 7.2 A Sample Conclusion

In this brief talk, I identified four main reasons why sports and education should be separated:

Here the speaker repeats his main assertion or thesis.

- Sports programs drain funds from other activities and programs.
- Sports programs divert attention, time, and energy away from more important subjects.
- Sports programs create an in-group and an out-group.
- Sports programs set up unrealistic goals.

The speaker summarizes the four points he made in the speech.

When school issues come up for a vote or for debate, think about these reasons as to why sports and education should be separated. Or, when your nephew or niece or daughter or son asks about playing sports, consider discussing the very real disadvantages of sports in education.

This brief motivation is an attempt to get the listeners to apply what's been said in the speech into their own lives.

By the way, I still enjoy playing basketball; it's a great sport. It just doesn't belong in schools.

Here the speaker closes in a way that signals the end of the speech.

Transitions

Because members of your audience will hear your speech just once, they must understand it as you speak it, or your message will be lost. Transitions will help your listeners understand your speech more accurately.

Transitions are words, phrases, or sentences that help your listeners follow the development of your thoughts and arguments and get an idea of where you are in your speech.

You can think of transitions as serving four functions: to connect, to preview, to review, and to signal where the speaker is in the speech. All of these functions work to provide coherence to your speech and to make it easier for the audience to follow your train of thought.

transitions
Words, phrases, or sentences that help your listeners follow the development of your thoughts and arguments and get an idea of where you are in your speech.

CONNECTIVES

Use connective transitions to connect the major parts of your speech. Use transitions in at least the following places:

- between the introduction and the body of the speech
- between the body and the conclusion
- between the main points in the body of the speech

You might say, for example, *Now that we have a general idea of… we can examine it in more detail.* This helps the listener see that you've finished your introduction and are moving into the first main point. Or you might say, *Not only are prison sentences too long, they are often incorrect.* This would help the listener see that you've concluded your argument about the length of prison sentences and are now going to illustrate that sentences are often incorrect. Other common phrases useful as connective transitions include: *In contrast to… consider also…, Not only… but also…, In addition to… we also need to look at…,* and *Not only should we… but we should also….* These transitions are generally indicated in your outline in square brackets. Here is how Alisha Forbes (2012) connected her previous discussion of the problems with the discussion of three solutions:

> If something is not done, this problem will become a never ending cycle. Saving our economy through the investment of children is possible through awareness, partnership, and volunteerism.

PREVIEWS

Preview transitions help the audience get a general idea of where you're going. For example, you might want to signal the part of your speech you're approaching and say something like *By way of introduction...*, or *In conclusion..., Now, let's discuss why we are here today...*, or *So, what's the solution? What should we do?*

At other times, you might want to announce the start of a major proposition or piece of evidence and say something like *An even more compelling argument..., A closely related problem..., My next point...*, or *If you want further evidence, just look at...*

Here is how Andrew Eilola (2012) of Concordia College uses a preview transition:

> Now that we've delved into the problems of veteran homelessness, let's examine the causes that enable them to remain in existence today. They are two-fold: soldiers have trouble transitioning and there is a benefits backlog.

REVIEWS

It often helps to provide periodic reviews (sometimes called internal summaries), especially if your speech is long or complex. This review transition is a statement that reviews in brief what you've already said. It's a statement that usually recaps some major subdivision of your speech. Incorporate internal summaries into your speech—perhaps working them into the transitions connecting your main points. Notice how the internal summary presented below reminds listeners of what they've just heard and previews what they'll hear next:

> Inadequate recreational facilities, poor schooling, and a lack of adequate role models seem to be the major problems facing our youngsters. Each of these, however, can be remedied and even eliminated. Here's what we can do.

SIGNPOSTS

Signpost transitions are individual words that tell listeners where you are in your speech and would include such terms as

> First,...
>
> A second argument...
>
> Next, consider...
>
> Thus,...
>
> Therefore,...
>
> So, as you can see...
>
> It follows, then, that...

In connection with these suggestions, see Table 7.1, which identifies some common faults that you'll want to avoid.

Outline the Speech

7.4 Explain how to create preparation and delivery outlines.

outline

A blueprint or pattern for a speech.

The **outline** is a blueprint for your speech; it lays out the elements of the speech and their relationship to one another. With this outline in front of you, you can see at a glance all the elements of organization considered here—the introduction and conclusion, the transitions, the main points and their relationship to the thesis and purpose, and the adequacy of the supporting materials. Like a blueprint for a building, the outline enables you to spot weaknesses that might otherwise go undetected.

Begin outlining at the time you start constructing your speech. Don't wait until you've collected all your material, but begin outlining as you're collecting material, organizing it, and styling it. In this way you'll take the best advantage of one of the major functions of an outline—to tell you where change is needed.

TABLE 7.1 Common Faults in Introductions, Conclusions, and Transitions

Your Speech	Faults	Correctives
In your introduction:	Don't apologize (generally).	In the United States and western Europe, an apology may be seen as an excuse and so is to be avoided. In certain other cultures (those of Japan, China, and Korea are good examples), however, speakers are expected to begin with an apology. It's a way of complimenting the audience.
	Avoid promising something you won't deliver.	The speaker who promises to tell you how to make a fortune in the stock market or how to be the most popular person on campus (and fails to deliver such insight) quickly loses credibility.
	Avoid gimmicks that gain attention but are irrelevant to the speech or inconsistent with your treatment of the topic.	For example, slamming a book on the desk or telling a joke that bears no relation to your speech may accomplish the limited goal of gaining attention, but quickly audience members see that they've been fooled and will resent it.
	Don't introduce your speech with weak statements.	Statements such as "I'm really nervous, but here goes" or "Before I begin my talk, I want to say…" will make audience members uncomfortable and will encourage them to focus on your delivery rather than on your message.
In your conclusion:	Don't introduce new material.	Instead, use your conclusion to reinforce what you've already said and to summarize.
	Don't dilute your position.	Avoid being critical of your own material or your presentation. Saying, for example, "The information I presented is probably dated, but it was all I could find" or "I hope I wasn't too nervous" will detract from the credibility you've tried to establish.
	Don't drag out your conclusion.	End crisply.
In your transitions:	Avoid too many or too few transitions.	Either extreme can cause problems. Use transitions to help your listeners, who will hear the speech only once, to understand the structure of your speech.
	Avoid transitions that are out of proportion to the speech parts they connect.	If you want to connect the two main points of your speech, you need something more than just "and" or "the next point." In contrast, if you want to connect two brief examples, then a simple "another example occurs when…" will do.

Constructing the Outline

After you've completed your research and have mapped out an organizational plan for your speech, put this plan (this blueprint) on paper. That is, construct what is called a **preparation outline** of your speech, using the following guidelines.

preparation outline
A thorough outline (or blueprint) of the speech.

PREFACE THE OUTLINE WITH IDENTIFYING DATA

Before you begin the outline proper, identify the general and specific purposes as well as your thesis. You also may want to include a working title—a title that you may change as you continue to polish and perfect your speech. This prefatory material should look something like this:

What Do Media Do?

General purpose:	To inform
Specific purpose:	To inform my audience of four functions of the media
Thesis:	The media serve four functions.

These identifying notes are not part of your speech proper. They're not, for example, mentioned in your oral presentation. Rather, they're guides to the preparation of the speech and the outline. They're like road signs to keep you going in the right direction and to signal when you've gone off course.

OUTLINE THE INTRODUCTION, BODY, AND CONCLUSION AS SEPARATE UNITS

The introduction, body, and conclusion of the speech, although intimately connected, should be labeled separately and should be kept distinct in your outline. Like the identifying data above, these labels are not spoken to the audience but are further guides to your preparation.

By keeping the introduction, body, and conclusion as separate units, you'll be able to see at a glance if they do, in fact, serve the functions you want them to serve. You'll be able to see where there are problems and where repair is necessary. At the same time, make sure that you examine and see the speech as a whole—in which the introduction leads to the body and the conclusion summarizes your main points and brings your speech to a close.

INSERT TRANSITIONS

Insert [using square brackets] transitions between the introduction and the body, between the body and the conclusion, among the main points of the body, and wherever else you think they might be useful.

APPEND A LIST OF REFERENCES

Some instructors require that you append a list of references to the written preparation outline of each of your speeches. If this is requested, then place the list at the end of the outline or on a separate page. Some instructors require that only sources cited in the speech be included in the list of references, whereas others require that the full list of sources consulted be provided (those mentioned in the speech as well as those not mentioned).

Whatever the specific requirements in your course, remember that source citations will prove most effective with your audience if you carefully integrate them into the speech. It will count for little if you consult the latest works by the greatest authorities but never mention this to your audience. So, when appropriate, weave into your speech the source material you've consulted. In your outline, refer to the source material by the author's name, date, and page number in parentheses; then provide the complete citation in your list of references.

In your actual speech it might prove more effective to include the source with your statement. It might be phrased something like this:

> Sheena Lyenar, in her 2010 *The Art of Choosing*, argues that to be able to make choices, we need to first evaluate all the possible options.

USE A CONSISTENT SET OF SYMBOLS

The following is the standard, accepted sequence of symbols for outlining.

  I.
     A.
       1.
         a.
           (1)
             (a)

Begin the introduction, the body, and the conclusion with Roman numeral I. Treat each of the three major parts as a complete unit.

Not This	This
Introduction	Introduction
I.	I.
II.	II.
Body	Body
III.	I.
IV.	II.
V.	III.
Conclusion	Conclusion
VI.	I.
VII.	II.

USE COMPLETE DECLARATIVE SENTENCES

Phrase your ideas in the outline in complete declarative sentences rather than as questions or as phrases. This will further assist you in examining the essential relationships. It's much easier, for example, to see if one item of information supports another if both are phrased in the declarative mode. If one is a question and one is a statement, this will be more difficult.

Sample Outlines

Now that the principles of outlining and organization are clear, here are some specific examples to illustrate how these principles are used in specific outlines. The accompanying Public Speaking Sample Assistant boxes present a variety of outlines.

PREPARATION OUTLINES

The preparation outline is the main outline that you construct and—in most learning environments—turn in to your instructor. It is a detailed blueprint for your speech. A preparation outline following a topical organization is presented in the accompanying Public Speaking Sample Assistant box. Another preparation outline following a motivated sequence pattern is provided in Chapter 10.

JOURNAL 7.4 PUBLIC SPEAKING CHOICE POINT

The Value of Outlines

Sammy has considerable apprehension in giving a speech. *What choices does Sammy have for using his outline to help reduce his apprehension?*

TEMPLATE OUTLINES

A **template outline**, like the templates you use for writing letters, résumés, greeting cards, or business cards, is a pre-established format into which you insert your specific information. A sample template outline for a speech using a topical organization pattern is presented in the Public Speaking Sample Assistant box. Note that in this template outline there are three main points (I, II, and III in the body). These correspond to the III A, B, and C of the introduction (in which you'd orient the audience) and to the I A, B, and C of the conclusion (in which you'd summarize your main points). The transitions are signaled by square brackets. As you review this outline, the faintly printed watermarks will remind you of the functions of each outline item.

template outline
An outline in which the essential parts of the speech are identified with spaces for these essential parts to be filled in; a learning device for developing speeches.

DELIVERY OUTLINES

After you construct your preparation outline, you can begin to construct your **delivery outline**, an outline consisting of key words or phrases that will assist you in

delivery outline
A brief outline of a speech that the speaker uses during the actual speech presentation.

ETHICAL CHOICE POINT

Constructing an Outline

You have a speech due next week, and you're having trouble constructing your outline. But your friend, who is great at developing outlines, offers to help you write it. You could really use the help; also, in the process you figure you'll learn something about outlining. And besides, you'll fill in the outline, type it up, and present the speech. *What are some of your ethical choices for getting a decent outline and yet not being dishonest?*

PUBLIC SPEAKING Sample Assistant

PREPARATION OUTLINE WITH ANNOTATIONS (TOPICAL ORGANIZATION)

Self-Disclosure

General purpose: To inform

Specific purpose: To inform my audience of the advantages and disadvantages of self-disclosing

Thesis: Self-disclosure has advantages and disadvantages.

Generally, the title, thesis, and general and specific purposes of the speech preface the outline. When the outline is an assignment that is to be handed in, additional information may be requested.

Introduction

I. We've all heard them:
   A. I'm in love with my nephew.
   B. My husband is not my baby's father.
   C. I'm really a woman.

Note the general format for the outline: the headings (introduction, body, and conclusion) are clearly labeled, and the sections are separated visually.

These brief statements are designed to grab attention and perhaps a laugh but also to introduce the nature of the topic.

II. We've all disclosed.
   A. Sometimes it was positive, sometimes negative, but always significant.
   B. Knowing the potential consequences will help us make better decisions.

This introduction serves the three functions discussed in the text: it gains attention; establishes an S–A–T connection (by noting that all of us, speaker and audience, have had this experience); and orients the audience (by identifying the three major ideas of the speech).

The speaker seeks to establish a speaker–audience–topic connection.

III. We look at this important form of communication in three parts:
   A. First, we look at the nature of self-disclosure.
   B. Second, we look at the potential rewards.
   C. Third, we look at the potential risks.

   [Let's look first at the nature of this type of communication.]

The speaker orients the audience and explains the three parts of the speech. The use of guide phrases (*first, second, third*) helps the audience fix clearly in mind the major divisions of the speech.

Body

I. Self-disclosure is a form of communication (Erber & Erber, 2011; Petronio, 2000).
   A. S-D is about the self.
      1. It can be about what you did.
      2. It can be about what you think.
   B. S-D is new information.
   C. S-D is normally about information usually kept hidden.
      1. It can be something about which you're ashamed.
      2. It can be something for which you'd be punished in some way.

   [Knowing what self-disclosure is, we can now look at its potential rewards.]

This transition cues the audience that the speaker will consider the first of the major parts of the speech. Notice that transitions are inserted between all major parts of the speech. Although they may seem too numerous in this abbreviated outline, they'll be appreciated by audience members because the transitions will help them follow and understand your speech.

Notice the parallel structure; each section in the body is phrased in similar style. Although this may seem unnecessarily redundant, it will help your audience follow your speech more closely and will also help you in logically structuring your thoughts.

These examples would be recounted in greater detail in the actual speech. One of the values of outlining these examples is that you'll be able to see at a glance how many you have and how much time you have available to devote to each example. Examples, especially personal ones, have a way of growing beyond their importance to the speech.

This transition provides closure of one topic before turning to another.

II. Self-disclosure has three potential rewards.
   A. It gives us self-knowledge.
   B. It increases communication effectiveness (Schmidt & Cornelius, 1987).
   C. It improves physiological health (Sheese, Brown, & Graziano, 2004).

Another useful transition.

[Although these benefits are substantial, there are also risks.]

III. Self-disclosure has three potential risks.
   A. It can involve personal risks.
      1. This happened to a close friend.
      2. This also happened with well-known celebrities.
   B. It can involve relationship risks (Petronio, 2000).
      1. This happens on *Jerry Springer* five times a week.
      2. It also happened to me.
   C. It can involve professional risks (Fesko, 2001; Korda, 1975).
      1. This occurred recently at work.
      2. There are also lots of political examples.

[Let me summarize this brief excursion into self-disclosure.]

Conclusion

I. Self-disclosure is a type of communication.
   A. It's about the self and concerns something new and something that you usually keep hidden.
   B. Self-disclosure can lead to increased self-knowledge, better communication, and improved health.
   C. Self-disclosure can also create risks to your personal, relational, and professional lives.

II. Self-disclosure is not only an interesting type of communication; it's also vital.
   A. You may want to explore this further by simply typing "self-disclosure" in your favorite search engine.
   B. If you want a more scholarly presentation, take a look at Sandra Petronio's *Balancing the Secrets of Private Disclosures* in the library or online.

III. The bottom line, of course: Should you self-disclose?
   A. Yes.
   B. No.
   C. Maybe.

References

Erber, R., & Erber, M. W. (2011). *Intimate relationships: Issues, theories, and research,* 2nd ed. Boston: Allyn & Bacon.

Fesko, S. L. (2001). Disclosure of HIV status in the workplace. *Health and Social Work, 25,* 235–244.

Korda, M. (1975). *Power! How to get it, how to use it.* New York: Ballantine.

Petronio, S. (Ed.). (2000). *Balancing the secrets of private disclosures.* Mahwah, NJ: Erlbaum.

Schmidt, T. O., & Cornelius, R. R. (1987). Self-disclosure in everyday life. *Journal of Social and Personal Relationships, 4,* 365–373.

Sheese, B. E., Brown, E. L, & Graziano, W. G. (2004). Emotional expression in cyberspace: Searching for moderators of the Pennebaker disclosure effect via e-mail. *Health Psychology, 23* (September), 457–464.

Each statement in the outline is a complete sentence. You can easily convert this outline into a phrase or key-word outline for use in delivery (see the delivery outline in the accompanying Public Speaking Sample Assistant). The full sentences, however, will help you more clearly see relationships among items.

References are integrated throughout the outline just as they would be in a term paper. In the actual speech, the speaker might say something like "Communication theorist Sandra Petronio presents evidence to show that…"

This first part of the conclusion summarizes the major parts of the speech. The longer the speech, the more extensive the summary should be.

Notice that the Introduction's III A, B, and C correspond to the Body's I, II, and III, and to the Conclusion's I A, B, and C. This pattern will help you emphasize the major ideas in your speech—first in the orientation, second in the body of the speech, and third in the conclusion's summary.

This step, in which the speaker motivates the listeners to continue learning about self-disclosure, is optional in informative speeches. In persuasive speeches, you'd use this step to encourage listeners to act on your purpose—to vote, to donate time, to give blood, and so on.

This step provides closure; it makes it clear that the speech is finished. It also serves to encourage reflection on the part of audience members as to their own self-disclosing communication.

This reference list includes only the sources cited in the speech.

A TEMPLATE OUTLINE (TOPICAL ORGANIZATION)

Here's a template outline—a kind of template for structuring a speech. This particular outline would be appropriate for a speech using a topical organization pattern.

Template Outline

General purpose:
your general aim (to inform, to persuade, to entertain)

Specific purpose:
what you hope to achieve from this speech

Thesis:
your main assertion; the core of your speech

INTRODUCTION

I. gain attention

II. establish speaker–audience–topic connection

III. orient audience

   A. first main point; same as I in body

   B. second main point; same as II in body

   C. third main point; same as III in body

[Transition:]
connect the introduction to the body

BODY

I. first main point

   A. support for I (the first main point)

   B. further support for I

   [Transition:]
   connect the first main point to the second

II. second main point

   A. support for II (the second main point)

   B. further support for II

   [Transition:]
   connect the second main point to the third

III. third main point

   A. support for III

   B. further support for III

   [Transition:]
   connect the third main point (or all main points) to the conclusion

CONCLUSION

I. summary _____

   A. first main point; same as I in body _____

   B. second main point; same as II in body _____

   C. third main point; same as III in body _____

II. motivation _____

III. closure _____

REFERENCES

1. _____

2. _____

3. _____

delivering the speech. Resist the temptation to use your preparation outline to deliver the speech. If you do use your preparation outline, you'll tend to read from it instead of presenting an extemporaneous speech in which you attend to and respond to audience feedback.

Instead, construct a brief delivery outline that will assist rather than hinder your delivery of the speech. A sample delivery outline based on the full-sentence preparation outline provided earlier is presented in the Public Speaking Sample Assistant box.

Note first that the outline is brief enough so you'll be able to use it effectively without losing eye contact with the audience. The outline uses abbreviations (for example, *S-D* for *self-disclosure*) and phrases rather than complete sentences. This helps to keep the outline brief and also helps you to scan your message more quickly.

At the same time, however, the delivery outline is detailed enough to include all essential parts of your speech, including transitions. Be careful that you don't omit essential parts even if you're convinced that you couldn't possibly forget them. Normal apprehension may cause you to do exactly that.

VIEWPOINTS
Delivery Outline Mistakes

What mistakes do you see speakers make in using their delivery outlines?

PUBLIC SPEAKING Sample Assistant

A PHRASE/KEY-WORD DELIVERY OUTLINE

Self-Disclosure

PAUSE!

Look Over the Audience!

Introduction

I. We've heard them:

   A. "I'm in love with my nephew."

   B. "My husband is not my baby's father."

   C. "I'm really a woman."

II. We've all S-D

   A. sometimes 1, 2, significant

   B. consequences = better decisions

III. 3 parts: (WRITE ON BOARD)

   A. nature of S-D

   B. rewards

   C. risks

[1st = type of communication]

PAUSE, STEP FORWARD

Body

I. S-D: communication

   A. about self

   B. new

   C. hidden information

[knowing what self-disclosure is, now rewards]

II. 3 rewards

   A. self-knowledge

   B. communication effectiveness

   C. physiological health

[benefits substantial, there are also risks]

PAUSE!

III. 3 risks

   A. personal

   B. relationship

   C. professional

[summarize: S-D]

Conclusion

I. S-D = communication

   A. about self, new, and usually hidden

   B. rewards: increased self-knowledge, better communication, and improved health

   C. risks: personal, relational, and professional

II. S-D not only interesting, it's vital

   A. explore further "S-D" into www

   B. scholarly: Sandra Petronio's *Boundaries*

III. Should you S-D?

   A. yes

   B. no

   C. maybe

PAUSE!

Any Questions?

This outline contains delivery notes specifically tailored to your own needs; for example, pause suggestions and guides to using visual aids.

The delivery outline is clearly divided into an introduction, body, and conclusion and uses the same numbering system as the preparation outline.

Rehearse with your delivery outline, not with your full-sentence preparation outline. This suggestion is simply a specific application of the general rule: Make rehearsals as close to the real thing as possible.

SUMMARY: ORGANIZE YOUR SPEECH (STEPS 5, 6, AND 7)

This chapter has covered ways to organize the body of the speech; prepare the introduction, conclusion, and transitions; and outline the speech. A well-organized speech will be easier for you to remember and also easier for the audience to follow and remember.

Develop Your Main Points (Step 5)

7.1 Explain how to develop main points that are limited in number, focus on your audience, and are worded effectively.

1. Select the points that are most important to your thesis; combine those that have a common focus; select those that are most relevant to your audience; use few main points (two, three, or four work best); phrase your main points in parallel style; and separate your main points avoiding any overlap.

Organize Your Main Points (Step 6)

7.2 Explain the major organizational patterns.

2. In a temporal pattern your main ideas are arranged in a time sequence.
3. In a spatial pattern your main ideas are arranged in a space pattern—for example, left to right.
4. In a topical pattern your main ideas (equal in value and importance) are itemized.
5. In a problem–solution pattern your main ideas are divided into problems and solutions.
6. In a cause–effect pattern your main ideas are arranged into causes and effects.
7. In a structure-function pattern the speech may divided into 2 parts: structure and function or each item (say, organ of the body) may be discussed in terms of its structure and its function.
8. In a comparison-and-contrast pattern your main points might be the main divisions of your topic and you would identify similarities and differences.
9. In a pro-and-con pattern the advantages and disadvantages of, say, two proposals are explained.
10. In a claim-and-proof pattern your thesis is your claim and each main point would be support for your claim.
11. In the multiple-definition pattern each of your main points would consist of a different type of definition.
12. In the Who? What? Why? Where? When? pattern each of your main points answers one of these questions.

13. In the fiction–fact pattern you identify the untrue beliefs (the fictions) and then dispute them with the facts.
14. In selecting an organizational pattern, take into consideration the cultural backgrounds of your listeners, especially the extent to which they are from low-context or high-context cultures.

Construct Your Introduction, Conclusion, and Transitions (Step 7)

7.3 Explain the characteristics of effective introductions, conclusions, and transitions.

15. Construct your introduction so it:
    - Gains attention.
    - Establishes a connection among speaker, audience, and topic.
    - Orients the audience.
16. Construct your conclusion so it:
    - Summarizes your speech or some aspect of it.
    - Motivates your audience.
    - Provides crisp closure.
17. Use transitions to help the audience understand the flow of your speech. Use transitions to connect, preview, and review and to provide signposts.
18. Avoid the common problems of introductions, conclusions, and transitions:
    - Don't apologize.
    - Avoid promising what you won't deliver.
    - Don't rely on gimmicks.
    - Don't preface your introduction.
    - Avoid ineffective opening lines.
    - Don't introduce new material in your conclusion.
    - Don't dilute your position.
    - End crisply; don't drag out your conclusion.
    - Avoid too many or too few transitions.
    - Avoid transitions that are out of proportion to the parts of the speech they connect.

Outline the Speech

7.4 Explain how to create preparation and delivery outlines.

19. Outlines may vary from complete sentence outlines to those with just key words and phrases. In constructing your outline: Preface the outline with identifying data; outline the introduction, body, and conclusion as separate units; insert transitions in square brackets; append a list of references (if required); use a consistent set of symbols; and use complete declarative sentences (for your preparation outline).

KEY TERMS: ORGANIZE YOUR SPEECH (STEPS 5, 6, AND 7)

attention
body
cause–effect pattern
claim-and-proof pattern
comparison and contrast
 pattern
delivery outline
fiction–fact pattern

high-context culture
low-context culture
multiple-definition pattern
orientation
outline
preparation outline
problem–solution pattern
pro-and-con pattern

spatial pattern
structure-function pattern
template outline
temporal pattern
topical pattern
transitions
Who? What? Why? Where? When?
 pattern

PUBLIC SPEAKING EXERCISES

7.1 Generating Main Points

One of the skills in organizing a speech is to ask a strategic question of your thesis and from the answer to generate your main points. Below are 10 thesis statements suitable for a variety of informative or persuasive speeches. For each thesis statement, ask a question and generate two, three, or four main points that would be suitable for an informative or persuasive speech.

Here's an example to get you started:

Thesis statement:	Mandatory retirement should be abolished.
Question:	Why should mandatory retirement be abolished?

I. Mandatory retirement leads us to lose many of the most productive workers.

II. Mandatory retirement contributes to psychological problems of those forced to retire.

III. Mandatory retirement costs businesses economic hardship because they have to train new people.

1. Buy American.
2. Tax property assets owned by religious organizations.
3. Require adoption agencies to reveal the names of birth parents to all adopted children when they reach 18 years of age.
4. Permit condom distribution in all junior and senior high schools.
5. Permit single people to adopt children.
6. Ban all sales of fur from wild animals.
7. Decriminalize soft drug sales.
8. Require all students at this college to take courses on cultural diversity.
9. Legalize marijuana in all stages.
10. Eliminate football from all high schools and colleges.

7.2 Constructing Introductions and Conclusions

Prepare an introduction and a conclusion for a speech on one of the theses listed. Be prepared to explain the methods you used to accomplish each of these aims.

1. College isn't for everyone.
2. No jail time should be imposed for first offenders of the drug laws.
3. Each of us should donate our organs to science after our death.
4. Laws restricting Sunday shopping should be abolished.
5. Suicide and its assistance by others should be legalized.
6. Gambling should be legalized in all states.
7. College athletics should be abolished.
8. Animal experimentation by the cosmetics industry should be illegal.
9. Divorce should be granted immediately when there's mutual agreement.
10. Privatization of elementary and high schools should be encouraged.

7.3 Scrambled Outline

Here is a scrambled outline of a speech on apologies. It contains an introduction and a conclusion, each serving the three functions identified here, and four transitions. Arrange these into a proper outline.

1. Be specific.
2. After some pretty bad apologies that cost me two important relationships, I learned the basics of effective apologies—a skill that will help you now and in the future.
3. In this brief exploration we looked at the definition, purposes, and rules of effective apologies.
4. Apologies encourage others to maintain a positive image of you.
5. To acquire this skill we need to understand what an apology is, the purposes of apologies, and the characteristics of an effective apology.
6. It could be about something you did.
7. An apology is an expression of regret.
8. Now that we have a general idea of what an apology is, we can look at the purposes it serves.
9. Apologies serve two major purposes.
10. These purposes will best be served with an apology that is effectively composed.
11. An effective apology can be crafted by following four rules.
12. Express regret.
13. Give assurance that this will not happen again.
14. It could be about something you said.
15. Apologies help repair your relationship.
16. Omit excuses.
17. Let's look first at what an apology is.
18. As we've seen, an apology is an expression of sorrow or regret for having said or done something you shouldn't have.
19. Who hasn't ever had to apologize? Anyone?
20. The Web is flooded with very logical and very practical advice on apologies for both business and relationships. Just search for *apologies*.
21. Apologies won't solve all problems created by saying or doing something you shouldn't have, but they can help if expressed effectively. Good luck with your next apology.

CHAPTER 8

WORD, REHEARSE, AND PRESENT YOUR SPEECH

(STEPS 8, 9, AND 10)

Cultivating an effective delivery style
is no simple process.

CHAPTER TOPICS

Word Your Speech (Step 8)

Rehearse Your Speech (Step 9)

Present Your Speech (Step 10)

Effective Vocal Delivery

Effective Bodily Action

LEARNING OBJECTIVES

8.1 Define *clarity, vividness, appropriateness, personal style,* and *cultural sensitivity* and some of the guidelines for achieving these qualities in public speaking and achieving sentences of maximum effectiveness.

8.2 Explain the suggestions for effective and efficient speech rehearsal.

8.3 Identify the methods of presentation and the suggestions for using these methods effectively.

8.4 Explain the characteristics of effective vocal delivery in public speaking.

8.5 Explain the characteristics of effective bodily action.

Your success as a public speaker depends heavily on the way you express your ideas: on the words you select and the way you phrase your sentences. The first section of this chapter will focus on this crucial process of wording your speech for maximum impact and effectiveness. Remaining sections will cover ways to rehearse your speech and the varied presentation methods.

Word Your Speech (Step 8)

8.1 Define *clarity*, *vividness*, *appropriateness*, *personal style*, and *cultural sensitivity* and some of the guidelines for achieving these qualities in public speaking and achieving sentences of maximum effectiveness.

When you're reading, you can look up an unfamiliar word, reread difficult portions, or look up an unfamiliar word or check a reference. When you're listening, you don't have this luxury. Because of differences between reading and listening and because your listeners will hear your speech only once, your talk must be instantly intelligible.

Researchers who have examined a great number of speeches and writings have found several important differences among them (Akinnaso, 1982; DeVito, 1981). Generally, **oral style**, the style of spoken language, consists of shorter, simpler, and more familiar words than does written language. For most speeches, this "oral style" is appropriate. The specific suggestions offered throughout this section will help you to style a speech that will retain the best of the oral style while maximizing comprehension and persuasion.

Clarity

Clarity in speaking style should be your primary goal. Here are some guidelines to help you make your meanings clear:

- **Be economical.** Don't waste words. Get rid of the clutter, the words that don't add anything to your meaning. Notice the wasted words in expressions such as "at 9 a.m. *in the morning*," "we *first* began the discussion," "I *myself personally*," and "blue *in color*." By withholding the italicized terms, you eliminate unnecessary words and move closer to a more economical and clearer style.

- **Use specific terms and numbers.** Be specific to create a clearer and more detailed picture. Don't say "dog" when you want your listeners to picture a St. Bernard. Don't say "car" when you want them to picture a limousine. The same is true of numbers. Don't say "earned a good salary" if you mean "earned $90,000 a year." Don't say "taxes will go up" when you mean "taxes will increase 7 percent."

- **Use short, familiar terms.** Generally, favor the short word over the long, the familiar over the unfamiliar, and the more commonly used over the rarely used term. Use *harmless* instead of *innocuous*, *clarify* instead of *elucidate*, *use* instead of *utilize*, *find out* instead of *ascertain*, *expense* instead of *expenditure*.

- **Carefully assess idioms. Idioms** are expressions that are unique to a specific language and whose meaning cannot be deduced from the individual words used. Expressions such as "kick the bucket" and "doesn't have a leg to stand on" are idioms. Either you know the meaning of the expression or you don't; you can't figure it out from the definitions of the individual words. Idioms give your speech a casual and informal style, making your speech sound like speech and not like a written essay. But idioms can create problems for audience members who are not native speakers of your language.

oral style
The style of spoken discourse that, when compared with written style, consists of shorter, simpler, and more familiar words; more qualification, self-reference terms, allness terms, verbs, and adverbs; and more concrete terms and terms indicative of consciousness of projection—for example, "as I see it."

clarity
A quality of speaking style that makes a message easily intelligible.

idioms
Expressions that are unique to a specific language and whose meaning cannot be deduced simply from an analysis of the individual words.

figure of speech
Stylistic device and way of expressing ideas that is used to achieve special effects.

alliteration
A figure of speech in which the initial sound in two or more words is repeated.

hyperbole
A figure of speech in which something is exaggerated for effect but is not intended to be taken literally.

irony
A figure of speech employed for special emphasis in which a speaker uses words whose literal meaning is the opposite of the speaker's actual message or intent.

metaphor
A figure of speech in which there is an implied comparison between two unlike things; for example, "That CEO is a jackal."

simile
A figure of speech in which a speaker compares two unlike things using the words *like* or *as*.

synecdoche
A figure of speech in which a part of an object is used to stand for the entire object as in *green thumb* for *gardener*.

metonymy
A figure of speech in which some particular thing is referred to by something with which it is closely associated, for example, *Rome* for the *Catholic Church* or the *White House* for the *U.S. government*.

antithesis
A figure of speech in which contrary ideas are presented in parallel form, as in Charles Dickens's opening lines in *A Tale of Two Cities*: "It was the best of times, it was the worst of times."

personification
A figure of speech in which human characteristics are attributed to inanimate objects for special effect; for example, "After the painting, the room looked cheerful and energetic."

rhetorical question
A question that is used to make a statement or to produce a desired effect rather than secure an answer.

oxymoron
A term or phrase that combines two normally opposite qualities as in *bittersweet*.

- **Vary the levels of abstraction.** Combining high abstraction (i.e., the very general) and low abstraction (i.e., the very concrete) seems to work best. Too many generalizations will be vague and difficult for your audience to comprehend, but too many specifics will leave them wondering what the big picture is.

Vividness

Select words that make your ideas vivid, that make them come alive in the listeners' minds.

- **Use active verbs.** Favor verbs that communicate activity. Try selecting verbs that will enable listeners to visualize an action—verbs like *dance, climb*, and *run*, for example.
- **Use imagery.** Inject vividness into your speech by appealing to the audience's senses, especially their visual, auditory, and tactile senses. Using imagery can make your listeners see, hear, and feel what you're talking about. *Visual imagery* enables you to describe people or objects in images the audience can see. When appropriate, describe visual qualities such as height, weight, color, size, shape, length, and contour. Let your audience see the sweat pouring down the faces of coal miners. *Auditory imagery* helps you appeal to the audience's sense of hearing. Let listeners hear the car screeching or roar of angry tenants. *Tactile imagery* enables you to make the audience feel the temperature or texture you're talking about. Let listeners feel the cool water running over their bodies, the fighter's punch, or the sand beneath their feet.
- **Use figures of speech.** A **figure of speech** is a stylistic device in which words are used beyond their literal meaning. One of the best ways to achieve vividness is to use figures of speech: (**alliteration, hyperbole, irony, metaphor, simile, synecdoche, metonymy, antithesis, personification, rhetorical questions,** and **oxymorons**). Table 8.1 defines and illustrates each of these. As you read this table try applying these to such bland phrases as "a wonderful meal," "he made a fortune," "the thief was big," "the apartment was a mess," or "she lived a good life."

Appropriateness

Appropriate language is consistent in tone with your topic, your audience, and your own self-image. It's language that does not offend anyone or make anyone feel uncomfortable and seems natural given the situation. Here are some guidelines to help you choose appropriate language.

- **Speak at the appropriate level of formality.** Although public speaking usually takes place in a somewhat formal situation, relatively informal language seems to work best in most situations. One way to achieve a more informal style is to use contractions: *don't* instead of *do not*, *wouldn't* instead of *would not*. Contractions give a public speech the sound and rhythm of conversation—a quality that listeners generally like.
- **Avoid written-style expressions.** Avoid expressions that are more familiar in writing, such as "the former" or "the latter" as well as expressions such as "the argument presented above." These make listeners feel you're reading to them rather than talking with them.
- **Avoid slang, vulgarity, and offensive expressions.** Be careful not to offend audience members with language that embarrasses them or makes them think you have little respect for them. Although your listeners may use such expressions, they generally resent their use by public speakers.

TABLE 8.1   Ten Popular Figures of Speech

Figure	Definition	Examples
Alliteration	the repetition of the same initial sound in two or more words	*fifty famous flavors* *the cool, calculating leader*
Hyperbole	the use of extreme exaggeration	*He cried like a faucet.* *I'm so hungry I could eat a whale.*
Irony	the use of a word or sentence whose literal meaning is the opposite of that which is intended	A teacher handing back failing examinations might say, *So pleased to see how hard you all studied.*
Metaphor	an implied comparison between two unlike things	*She's a lion when she wakes up.* *He's a real bulldozer.*
Simile	like metaphor, compares two unlike objects but uses the word *like* or *as*	*The manager is as gentle as a lamb.* *Pat went through the problems like a high-speed drill.*
Synecdoche	using a part of an object to stand for the whole object	*all hands were on deck* (in which *hands* stands for "sailors" or "crew members") *green thumb* (for "expert gardener")
Metonymy	the substitution of a name for a title with which it's closely associated	*City Hall issued the following news release* (in which *City Hall* stands for "the mayor" or "the city council")
Antithesis	the presentation of contrary or polar opposite ideas in parallel form	*My loves are many, my enemies are few.* *It was the best of times, it was the worst of times* (from Charles Dickens's opening to *A Tale of Two Cities*).
Personification	the attribution of human characteristics to inanimate objects	*This room cries out for activity.* *My car is tired.*
Rhetorical questions	questions that are used to make a statement or to produce a desired effect rather than secure an answer	*Do you want to be popular?* *Do you want to get well?*
Oxymoron	a term or phrase that combines two normally opposite qualities	*bittersweet, the silent roar, poverty-stricken millionaires, the ignorant genius, a war for peace*

Personal Style

Audiences favor speakers who use a personal rather than an impersonal style—who speak *with* them rather than *at* them. A personal style—one that uses pronouns, direct questions to the audience, and **immediacy**—makes the audience feel more involved with the speaker and the speech topic.

immediacy

A quality of interpersonal effectiveness; a sense of contact and togetherness; a feeling of interest in and liking for the other person.

- **Use personal pronouns.** Say "I," "me," "he," "she," and "you." Avoid expressions such as the impersonal *one* (as in "One is led to believe that…"), *this speaker*, and *you, the listeners.* These expressions are overly formal and distance the audience, creating barriers rather than bridges.

- **Direct questions to the audience.** Involve audience members by asking them questions. With a small audience, you might even take brief responses. With larger audiences, you might ask the question, pause to allow audience members time to consider their responses, and then move on. When you direct questions to your listeners, you make them feel they are part of the experience.

- **Create immediacy.** Create immediacy (a closeness with your audience) by referring directly to your listeners, using *you;* say; "*You'll* enjoy reading…" instead of "Everyone will enjoy reading…" Refer to commonalities between you and the audience and to shared experiences and goals: for example, "We all need a more responsive PTA."

Power

Public speaking, perhaps even more than interpersonal or small group communication, often requires a powerful style—a style that is certain, definite, and persuasive. The first step toward achieving a powerful style of speech is to eliminate the powerless forms that you may use now. The following is a list of the major characteristics of powerless speech (Grant, 2016; Dillard & Marshall, 2003; Johnson, 1987; Kleinke, 1986; Lakoff, 1975; Molloy, 1981; Timmerman, 2002).

- **Hesitations** make you sound unprepared and uncertain: "I, er, want to say that, ah, this one is, er, the best, you know?"
- **Too many intensifiers** make your speech monotonous and don't allow you to stress what you do want to emphasize: "Really, this was the greatest; it was truly awesome, phenomenal."
- **Disqualifiers** signal a lack of competence and a feeling of uncertainty: "I didn't read the entire article, but…," "I didn't actually see the accident, but…"
- **Self-critical statements** signal a lack of confidence and may make public your own inadequacies: "I'm not very good at this," "This is my first public speech."
- **Slang and vulgar language** signal a lack of awareness of the speaking situation and hence little power: "No problem!" "What the hell?!"

Cultural Sensitivity

cultural sensitivity
An awareness of and sensitivity to the rules for communicating in varied cultural settings.

Cultural sensitivity refers to an attitude and way of behaving in which you're aware of and acknowledge cultural variation. It's a quality that you'll want to demonstrate in your own public speeches, and you should expect other speakers to as well. Here are a few guidelines to keep in mind.

- **Use appropriate cultural identifiers.** The best guide to follow here is to use the terms that the people you're talking about prefer and that your audience sees as appropriate. So, if you're talking about transgendered people and aren't sure of the proper terminology, look it up. And, while you're at it, check your pronunciation of unfamiliar terms against an audio dictionary. It will be time well spent; after all, you don't want to alienate members of your audience or have them think you're insensitive. If you err, err on the side of over-politeness, of being overly culturally sensitive.

inclusive language
Language that includes all people and all cultures rather than terms that are specific to any one specific cultural group.

- **Use inclusive language.** Try to use **inclusive language**, language that includes all people and all cultures rather than terms that are specific to any one specific cultural group. For example, if you're referring to religious worship in general then *house of worship* is more inclusive than *church* or *mosque* or *temple*. If you're talking about a specific house of worship then, of course, use the more specific and unique term.

stereotyping
Using a generalized designation for a group of people that fails to acknowledge individual differences; using language that implies that all people of a group are the same.

- **Avoid stereotyping.** Avoid **stereotyping**, implying that all members of a particular group are the same and that they can be described easily and without taking into consideration individual differences. Not all white people are alike, not all gay men are alike, not all women are alike, and not all 80-year-olds are alike. Also, avoid occupational stereotyping—for example, making the pilot or doctor a male and the flight attendant or nurse a woman. Also, avoid identifying the sex or race or age or affectional orientation when it's not relevant, as in the *female mathematician*, the *African American college president*, the *80-year-old professor*, or the *gay athlete*. **Avoid any terms or phrases that might be perceived as sexist, racist, heterosexist, or ageist.** For example, avoid making the hypothetical person a male or using the masculine pronouns (*he, him, his*) generically; instead use the plural (*they, them, their*) or say "she or he" or "he or she."

VIEWPOINTS
Word Choice

Of all the qualities of effective word choice which do you think is the most important in an informative speech? In a persuasive speech?

Sentence Construction

Effective public speaking style also requires careful attention to the construction of sentences. Here are some guidelines that will help you achieve a clear, vivid, appropriate, personal, and powerful speaking style.

- **Use short rather than long sentences.** Short sentences are more forceful and economical. They are easier to understand and to remember. Listeners don't have the time or inclination to unravel long and complex sentences. Help them to listen more efficiently by using short rather than long sentences.

- **Use direct rather than indirect sentences.** Direct sentences are easier to understand. They are also more forceful. Instead of saying, "I want to tell you the three main reasons why we should not adopt the Bennett Proposal," say, "We should not adopt the Bennett Proposal. Let me give you three good reasons."

- **Use active rather than passive sentences.** Active sentences are easier to understand. They also make your speech livelier and more vivid. Instead of saying, "The lower court's original decision was reversed by the Supreme Court," say, "The Supreme Court reversed the lower court's decision." Instead of saying, "The change was favored by management," say, "Management favored the change."

- **Use positive rather than negative sentences.** Positive sentences are easier to comprehend and to remember (Clark, 1974; DeVito, 1976). Notice how the positive sentences are easier to understand than the negative sentences.

Positive Sentences	Negative Sentences
The director rejected the proposal.	The director did not accept the proposal.
This committee works outside normal channels.	This committee does not work within the normal channels.

- **Vary the Type and Length of Sentences.** The advice to use short, direct, active, and positive sentences is valid most of the time. But too many sentences of the same type or length will make your speech sound boring. Use variety, but generally follow the guidelines.

JOURNAL 8.1 PUBLIC SPEAKING CHOICE POINT

Speaking Style

Rochelle is asked to give a presentation on the library's new and complex online services to a group of faculty members. *What kinds of advice would you give Rochelle concerning her speaking style? For example, should she strive for a personal or an impersonal style? Should she signal immediacy or distance? Would your advice differ if Rochelle's audience were a freshman communication class instead of faculty members?*

Rehearse Your Speech (Step 9)

8.2 Explain the suggestions for effective and efficient speech rehearsal.

Through rehearsal you can develop delivery skills that will help you achieve the purposes of your speech. Rehearsal also will enable you to time your speech and to see how the speech will flow as a whole. Additionally, rehearsal will help you test out your presentation aids, detect any technological problems, and resolve them. And, of course, through rehearsal you'll learn your speech, so you'll be more confident when you deliver it. This confidence will help to reduce your apprehension. The following procedures should assist you in achieving these goals.

Rehearse the Speech as a Whole

Rehearse the speech from beginning to end. Don't rehearse the speech in parts. Rehearse it from getting out of your seat, through the introduction, body, and conclusion, to returning to your seat. Be sure to rehearse the speech with all the examples and illustrations (and audiovisual aids, if any) included. This will enable you to connect the parts of the speech and to see how they interact with one another.

Time the Speech

Time the speech during each rehearsal. Make any necessary adjustments on the basis of this timing. If you're using computer presentation software, you'll be able to time your speech very precisely. Such software will also enable you to time the individual parts of your speech so you can achieve the balance you want—for example, you might want to spend twice as much time on the solutions as on the problems, or you might want to balance the introduction and conclusion so that each constitutes about 10 percent of your speech.

Approximate the Actual Speech Situation

Rehearse the speech under conditions as close as possible to those under which you'll deliver it. If possible, rehearse the speech in the same room where you'll present it. If this is impossible, try to simulate the actual conditions as closely as you can—in your living room or even in a bathroom. If possible, rehearse the speech in front of supportive listeners; one study found that students who practiced their speeches before an audience received higher grades than those who practiced without an audience (Smith & Frymier, 2006). It's always helpful (especially for your beginning speeches) if your listeners are supportive rather than critical—but merely having listeners present during your rehearsal will further simulate the conditions under which you'll eventually speak. Get together with two or three other students in an empty classroom where you can each serve as speaker and listener.

Incorporate Changes and Delivery Notes

Don't interrupt your rehearsal to make notes or changes; if you do, you may never experience the entire speech from beginning to end. But do make any needed changes in the speech between rehearsals. While making these changes, note any words whose pronunciation or articulation you wish to check. Also, insert pause notations, "slow down" warnings, and other delivery suggestions into your outline.

If possible, record your speech (ideally on video) so you can hear exactly what your listeners will hear: your volume, rate, pitch, articulation and pronunciation, and pauses. You'll then be in a better position to improve these qualities.

Rehearse Often

Rehearse the speech as often as seems necessary. Rehearse the speech at least three or four times; less than this is sure to be too little. And rehearse the speech as long as your rehearsals continue to produce improvements in the speech or in your delivery.

Undertake a Long-Term Delivery Improvement Program

To become a truly effective speaker, you may need to undertake a long-term delivery improvement program. Approach this project with a positive attitude: Tell yourself that you can do it and that you will do it.

- **Seek feedback.** Secure feedback from someone whose opinion and insight you respect. Your public speaking instructor may be a logical choice, but someone majoring in communication or working in a communication field might also be appropriate. Get an honest and thorough appraisal of both your voice and your bodily action.
- **See, hear, and feel the differences between effective and ineffective patterns.** For example, is your pitch too high or your volume too loud? An audio recorder will be very helpful. Learn to sense your rigid posture or your lack of arm and hand gestures. Once you've perceived these voice and/or body patterns, concentrate on learning more effective habits. Practice a few minutes each day. Avoid becoming too conscious of any source of ineffectiveness. Just try to increase your awareness and work on one problem at a time. Do not try to change all your patterns at once.
- **Seek additional feedback on the changes.** Make certain that listeners agree that the new patterns you're practicing really are more effective. Remember that you hear yourself through bone conduction as well as through air transmission. Others hear you only through air transmission. So what you hear and what others hear will be different.
- **For voice improvement, consult a book on voice and diction.** Such books will provide exercises for practice and additional information on the nature of volume, rate, pitch, and quality.

JOURNAL 8.2 PUBLIC SPEAKING CHOICE POINT

Vocalized Pauses

Millie's normal speech is extremely rapid, and she needs to slow down when she gives her speeches. *What are some of the things Millie can do during rehearsal to make sure she speaks at a normal rate?*

- **If difficulties persist, see a professional.** For voice problems, see a speech clinician. Most campuses have a speech clinic, and you can easily avail yourself of its services. For bodily action difficulties, talk with your public speaking instructor.
- **Seek professional help if you're psychologically uncomfortable with any aspect of your voice or bodily action.** It may be that all you have to do is to hear yourself or see yourself on a video—as others hear and see you—to convince yourself that you sound and look just fine. Regardless of what is causing this discomfort, however, if you're uncomfortable, do something about it. In a college community there's more assistance available to you at no cost than you'll ever be offered again. Make use of it.

With these rehearsal guidelines in mind, consider your actual presentation, beginning with defining what makes for an effective public speaking presentation.

Present Your Speech (Step 10)

8.3 Identify the methods of presentation and the suggestions for using these methods effectively.

This last step is the reason for all the others and will prove challenging, exciting, scary, difficult, and much more. Here we define the nature of effective presentation, the methods of presentation you might use, and ways to use your voice and bodily action to best advantage.

The Nature of an Effective Presentation

Perhaps the most important characteristic of effective public speaking presentation is that it depends. What makes for effectiveness in one situation and with one speaker will not necessarily prove effective in another situation with a different speaker. And to complicate matters just a bit, audiences differ in what they consider effective delivery—some audiences expect and enjoy a lively entertaining style while others will prefer a more subtle, intellectualized presentation.

You'll want to develop a presentation style that works for you while remaining flexible in adjusting that presentation style to the uniqueness of the specific public speaking situation. Nevertheless, amid these qualifications we can offer a few suggestions as to what constitutes effective presentation.

- **Comfortable.** Your presentation style should be comfortable to you. It should feel natural to you, and it should look natural to the audience. It should not appear phony or in any way unnatural.
- **Consistent.** Your presentation style should be consistent with all the other public speaking factors you've considered throughout your preparation. If your speech is on a humorous topic, then your presentation style is likely to be lighthearted. If your speech were on a more somber topic (such as the death penalty), then your presentation style would likely be fairly serious.
- **Interesting.** Your presentation should add interest and some variety into your speech. Much like your language contributes to the interest of your speech, so does your delivery. If you stand motionless, it's not likely to prove terribly interesting. At the same time, you don't want to run around the room just to add interest that, in this case, would draw attention away from your speech.
- **Contributes to the speech.** Your presentation style should contribute to your speech; it should add some degree of clarity to what you're saying. For example, moving a half step forward or to the side when introducing a main point might help reinforce your verbal transition. In addition, your presentation

style—whatever that is—should not call attention to itself and away from the message of your speech. Your presentation style should reinforce your verbal message.

Methods of Presentation

Public speakers vary greatly in their methods of presentation. Some speak off the cuff, with no apparent preparation (impromptu); others read their speeches from the printed text (manuscript). Some construct a detailed outline and create the speech itself at the moment of delivery (extemporaneous).

Still others memorize their speeches—a method that is not recommended. The major disadvantage of a **memorized speech** (actually more of an oral interpretation presentation than a public speech) is that you might forget your speech. In a memorized speech each sentence cues the recall of the following sentence. Thus, when you forget one sentence, you may forget the rest of the speech. Another disadvantage is that memorizing makes it virtually impossible to adjust to audience feedback. And if you're not going to adjust to feedback, you lose the main advantage of face-to-face contact.

memorized speech
A method of oral presentation in which the entire speech is committed to memory and then recited.

Here we'll consider the impromptu, manuscript, and extemporaneous methods of presentation along with some general suggestions for using each method. These delivery suggestions—as you'll see—will also prove helpful in managing your apprehension. As you develop more control and comfort over your voice and bodily action in public speaking, you'll relax and feel more comfortable. These feelings will then help reduce your fear of public speaking.

SPEAKING IMPROMPTU

When you give an **impromptu speech**, you speak without any specific preparation or advance thinking. You and the topic meet for the first time, and immediately the speech begins. On some occasions you will not be able to avoid speaking impromptu. In a classroom, after someone has spoken, you may comment on the speech you just heard in a brief impromptu speech of evaluation. In asking or answering questions in an interview situation, you're giving impromptu speeches, albeit extremely short ones. At meetings you may find yourself speaking impromptu as you explain a proposal or defend a plan of action; these, too, are impromptu speeches. The ability to speak impromptu effectively depends on your general public speaking ability. The more proficient a speaker you are, the better you'll be able to function impromptu.

impromptu speech
A speech given without any explicit prior preparation.

The impromptu experience provides excellent training in different aspects of public speaking, such as maintaining eye contact; responding to audience feedback; gesturing; organizing ideas; and developing examples, arguments, and appeals. The major disadvantage of speaking impromptu is that it does not permit attention to details of public speaking such as audience adaptation, research, and style.

When you are called upon to speak impromptu, the following suggestions should prove useful.

- **Don't apologize.** Everyone has difficulty speaking impromptu, and there's no need to emphasize any problems you may have.
- **Be positive.** Don't express verbally or nonverbally any displeasure or any negative responses to the experience, the topic, the audience, or even yourself. Approach the entire task with a positive attitude and a positive appearance. It will help make the experience more enjoyable both for you and for your audience.
- **Pre-plan as much as you can.** When you have to speak impromptu, jot down two or three subtopics that you'll cover and perhaps two or three bits of supporting material that you'll use in amplifying these two or three subtopics.
- **Develop your conclusion.** It will probably be best to use a simple summary conclusion in which you restate your main topic and the subtopics that you discussed.

- **Develop an introduction.** Here it will probably be best simply to identify your topic and orient audience members by telling them the two or three subtopics that you'll cover.

SPEAKING FROM MANUSCRIPT

manuscript speech
A speech designed to be read verbatim from a script.

With a **manuscript speech**, you write out the entire speech exactly as you want it to be heard by your audience and read it to the audience. Because the manuscript method allows you to control exactly what you'll say, it may be the logical method to use in politics, for example, where an ambiguous phrase might prove insulting or belligerent and cause serious problems.

One of the major advantages of a manuscript speech is that you control the timing precisely. This is particularly important when you are delivering a speech that will be recorded (on television, for example). Also, there's no danger of forgetting an important point; everything is there for you on paper. Still another advantage is that the manuscript method allows you to use the exact wording you (or a team of speech writers) want. The most obvious disadvantage is that it's difficult to read a speech and sound natural and non-mechanical. Reading material from the printed page or a teleprompter with liveliness and naturalness is itself a skill that is difficult to achieve without considerable practice. Audiences don't like speakers to read their speeches. Also, reading a manuscript makes it difficult to respond to feedback from your listeners. And when the manuscript is on a stationary lectern, as it most often is, it's impossible for you to move around. You have to stay in one place. The speech controls your movement or, rather, your lack of movement.

When speaking from manuscript, consider the following suggestions.

- **Listen to your own words.** Write out your speech with an eye to oral presentation. Try to hear what your words will sound like as you write them down.
- **Mark up your manuscript with delivery notes.** Write in pause points—especially important in manuscript speaking because of the tendency to read quickly. Underline or boldface key terms that you want to stress.
- **Maintain eye contact.** Even though you're reading from manuscript, you are still delivering a speech and it should sound as natural and extemporaneous as possible. Rehearse your speech so you can alternate looking at the manuscript with looking at the audience.
- **Make your manuscript readable.** Use large fonts that you'll be able to see easily without squinting or putting the manuscript up to your nose. Format page breaks so they coincide with natural breaks in the speech. Don't separate sentences or even main points on two different pages.
- **Make your manuscript practical.** Use only one side of the paper and number the pages clearly to reduce any chance of losing your place.
- **Commit some opening and closing to memory.** Even when speaking from manuscript, memorize your first few opening lines and your last few closing lines. In this way you'll be able to maintain eye contact with the audience during these two most crucial times.

SPEAKING EXTEMPORANEOUSLY

extemporaneous speech
A speech that is thoroughly prepared and organized in detail and in which certain aspects of style are predetermined.

An **extemporaneous speech** involves thorough preparation and a commitment to memory of the main ideas and their order (and, if you wish, your introduction and conclusion). There is, however, no commitment to exact wording for the remaining parts of the speech.

Extemporaneous delivery is useful in most speaking situations. Good college lecturers use the extemporaneous method. They prepare thoroughly and know what they want to say and in what order they want to say it, but they have given no commitment to exact wording.

One advantage of this method is that it allows you to respond easily to feedback. Should audience feedback suggest that a point needs clarification, for example, you can rephrase the idea or give an example. Extemporaneous delivery is the method that comes closest to conversation—a kind of "enlarged conversation." With this method you can move about and interact with the audience.

Here are a few guidelines for using the extemporaneous method—the method recommended for your classroom speeches and for most of the speeches you'll deliver throughout your life.

- **Memorize the opening and closing lines.** This will help you focus your complete attention on the audience and will put you more at ease. Similarly, memorize the main points and the order in which you'll cover them; this will free you from relying on your notes and will make you feel more in control of the speech and of the entire speech-making situation.

- **Speak naturally.** Listeners will enjoy your speech and believe you more if you speak as if you were conversing with a small group of people. Don't allow your delivery to call attention to itself. Your ultimate aim should be to deliver the speech so naturally that the audience won't even notice your delivery.

- **Use delivery to reinforce your message.** All aspects of your delivery—your voice, bodily action, and general appearance, for example—should work together to make your ideas instantly intelligible to your audience.

- **Vary your delivery.** Variety in voice and bodily action will help you maintain your listeners' attention. Vary your vocal volume and your rate of speaking. In a similar way, avoid standing in exactly the same position throughout the speech. Use your body to express your ideas, to communicate to the audience what is going on in your head.

- **Create immediacy with delivery.** Make your listeners feel that you're talking directly and individually to each of them: Maintain appropriate eye contact with the audience members, talk directly to your audience and not to your notes or to your visual aids, smile when it's appropriate and consistent with your speech purpose, and maintain a physical closeness that reinforces a psychological closeness (don't stand behind the desk or lectern).

- **Be expressive.** You can do this by allowing your facial muscles and your entire body to reflect and echo your inner involvement. Use gestures appropriately. Too few gestures may signal lack of involvement; too many may communicate uneasiness, awkwardness, or anxiety. Carefully read the feedback signals sent by your audience and respond to these signals with verbal, vocal, and bodily adjustments.

The remaining sections of this chapter will explain how you can use your voice and your bodily action to most effectively communicate your thoughts and feelings. In conjunction with reading about what makes for effective presentation, visit the variety of websites (YouTube especially) that contain videos of speeches. And, of course, the TED speakers are uniformly excellent models. These videos will enable you to see effective delivery in action.

JOURNAL 8.3 PUBLIC SPEAKING CHOICE POINT

Presentation Methods

Gary is planning to give a speech on the campus television station appealing to students to vote for him as class president. *What are some of Gary's choices for presenting this speech? What are the advantages and disadvantages of each?*

Effective Vocal Delivery

8.4 Explain the characteristics of effective vocal delivery in public speaking.

You can achieve effective vocal delivery by mastering your volume, rate, pitch, pauses, articulation, and pronunciation. Let's look at each in turn.

Volume

volume
The relative intensity of the voice.

The word *volume* refers to the relative intensity of the voice. (The word *loudness* refers to the hearer's perception of that relative intensity.) In an adequately controlled voice, **volume** will vary according to several factors. For example, the distance between you and your listeners, the competing noise, and the emphasis you wish to give an idea will all influence your volume.

Problems with volume are easy to identify in others, though difficult to recognize in ourselves. One obvious problem is a voice that is too soft. When speech is so soft that listeners have to strain to hear, they'll soon tire of expending so much energy. On the other hand, a voice that is too loud will prove disturbing because it intrudes on listeners' psychological space; it also may communicate aggressiveness and give others the impression that you are difficult to get along with.

The most common problems are too little volume variation and variation that falls into an easily predictable pattern. If audience members can predict volume changes, they'll focus on that pattern and not on what you're saying.

Another major problem is fading away at the end of sentences. Some speakers begin sentences in an appropriate volume but end them at an extremely low volume. Be careful to avoid this tendency; when finishing sentences, make sure the audience is able to hear you at an appropriate volume.

Rate

rate
The speed at which you speak, generally measured in words per minute.

Your speech **rate** is the speed at which you speak. About 150 words per minute seems to be the average for speaking as well as for reading aloud. The problems with rate are speaking too fast or too slow, speaking with too little variation, or speaking with too predictable a pattern. If you talk too fast, you deprive your listeners of time they need

to understand and digest what you're saying; they may simply decide not to spend the energy needed to understand your speech. If your rate is too slow, your listeners' attention may wander to matters unrelated to your speech. Speak at a pace that engages the listeners and allows them time for reflection without boring them.

Use variations in rate to call attention to certain points and to add variety. For example, if you speak of the dull routine of an assembly line worker at a rapid and varied pace or of the wonder of a circus with no variation in rate, you're surely misusing this important vocal dimension. Again, if you're interested in and conscious of what you're saying, your rate variations should flow naturally and effectively.

Pitch

Pitch is the relative highness or lowness of your voice as perceived by your listener. More technically, pitch results from the rate at which your vocal cords vibrate. If they vibrate rapidly, listeners will perceive your voice as having a high pitch. If they vibrate slowly, they'll perceive it as having a low pitch.

pitch
The highness or lowness of the vocal tone.

Pitch changes often signal changes in the meanings of many sentences. The most obvious is the difference between a statement and a question. Thus, the difference between the declarative sentence "So this is the proposal you want me to support" and the question "So this is the proposal you want me to support?" is inflection or pitch. This, of course, is obvious. But note that depending on where the inflectional change is placed, the meaning of the sentence changes drastically. Note also that all of the following questions contain exactly the same words, but they each ask a different question when you emphasize different words:

- Is **this** the proposal you want me to support?
- Is this the proposal you want **me** to support?
- Is this the proposal you want me to **support**?

The obvious problems with pitch are levels that are too high, too low, or too patterned. Neither of the first two problems is common in speakers with otherwise normal voices, and with practice you can correct a pitch pattern that is too predictable or monotonous. As you gain speaking experience, pitch changes will come naturally from the sense of what you're saying. Because each sentence is somewhat different from every other sentence, there should be a normal variation—a variation that results not from some predetermined pattern but rather from the meanings you wish to convey to the audience.

Pauses

Pauses come in two basic types: filled and unfilled. **Filled pauses** are pauses in the stream of speech that you fill with vocalizations such as *er, um, ah, well, like, you know what I mean, like I mean,* and *you know*. Filled pauses are generally ineffective and are likely to make you appear hesitant, unprepared, and unsure of yourself.

filled pauses
Interruptions in speech that are filled with such vocalizations as *er* or *um*.

Unfilled pauses —silences interjected into the normally fluent stream of speech— can be effective in public speaking if used correctly. Here are just a few examples of places where unfilled pauses—silences of a second or two—should prove effective.

unfilled pauses
Silences of unusually long duration.

- **Pause before beginning your speech.** Don't start your speech as soon as you get to the front of the room; instead, position yourself so you feel comfortable. Then scan the audience and begin your speech.
- **Pause at transitional points.** These pauses will help you signal that you're moving from one part of the speech to another or from one idea to another.
- **Pause at the end of an important assertion.** This will give the audience time to think about the significance of what you're saying.

- **Pause after asking a rhetorical question.** This will give your listeners time to think about how they'd answer the question.
- **Pause before an important idea.** This will help signal that what comes next is especially significant.
- **Pause before asking for questions.** If there's a question period following your speech and you're in charge of it, pause after you've completed your conclusion and ask audience members if they have any questions.
- **Pause after the last sentence of your conclusion.** Continue to maintain eye contact with the audience, and then walk, do not run, back to your seat. Once you are back in your seat, focus on the class activity taking place.

Articulation

articulation

The movements of the speech organs as they modify and interrupt the air stream from the lungs, forming sounds.

Articulation consists of the movements the speech organs make as they modify and interrupt the air stream you send from the lungs. Different movements of these speech organs (for example, the tongue, lips, teeth, palate, and vocal cords) produce different sounds. Our concern here is to identify the major problems in articulation.

The three major articulation problems are omission, substitution, and addition of sounds or syllables. These problems occur both in native speakers of English and in speakers whose first language is not English. Fortunately, they can be easily corrected with informed practice.

ERRORS OF OMISSION

Omitting sounds or even syllables is a major articulation problem—but one easily overcome with concentration and practice. Here are some examples.

Not This	This
gov-a-ment	gov-ern-ment
hi-stry	hi-story
wanna	want to
studyin	studying
a-lum-num	a-lum-i-num
comp-ny	comp-a-ny

ERRORS OF SUBSTITUTION

Substituting an incorrect sound for the correct one is another easily corrected problem. Among the most common errors are substituting *d* for *t* and *d* for *th*.

Not This	This
wader	waiter
dese	these
ax	ask
undoubtebly	undoubtedly
beder	better
ekcetera	etcetera

ERRORS OF ADDITION

When there are errors of addition, sounds are added where they don't belong. Some examples include:

Not This	This
acrost	across
athalete	athlete
Americer	America
idear	idea
filim	film
lore	law

JOURNAL 8.4 PUBLIC SPEAKING CHOICE POINT

Mispronunciation

In giving his speech Michael realizes that he mispronounced a key word twice and saw that some members of the audience noticed the mistake. *What are some of Michael's options for dealing with this?*

If you make any of these errors, you can easily correct them. First, become conscious of your own articulation patterns (and of any specific errors you may be making). Then listen carefully to the articulation of prominent speakers (for example, broadcasters), comparing their speech patterns with your own. Practice the correct patterns until they become part of your normal speech behavior.

Pronunciation

Pronunciation is the production of syllables or words according to some accepted standard, as identified in any good dictionary. Among the most widespread pronunciation problems are putting the accent (stress or emphasis) on the wrong syllable and pronouncing sounds that should remain silent. Both of these pronunciation problems may result from learning English as a second language. For example, a person may use the accent system of his or her first language to pronounce words in English that may have a different accent system. Similarly, in many languages, all letters that appear in a word are pronounced in speech, whereas in English some letters are silent.

pronunciation
The production of syllables or words according to some accepted standard as presented, for example, in a dictionary.

ERRORS OF ACCENT
Here are some common examples of words accented incorrectly.

Not This	This
New Orleáns	New Órleans
ínsurance	insúrance
orátor	órator

ERRORS OF PRONOUNCING SILENT SOUNDS
For some words correct pronunciation means not articulating certain sounds, as in the following examples.

Not This	This
often	offen
homage	omage
Illinois	Illinoi
even-ing	eve-ning

Here are additional words that are often mispronounced: abdomen, accessory, arctic, buffet, cavalry, clothes, costume, diagnosis, especially, espresso, February, foliage, forehead, forte, herb, hierarchy, library, nausea, nuclear, probably, prostate, realtor, relevant, repeat, salmon, sandwich, similar, strength, substantive, and xenophobia.

The best way to deal with pronunciation problems is to look up any term you're not sure of in an audio dictionary. Make it a practice to look up words you hear others use that seem to be pronounced incorrectly as well as those words that you wish to use yourself but are not sure how to pronounce.

Effective Bodily Action

8.5 Explain the characteristics of effective bodily action.

You speak with your body as well as with your mouth. The total effect of the speech depends not only on what you say but also on the way you present it. It depends on your movements, gestures, and facial expressions as well as on your words. Here we'll consider some of the most essential aspects of bodily action: general appearance, eye contact, facial expression, posture, gestures, movement, proxemics, the use of notes, and handling questions.

General Appearance

Public speaking is usually a more formal type of communication than most others, so you need to give some attention to your general appearance.

First, discover what the accepted and appropriate attire for the occasion is. For your classroom speeches, you'll probably be fine if you dress as you might for a conference with the dean or chair of your department. That is, try to dress perhaps one level above your everyday attire.

Second, dress comfortably but not too casually. Comfortable clothing will make you feel more at ease and will help you to be yourself. If you're in doubt as to how casual you should be, err on the side of formality; wear the tie, nice shoes, or dress.

Third, avoid excess in just about anything you can think of. Too much jewelry or especially wild colors are likely to call attention to your manner of dress instead of to what you're saying.

Eye Contact

The most important single aspect of bodily communication is eye contact. The two major problems with eye contact are inappropriate eye contact and eye contact that does not cover the audience fairly. In much of the United States, listeners perceive speakers who don't maintain enough eye contact as distant, unconcerned, and less trustworthy than speakers who look directly at their audience. Consequently, it's generally best to maintain relatively focused eye contact with your audience. Use your eyes to communicate your concern for and interest in what you're saying and to convey your confidence and commitment. Avoid staring blankly through audience members or glancing over their heads, at the floor, or out the window. Also, be careful when using slides or any presentation aid that you continue to maintain eye contact with the audience. In other cultures—for example, in many Asian cultures—focused eye contact may prove embarrassing to audience members, so in such cultures, it's often best to scan the audience without locking eyes with specific listeners.

Involve all listeners in the public speaking transaction. Communicate equally with the members on the left and on the right, in both the back and the front. Eye contact will also enable you to secure audience feedback—to see if your listeners are interested or bored or puzzled. Use eye contact to gauge listeners' levels of agreement and disagreement.

Facial Expression

Facial expressions are especially important in communicating emotions—anger and fear, boredom and excitement, doubt and surprise. If you feel committed to and believe in your thesis, you'll probably display your meanings appropriately and effectively.

Nervousness and anxiety, however, may at times prevent you from relaxing enough so that your emotions come through. Fortunately, time and practice will allow you to relax, and the emotions you feel will reveal themselves appropriately and automatically.

Generally, members of one culture will be able to recognize the emotions displayed facially by members of other cultures. But there are differences in what each culture considers appropriate to display in public. Each culture has its own "display rules" (Ekman, Friesen, & Ellsworth, 1972). For example, Japanese–Americans watching a stress-inducing film spontaneously displayed the same facial emotions as did other Americans when they thought they were unobserved. But when an observer was present, the Japanese–Americans masked (tried to hide) their emotional expressions more than did the other Americans (Gudykunst & Kim, 1992).

Posture

When delivering your speech, stand straight but not stiff. Try to communicate a command of the situation without communicating the discomfort that is actually quite common for beginning speakers.

Avoid the common mistakes of posture: Avoid putting your hands in your pockets or clasping them in front of or behind your back, and avoid leaning on the desk, the lectern, or the whiteboard. With practice you'll come to feel more at ease and will communicate this by the way you stand before the audience.

Gestures

Gestures in public speaking help illustrate your verbal messages. We gesture for this purpose regularly in conversation. For example, when saying "Come here," you probably move your head, hands, arms, and perhaps your entire body to motion the listener in your direction. Your body, as well as your verbal message, says "Come here."

Avoid using your hands to preen, however. For example, avoid fixing your hair or adjusting your clothing; don't fidget with your watch, ring, or jewelry. Effective bodily action is spontaneous and natural to you as the speaker, to your audience, and to your speech. If gestures seem planned or rehearsed, they'll appear phony and insincere. As a general rule, don't do anything with your hands that doesn't feel right for you; the audience will recognize it as unnatural. If you feel relaxed and comfortable with yourself and your audience, you'll generate natural bodily action without conscious or studied attention.

Movement

In public speaking, movement can often be of help. Movement keeps both you and the audience more alert. Even when speaking behind a lectern, you can give the illusion of movement. You can step back or forward or flex your upper body so it appears that you're moving more than you are.

If you're using a lectern, you may wish to signal transitions by stepping to the side or in front of it and then behind it again as you move from one point to another. You may wish to lean over the lectern when, say, posing a question to your listeners or advancing a particularly important argument. But never lean on the lectern; never use it as support.

Avoid the three problems of movement: too little, too much, and too patterned. Speakers who move too little often appear strapped to the podium, afraid of the audience, or too uncommitted to involve themselves fully. With too much movement the audience begins to concentrate on the movement itself, wondering where the speaker will wind up next. With movement that is too patterned, the audience may become bored—too steady and predictable a rhythm quickly becomes tiring. The audience will often view the speaker as nonspontaneous and uninvolved.

Use whole-body movements to emphasize transitions and to emphasize the introduction of a new and important assumption, bit of evidence, or closely reasoned argument. Thus, when making a transition, you might take a step forward to signal that something new is coming. Use whole-body movements (as well as hand gestures and eye movements) when referring to your presentation aids.

Approaching the Lectern

Perhaps the first movement of the speaker that the audience sees is walking to the lectern, podium, or front of the room. *What mistakes do you see some speakers make? What makes for an effective entrance?*

proxemics

The study of the communicative function of space; the study of how people unconsciously structure their space—the distance between people in their interactions, the organization of space in homes and offices, and even the design of cities.

Proxemics

Proxemics, or the way you use space in communication, can be a crucial factor in public speaking. Consider the spaces between you and your listeners and among the listeners themselves. If you stand too close to your listeners, they may feel uncomfortable, as if their personal space is being violated. If you stand too far away from your audience, you may be perceived as uninvolved, uninterested, or uncomfortable.

Recognize too that there are often cultural differences in the expectations of where a speaker should stand. One useful rule to follow is to watch where your instructors and other speakers stand and adjust your own position accordingly. At the same time, keep your eyes on audience members for signs that you are standing too far away (perhaps you'll see them leaning toward you or with puzzled looks) or too close (they may literally lean back in their chairs). If you do notice such signs, just adjust your distance gradually without calling attention to the fact that you're changing the distance.

Using Notes

For some speeches it may be helpful for you to use notes—for example, an abbreviated outline on one piece of paper or on one or a few index cards. To make the most effective use of such notes, keep in mind the following guidelines.

- **Keep your notes to a minimum.** The fewer notes you take with you, the better off you'll be. One reason so many speakers bring notes with them is that they want to avoid the face-to-face interaction required. With experience, however, you should find this face-to-face interaction the best part of the public speaking experience.

- **Resist the temptation to bring the entire speech outline with you.** You may rely on it too heavily and lose direct contact with the audience. Bring with you as much information as you absolutely need but never so much that it will interfere with your direct contact with the audience.

- **Use your notes with "open subtlety."** Don't make your notes more obvious than necessary. Don't gesture with your notes and thus make them more obvious than they need be. At the same time, don't try to hide them. Use them openly and honestly but gracefully, with "open subtlety." To do this effectively, you'll have to know your notes intimately. Rehearse at least twice with the same notes that you'll take with you to the speaker's stand.

■ **Don't allow your notes to prevent directness.** When using your notes, pause to look at them. Then regain eye contact with the audience and continue your speech. Don't read from your notes; just take cues from them. The one exception to this is an extensive quotation or complex set of statistics that you have to read; read it and then, almost immediately, resume direct eye contact with the audience.

ETHICAL CHOICE POINT
To Correct an Error or Not?

During a speech on HIV infection, you mention that the rate of HIV infection in women has increased by 10 percent over the past several years. You meant to say that the rate had decreased, but—probably because of nervousness—you said exactly the opposite of what you intended. Even though no one asks you about this during the question-and-answer session following your speech, you wonder if you should correct yourself. The problem, you feel, is that if you do correct yourself, the audience may question your entire speech, and this could undercut a message that you feel very strongly about. *What are your ethical choices for presenting information accurately but also being persuasive in a cause you believe in deeply?*

Handling Questions

In many public speaking situations, a question-and-answer period will follow the speech, so be prepared to answer questions. Generally, a question-and-answer session is helpful because the ensuing dialogue gives the speaker an opportunity to talk more about something he or she is interested in. In some cases, too, there seems an ethical obligation for the speaker to entertain questions; after all, if audience members sat through what the speaker wanted to say, the speaker should listen to what they want to say.

In most public speaking situations, the question-and-answer session focuses on the message of the speaker. In the public speaking classroom, the question-and-answer session may focus, in whole or in part, on the speech preparation, the effectiveness of organization, the style of language and delivery, or the sufficiency of the evidence. In either case, here are 10 suggestions for making this Q&A session more effective.

1. **Anticipate questions.** Anticipate questions you're likely to be asked and prepare answers to them as you're preparing your speech.
2. **Encourage questions.** If you wish to encourage questions, preface the question period with some kind of encouraging statement; for example, "I know you have lots of questions—especially on how the new health program will work and how we'll finance it. I'll be happy to respond to your questions. Anyone?"
3. **Maintain eye contact with the audience.** Let audience members know that you're still speaking with them.
4. **Ask for clarification and repeat if necessary.** After you hear a question, pause to think about the question and about your answer. If you're not sure what the question is asking you, seek clarification. There's no sense answering a question that wasn't asked. If you suspect that some members of the audience didn't hear the question, repeat it; then begin your answer.
5. **Be discerning.** You don't have to answer every question just because you're asked. If a question is too personal or you just don't want to get into that area, avoid responding by saying something like "I'd like to stick to the matter at hand" or "That's a great question, but I really don't think this is the place to discuss that."

6. **Control defensiveness.** Don't assume that a question is a personal attack. Assume, instead, that the question is an attempt to secure more information or perhaps to challenge a position you've taken.

7. **Show your appreciation.** If appropriate, thank the questioner or note that it's a good question. This will encourage others also to ask questions. This can be overdone, so be sure to avoid making this an automatic preface to each answer.

8. **Don't bluff.** If you're asked a question and you don't know the answer, say so. If appropriate, note that you'll try to find the answer and get back to the questioner.

9. **Reinforce your main ideas.** Consider the usefulness of a persuasive answer. Q&A sessions often give you opportunities to further advance your purpose by connecting the question and its answer with one or more of your major points: "I'm glad you asked about child care because that's exactly the difference between the two proposals we're here to vote on. The plan I'm proposing..."

10. **Don't allow one person to dominate the Q&A session.** Avoid getting into a debate with one person and neglecting your larger audience. Often there is an unstated rule that each questioner may also ask one follow-up question. If that is in effect, you'll want to follow it. Just be careful that this doesn't become a private dialogue.

JOURNAL 8.5 PUBLIC SPEAKING CHOICE POINT

Audience Questions

After giving what you thought was a most provocative speech, no one in the audience asks a question—as they have of the other speakers. *What are some of the things you might do to encourage questions?*

SUMMARY: WORD, REHEARSE, AND PRESENT YOUR SPEECH (STEPS 8, 9, AND 10)

In this chapter we looked at how language works and at how you can use language to better achieve your public speaking goals. We also looked at some guidelines for effective rehearsal, the varied methods of presentation, and effective vocal and body delivery.

Word Your Speech (Step 8)

8.1 Define *clarity, vividness, appropriateness, personal style,* and *cultural sensitivity* and some of the guidelines for achieving these qualities in public speaking and achieving sentences of maximum effectiveness.

1. Clarity: Be economical; use specific terms and numbers; use short, familiar terms; carefully assess idioms; and vary the level of abstraction.

2. Vividness: Use active verbs, use imagery, and use figures of speech.

3. Appropriateness: Speak on the appropriate level of formality; avoid written-style expressions; and avoid slang and vulgar terms.

4. Personal style: Use personal pronouns, direct questions to the audience, and create immediacy.

5. Use powerful sentences, avoiding hesitations, too many intensifiers, disqualifiers, self-critical statements, and slang.

6. Construct sentences that are short rather than long, direct rather than indirect, active rather than passive, and positive rather than negative.

Rehearse Your Speech (Step 9)

8.2 Explain the suggestions for effective and efficient speech rehearsal.

7. Follow these rehearsal guidelines: Rehearse the speech as a whole, time the speech, approximate the actual speech situation as best you can, incorporate changes and delivery notes, and rehearse often.

8. In addition, consider undertaking a long-term delivery program.

Present Your Speech (Step 10)

8.3 Identify the methods of presentation and the suggestions for using these methods effectively.

9. Effective public speaking presentation is comfortable and consistent, maintains interest, and contributes to the overall effect of the speech.

10. Impromptu: speaking without preparation; useful in certain aspects of public speaking.

11. Manuscript: reading from a written text; useful when exact timing and wording are essential.

12. Extemporaneous: speaking after thorough preparation and memorization of the main ideas; useful in most public speaking situations.

Effective Vocal Delivery

8.4 Explain the characteristics of effective vocal delivery in public speaking.

13. Volume: Avoid speech that is overly soft, loud, or unvaried, and be sure not to fade away at ends of sentences.

14. Rate: Avoid speaking too fast, too slowly, with too little variation, or in too predictable a pattern.

15. Pitch: Avoid a pitch that is overly high, low, or monotonous or that falls into too predictable a pattern.

16. Pauses: Use pauses to signal transitions between parts of the speech, give the audience time to think, allow listeners to ponder rhetorical questions, and signal the approach of especially important ideas.

17. Articulation: Errors of articulation include omission, substitution, and addition.

18. Pronunciation: Errors of pronunciation include using the wrong accent and pronouncing silent sounds.

Effective Bodily Action

8.5 Explain the characteristics of effective bodily action.

19. Present an appropriate general appearance.

20. Maintain eye contact.

21. Allow facial expressions to convey thoughts and feelings.

22. Use posture to communicate command of the speech experience.

23. Dress comfortably and at an appropriate level of formality.

24. Gesture naturally.

25. Move around a bit.

26. Position yourself neither too close to nor too far from the audience.

27. Use a few notes, but use them with "open subtlety" so they don't prevent your maintaining direct contact with your audience.

28. Treat the question-and-answer session as an extension of your speech, following the same general principles of effectiveness you followed in preparing and presenting your speech.

KEY TERMS: WORD, REHEARSE, AND PRESENT YOUR SPEECH (STEPS 8, 9, AND 10)

alliteration
antithesis
articulation
cultural sensitivity
clarity
extemporaneous speech
figure of speech
filled pauses
hyperbole
idioms
immediacy

impromptu speech
inclusive language
irony
manuscript speech
memorized speech
metaphor
metonymy
oral style
oxymoron
personification
pitch

pronunciation
proxemics
rate
rhetorical question
simile
stereotyping
synecdoche
unfilled pauses
volume

PUBLIC SPEAKING EXERCISES

8.1 Distinguish Between Commonly Confused Words

Using the wrong term is likely to divert audience attention from your main ideas and perhaps damage your credibility. When in doubt, check it out. Many words, because they sound alike or are used in similar situations, are commonly confused. Underline the word in parentheses that you would use in each sentence.

a. He (accepted, excepted) the award and thanked everyone (accept, except) the producer.

b. The professor (affected, effected) her students greatly and will now (affect, effect) a complete curriculum overhaul.

c. Are you deciding (between, among) red and green or (between, among) red, green, and blue?

d. I (can, may) scale the mountain but I (can, may) not reveal its hidden path.

e. The table was (cheap, inexpensive) but has great style whereas the chairs cost a fortune but look (cheap, inexpensive).

f. The explorer's dream was to (discover, invent) uncharted lands but also to (discover, invent) computer programs.

g. She was (explicit, implicit) in her detailed description of the crime but made only (explicit, implicit) observations concerning the perpetrator.

h. He was evasive and only (implied, inferred) that he'd seek a divorce. You can easily (imply, infer) his reasons.

i. The wedding was (tasteful, tasty) and the food really (tasteful, tasty).

j. The student seemed (disinterested, uninterested) in the test while, in assigning grades, the teacher was always (disinterested, uninterested).

Here are the principles that govern correct usage: (1) Use *accept* to mean "to receive" and *except* to mean "with the exclusion of." (2) Use to *affect* to mean "to have an effect or to influence" and to *effect* to mean "to produce a result." (3) Use *between* when referring to two items and *among* when referring to more than two items. (4) Use *can* to refer to ability and *may* to refer to permission. (5) Use *cheap* to refer to something that is inferior and *inexpensive* to describe something that costs little. (6) Use *discover* to refer to the act of finding something out or learning something previously unknown, and use *invent* to refer to the act of originating something new. (7) Use *explicit* to mean "specific" and *implicit* to describe something that's indicated but not openly stated. (8) Use to *imply* to mean "to state indirectly" and to *infer* to mean "to draw a conclusion." (9) Use *tasteful* to refer to good taste and *tasty* to refer to something that tastes good. (10) Use *uninterested* to refer to a lack of interest, and use *disinterested* to mean "objective or unbiased."

8.2 Giving Life to Your Sentences

Here are some rather bland sentences. Improve each of them by making them clearer, more vivid, more appropriate, and more personal.

1. The teacher was discussing politics.
2. The player scored.
3. Only three of the previously mentioned people agreed.
4. The children each received presents.
5. I read the review of the movie.
6. The couple rented a great car.
7. The detective wasn't much help.
8. The animal approached the baby.
9. He walked up the steep hill.
10. They played games.
11. The cat climbed the fence.
12. The house is in the valley.

INFORMING YOUR AUDIENCE

The principles of informative speaking will prove useful in just about all your messages.

CHAPTER TOPICS

Principles of Informative Speaking

Speeches of Description

Speeches of Definition

Speeches of Demonstration

LEARNING OBJECTIVES

9.1 Identify the principles of informative speaking.

9.2 Define the speech of description.

9.3 Define the speech of definition.

9.4 Define the speech of demonstration.

One of the important types of speeches you'll be called upon to deliver is the informative speech, the subject of this chapter. We'll first look at some key principles for communicating information, and then we'll examine the varied types of informative speeches and see how you can develop each type most effectively.

Principles of Informative Speaking

9.1 Identify the principles of informative speaking.

To communicate information is to tell your listeners something they don't know, something new. Recall the characteristics of a good topic:

- substantive (deals with matters of substance)
- appropriate (to you as the speaker and also to the audience and the occasion)
- culturally sensitive (recognizing the cultural norms present in most diverse audiences)

In **informative speaking** you may inform your audience about a new way of looking at old things or an old way of looking at new things. You may discuss a theory not previously heard of or a familiar concept not fully understood. You may talk about events that the audience may be unaware of or explain happenings they may have misconceptions about. Regardless of what type of informative speech you intend to give, the following guidelines should help.

informative speaking
Speaking to convey information, something that is not already known.

Focus on Your Audience

Your audience will—to some extent—influence the information you'll present and how you'll present it. Consequently, it's wise to look to your audience as a first principle. So, let's say you want to give an informative speech on Microsoft's new edition of Windows. This will provide a good illustration of how the same topic can be pursued with different goals in mind.

- To an audience of dedicated Mac users, the information may be entirely new, so your goal will be to introduce a topic unknown to the audience.
- To an audience of dedicated Mac users who think there's little or no difference between the systems, you'll be clarifying misconceptions.
- To an audience of students using a previous version of Windows, you may wish to demonstrate how this new operating system is different. For example, you might explain the ways in which the new version is superior to the current version.

As you can appreciate, each of these speeches would have to be somewhat different depending on the knowledge and experience of the audiences.

Stress Relevance and Usefulness

Listeners remember information best when they see it as relevant and useful to their own needs or goals. Notice that as a listener you regularly demonstrate this principle of relevance and usefulness. For example, in class you may attend to and remember the stages in the development of language in children simply because you'll be tested on the information and you want to earn a high grade. Or you may remember a given piece of information because it will help you make a better impression in your job interview, make you a better parent, or enable you to deal with relationship problems. Like you, listeners attend to information that will prove useful to them.

If you want the audience to listen to your speech, relate your information to its members' needs, wants, or goals. Throughout your speech, but especially in the beginning, make sure your listeners know that the information you're presenting is or will be relevant and useful to them now or in the immediate future. For example, you might say something like:

> We all want financial security. We all want to be able to buy those luxuries we read so much about in magazines and see every evening on television. Wouldn't it be nice to be able to buy a car without worrying about where you're going to get the down payment or how you'll be able to make the monthly payments? Actually, that is not an unrealistic goal, as I'll demonstrate in this speech. In fact, I'll show you several investment strategies that have enabled many people to increase their income by as much as 20 percent.

Limit the Amount of Information

There's a limit to the amount of information that a listener can take in at one time. Resist the temptation to overload your listeners with information. Instead of enlarging the breadth of information you communicate, expand its depth. It's better to present two new items of information and explain these in depth with examples, illustrations, and descriptions than to present five items without this needed amplification. The speaker who attempts to discuss the physiological, psychological, social, and linguistic differences between men and women, for example, is clearly trying to cover too much and is going to be forced to cover these areas only superficially, with the result that little new information will be communicated. Even covering one of these areas completely is likely to prove difficult. Instead, select one subdivision of one area—say, language development or differences in language problems—and develop that in depth.

Adjust the Level of Complexity

As you know from attending college classes, information can be presented in very simple or very complex form. Adjusting the level of complexity on which you communicate your information is crucial. This adjustment should depend on the wide variety of factors considered throughout this book, for example, the level of knowledge your audience has, the time you have available, the purpose you hope to achieve, or the topic on which you're speaking. If you simplify a topic too much, you risk boring or, even worse, insulting your audience. On the other hand, if your talk is too complex, you risk confusing your audience and failing to communicate your message.

Generally, beginning speakers err by being too complex and not realizing that a 5- or 10-minute speech isn't long enough to make an audience understand sophisticated concepts or complicated processes. At least in your beginning speeches, try to keep it simple rather than complex. Make sure the words you use are familiar to your audience; alternatively, explain and define any unfamiliar terms as you use them. For example, remember that jargon and technical vocabulary familiar to a sound engineer may not be familiar to the person who listens to music for pleasure on Spotify. Always see your topic from the point of view of audience members; ask yourself how much they know about your topic and its particular terminology.

Relate New Information to Old

Listeners will learn information more easily and retain it longer when you relate it to what they already know. So relate the new to the old, the unfamiliar to the familiar, the unseen to the seen, the untasted to the tasted. Here, for example, Betsy Heffernan, a student from the University of Wisconsin (Reynolds & Schnoor, 1991), relates the problem of sewage to a familiar historical event.

During our nation's struggle for independence, the citizens of Boston were hailed as heroes for dumping tea into Boston Harbor. But not to be outdone, many modern day Bostonians are also dumping things into the harbor: five thousand gallons of human waste every second. The New England Aquarium of Boston states that since 1900, Bostonians have dumped enough human sewage into the harbor to cover the entire state of Massachusetts chest deep in sludge. Unfortunately, Boston isn't alone. All over the country, bays, rivers, and lakes are literally becoming cesspools.

Vary the Levels of Abstraction

You can talk about freedom of the press in the abstract by talking about the importance of getting information to the public, by referring to the Bill of Rights, and by relating a free press to the preservation of democracy. But you can also talk about freedom of the press on a low level of abstraction, a level that is specific and concrete; for example, you can describe how a local newspaper was prevented from running a story critical of the town council or how Lucy Rinaldo was fired from the *Accord Sentinel* after she wrote a story critical of the mayor.

Varying the **levels of abstraction**—combining high abstraction (the very general) and low abstraction (the very specific)—seems to work best. Too many generalizations without the specifics or too many specifics without the generalizations will prove less effective than the combination of abstract and specific.

Figure 9.1 presents an example of how the levels of abstraction might be varied.

levels of abstraction

The different levels of specificity ranging from the highly abstract to the very concrete.

Figure 9.1 A Sample of Varied Abstraction

Note that in the first paragraph we have a relatively abstract description of homelessness. In the second paragraph, we get into specifics. In the last paragraph, the abstract and the concrete are connected.

Here the speaker begins with relatively general or abstract statements.

Here the speaker gets to specifics—the refrigerator box, the blanket, the plastic bottles, for example.

Homelessness is a serious problem for all metropolitan areas throughout the country. It's currently estimated that there are now more than 200,000 homeless in New York City alone. But what is this really about? Let me tell you what it's about.

It's about a young man. He must be about 25 or 30, although he looks a lot older. He lives in a cardboard box on the side of my apartment house. We call him Tom, although we really don't know his name. All his possessions are stored in this huge box. I think it was a box from a refrigerator. Actually, he doesn't have very much, and what he has easily fits in this box. There's a blanket my neighbor threw out, some plastic bottles Tom puts water in, and some Styrofoam containers he picked up from the garbage from Burger King. He uses these to store whatever food he finds.

What is homelessness about? It's about Tom and 200,000 other "Toms" in New York and thousands of others throughout the rest of the country. And not all of them even have boxes to live in.

The conclusion combines the specific (Tom) with the more general (200,000 homeless people and thoughts of others throughout the country) and (again) the specific of the box.

ETHICAL CHOICE POINT

Informing or Persuading?

You want to raise money for repairs of the local children's community center and plan to give your persuasive speech on this topic. Right now, however, you have to give a speech of description, and you wonder if it would be ethical for you to give this speech of description detailing all the problems with the center. You want to be truthful, but you also want the audience to conclude that the community center needs money for repairs. You wonder if it would be unethical to deliver a speech of information that is actually persuasive in large part. *What are your ethical choices in this situation?*

Make Your Speech Easy to Remember

The principles of public speaking (principles governing use of language, delivery, and supporting materials, for example) will all help your listeners remember your speech. If you stress interest and relevance—as already noted—audience members are more likely to remember what you say because they will see it as important and relevant to their own lives. Here are a few more suggestions.

- **Repeat the points you want the audience to remember.** Help audience members to remember what you want them to remember by repeating your most important points.

- **Use signposts.** Guide your audience's attention to your most memorable points by saying, for example, "the first point to remember is that…," "the argument I want you to remember when you enter that voting booth is…."

- **Use internal summary transitions.** Internal summary transitions will remind the audience of what you have said and how it relates to what is to follow. This kind of repetition will reinforce your message and help your listeners remember your main points.

- **Pattern your messages.** If audience members can see the logic of your speech, they'll be better able to organize what you say in their own minds. If they can see that you're following a temporal pattern or a spatial pattern, for example, it will be easier for them to retain more of what you say because they'll have a framework into which they can fit what you say.

- **Focus audience attention.** The best way to focus the listeners' attention is to tell them to focus their attention. Simply say, "I want you to focus on three points that I will make in this speech. First,…" or "What I want you to remember is this:…."

JOURNAL 9.1 PUBLIC SPEAKING CHOICE POINT

Memorable Speeches

With your next speech in mind, what are some of your choices for making your speech memorable?

Now that the principles of informative speaking have been identified, let's consider the main types of informative speeches.

speeches of description
Informative speeches in which you explain an object, person, event, or process.

- **Speeches of description** are speeches in which you describe an object (the human heart) or person (a genius, artist, or Picasso) or describe an event (a hurricane) or process (adopting a child).

VIEWPOINTS
The Principles in Cooking

Watch a cooking program from start to finish. *How many of the seven principles discussed earlier in this chapter can you identify? In what ways might you use these same principles as you prepare your next speech?*

- **Speeches of definition** are speeches in which you define a term (linguistics), a system or theory (evolution), or similar and dissimilar terms (nature/nurture, communism/socialism).
- **Speeches of demonstration** are speeches in which you show how to do something (protecting yourself against identity theft) or how something works (search spiders).

speeches of definition
Informative speeches devoted to explaining the meaning of a concept.

speeches of demonstration
Informative speeches in which the speaker shows the audience how to do something or how something operates.

Speeches of Description

9.2 Define the speech of description.

In a speech of description, you're concerned with explaining an object, person, event, or process. Here are a few examples.

Describing an Object or Place

- the parts of a smartphone
- the geography of Africa
- the hierarchy of a university
- the modern hospital
- the components of a computer system

Describing a Person, Real or Generalized

- the power of Nancy Pelosi, Bill Gates, Tiger Woods, or Angela Merkel
- the significance of Benjamin Franklin, Rosa Parks, or Quentin Tarantino
- the happy and the sad
- the contributions of a philanthropist, real or ideal
- the vegan and the vegetarian

Describing an Event or Process

- the growth and decline of Occupy Wall Street
- the events leading to the war with Iraq
- organizing a bodybuilding contest
- purchasing stock online
- how a child acquires language

Thesis

The thesis of a speech, as explained in Chapter 3, is your single most important concept; it is what you most want your audience to remember. The thesis of a speech of description simply states what you'll describe in your speech. For example:

- The child acquires language in four stages.
- There are three steps to purchasing stock online.
- Four major events led to the war with Iraq.

Main Points

The main points of your speech are the major subdivisions of the thesis. You derive your main points from the thesis by asking strategic questions. For example:

- What are the four stages in child language acquisition?
- What are the three steps to purchasing stock online?
- What events led to the war with Iraq?

JOURNAL 9.2 PUBLIC SPEAKING CHOICE POINT

Describing

Juliet wants to give a speech describing Second Life, the virtual reality game she has become a passionate fan of. Some members of her audience have a fairly negative view of virtual gaming, thinking it is a waste of time or worse, but she knows that others hold positive views. Juliet wants to acknowledge her understanding of these diverse attitudes. *What are Juliet's options for introducing this topic? If you were Juliet, what would you say? How can she keep her speech informative without interjecting her own passions on the subject?*

Support

Obviously you don't want simply to list your main points but to flesh them out—to make them memorable, interesting, and, most of all, clear. You do this by using a variety of materials that amplify and support your main ideas; you include examples, illustrations, testimony, and statistics. So, in describing the babbling stage of language learning, you might give examples of babbling, the age at which babbling first appears, the period of time that babbling lasts, or the differences between the babbling of girls and boys.

Because this is a speech of description, give extra consideration to the types of description you might use in your supporting materials. Try to describe the object or event with lots of different descriptive categories. With physical categories, for example, ask yourself questions such as these: What color is it? How big is it? What is it shaped like? How much does it weigh? What is its volume? How attractive/unattractive is it? Also consider social, psychological, and economic categories. In describing a person, for example, consider such categories as friendly/unfriendly, warm/cold, rich/poor, aggressive/meek, and pleasant/unpleasant.

Consider how you might use presentation aids. In describing an object or a person, show your listeners a picture; show them the inside of a telephone, pictures of the brain, the skeleton of the body. In describing an event or process, show them a diagram or flowchart to illustrate the stages or steps; for example, the steps involved in buying stock, in publishing a newspaper, in putting a parade together.

Organization

Consider using a spatial or a topical organization when describing objects and people. Consider using a temporal pattern when describing events and processes. For example, if you were to describe the layout of Philadelphia, you might start from the north and work down to the south (using a spatial pattern). If you were to describe the achievements of Thomas Edison, you might select Edison's three or four major contributions and discuss each of these equally (using a topical pattern).

If you were describing the events leading up to Iraq War, you might use a temporal pattern, starting with the earliest and working up to the latest. A temporal pattern also would be appropriate for describing how a hurricane develops or how a parade is put together.

Consider the Who? What? Where? When? Why? pattern of organization. These journalistic categories are especially useful when you want to describe an event or a process. For example, if you're going to describe how to purchase a house, you might want to consider the people involved (who?), the steps you have to go through (what?), the places you'll have to go (where?), the time or sequence in which the steps have to take place (when?), and the advantages and disadvantages of buying the house (why?).

Here are two examples showing the bare bones of how a descriptive speech might look. In this first example, the speaker describes four suggestions for reducing energy bills. Notice that the speaker derives the main points from asking a question of the thesis.

General purpose:	To inform
Specific purpose:	To describe how you can reduce energy bills
Thesis:	Energy bills can be reduced. (How can energy bills be reduced?)

    I. Caulk window and door seams.

    II. Apply weather stripping around windows and doors.

    III. Insulate walls.

    IV. Install storm windows and doors.

In this second example, the speaker describes the way fear works in intercultural communication.

General purpose:	To inform
Specific purpose:	To describe the way fear works in intercultural communication
Thesis:	Fear influences intercultural communication. (How does fear influence intercultural communication?)

    I. We fear disapproval.

    II. We fear embarrassing ourselves.

    III. We fear being harmed.

In delivering such a speech, a speaker might begin by saying:

> Three major fears interfere with intercultural communication. First, we fear disapproval—from members of our own group as well as from members of the other person's group. Second, we fear embarrassing ourselves, even making fools of ourselves, by saying the wrong thing or appearing insensitive. And third, we may fear being harmed—our stereotypes of the other group may lead us to see its members as dangerous or potentially harmful to us.
>
> Let's look at each of these fears in more detail. We'll be able to see clearly how they influence our own intercultural communication behavior.
>
> Consider, first, the fear of disapproval.

The speaker would then amplify and support this fear of disapproval. This could be achieved by giving examples of disapproval seen in his or her own experience, the testimony of communication theorists on the importance of such fear, or research findings on the effects that such fear might have on intercultural communication.

Speeches of Definition

9.3 Define the speech of definition.

What is leadership? What is a born-again Christian? What is the difference between sociology and psychology? What is a cultural anthropologist? What is safe sex? These are all topics for informative speeches of definition.

A definition is a statement of the meaning of a term. In giving a speech of definition (as opposed to using a definition as a form of supporting material, as explained in Chapter 5), you may focus on defining a term, defining a system or theory, or pinpointing the similarities and/or differences among terms or systems. A speech of definition may be on a subject new to the audience or may present a familiar topic in a new and different way. Here are a few examples.

Defining a Term

- What is leadership?
- What is fracking?
- What is perjury?
- What is ADHD?
- What is self-esteem?
- What is diabetes?

Defining a System or Theory

- What is General Systems Theory?
- What is the classical theory of public speaking?
- Communism: its major principles

- What is virtual reality?
- What is futurism?

Defining Similar and Dissimilar Terms or Systems
- Robbery, burglary, and theft
- What do Christians and Muslims have in common?
- Facebook and Google or Google and Bing (or Yahoo!)
- Nature and nurture
- Text and online dictionaries: What's the difference?
- Oedipus and Electra: How do they differ?

Thesis

The thesis in a speech of definition is a statement identifying the term or system and your intention to define it or to contrast it with other terms; for example, "Christianity and Islam have much in common" or "There are three main differences between print and online dictionaries."

Main Points

You derive the main points for a speech of definition by asking questions of your thesis; for example, if your thesis is "Christianity and Islam have much in common," then the logical question is, What are they? What do Christianity and Islam have in common? Your answers to this question would then constitute your main points. If your thesis is that text and online dictionaries differ in three major ways, then the logical question is, What are the three ways? How do text and online dictionaries differ? Here your main points would be the ways in which these dictionaries differ.

Support

Once you have each of your main points, support them with examples, testimony, and the like. For example, one of your main points in the Christianity–Islam example may be that both religions believe in the value of good works. You might then quote from the New Testament and from the Quran to illustrate this belief, or you might give examples of noted Christians and Muslims who exemplified this characteristic, or you might cite the testimony of religious leaders who talked about the importance of good works.

JOURNAL 9.3 PUBLIC SPEAKING CHOICE POINT

Defining the Ideal Friend

Let's say you're preparing a speech of definition on the ideal friend. *What are some of the ways in which you can define the ideal friend and at the same time follow/apply the principles of informative speaking discussed earlier?*

Organization

In addition to the obvious organizational pattern of multiple definitions, consider using a topical order, in which each main idea is treated equally. In either case, however, proceed from the known to the unknown. Start with what your audience knows and

work up to what is new or unfamiliar. Let's say you want to explain the concept of phonemics (with which your audience is totally unfamiliar). The specific idea you wish to get across is that each phoneme stands for a unique sound. You might proceed from the known to the unknown and begin your definition with something like this:

> We all know that in the written language each letter of the alphabet stands for a unit of the written language. Each letter is different from every other letter. A *t* is different from a *g*, and a *g* is different from a *b*, and so on. Each letter is called a "grapheme." In English we know we have 26 such letters.
>
> We can look at the spoken language in much the same way. Each sound is different from every other sound. A *t* sound is different from a *d*, and a *d* is different from a *k,* and so on. Each individual sound is called a "phoneme."
>
> Now, let me explain in a little more detail what I mean by a "phoneme."

Here are two examples of how you might go about constructing a speech of definition. In this first example the speaker explains the parts of a résumé and follows a spatial order, going from the top to the bottom of the page.

General purpose:	To inform
Specific purpose:	To define the essential parts of a résumé
Thesis:	There are four major parts to a résumé. (What are the four major parts of a résumé?)

   I. Identify your career goals.

   II. Identify your educational background.

   III. Identify your work experience.

   IV. Identify your special competencies.

In this second example the speaker selects three major types of lying for discussion and arranges these in a topical pattern.

General purpose:	To inform
Specific purpose:	To define lying by explaining the major types of lying
Thesis:	There are three major kinds of lying. (What are the three major kinds of lying?)

   I. Concealment is the process of hiding the truth.

   II. Falsification is the process of presenting false information as if it were true.

   III. Misdirection is the process of acknowledging a feeling but misidentifying its cause.

In delivering such a speech, a speaker might begin the speech by saying:

> A lie is a lie is a lie. True? Well, not exactly. Actually, there are a number of different ways we can lie. We can lie by concealing the truth. We can lie by falsification, by presenting false information as if it were true. And we can lie by misdirection, by acknowledging a feeling but misidentifying its cause.
>
> Let's look at the first type of lie—the lie of concealment. Most lies are lies of concealment. Most of the time when we lie we simply conceal the truth. We don't actually make any false statements. Rather we simply don't reveal the truth. Let me give you some examples I overheard recently.

Speeches of Demonstration

9.4   Define the speech of demonstration.

Whether in using demonstration within a speech or in giving a speech devoted entirely to demonstration, you show the audience how to do something or how something operates. This speech is sometimes called a speech of process because the emphasis is on showing the audience how to perform some process or how some process works. Here are some examples of topics of speeches of demonstration.

Demonstrating How to Do Something

- how to insulate your house
- how to set up a blog
- how to trace your ancestry
- how to give mouth-to-mouth resuscitation
- how to drive defensively
- how to develop a budget

Demonstrating How Something Operates

- how does LinkedIn work
- how do you install Google Hangouts
- how does the liquid lens work

VIEWPOINTS

Informative Speaking on the Job

In what ways might the ability to prepare and present an effective informative speech be beneficial to you in your chosen profession?

- how the body maintains homeostasis
- how a hurricane develops
- how a heart bypass operation is performed

Thesis

The thesis for a speech of demonstration identifies what you will show the audience how to do or how something operates. For example:

- E-mail works through a series of electronic connections from one computer to a server to another computer.
- You can insulate your house in three different ways.
- Developing a budget involves following four steps.

JOURNAL 9.4 PUBLIC SPEAKING CHOICE POINT

Unexpected Happenings

Harry, a first-year culinary arts student, is the third speaker in a series of five, demonstrating how to prepare stir-fried vegetables. Unfortunately, the first speaker, a fourth-year student, presented a really excellent speech on the exact same dish. *What are some of Harry's options for dealing with this situation? If you were Harry, what would you say (if anything) in reference to the earlier speaker?*

Main Points

You can then derive your main points by asking a simple how or what question of your thesis:

- How do these electronic connections work?
- What are the ways of insulating a house?
- What are the steps to developing a budget?

In the first example, your main points would be the ways in which the electronic connections work. In the second, they would be the ways you can insulate. And, in the third example, your main points would be the steps you should follow in developing a budget.

Support

You then support each of your main ideas with a variety of materials. For example, you might show diagrams of houses that use different burglarproofing methods, demonstrate how various locks work, or show how different security systems work.

Presentation aids are especially helpful in speeches of demonstration. Good examples of visual aids are the signs in restaurants demonstrating the Heimlich maneuver. These signs demonstrate the sequence of steps with pictures as well as words. The combination of verbal and graphic information makes it easy to understand this important process. In a speech on the Heimlich maneuver, however, it might be best to use only the pictures so the written words would not distract your audience from your oral explanation.

Organization

In most cases a temporal pattern will work best in speeches of demonstration. Demonstrate each step in the sequence in which it's to be performed. In this way, you'll avoid one of the major difficulties in demonstrating a process—backtracking. Don't skip steps, even if you think they're familiar to the audience. They may not be. Connect each step to the next with appropriate transitions. For example, in explaining the Heimlich maneuver, you might say:

> Now that you have your arms around the choking victim's chest, your next step is to...

Assist your listeners by labeling the steps clearly; for example, "the first step," "the second step," and so on.

It's often helpful when demonstrating to give a broad general picture and then present each step in turn. For example, suppose you were talking about how to prepare a wall for painting. You might begin with a general overview to give your listeners a general idea of the process, saying something like this:

> In preparing the wall for painting, you want to make sure that the wall is smoothly sanded, free of dust, and dry. Sanding a wall isn't like sanding a block of wood. So let's look at the proper way to sand a wall.

Here are two examples of the speech of demonstration. In this first example, the speaker explains the proper way to paint a wall by rag rolling. As you can see, the speaker uses a temporal organizational pattern and covers three stages in the order in which they would be performed.

General purpose: To inform

Specific purpose: To demonstrate how to rag roll

Thesis: Rag rolling is performed in three steps. (What are the three steps of rag rolling?)

    I. Apply the base coat of paint.

    II. Apply the glaze coat.

    III. Roll a rag through the wet glaze.

In the next example, the speaker identifies and demonstrates how to listen actively.

General purpose: To inform

Specific purpose: To demonstrate three techniques of active listening

Thesis: We can become active listeners. (How can we become active listeners?)

    I. Paraphrase the speaker's meaning.

    II. Express understanding of the speaker's feelings.

    III. Ask questions.

In delivering the speech, the speaker might begin by saying:

> Active listening is a special kind of listening. It's listening with total involvement, with a concern for the speaker. It's probably the most important type of listening you can engage in. Active listening consists of three steps: paraphrasing the speaker's meaning, expressing understanding of the speaker's feelings, and asking questions.
>
> Your first step in active listening is to paraphrase the speaker's meaning. What is a paraphrase? A paraphrase is a restatement in your own words of the speaker's meaning. That is, you express in your own words what you think the speaker meant. For example, let's say that the speaker said....

SUMMARY: INFORMING YOUR AUDIENCE

This chapter considered the informative speech, first surveying some general principles and then examining three main types of informative speaking (speeches of description, definition, and demonstration).

Principles of Informative Speaking

9.1 Identify the principles of informative speaking.

1. Among the principles of communicating information are:
   - Focus on your audience.
   - Stress the relevance and the usefulness of the information to your audience.
   - Limit the amount of information you communicate.
   - Adjust the level of complexity.
   - Relate new information to old.
   - Vary the levels of abstraction.
   - Make your speech easy to remember.

Speeches of Description

9.2 Define the speech of description.

2. Speeches of description examine a process or procedure, an event, an object, or a person.

Speeches of Definition

9.3 Define the speech of definition.

3. Speeches of definition define a term, system, or theory or similarities and/or differences among terms.

Speeches of Demonstration

9.4 Define the speech of demonstration.

4. Speeches of demonstration show how to do something or how something operates.

KEY TERMS: INFORMING YOUR AUDIENCE

informative speaking
levels of abstraction
speeches of definition

speeches of demonstration
speeches of description

PUBLIC SPEAKING EXERCISES

9.1 Defining Terms

Speeches of Definition

Select one of the following terms and define it, using at least three of the different types of definition considered in Chapter 5 (etymology, authority, negation, specific examples, or direct symbolism): communication, love, conflict, leadership, audience. You'll find it helpful to visit a few online dictionaries or thesauruses.

9.2 A 2-Minute Informative Speech

Prepare and deliver a 2-minute informative speech in which you do one of the following:

- Explain a card game: Explain the way a card game such as solitaire, poker, gin rummy, bridge, canasta, or pinochle is played.

- Explain a board game: Explain the way a board game such as chess, backgammon, Chinese checkers, Go, Othello, Scrabble, Yahtzee, or Monopoly is played.

- Explain food preparation: Explain how to make a pie, a soup, a western omelet, a pizza, roast beef, a dip, or a casserole (any kind you'd like).

- Explain a sport: Explain the way a sport such as football, baseball, basketball, hockey, soccer, tennis, or golf is played.

PERSUADING YOUR AUDIENCE

→ Most public speeches are persuasive in intent.

CHAPTER TOPICS

Principles of Persuasive Speaking

The Three Persuasive Proofs

Persuasive Speeches of Fact, Value, and Policy

LEARNING OBJECTIVES

10.1 Paraphrase the principles of persuasive speaking.

10.2 Explain the three persuasive proofs (logical, emotional, and credibility).

10.3 Explain the nature of speeches of fact, value, and policy and the guidelines for preparing such speeches.

The previous chapter focused on informative speaking; it examined the essential principles for communicating information and the varied types of informative speeches. This chapter looks at persuasive speaking, specifically the essential principles of persuasion, the three types of proof, and the types of persuasive speeches you might give. Table 10.1 identifies some of the major differences between speeches that aim primarily to inform and speeches that aim primarily to persuade and provides a useful transition between these two chapters.

Principles of Persuasive Speaking

10.1 Paraphrase the principles of persuasive speaking.

You can become more successful in strengthening or changing attitudes or beliefs and in moving your listeners to action by following these guidelines for persuasive speaking. Some of these can be explained very simply in two or three paragraphs; others are more complex and need more elaboration. All, however, will help you become a more persuasive public speaker.

Keep Your Goal Always in Mind

Persuasion refers to the process of influencing another person's attitudes, beliefs, values, and/or behaviors. In your persuasive speeches, you may want to accomplish any one of the following two general goals.

- **To change attitudes, beliefs, or values.** Change might involve strengthening existing attitudes and beliefs as many religious sermons and public service announcements often do. Or you may want to change what the audience thinks or believes about, for example, the Middle East, same-sex marriage, proper diet, or a political candidate.
- **To motivate to action.** Ultimately, your goal is to get people to do something—for example, to vote for one person rather than another, to donate money to a fund for the homeless, or to take a course in criminology.

It's useful to think of influence as occurring on a *persuasion continuum* ranging from one extreme to another. Let's say that you want to give a persuasive speech on guns on campus. You might visualize your audience as existing on a continuum ranging from strongly in favor to strongly opposed, as shown in Figure 10.1. Your task is to move your audience in the direction of your persuasive purpose. You can

TABLE 10.1   Differences between Informative and Persuasive Speeches

Element of Speech	Informative Speeches (e.g., classroom lectures, demonstrations of how things work)	Persuasive Speeches (e.g., political speeches, religious sermons)
Topic/subject	Significant but generally noncontroversial	Significant and controversial or debatable
Purpose	To communicate new information to listeners	To change the attitudes, beliefs, or behaviors of listeners
Thesis	States the central idea of the speech	States the debatable position to be argued
Support	Primarily examples, definitions, numerical data, and presentation aids	In addition to informative support, relies heavily on logical, emotional, and credibility support

Figure 10.1 The Persuasion Continuum

center your message on strengthening, weakening, or changing your listeners' attitudes, beliefs, or values about guns on campus; or you can center your message on moving the listeners to act—to protest, write letters, or sign a petition. If your purpose is to persuade the audience to oppose guns on campus, then in Figure 10.1, any movement toward the right will be successful persuasion; if your purpose is to persuade listeners to support guns on campus, then any movement toward the left will be successful persuasion. Realize, however, that it's possible to give a speech in which you hope to move listeners in one direction but actually move them in the opposite direction. This "negative persuasion" can occur, for example, when the audience perceives the speaker as dishonest or self-promoting or ill-informed. *Have you ever witnessed negative persuasion?*

Be Culturally Sensitive

Cultural differences are especially important in persuasion; the appeals you'd use to influence one cultural group would not be the same you'd use for a different group. You can appreciate the importance of this by looking at seven dimensions of culture with persuasive strategies in mind:

Individualist cultures, collectivist cultures, high-power-distance cultures, low-power-distance cultures, high-ambiguity-tolerant cultures, low-ambiguity-tolerant cultures, masculine cultures, feminine cultures, high-context cultures, low-context cultures, short-term-oriented cultures, long-term-oriented cultures, indulgent cultures and **restrained cultures** (Hall, 1976; Hall & Hall, 1987; Hofstede, Hofstede, & Minkov, 2010; Singh & Pereira, 2005).

- **Individualist and collectivist cultures.** *Individualist cultures* (such as the United States, Australia, United Kingdom, Netherlands, Canada, New Zealand, Italy, Belgium, Denmark, and Sweden) emphasize the individual, individual success, and individual responsibility. *Collectivist cultures* (such as Guatemala, Ecuador, Panama, Venezuela, Colombia, Indonesia, Pakistan, China, Costa Rica, and Peru), on the other hand, emphasize the group or family or organization as more important than the individual. In appealing to members of individualistic cultures, you'll want to emphasize such themes as independence, nonconformity, and uniqueness. You'll also be well advised to stress your competence; if you don't, your listeners may assume it's because you don't have any. In a speech to members of a collectivist culture, however, successful appeals will emphasize the importance of family, of loyalty (to brand names or local organizations), and of national identity and pride (Dillard & Marshall, 2003; Han & Shavitt, 1994). In collectivist cultures, to stress your own competence or that of your corporation may prove insulting; it may be taken as a suggestion that your audience members are inferior or that their corporations are not as good as yours.

- **High- and low-power-distance cultures.** In *high-power-distance cultures* (such as Mexico, Brazil, India, and the Philippines), there is a large difference between those who have and those who don't have power. In *low-power-distance* cultures (such as Denmark, New Zealand, Sweden, and to a lesser extent the United States), there is little difference. When you are addressing members of a high-power-distance culture, references to important and prominent people and to what they believe and advocate will prove effective. In a low-power-distance

individualist cultures
Cultures in which the individual's rather than the group's goals and preferences are given primary importance. Opposed to *collectivist cultures.*

collectivist cultures
Cultures in which the group's goals rather than the individual's are given primary importance and where, for example, benevolence, tradition, and conformity are given special emphasis. Opposed to *individualist cultures.*

high-power-distance cultures
Cultures in which power is concentrated in the hands of a few; there's a great difference between the power held by these people and the power of the ordinary citizen. Opposed to *low-power-distance cultures.*

low-power-distance cultures
Cultures in which power is relatively evenly distributed throughout the citizenry. Opposed to *high-power-distance cultures.*

high-ambiguity-tolerant cultures
Cultures that are accepting of ambiguity and do not feel threatened by unknown situations; uncertainty is a normal part of life and people accept it as it comes.

low-ambiguity-tolerant cultures
Cultures that are uncomfortable with ambiguity, do much to avoid uncertainty, and have a great deal of anxiety about not knowing what will happen next.

masculine cultures
Cultures that view men as assertive, oriented to material success, and strong and view women, on the other hand, as modest, focused on the quality of life, and tender. Masculine cultures emphasize success and so socialize their people to be assertive, ambitious, and competitive. Opposed to *feminine cultures.*

feminine cultures

Cultures that encourage both men and women to be modest, oriented to maintaining the quality of life, and tender. Feminine cultures emphasize the quality of life. Opposed to *masculine cultures*.

high-context cultures

Cultures in which much of the information in communication is in the context or in the person rather than explicitly coded in the verbal message. Opposed to *low-context cultures*.

low-context cultures

Cultures in which most of the information in communication is explicitly stated in the verbal messages. Individualist cultures are usually low-context cultures. Opposed to *high-context cultures*.

short-term-oriented cultures

Cultures in which people look more to the past and the present; these cultural members spend their resources for the present and want quick results from their efforts. Opposed to *long-term-oriented cultures*.

long-term-oriented cultures

Cultures that promote the importance of future rewards and so, for example, members of these cultures are more apt to save for the future and to prepare for the future academically. Opposed to *short-term-oriented cultures*.

indulgent cultures

Cultures that emphasize the gratification of desires and a focus on having fun and enjoying life. Opposed to *restrained cultures*.

restrained cultures

Cultures that foster the curbing of immediate gratification and regulate it by social norms. Opposed to *indulgent cultures*.

culture, however, these appeals will prove less effective than will, say, references to or testimonials from people much like the people you want to influence.

- **High- and low-ambiguity-tolerant cultures.** In some cultures, people do little to avoid uncertainty and have little anxiety about not knowing what will happen next. In other cultures, however, uncertainty is strongly avoided and there is much anxiety about uncertainty. Members of *high-ambiguity-tolerant cultures* don't feel threatened by uncertainty; such cultures include, for example, Singapore, Jamaica, Denmark, Sweden, Hong Kong, Ireland, Great Britain, Malaysia, India, Philippines, and the United States. Members of *low-ambiguity-tolerant cultures* do much to avoid uncertainty and have much anxiety about not knowing what will happen next; these cultures include, for example, Greece, Portugal, Guatemala, Uruguay, Belgium, El Salvador, Japan, Yugoslavia, Peru, France, Chile, Spain, and Costa Rica. Audiences high in uncertainty avoidance want information from experts (or supported by experts)—they want to know very clearly where they can go for information and guidance. These audiences also value tradition, so appeals to the past will prove effective. Audiences low in uncertainty avoidance are more ready to accept the new and the different.

- **Masculine and feminine cultures.** *Masculine cultures* emphasize stereotypically masculine values of strength, status, and success; examples include Japan, Austria, Venezuela, Italy, Switzerland, Mexico, Ireland, Jamaica, Great Britain, and Germany. *Feminine cultures* emphasize stereotypically feminine values of intimacy, relationships, and fidelity; for example, Sweden, Norway, Netherlands, Denmark, Costa Rica, Yugoslavia, Finland, Chile, Portugal, and Thailand. The message here is clear; audience members with "masculine" cultural beliefs will be motivated by appeals to achievement, adventure, and enjoyment and will welcome the "hard sell." Listeners from cultures high in "femininity" will be motivated by "soft sell" appeals and by appeals to harmony and aesthetic qualities. It should be mentioned that some may find these terms likely to further stereotyping and offer substitutes such as *achievement orientation* versus *people orientation*. *Masculine* and *feminine*, however, are the terms under which this research is conducted and the terms you'd use in your Internet searches, so they are used here with the caveat that they are intended to capture the way lots of people think of these two cultural orientations and not to further stereotyping (Lustig & Koester, 2013).

- **High- and low-context cultures.** In *high-context cultures*, information is part of the context and does not have to be verbalized explicitly (for example, Japanese, Arabic, Latin American, Thai, Korean, Apache, and Mexican cultures). In *low-context cultures*, information is made explicit and little is taken for granted (for example, Germany, Sweden, Norway, and the United States). Listeners from high-context cultures will favor appeals that are indirect and implied; listeners from low-context cultures will want detail, directness, and explicitness.

- **Short- and long-term-oriented cultures.** *Short-term-oriented cultures* (Puerto Rico, Ghana, Egypt, Trinidad, Nigeria, and Dominican Republic are examples) teach an orientation that emphasizes the present with such beliefs as *spend now* and *enjoy yourself now*. Appeals that are addressed to these present and immediate concerns of how to enjoy yourself will likely prove effective here. *Long-term-oriented cultures* (South Korea, Taiwan, Japan, China, Ukraine, and Germany are examples) teach an orientation that promotes the importance of future rewards and would be especially persuaded by appeals that address these future rewards, for example, the promise of wealth or promotion, the importance of saving, the need for a healthy diet, and the importance of insurance.

- **Indulgent and restrained cultures.** These types of cultures differ in their emphasis on indulgence or restraint. *Indulgent cultures* (Venezuela, Mexico, Puerto Rico, El Salvador, Nigeria, and Colombia are examples) are concerned with two main values: (1) the feeling that you may do as you wish, that you aren't obligated to do what others want you to do, and (2) having leisure time. Together, these values define happiness—a major concern of cultures high in indulgence. *Restrained cultures* (Pakistan, Egypt, Latvia, Ukraine, Albania, and Belarus are examples) foster the curbing of gratification; too much fun is not honorable. Appeals to be thrifty or to save or study for the future, for example, are likely to be well received by cultures low in indulgence (they're looking toward the future) and less well received by cultures high in indulgence (they want to enjoy themselves now). Similarly, friendships are more highly valued in indulgent than in restrained cultures, and so examples and appeals to the importance of friendship will be received very differently by the different cultures.

Identify with Your Audience

A closely related principle is that of identification, a process of demonstrating a similarity with your audience. If you can show audience members that you and they share important attitudes, beliefs, and values, you'll clearly advance your persuasive goal. Other similarities are also important. For example, in some cases similarity of cultural, educational, or social background may help you identify yourself with your audience. Be aware, however, that insincere or dishonest identification is likely to backfire and create problems. So avoid even implying similarities between yourself and your audience that don't exist.

As a general rule, never ask the audience to do what you have not done yourself; always demonstrate that you have done what you want the audience to do. If you don't, the audience will rightfully ask, "Why haven't you done it?" In addition, besides doing whatever it may be, show your listeners that you're pleased to have done it. For example, tell them of the satisfaction you derived from donating blood or from reading to blind students.

Secure a *Yes* Response

Research evidence clearly supports the importance of securing a *yes response* in influencing further compliance (Goldstein, Martin, & Cialdini, 2008). If you can get your listeners to give a yes response to some related issue, they will be more likely to give another *yes* response (ideally to your thesis). Even if the *yes* response is to some small request, it will still pave the way to a *yes* response for a larger request. For example, when homeowners first agreed to install a small "drive safely" sign in their window, they were more likely to agree to a major request (installing a large sign on their perfectly manicured lawns) than were those homeowners who were not asked to install the small sign first.

Anticipate Selective Exposure

People listen in accordance with the principle of **selective exposure**. This principle or law has two parts: It states that (1) listeners actively seek out information that supports their opinions, beliefs, values, decisions, and behaviors; and (2) listeners actively avoid information that contradicts their existing opinions, beliefs, attitudes, values, decisions, and behaviors. People exercise selective exposure most often when their confidence in their own opinions and beliefs is weak.

If you want to persuade an audience that holds attitudes different from your own, anticipate selective exposure operating and proceed inductively; that is, hold back on your thesis until you've given your evidence and argument. Only then relate this evidence and argument to your initially contrary thesis. If you were to present them with your thesis first, your listeners might tune you out without giving your position a fair hearing. So become thoroughly familiar with the attitudes of your audience if you want to succeed

selective exposure

A principle of persuasion that argues that listeners actively seek out information that supports their opinions, beliefs, and values while actively avoiding information that would contradict these opinions, beliefs, and values.

in making these necessary adjustments and adaptations. Let's say you're giving a speech on the need to reduce spending on college athletic programs. If your audience were composed of listeners who agreed with you and wanted to cut athletic spending, you might lead with your thesis. Your introduction might go something like this:

> Our college athletic program is absorbing money that we can more profitably use for the library, science labs, and language labs. Let me explain how the money now going to unnecessary athletic programs could be better spent in these other areas.

On the other hand, suppose you were addressing alumni who strongly favored the existing athletic programs. In this case, you might want to lead with your evidence and then state your thesis.

> Our college library, science labs, and computer labs are badly in need of upgrades. Let's see how we can all profit from these upgrades and then we'll consider from where this money might come.

Use Positive Labeling

People generally act in ways consistent with the way in which they are labeled, especially if the label is a favorable one that reflects positively on the individual. So if you describe your listeners as possessing a particular attitude or trait (and for ethical reasons, you need to truly believe that they actually do possess such attitudes or traits), they'll be more apt to act in accordance with the label (Goldstein, Martin, & Cialdini, 2008). For example, let's say that you want to motivate your audience to devote time to working with students who have learning disabilities. If you describe audience members as caring, compassionate, and helpful, for example, they'll be more apt to think of themselves in that way and be more apt to agree to requests that other caring, compassionate, and helpful people do.

Ask for Reasonable Amounts of Change

The greater and more important the change you want to encourage in your audience, the more difficult your task will be. Put in terms of the continuum of persuasion introduced earlier, this principle suggests that you'll be more successful if you ask for small movements in the direction of your speech purpose. The reason is simple: As listeners

VIEWPOINTS

Negative Labeling

In what ways might negative labeling be used as a persuasive strategy?

we normally demand a greater number of reasons and a lot more evidence before we make important choices—such as, say, deciding to change careers, move to another state, or invest in stocks.

On the other hand, we may be more easily persuaded (and demand less evidence) on relatively minor issues—whether to take a course in "Small Group Communication" rather than "Persuasion" or to give to the United Heart Fund instead of the American Heart Fund.

Generally, people change gradually, in small degrees over a long period of time. Persuasion, therefore, is most effective when it strives for small changes and works over a period of time. For example, a persuasive speech stands a better chance when it tries to get a drinker to attend just one AA meeting rather than advocating giving up alcohol for life. If you try to convince audience members to change their attitudes radically or to engage in behaviors to which they're initially opposed, your attempts may backfire. In this type of situation, listeners may tune you out, closing their ears to even the best and most logical arguments.

In your classroom speeches, set reasonable goals for what you want the audience to do. Remember you have only perhaps 10 minutes, and in that time you cannot move the proverbial mountain. Instead, ask for small, easily performed behaviors. Encourage your listeners to visit a particular website (perhaps even one dedicated to beliefs or values that they do not currently share), to vote in the next election, or to buy the new virus protection software.

Provide Social Proof

You provide **social proof** when you give your listeners examples of other people doing what you want them to do (Cialdini, 2013; Goldstein, Martin, & Cialdini, 2008; Surowiecki, 2005). So, let's say you want your listeners to turn off their cell phones during classes. How might you achieve this? Consider these two alternatives:

social proof
Examples of other people who do or don't do as you want the audience to do.

1. So many people leave on their cell phones, which annoy others. This is just an example of gross inconsideration for the rights of others.

2. So many people are turning off their cell phones and acting with consideration for others.

Which strategy is likely to prove more effective? In the first, you offer what is called *negative* social proof—you're showing your listeners that many people do what they should *not* do. And, they may reason, if everyone is doing it, why shouldn't I? In the second, you offer *positive* social proof—you're showing your listeners that many people do what you want them to also do. And, again, they are more likely to do what others are doing—in this case, what you want them to do. This "herd instinct" is a powerful impulse.

Follow a Motivated Sequence

One time-honored principle of persuasion is the **motivated sequence**, a persuasive strategy and way of organizing your speech. In the motivated sequence, you do five things: (1) gain attention, (2) establish a need for a change, (3) advance a proposal to satisfy the need, (4) visualize for audience members what things would be like were they to do what you suggest, and (5) move them to action (German, Gronbeck, Ehninger, & Monroe, 2013). Let's explain each in more detail.

motivated sequence
A persuasive strategy consisting of five steps: attention, need, satisfaction, visualization, and action.

1. **Attention.** Your first step is to persuade audience members to give you their undivided attention. If you execute this step effectively, your audience should be eager to hear what you have to say. You can gain audience attention by, for example, asking a rhetorical question, referring to specific audience members, or using a dramatic or humorous story. These and other ways of gaining attention are discussed more fully in Chapter 7.

2. **Need.** Second, prove to listeners that they need to learn or do something. You can establish need in three ways:

   1. State the need or problem as it exists or will exist.
   2. Illustrate the need with specific examples, illustrations, statistics, testimony, and other forms of support.
   3. Point to how this need affects your specific listeners—for example, their financial status, career goals, or individual happiness.

For example, in a speech to convince people in their 60s and 70s to purchase home computers, you might say the following:

> A survey of persons in their 60s and 70s reported that one of their greatest needs was easy and rapid access to medical information. If you are like those in this survey, then the home computer may be your answer.

3. **Satisfaction.** Third, present the "solution" that satisfies the need you demonstrated in step 2. This step should convince audience members that what you are informing them about or persuading them to do will satisfy the need. You answer the question "How will the need be satisfied by what I am asking the audience to learn, believe, or do?" This step usually contains two types of information:

   1. a clear statement (with examples and illustrations if necessary) of what you want audience members to learn, believe, or do; and
   2. a statement of how or why what you are asking them to learn, believe, or do will lead to satisfying the need identified in step 2. For example, you might say

   > With a home computer, you'll be able to get information on thousands of potential drug interactions in seconds.

You might then show your listeners, perhaps with an actual demonstration, how this would be done.

4. **Visualization.** Fourth, intensify the audience's feelings or beliefs; take listeners beyond the present place and time and help them imagine what it would be like if the need were satisfied (with the solution suggested in step 3). You can accomplish this by (1) demonstrating the positive benefits to be derived if this advocated proposal were put into operation or (2) demonstrating the negative consequences that will occur if your plan is not followed. You could also combine the two methods and demonstrate both the positive benefits of your plan and the negative effects of the existing situation or of a competing proposal. For example, you might say something like this:

> With one simple click, you'll be able to stay at home and get valuable medical information instead of fighting traffic and wasting time.

You might then demonstrate with a specific example how they would find this information.

5. **Action.** Tell the audience what they should do to satisfy the need you have identified. Your goal is to move the audience in a particular direction. Here are three ways to accomplish this step:

   1. State exactly what audience members should do.
   2. Appeal to their emotions.
   3. Give them guidelines for future action.

   For example:

   > Read this pamphlet, "Life on the Computer after 60," and go to your nearest computer store and talk with the salespeople.

Or you might suggest that they consider taking an appropriate adult education course at the local community college.

Notice that if you limit your persuasive purpose to strengthening or changing attitudes or beliefs, you must go at least as far as visualization. If you aim to get your listeners to behave in a certain way, you'll need to go all the way through the action step.

Table 10.2 provides a way of looking at the motivated sequence in terms of audience responses and some cautions to observe in using the motivated sequence.

The accompanying Public Speaking Sample Assistant illustrates the organizational structure of a speech following the motivated sequence.

TABLE 10.2 The Motivated Sequence as a Persuasive Strategy

Step and Purpose	Audience Question Speaker Should Answer	Ideal Audience Response	Cautions
Attention: Focus listeners' attention on you and your message.	Why should I listen? Is this worth my time?	■ This sounds interesting. ■ Tell me more.	Make attention relevant to speech topic.
Need: Demonstrate that there is a problem that affects them.	Why do I need to know or do anything?	■ OK, I understand; there's a problem. ■ Something needs to be done.	Don't overdramatize the need.
Satisfaction: Show listeners how they can satisfy the need.	How can I do anything about this?	■ I can change things. ■ I know what I can do. ■ I'm empowered.	Answer any objections listeners might have to your plan.
Visualization: Show listeners what the situation will be like with the need satisfied.	How would anything be different or improved?	■ *Wow!* Things look a lot better this way. ■ That change was really needed.	Be realistic; don't visualize the situation as perfect.
Action: Urge listeners to act.	What can I do to effect this change?	■ Let me sign up. ■ Here's my contribution. ■ I'll participate.	Be specific. Ask for small changes and behaviors.

PUBLIC SPEAKING Sample Assistant

A PREPARATION OUTLINE WITH ANNOTATIONS (MOTIVATED SEQUENCE ORGANIZATION)

This outline illustrates how you might construct an outline and a speech using the motivated sequence. In a longer speech, if you wanted to persuade an audience to establish a youth center, you might want to select two or three general arguments rather than limiting yourself to the one argument about reducing juvenile crime.

The Youth Center

General purpose: To persuade

Specific purpose: To persuade my listeners to vote in favor of Proposition 14 establishing a community youth center

Thesis: A youth center will reduce juvenile crime.

I. If you could reduce juvenile crime by some 20 percent by just flipping a lever, would you do it?
   A. Thom's drug store was broken into by teenagers.
   B. Loraine's video store windows were broken by teenagers.

I. Attention step

The speaker asks a question to gain attention and follows it with specific examples that audience members have experienced. The question and examples focus on one issue: the need to reduce juvenile crime. If the speech were a broader one that included other reasons for the center, then these would be previewed here as well.

II. Juvenile crime is on the rise.

A. The overall number of crimes has increased.

1. In 2003 there were 32 juvenile crimes.

2. In 2010 there were 47 such crimes.

3. In 2013 there were 63 such crimes.

B. The number of serious crimes also has increased.

1. In 2003 there were 30 misdemeanors and 2 felonies.

2. In 2013 there were 35 misdemeanors and 28 felonies.

III. A youth center will help reduce juvenile crime.

A. Three of our neighboring towns reduced juvenile crime after establishing a youth center.

1. In Marlboro there was a 20 percent decline in overall juvenile crime.

2. In both Highland and Ellenville the number of serious crimes declined 25 percent.

B. The youth center will not increase our tax burden.

1. New York State grants will pay for most of the expenses.

2. Local merchants have agreed to pay any remaining expenses.

IV. Juvenile crime will decrease as a result of the youth center.

A. If we follow the example of our neighbors, our juvenile crime rates are likely to decrease by 20 to 25 percent.

B. Thom's store would not have been broken into.

C. Loraine's windows would not have been broken.

V. Vote *yes* on Proposition 14.

A. In next week's election, you'll be asked to vote on Proposition 14, establishing a youth center.

B. Vote yes if you want to help reduce juvenile crime.

C. Urge your family members, your friends, and your work colleagues also to vote *yes*.

II. Need step

The speaker states the need directly and clearly and shows that a problem exists. The speaker then demonstrates that the rise in crime is significant both in absolute numbers and in the severity of the crimes. To increase the listeners' ability to understand these figures, it would help if these figures were written on a whiteboard, on a prepared chart, or on PowerPoint slides. In a longer speech, other needs might also be identified in this step; for example, the need to offer teenagers a place where they can learn useful vocational and social skills.

III. Satisfaction step

In this step the speaker shows the listeners that the proposal to establish a youth center has great benefits and no significant drawbacks.

The speaker argues that the youth center will satisfy the need to reduce juvenile crime by showing statistics from neighboring towns. The speaker also answers the objection and removes any doubts about increased taxes. If the speaker had reason to believe that listeners might have other possible objections, those objections, too, should be answered in this step.

IV. Visualization step

Here the speaker visualizes what the town would be like if the youth center were established, using both the statistics developed earlier and the personal examples introduced at the beginning of the speech.

V. Attention step

In this step the speaker asks listeners to take specific actions—to vote in favor of the youth center and to urge others to do the same. The speaker also reiterates the main theme of the speech; namely, that the youth center will help reduce juvenile crime.

JOURNAL 10.1 PUBLIC SPEAKING CHOICE POINT

Using The Motivated Sequence

Gus wants to give a speech opposing a proposed youth center, arguing that the way to fight youth crime is by mandating harsher sentences for all youth crimes. He wants to use the motivated sequence pattern. *Following the steps described previously, how might Gus craft a persuasive argument?*

The Three Persuasive Proofs

10.2 Explain the three persuasive proofs (logical, emotional, and credibility).

Classical rhetoric (as well as contemporary research) identifies three kinds of persuasive proofs: **logical proof** (or *logos*), **emotional proof** (or *pathos*), and **credibility proof** (or *ethos*).

Logical Proof (*Logos*)

When a speaker persuades listeners with logical proof the arguments focus on facts and evidence rather than on emotions or credibility claims. Not surprisingly, when listeners are persuaded by logical proof, they are more likely to remain persuaded over time and are more likely to resist counterarguments that may come up in the future (Petty & Wegener, 1998). We'll look at the three main categories of logical appeals and then at some fallacies of reasoning.

REASONING FROM SPECIFIC INSTANCES AND GENERALIZATIONS

In **reasoning from specific instances** (or examples), you examine several specific instances and then conclude something about the whole. This form of reasoning, known as *induction*, is useful when you want to develop a general principle or conclusion but cannot examine the whole. For example, you visit several Scandinavian cities and conclude something about the whole of Scandinavia. Critically analyze reasoning from specific instances (your own or those of speakers you're listening to) by asking the following questions.

- **Were enough specific instances examined?** Two general guidelines will help you determine how much is enough. First, the larger the group you wish to cover with your conclusion, the greater the number of specific instances you should examine. If you wish to draw conclusions about members of an entire country or culture, you'll have to examine a considerable number of people before drawing even tentative conclusions. On the other hand, if you're attempting to draw a conclusion about a bushel of 100 apples, sampling a few is probably sufficient. Second, the greater the diversity of items in the class, the more specific instances you will have to examine. Some classes or groups of items are relatively similar, whereas others are more different; this will influence how many specific instances constitute a sufficient number. Pieces of spaghetti in boiling water are all about the same; thus, sampling one usually tells you something about all the others. On the other hand, Scandinavian cities are very different from one another, so valid conclusions about the entire range of countries will require a much larger sample.

- **Are there significant exceptions?** When you examine specific instances and attempt to draw a conclusion about the whole, take into consideration the exceptions. Thus, if you examine the GPA of computer science majors and discover that 70 percent have GPAs above 3.5, you may be tempted to draw the conclusion that computer science majors are especially bright. But what about the 30 percent who have lower GPAs? How much lower are these scores? This may be a significant exception that must be taken into account when you draw your conclusion and would require you to qualify your conclusion in significant ways. Exactly what kind of or how many exceptions will constitute "significant exceptions" will depend on the unique situation.

REASONING FROM CAUSES AND EFFECTS

In **reasoning from causes and effects**, you may go in either of two directions. You may reason from cause to effect (from observed cause to unobserved effect) or from effect to cause (from observed effect to unobserved cause). In testing your own reasoning from cause to effect or from effect to cause and in evaluating the causal reasoning of others, ask yourself the following questions:

---

logical proof
The presentation of evidence and reasoned argument to support an assertion.

logos
From the Greek, another term for *logical proof.*

emotional proof
The presentation of appeals to the feelings, needs, desires, and wants of others in order to persuade them.

pathos
From the Greek, another term for *emotional proof.*

credibility proof
The presentation of an individual's qualifications (competence, character, and charisma) to support the individual's arguments.

ethos
From the Greek, another term for *credibility proof.*

reasoning from specific instances
A form of reasoning in which several specific instances are examined and then a conclusion about the whole is formed.

reasoning from causes and effects
A form of reasoning in which you reason that certain effects are due to specific causes or that specific causes produce certain effects.

■ **Might other causes be producing the observed effect?** If you observe a particular effect (say, high crime or student apathy), you need to ask if causes other than the one you're postulating might be producing these effects. Thus, you might postulate that poverty leads to high crime, but there might be other factors actually causing the high crime rate. Or poverty might be one cause but not the most important cause. Therefore, explore the possibility of other causes producing the observed effects.

■ **Is the causation in the direction postulated?** If two things occur together, it's often difficult to determine which is the cause and which is the effect. For example, a lack of interpersonal intimacy and a lack of self-confidence often occur in the same person. The person who lacks self-confidence seldom has intimate relationships with others. But which is the cause and which is the effect? It might be that the lack of intimacy "causes" low self-confidence; it might also be, however, that low self-confidence "causes" a lack of intimacy. Of course, it might also be that some other previously unexamined cause (a history of negative criticism, for example) might be producing both the lack of intimacy and the low self-confidence.

REASONING FROM SIGN

reasoning from sign
A form of reasoning in which the presence of certain signs (clues) are interpreted as leading to a particular conclusion.

Reasoning from sign involves drawing a conclusion on the basis of the presence of clues or symptoms that frequently occur together. Medical diagnosis is a good example of reasoning by sign. The general procedure is simple. If a sign and an object, event, or condition are frequently paired, the presence of the sign is taken as proof of the presence of the object, event, or condition. For example, fatigue, extreme thirst, and overeating serve as signs of hyperthyroidism because they frequently accompany the condition. In using reasoning from sign and in evaluating the reasoning by sign of others, ask yourself the following questions:

■ **Do the signs necessitate the conclusion drawn?** Given extreme thirst, overeating, and fatigue, how certain may you be of the "hyperthyroid" conclusion? With most medical and legal matters we can never be absolutely certain, but we can be certain beyond a reasonable doubt.

■ **Are there other signs that point to the same conclusion?** In the thyroid example, extreme thirst could be brought on by any number of factors. Similarly, the fatigue and the overeating could be attributed to other causes. Yet taken together, the three signs seem to point to only one reasonable diagnosis. Generally, the more signs that point toward the conclusion, the more confidence you can have that it's valid.

■ **Are there contradictory signs?** Are there signs pointing toward contradictory conclusions? For example, if the butler had a motive and a history of violence (signs supporting the conclusion that the butler was the murderer) but also had an alibi (a sign pointing to the conclusion of innocence), then the conclusion of guilt would have to be reconsidered or discarded.

LISTENING TO LOGICAL ARGUMENTS AND THE FALLACIES OF REASONING

When listening to logical or seemingly logical arguments, in addition to asking yourself the questions suggested for the various types of reasoning, also listen for what are called the *fallacies of reasoning*: arguments that appear to address issues but really don't. Here are just six such fallacies: **anecdotal evidence, appeal to tradition, testimonial, transfer, thin entering wedge,** and **agenda-setting** (Herrick, 2004; Lee & Lee, 1972, 1995; Pratkanis & Aronson, 1991). Learn to spot fallacies in the speeches of others, and be sure to avoid them in your own speeches.

anecdotal evidence
A fallacious persuasive tactic in which the speaker offers specific examples or illustrations as "proof."

■ **Anecdotal evidence.** Often you'll hear people use *anecdotal evidence* to "prove" a point: "Men are like that; I know because I have three brothers." "That's the way Japanese managers are; I've seen plenty of them." One reason this type of "evidence" is inadequate is that it relies on too few observations; it's usually a clear case of over-generalizing on the basis of too few instances. A second reason anecdotal evidence is inadequate is that one person's observations may be unduly clouded by his or her own attitudes and beliefs; your personal attitudes toward men or Japanese-style management, for example, may influence your perception of their behaviors.

- **Appeal to tradition.** Often used as an argument against change, the *appeal to tradition* claims that some proposed innovation is wrong or should not be adopted because it was never done before. This fallacious argument is used repeatedly by those who don't want change. But, of course, the fact that something has not been done before says nothing about its value or whether it should be done now.

- **Testimonial.** The *testimonial* technique involves using the image associated with some person to secure your approval (if you respect the person) or your rejection (if you don't respect the person). This is the technique of advertisers who use actors dressed up to look like doctors or plumbers or chefs to sell their products. Sometimes this technique takes the form of using only vague and general "authorities," as in "experts agree," "scientists say," "good cooks know," or "dentists advise."

- **Transfer.** In *transfer* the speaker associates her or his idea with something you respect (to gain your approval) or with something you detest (to gain your rejection). For example, a speaker might portray a proposal for condom distribution in schools as a means for "saving our children from AIDS" (to encourage acceptance) or as a means for "promoting sexual promiscuity" (to encourage disapproval). Sports-car manufacturers try to get you to buy their cars by associating them with high status and sex appeal; promoters of exercise clubs and diet plans attempt to associate them with health, self-confidence, and interpersonal appeal.

- **Thin entering wedge.** In using the *thin entering wedge*, a speaker argues against a proposal or new development on the grounds that it will be a "thin entering wedge" that will open the floodgates to all sorts of catastrophes (Chase, 1956). Though often based on no evidence, this argument has been used throughout history to oppose change. Some examples are "wedge" claims that school integration and interracial marriage will bring the collapse of American education and society, same-sex unions will destroy the family, and banning smoking in all public places will lead to the collapse of the restaurant industry.

- **Agenda-setting.** In *agenda-setting* a speaker contends that XYZ is the issue and that all others are unimportant and insignificant. This kind of fallacious appeal is heard frequently, as in "Balancing the budget is the key to the city's survival" or "There's only one issue confronting elementary education in our largest cities, and that is violence." In almost all situations, however, there are many issues and many sides to each issue. Often the person proclaiming that XYZ is the issue really means, "I'll be able to persuade you if you focus solely on XYZ and ignore the other issues."

appeal to tradition
A fallacy often used as an argument against change, as when a speaker claims that a proposed plan should not be adopted because it was never done before.

testimonial
A persuasive and often fallacious technique in which the speaker uses the authority or image of some positively evaluated person to gain your approval or of some negatively evaluated person to gain your rejection.

transfer
A persuasive technique in which a speaker associates an idea with something you respect to gain your approval or with something you dislike to gain your rejection.

thin entering wedge
A persuasive fallacy in which a speaker argues against a position on the grounds that it is a thin entering wedge that will open the floodgates to all sorts of catastrophes, though there is no evidence to support such results.

agenda-setting
A fallacy or pseudo-argument in which a speaker contends that only certain issues are important and others are not—in an attempt, for example, to focus attention on the strong points of a plan and divert attention from the weak points.

JOURNAL 10.2 PUBLIC SPEAKING CHOICE POINT

Selecting Arguments

Rose is preparing a persuasive speech on a question of policy, arguing that owners of phone-in psychic services should be prosecuted for fraud. *What are some of Rose's options for persuading her audience to accept her thesis?*

Emotional Proof (*Pathos*)

Emotional appeals (or motivational appeals) are appeals to your listeners' feelings, needs, desires, and wants and can be powerful means of persuasion (Wood, 2000). Specifically, when you use emotional appeals, you appeal to those forces that energize, move, or motivate people to develop, change, or strengthen their attitudes or ways of behaving. For example, one motive might be the desire for status. This desire might motivate someone to enter a high-status occupation or to dress a certain way.

Developed in the late 1960s, one of the most useful analyses of human motives remains Abraham Maslow's fivefold hierarchy of needs, reproduced in Figure 10.2 (Benson & Dundis, 2003; Maslow, 1970). One of the assumptions contained in this theory is that people seek to fulfill the needs at the lowest level first. Only when those needs are satisfied do the needs at the next level begin to influence behavior. For example, people would not concern themselves with the need for security or freedom from fear if they were starving (if their need for food had not been fulfilled). Similarly, they would not be concerned with friendship if their need for protection and security had not been fulfilled. The implication for you as a speaker is that you have to know what needs of your audience are unsatisfied. These are the needs you can appeal to in motivating them.

Here are several useful motivational appeals organized around Maslow's hierarchy. As you review these, try to visualize how you would use each one in your next speech.

Figure 10.2 Maslow's Hierarchy of Needs

How would you describe the satisfied and unsatisfied needs of members of your public speaking class? Which of these needs would, according to Maslow, be most motivating for your class?

SOURCE: Based on Abraham Maslow, *Motivation and Personality*. New York: HarperCollins, 1970.

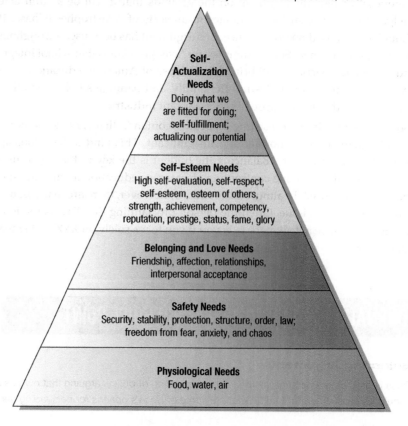

PHYSIOLOGICAL NEEDS

In many parts of the world, and even in parts of the United States, the basic physiological needs of people are not fully met. These are powerful motivating forces. In many of the poorest countries of the world, the speaker who promises to meet fundamental physiological needs is the one the people will follow. Most college students in the United States, however, have their physiological needs for food, water, and air well satisfied, so these issues will not prove helpful in motivating and persuading them.

SAFETY NEEDS

Those who do not have their basic safety and freedom-from-fear needs met will be motivated by appeals to security, protection, and freedom from physical harm and from psychological distress. You see appeals to this need in advertisements for burglar protection devices for home and car, in political speeches promising greater police protection on the streets and in schools, and in the speeches of motivational gurus who promise psychological safety and freedom from anxiety. Sometimes the safety motive is seen in individuals' desire for order, structure, and organization—motives clearly appealed to in advertisements for personal data assistants like cell phones and information management software. Many people fear what is unknown, and order and structure seem to make things predictable and hence safe.

BELONGING AND LOVE NEEDS

Belonging and love needs are extremely powerful; most people are motivated to love and be loved. If you can teach your audience how to be loved and how to love, your audience will be not only attentive but also grateful. We also want affiliation—friendship and companionship. We want to be a part of a group, despite our equally potent desire for independence and individuality. Notice how advertisements for singles clubs, cruises, and dating services appeal to this need for affiliation. On this basis alone they successfully gain the attention, interest, and participation of thousands.

SELF-ESTEEM NEEDS

We have a need for positive self-esteem: a favorable self-image, a view of ourselves that casts us in the best possible light. We want to see ourselves as self-confident, worthy, and contributing human beings. We want to see ourselves as achievers. In using the achievement motive, be explicit in stating how your speech, ideas, and recommendations will contribute to the listeners' achievements. Show your listeners how what you have to say will help them achieve the goals they seek, and you'll likely have an active and receptive audience.

SELF-ACTUALIZATION NEEDS

At the top of Maslow's hierarchy is the self-actualization motive; you have a desire to self-actualize—to become what you feel you're fit for. If you see yourself as a poet, you must write poetry. If you see yourself as a teacher, you must teach. Even if you don't pursue these as occupations, you nevertheless have a desire to write poetry or to teach. Appeals to self-actualization needs—to the yearning "to be the best you can be"—encourage listeners to strive for their highest ideals and are often welcomed by the audience.

LISTENING TO EMOTIONAL APPEALS

Emotional appeals are all around you, urging you to do all sorts of things—usually to buy a product or to support a position or cause. As you listen to these inevitable appeals, consider the following:

- **Emotional appeals do not constitute proof.** No matter how passionate the speaker's voice or bodily movement, no matter how compelling the language, passion does not prove the case a speaker is presenting.
- **Feelings are not open to public inspection.** You really can't tell with certainty what the speaker is feeling. The speaker may, in fact, be using facial management

techniques or clever speechwriters to communicate emotions without actually feeling them.

- **Emotional appeals may be used to divert attention from the lack of real evidence.** If emotional appeals are being used to the exclusion of argument and evidence or if you suspect that the speaker seeks to arouse your emotions so you forget that there's no evidence, ask yourself why.

- **Emotional appeals may be to high or low motives.** A speaker can arouse feelings of love and peace but also feelings of hatred and war. In asking for charitable donations, an organization may appeal to high motives, such as your desire to help those less fortunate than you, or to lower motives such as guilt and fear.

- **Be especially on the lookout for the appeal to pity.** This is what logicians call *argumentum ad misericordiam*, as in "I really tried to do the work, but I've been having terrible depression and find it difficult to concentrate."

Credibility Proof (*Ethos*)

Your credibility is the degree to which your audience regards you as a believable spokesperson. Credibility is not something you have or don't have in any objective sense; rather, it's a function of what the audience *thinks* of you. Before reading about this type of proof, ask yourself how an audience (say, this class) would most likely see you:

1. Knowledgeable?
2. A thorough researcher?
3. Informed about the subject matter?
4. Fair in the presentation of material (i.e., evidence and argument)?
5. Concerned with the audience's needs?
6. Honest; unlikely to bend the truth?
7. Assertive in personal style?
8. Enthusiastic about the topic and in general?
9. Active rather than passive?

These questions focused on the three qualities of credibility we'll discuss—competence, character, and charisma—and are based on a large body of research (Richmond, Wrench, & McCroskey, 2013). Items 1, 2, and 3 refer to your perceived competence: How capable do you seem to the audience? Items 4, 5, and 6 refer to

ETHICAL CHOICE POINT

Fear as a Persuasive Strategy?

You're a student teacher in an elementary school and are required to teach your eighth-grade class the unit on sex education. Your objective, which is mandated by the state syllabus but also is consistent with your own feeling, is to get students to avoid sexual relationships until they are much older. But you know from talking with students that many of them intend to have sexual relationships at the earliest opportunity; in fact, some are currently sexually active. You wonder if it would be ethical to use fear appeals to scare the students about the potential dangers of sex. For example, you could show them photos of people with advanced cases of sexually transmitted diseases, youngsters living in poverty because they now have children to support, and so on. You believe that attitudes and behavior should be motivated by reason and logic and so you wonder if it would be ethical to use such fear appeals. *Given that you want to be effective but also true to your beliefs, what are some of your ethical choices in this matter? What would you do?*

character: Does the audience see you as a good and moral person? Items 7, 8, and 9 refer to your charisma: Does the audience see you as dynamic and active? As you read about credibility, think about how you might go about increasing your own believability/credibility: your perceived competence, character, and/or charisma.

If your listeners see you as competent and knowledgeable, of good character, and charismatic or dynamic, they will find you credible. As a result, you'll be more effective in changing their attitudes or in moving them to do something.

What makes a speaker credible will vary from one culture to another. In some cultures, people would see competence as the most important factor in, say, their choice of a teacher for their preschool children. In other cultures, the most important factor might be the goodness or morality of the teacher or perhaps the reputation of the teacher's family. At the same time, each culture may define each of the factors in credibility differently. For example, *character* may mean following the rules of a specific religion in some cultures and following the individual conscience in others. To take another example, the Quran, the Torah, and the New Testament will be ascribed very different levels of credibility depending on the religious beliefs of the audience. And this will be true even when all three religious books say essentially the same thing on a given point.

COMPETENCE

Your perceived **competence** is the knowledge and expertise an audience thinks you have. The more knowledge and expertise the audience sees you as having, the more likely the audience will believe you. Similarly, you're likely to believe a teacher or doctor if you think he or she is knowledgeable on the subject at hand. You can demonstrate your competence to your audience in a variety of ways.

competence
One of the qualities that undergirds personal credibility; encompasses a person's ability and knowledge.

- **Tell listeners of your competence.** Let the audience know of any special experience or training that qualifies you to speak on this specific topic. If you're speaking on communal living and you've lived on a commune yourself, then say so in your speech. Tell the audience of your unique personal experiences when these contribute to your credibility. This recommendation to tell listeners of your competence applies (generally) to most audiences you'll encounter in the United States. But in some cultures—notably collectivist cultures such as those of Japan, China, and Korea, for example—to stress your own competence or that of your corporation may be taken as a suggestion that your audience members are inferior or that their corporations are not as good as yours. In other cultures—notably individualist cultures such as those of Scandinavia, the United States, and western Europe, for example—if you don't stress your competence, your listeners may assume it's because you don't have any.

- **Cite a variety of research sources.** Make it clear to your audience that you've thoroughly researched your topic. Do this by mentioning some of the books you've read, persons you've interviewed, and articles you've consulted. Weave these references throughout your speech. Don't bunch them together at one time.

- **Stress the competencies of your sources.** If your audience isn't aware of them, then emphasize the particular competencies of your sources. In this way it becomes clear to the audience that you've chosen your sources carefully so as to provide the most authoritative sources possible. For example, saying simply, "Senator Cardova thinks…" does nothing to establish the senator's credibility. Instead, consider saying something like "Senator Cardova, who headed the finance committee for three years and was formerly a professor of economics at MIT, thinks…."

CHARACTER

Audience members will see you as credible if they perceive you as being someone of high moral **character**, someone who is honest, and someone they can trust. When

character
One of the qualities of credibility; an individual's honesty and basic nature; moral qualities.

VIEWPOINTS

Establishing Credibility

Evelyn is planning a speech on baseball to a class that is 75 percent male. She fears, however, that simply because she's a woman, her audience is not going to perceive her as credible—even though she knows more about baseball than any other person in the room. *If you were Evelyn's speech coach, what would you advise her to do? On what principles of persuasion do you base your advice?*

audience members perceive your intentions as good for them (rather than for your own personal gain), they'll think you credible and they'll believe you. You can establish your high moral character in a number of ways.

- **Stress fairness.** If delivering a persuasive speech, stress that you've examined both sides of the issue (if indeed you have). If you're presenting both sides, then make it clear that your presentation is accurate and fair. Be particularly careful not to omit any argument the audience may already have thought of—this is a sure sign that your presentation isn't fair or balanced. Tell the audience that you would not advocate a position if you did not base it on a fair evaluation of the issues.

- **Stress concern for audience.** Make it clear to audience members that you're interested in their welfare rather than seeking self-gain. If audience members feel that you are "out for yourself," they'll justifiably downgrade your credibility. Make it clear that the audience's interests are foremost in your mind. Tell audience members how the new legislation will reduce *their* taxes, how recycling will improve *their* community, how a knowledge of sexual harassment will make *their* workplace more comfortable and stress free.

- **Stress concern for enduring values.** We view speakers who are concerned with small and insignificant issues as less credible than speakers who demonstrate a concern for lasting truths and general principles. Thus, make it clear to audience members that your position—your thesis—is related to higher-order values; show them exactly how this is true.

Here, for example, Kofi Annan (2006), in giving his farewell speech as secretary general of the United Nations on September 19, 2006, stressed his concern for enduring values:

> Yes, I remain convinced that the only answer to this divided world must be a truly United Nations. Climate change, HIV/AIDS, fair trade, migration, human rights—all these issues, and many more, bring us back to that point. Addressing each is indispensable for each of us in our village, in our neighborhood, and in our country. Yet each has acquired a global dimension that can only be reached by global action, agreed and coordinated through this most universal of institutions.

CHARISMA

Charisma is a combination of your personality and dynamism as seen by the audience. Audience members will perceive you as credible (and believable) if they like you and if they see you as friendly and pleasant rather than aloof and reserved. Similarly, audiences favor the dynamic speaker over the hesitant, nonassertive speaker. They'll perceive you as less credible if they see you as shy, introverted, and soft-spoken rather than as an extroverted and forceful individual. (Perhaps people feel that a dynamic speaker is open and honest in presenting herself or himself but that a shy, introverted individual may be hiding something.) As a speaker there's much that you can do to increase your charisma and, hence, your perceived credibility.

- **Demonstrate a positive outlook.** Show the audience that you have a positive orientation to the public speaking situation and to the entire speaker–audience encounter. We see positive and forward-looking people as more credible than negative and backward-looking people. Stress your pleasure at addressing the audience. Stress hope rather than despair; stress happiness rather than sadness.
- **Demonstrate enthusiasm.** The lethargic speaker, the speaker who somehow plods through the speech, is the very opposite of the charismatic speaker. Try viewing a film of Martin Luther King Jr. or Billy Graham speaking—they're totally absorbed with the speech and with the audience. They're excellent examples of the enthusiasm that makes a charismatic speaker.
- **Be emphatic.** Use language that is emphatic rather than colorless and indecisive. Use gestures that are clear and decisive rather than random and hesitant. Demonstrate a firm commitment to the position you're advocating; the audience will be much more likely to agree with a speaker who believes firmly in the thesis of the speech.

LISTENING TO CREDIBILITY APPEALS AND PERSONAL ATTACKS

When you listen to credibility appeals, evaluate them critically. Here are three questions you'll find helpful to ask in assessing credibility appeals:

- **Is the dimension of credibility used relevant?** For example, are the politician's family members (nice though they may be) relevant to his or her position on gun control or social security or immigration? Is the politician's former military service (or the lack of it) relevant to the issue being discussed?
- **Are credibility appeals being used instead of argument and evidence?** In typical examples of invalid credibility appeals, speakers may emphasize their educational background (to establish "competence"), appear at religious rituals (to establish "moral character"), or endeavor to present themselves as take-charge, alpha-type individuals (to demonstrate "charisma"). When done to divert attention from the issues or to mask the absence of evidence, such appeals are meaningless.
- **Are the credibility appeals true?** The actor who advertises toothpaste dressed as a dentist is still an actor doing a modeling job, not a dentist. Too often people unconsciously attribute credibility to a performance because of a uniform. Even when the endorser is a real dentist, remember that this dentist is getting paid for the endorsement. Although this doesn't necessarily make the endorsement false, it does (or should) make you wonder.

In addition to these general questions, become conscious of fallacious strategies that focus on attacking the person. Be alert for fallacies like the following in the speeches of others, and eliminate them from your own reasoning.

- **Personal interest attacks may take either of two forms.** In one form the speaker disqualifies someone from having a point of view because he or she isn't directly affected by an issue or proposal or doesn't have firsthand knowledge; for example, a speaker might dismiss an argument on abortion merely because the

charisma
One of the qualities of credibility; an individual's dynamism or forcefulness.

argument was made by a man. In another form the speaker disqualifies someone because he or she will benefit in some way from a proposal. For example, arguing that someone is rich, middle class, or poor and thus will benefit greatly from a proposed tax cut does not mean that the argument for the tax cut is invalid. The legitimacy of an argument can never depend on the gender (or culture) of the individual. Nor can it depend on the gain that a person may derive from the position advocated. The legitimacy of an argument can be judged only on the basis of the evidence and reasoning presented.

■ **Character attacks.** Often referred to as *ad hominem* arguments, character attacks involve accusing another person (usually an opponent) of some wrongdoing or of some character flaw. The purpose is to discredit the person or to divert attention from the issue under discussion. Arguments such as "How can we support a candidate who has smoked pot [or avoided the military]?" or "Do you want to believe someone who has been unfaithful on more than one occasion?" are often heard in political discussions but probably have little to do with the logic of the argument.

■ **Name-calling.** In name-calling, often referred to as "poisoning the well," the speaker gives an idea, a group of people, or a political philosophy a bad name ("bigoted," "soft on terrorism") to try to get listeners to condemn an idea without analyzing the argument and evidence. The opposite of name-calling is the use of "glittering generalities," in which the speaker tries to make you accept some idea by associating it with things you value highly ("democracy," "free speech," "academic freedom"). By using these "virtue words," the speaker tries to get you to ignore the evidence and simply approve of the idea.

Persuasive Speeches of Fact, Value, and Policy

10.3 Explain the nature of speeches of fact, value, and policy and the guidelines for preparing such speeches.

The three main types of persuasive speeches concern facts, values, and policy. Here we'll explain the nature and differences among these types of speeches and explain how you can construct such speeches by illustrating their theses, main points, support, and organization.

Persuasive Speeches on Questions of Fact

questions of fact
Issues revolving around potentially answerable questions.

Questions of fact concern what is or is not true, what does or does not exist, what did or did not happen. Some questions of fact are easily answered. These include many academic questions you're familiar with: Who was Aristotle? How many people use the Internet to get news? When was the first satellite launched? Questions of fact also include more mundane questions: What's on television? When is the meeting? What's Jenny's e-mail address? You can easily find answers to these questions by looking at some reference book, finding the relevant website, or asking someone who knows the answer.

The questions of fact that we deal with in persuasive speeches are a bit different. Although these questions also have answers, the answers are not that easy to find and in fact may never be found. The questions concern controversial issues for which different people have different answers. Daily newspapers and Internet websites abound in questions of fact.

For example, on May 21, 2016—from Google, Bing, and Yahoo! online news—there were such questions of fact as these: What effects does the Zika virus have on the brain? Does Facebook have an institutional bias? Is Katie Holmes pregnant with Jamie Foxx's baby? What caused the Egyptian air crash?

THESIS

For a persuasive speech on a question of fact, you'll formulate a thesis based on a factual statement such as:

- This company has a glass ceiling for women.
- The plaintiff was slandered (or libeled or defamed).
- The death was a case of physician-assisted suicide.
- Gay men and lesbians make competent military personnel.
- Television violence leads to violent behavior in viewers.

If you were preparing a persuasive speech on, say, the first example given above, you might phrase your thesis as "This company discriminates against women." Whether the company does discriminate is a question of fact; clearly the company either does or does not discriminate. Whether you can prove it does or it doesn't, however, is another issue.

MAIN POINTS

Once you've formulated your thesis, you can generate your main points by asking the simple question "How do you know this?" or "Why would you believe this is true (factual)?" The answers to one of these questions will enable you to develop your main points. The bare bones of your speech might then look something like this:

General purpose:	To persuade
Specific purpose:	To persuade my listeners that this company discriminates against women
Thesis:	This company discriminates against women. [How can we tell that this company discriminates against women?]

    I. Women earn less than men.
    II. Women are hired less often than men.
    III. Women occupy fewer managerial positions than men.

Make sure that you clearly connect your main points to your thesis in your introduction, when introducing each of the points, and again in your summary. Don't allow the audience to forget that when women earn lower salaries than men, it directly supports the thesis that this company discriminates against women.

JOURNAL 10.3 PUBLIC SPEAKING CHOICE POINT

Developing Main Points

Peggy wants to give a persuasive speech arguing that violent video games are harmful to children. *What are some of Peggy's options for the main points of the speech?*

SUPPORT

Having identified your main points, you will then begin searching for information to support them. Taking the first point, you might develop it something like this:

    I. Women earn less than men.

        A. Over the past 5 years, the average salary for editorial assistants was $6,000 less for women than it was for men.

        B. Over the past 5 years, the entry-level salaries for women averaged $4,500 less than the entry-level salaries for men.

        C. Over the past 5 years, the bonuses earned by women were 20 percent below the bonuses earned by men.

Some speeches focus entirely on a question of fact; the thesis itself is a question of fact. In other speeches, however, you may want just one of your main points to center on a question of fact. So, for example, let's say you're giving a speech advocating that a particular state give adoption rights to gay men and lesbians. In this case, one of your points might focus on a question of fact: You might seek to establish that gay men and lesbians make competent parents. Once you've established that, you'd then be in a better position to argue for adoption rights.

In a speech on questions of fact, you'll want to emphasize logical proof. Facts are your best support. The more facts you have, the more persuasive you'll be in dealing with questions of fact. For example, the more evidence you can find that women earn less than men, the more convincing you will be in proving that women do in fact earn less and, ultimately, that women are discriminated against.

Use the most recent materials possible. The more recent your materials, the more relevant they will be to the present time and the more persuasive they're likely to be. Notice, in our example, that if you said that in 2013 women earned on average $5,000 less than men, it would be meaningless in proving that the company discriminates against women *now*.

ORGANIZATION

Speeches on questions of fact probably fit most clearly into a topical organizational pattern, in which each reason for your thesis is given approximately equal weight. Notice, for example, that the outline of the speech under "Main Points" uses a topical order: Each of the reasons pointing to discrimination is treated as an equal main point.

Persuasive Speeches on Questions of Value

questions of value
Issues focused on what is good or bad, just or unjust.

Questions of value concern what people consider good or bad, moral or immoral, just or unjust. Bing, Yahoo!, and Google news (May 21, 2016) reported on such questions of value as these: Is it worth requiring DOJ attorneys to take ethics classes? Should the high school valedictorian have been banned from graduation for refusing to shave his beard? Should women be skeptical of Donald Trump? What does the United States hope to gain from sending tanks within miles of Russia?

Speeches on questions of value will seek to strengthen audiences' existing attitudes, beliefs, or values. This is true of much religious and political speaking; for example, people who listen to religious speeches usually are already believers, so these speeches strive to strengthen the beliefs and values the people already hold. In a religious setting, the listeners already share the speaker's values and are willing to listen. Speeches that seek to change audience values are much more difficult to construct. Most people resist change. When you try to get people to change their values or beliefs, you're fighting an uphill (though not necessarily impossible) battle.

Be sure that you clearly define the specific value on which you're focusing. For example, let's say that you're developing a speech to persuade high school students to attend college. You want to stress that college is of value, but what type of value do you focus on? The financial value (college graduates earn more money than nongraduates)? The social value (college is a lot of fun and a great place to make friends)? The intellectual value (college will broaden your view of the world and make you a more critical and creative thinker)? Once you clarify the type of value on which you'll focus, you'll find it easier to develop the relevant points. You'll also find it easier to locate appropriate supporting materials.

THESIS

Theses devoted to questions of value might look something like this:

- The death penalty is unjustifiable.
- Bullfighting is inhumane.
- Discrimination on the basis of affectional orientation is wrong.
- Chemical weapons are immoral.
- Human cloning is morally justified.
- College athletics minimize the importance of academics.

MAIN POINTS

As with speeches on questions of fact, you can generate the main points for a speech on a question of value by asking a strategic question of your thesis, such as "Why is this good?" or "Why is this immoral?" For example, you can take the first thesis given above and ask, "Why is the death penalty unjustifiable?" The answers to this question will give you the speech's main points. The body of your speech might then look something like this:

General purpose:	To persuade
Specific purpose:	To persuade my listeners that the death penalty is unjustifiable
Thesis:	The death penalty is unjustifiable. [Why is the death penalty unjustifiable?]

I. The criminal justice system can make mistakes.
II. The death penalty constitutes cruel and unusual punishment.
III. No one has the moral right to take another's life.

SUPPORT

To support your main points, search for relevant evidence. For example, to show that mistakes have been made in capital punishment cases, you might itemize three or four high-profile cases in which people were put to death and later, through DNA, found to have been innocent.

At times, and with certain topics, it may be useful to identify the standards you would use to judge something moral or justified or fair or good. For example, in the

VIEWPOINTS

Negative Audience

Alan is planning to give a speech arguing that certain lifestyle websites are inconsistent with a college's mission and therefore should be restricted. Alan knows that his audience is opposed to his position, so he wonders what main points will work best. *From what you know about persuasion and about your classmates, what advice would you give Alan?*

"bullfighting is inhumane" speech, you might devote your first main point to defining when an action can be considered inhumane. In this case, the body of your speech might look like this:

I. An inhumane act has two qualities.
   A. It is cruel and painful.
   B. It serves no human necessity.
II. Bullfighting is inhumane.
   A. It is cruel and painful.
   B. It serves no necessary function.

Notice that, in the example of capital punishment, the speaker aims to strengthen or change the listeners' beliefs about the death penalty. The speaker is not asking the audience to do anything about capital punishment, but merely to believe that it's not justified. However, you might also use a question of value as a first step toward persuading your audience to take some action. For example, once you got your listeners to see the death penalty as unjustified, you might then ask them to take certain actions—perhaps in your next speech—to support an anti–death penalty politician, to vote for or against a particular proposition, or to join an organization fighting against the death penalty.

ORGANIZATION

Like speeches on questions of fact, speeches on questions of value often lend themselves to topical organization. For example, the speech on capital punishment cited earlier uses a topical order. But even within this topical order there is another level of organization, an organization that begins with those items on which there is the least disagreement or opposition and moves on to the items on which your listeners are likely to see things very differently. It's likely that even listeners in favor of the death penalty would agree that mistakes can be made; and such listeners probably would be willing to accept evidence that mistakes have in fact been made—especially if you cite reliable statistical evidence and expert testimony. By starting with this issue, you secure initial agreement and can use that as a basis for approaching areas where you and the audience are more likely to disagree.

Persuasive Speeches on Questions of Policy

When you move beyond a focus on value to urging your audience to do something about an issue, you're then into a **question of policy**. For example, in a speech designed to convince your listeners that bullfighting is inhumane, you'd be focusing on a question of value. If you were to urge that bullfighting should therefore be declared illegal, you'd be urging the adoption of a particular policy. Items on Yahoo!, Bing, and Google news (May 21, 2016) that suggested questions of policy included these: What should the Affordable Care Act's position be on contraception? Should Mexico have extradited "El Chapo" to the US? Should the Federal Reserve increase interest rates? What should US policy be toward Russia's airstrikes in Syria?

questions of policy
Issues focused on what should or should not be done, what is and what is not a valuable policy.

Questions of policy concern what should be done, what procedures should be adopted, what laws should be changed; in short, what policy should be followed. In some speeches you may want to defend or promote a specific policy; in others you may wish to argue that a current policy should be discontinued.

THESIS

Persuasive speeches frequently revolve around questions of policy and may use theses such as the following:

- Hate speech should be banned on college campuses.
- Texting while driving should result in loss of license.
- Our community should adopt a zero tolerance policy for guns in schools.
- Recreational marijuana should be legalized.

- Abortion should be available on demand.
- Music CDs should be rated for violence and profanity

As you can tell from these examples, questions of policy almost invariably involve questions of values. For example, the argument that hate speech should be banned at colleges is based on the value judgment that hate speech is wrong. To argue for a zero tolerance policy on guns in schools implies that you think it's wrong for students or faculty to carry guns to school.

MAIN POINTS

You can develop your speech on a question of policy by asking a strategic question of your thesis. With policy issues, the question will be "Why should this policy be adopted?" or "Why should this policy be discontinued?" or "Why is this policy better than what we now have?" Taking our first example, we might ask, "Why should hate speech be banned on campus?" From the answers to this question, you would develop your main points, which might look something like this:

I. Hate speech encourages violence against women and minorities.

II. Hate speech denigrates women and minorities.

III. Hate speech teaches hate instead of tolerance.

SUPPORT

You would then support each main point with a variety of supporting materials that would convince your audience that hate speech should be banned from college campuses. For example, you might cite the websites put up by certain groups that advocate violence against women and minority members or quote from the lyrics of performers who came to campus. Or you might cite examples of actual violence that had been accompanied by hate speech or hate literature.

In some speeches on questions of policy, you might simply want your listeners to agree that the policy you're advocating is a good idea. In other cases you might want them to do something about the policy—to vote for a particular candidate, to take vitamin C, to diet, to write to their elected officials, to participate in a walkathon, to wear an AIDS awareness ribbon, and so on.

ORGANIZATION

Speeches on questions of policy may be organized in a variety of ways. For example, if the existing policy is doing harm, consider using a cause-to-effect pattern. If your policy is designed to solve a problem, consider the problem–solution pattern. For example, in a speech advocating zero tolerance for guns in school, the problem–solution pattern would seem appropriate; your speech would be divided into two basic parts:

I. Guns are destroying our high schools. [problem]

II. We must adopt a zero tolerance policy. [solution]

Questions of policy are often well suited to organization with the motivated sequence. Here is an example how a talk about hate speech might employ the motivated sequence.

Attention

I. Here are just a few of the examples of hate speech I collected right here on campus. [Show slides 1–7]

Need

II. Hate speech creates all sorts of problems.

A. Hate speech encourages violence.

B. Hate speech denigrates women and minorities.

C. Hate speech teaches intolerance.

Satisfaction

III. If we're to build an effective learning environment, hate speech must go.

Visualization

IV. Banning hate speech will help us build an environment conducive to learning.

  A. Students will not fear violence.

  B. Women and minorities will not feel as if they are second-class citizens.

  C. Tolerance can replace intolerance.

Action

V. Sign my petition urging the administration to take action, to ban hate speech.

If you're persuading your listeners that one policy will be more effective than another (say, that a new policy will be better than the present policy), then a comparison-and-contrast organization might work best. Here you might divide each of your main points into two parts—the present policy and the proposed plan—so as to effectively compare and contrast them on each issue. For example, the body of a speech urging a new health-care plan might look something like this:

I. The plans are different in their coverage for psychiatric problems.

  A. The present plan offers nothing for such problems.

  B. The proposed plan treats psychiatric problems with the same coverage as physical problems.

II. The plans differ in their deductibles.

  A. The present plan has a $2,000 deductible.

  B. The proposed plan has a $500 deductible.

III. The plans differ in the hospitalization allowances.

  A. In the present plan two days are allowed for childbirth; in the proposed plan four days are allowed.

  B. In the present plan all patients are assigned to large wards; in the proposed plan all patients are assigned to semiprivate rooms.

Table 10.3 summarizes the three types of persuasive speeches in terms of their purposes, examples of the types of questions such speeches deal with, and the questions the audience is likely to ask and that you will likely want to have answers for somewhere in your speech.

TABLE 10.3 Questions of Fact, Value, and Policy

Question Purposes	Examples	Questions Audience May Want Answered
Questions of Fact: To persuade listeners that something is true or false.	■ Higgins is guilty (not guilty). ■ What he did was criminal (legal). ■ The stock market will go much higher (much lower).	■ Is this the most likely interpretation of the issue? ■ Are other, more likely, explanations possible? ■ How do we know that this is true or that this is false?
Questions of Value: To persuade listeners in the value of something, that something is good, moral, or just.	■ Higgins deserves the chair (to go free). ■ Universal health care is essential (not essential).	■ Why is this good or just or the right thing to do? Are there alternatives that would be more just or fairer? ■ Is this war just (unjust)?
Questions of Policy: To persuade listeners that this is the policy to adopt or not adopt.	■ The verdict must be guilty (not guilty). ■ Plan B needs to be enacted (discarded). ■ The war needs to be continued (discontinued).	■ Might there be better courses of action to follow? ■ Are there downsides to this course of action?

SUMMARY: PERSUADING YOUR AUDIENCE

In this chapter we looked at the persuasive speech: its goals, the principles of persuasion, and the three main types of persuasive speeches.

Principles of Persuasive Speaking

10.1 Paraphrase the principles of persuasive speaking.

1. Among the important principles for persuasive speaking are:
   - Keep your persuasive goal in mind.
   - Be culturally sensitive.
   - Identify with your audience.
   - Secure a *yes* response.
   - Anticipate selective exposure.
   - Use positive labeling.
   - Ask for reasonable amounts of change.
   - Provide social proof.
   - Motivate your listeners.

The Three Persuasive Proofs

10.2 Explain the three persuasive proofs (logical, emotional, and credibility).

2. The three persuasive proofs are:
   - Logical proof, the evidence and arguments
   - Emotional proof, the motivational appeals
   - Credibility appeals

Persuasive Speeches of Fact, Value, and Policy

10.3 Explain the nature of speeches of fact, value, and policy and the guidelines for preparing such speeches.

3. Persuasive speeches on questions of fact focus on what is or is not true. In a speech on a question of fact:
   - Emphasize logical proof.
   - Use the most recent materials possible.
   - Use highly competent sources.
   - Clearly connect your main points to your thesis.

4. Speeches on questions of value focus on issues of good and bad, justice or injustice. In designing speeches to strengthen or change attitudes, beliefs, or values:
   - Define clearly the specific value on which you're focusing.
   - Begin with shared assumptions and beliefs, then progress gradually to areas of disagreement.
   - Use sources that the audience values highly.

5. Speeches on questions of policy focus on what should or should not be done, what procedures should or should not be adopted. In designing speeches to move listeners to action:
   - Prove that the policy is needed.
   - Emphasize that the policy you're supporting is practical and reasonable.
   - Show your listeners how the policy will benefit them directly.
   - When asking for action, ask for small, easily performed, and very specific behaviors.
   - Use an organizational pattern that best fits your topic.

KEY TERMS: PERSUADING YOUR AUDIENCE

agenda-setting
anecdotal evidence
appeal to tradition
character
charisma
collectivist cultures
competence
credibility proof
emotional proof

ethos
feminist cultures
high-ambiguity-tolerant cultures
high-context cultures
high-power-distance cultures
individualist cultures
indulgent cultures
logical proof
logos

long-term-oriented cultures
low-ambiguity-tolerant cultures
low-context cultures
low-power-distance cultures
masculine cultures
motivated sequence
pathos
questions of policy
questions of fact

questions of value	reasoning from specific instances	social proof
reasoning from causes and effects	restrained cultures	testimonial
reasoning from sign	selective exposure	thin entering wedge
	short-term-oriented cultures	transfer

PUBLIC SPEAKING EXERCISES

10.1 Constructing Motivational Appeals

Here are a few theses you might use or hear in a persuasive speech. Select one of these and develop two or three motivational appeals that you might use in a speech to members of this class.

- Universal health care is a human right.
- "In God we trust" should be removed from all U.S. currency.
- Capital punishment should be declared illegal.
- Smoking should be banned throughout the entire college (buildings and grounds).
- Community college education should be free to all high school graduates.
- Tenure for teachers should be abolished.

10.2 Questions of Fact, Value, and Policy

Understanding how purposes and theses can be identified from a wide variety of questions of fact, value, and policy will help you construct more effective speeches. To develop this understanding, select an Internet news website (Google, Bing, Yahoo!, the Huffington Post, or any national newspaper or magazine site will work well) and identify the questions of fact, value, and policy covered in this one issue (as was done in this chapter). From these, select one question of fact, value, or policy and develop a general purpose, a specific purpose, a thesis that would be appropriate for a speech in this class, and two or three main ideas that you might want to develop based on this thesis.

SPEAKING ON SPECIAL OCCASIONS

→ Special occasions often call for public speaking.

CHAPTER TOPICS

LEARNING OBJECTIVES

CHAPTER TOPICS	LEARNING OBJECTIVES
The Introduction Speech	**11.1** Explain the introduction speech and the guidelines for preparing the speech.
The Presentation or Acceptance Speech	**11.2** Explain the presentation and acceptance speeches and the guidelines for preparing the speeches.
The Speech to Secure Goodwill	**11.3** Explain the speech to secure goodwill and the guidelines for preparing the speech.
The Dedication Speech	**11.4** Explain the dedication speech and the guidelines for preparing the speech.
The Commencement Speech	**11.5** Explain the commencement speech and the guidelines for preparing the speech.
The Inspirational Speech	**11.6** Explain the inspirational speech and the guidelines for preparing the speech.
The Eulogy	**11.7** Explain the eulogy and the guidelines for preparing the speech.
The Farewell Speech	**11.8** Explain the farewell speech and the guidelines for preparing the speech.
The Toast	**11.9** Explain the toast and the guidelines for preparing the speech.

n addition to the many varieties of informative and persuasive speeches, there are several types of speeches usually called "special occasion speeches" with which you'll want to achieve some familiarity. In this chapter we'll consider speeches to introduce someone, to present or accept an award, to secure goodwill or apologize, to dedicate something, to congratulate a graduating class (the commencement speech), to eulogize someone, to bid farewell, and to toast.

Like all forms of communication, the special occasion speech must be developed with a clear understanding of the influence of culture. For example, the discussion of the speech of introduction suggests that you not oversell the speaker; excessive exaggeration is generally evaluated negatively in much of the United States. On the other hand, exaggerated praise often is expected in some Latin cultures.

Similarly, the discussion of the speech of goodwill suggests that you present yourself as being worthy of the goodwill rather than as a supplicant begging for it. In some cultures, however, this attitude might be seen as arrogant and disrespectful to the audience. In some Asian cultures, for example, pleading for goodwill would be seen as suitably modest and respectful of the audience.

The Introduction Speech

11.1 Explain the introduction speech and the guidelines for preparing the speech.

introduction speech

A special occasion speech designed to introduce the speaker himself or herself to an audience or a speech designed to introduce another speaker or group of speakers.

The **introduction speech** considered here is a bit different and is usually designed to introduce a speaker or a topic that a series of speakers will address. For example, before a speaker addresses an audience, another speaker often sets the stage by introducing both the speaker and the topic. At conventions, where a series of speakers address an audience, a speech of introduction might introduce the general topic on which the speakers will focus and perhaps provide connecting links among the several presentations.

In a speech of introduction, your main purpose is to gain the attention and arouse the interest of the audience. The speech of introduction is basically informative and follows the general patterns already discussed for an informative speech. The main difference is that instead of discussing a topic's issues, you discuss who the speaker is and what the speaker will talk about. In your speeches of introduction, follow these general principles:

- **Establish the significance of the speech.** Focus the audience's attention and interest on the main speaker and on the importance of what the speaker will say.

- **Establish relevant connections among the speaker, the topic, and the audience.** Answer your listeners' inevitable question: Why should we listen to this speaker on this topic?

- **Stress the speaker's credibility.** For example, tell the audience what has earned this speaker the right to speak on this topic to this audience (see Chapter 10).

- **Speak in a style and manner that are consistent with the main speech.** Introduce the speaker with the same degree of formality that will prevail during the actual speech. Otherwise, the speaker will have to counteract an inappropriate atmosphere created by the speech of introduction.

- **Be brief (relative to the length of the main speech).** If the main speech is to be brief—say, 10 to 20 minutes—your introduction should be no longer than 1 or 2 minutes. If, on the other hand, the main speech is to be an hour long, then your introduction might last 5 to 10 minutes or even longer.

- **Don't cover the substance of the topic the speaker will discuss.** Also remember that clever stories, jokes, startling statistics, or historical analogies, which are often effective in speeches of introduction, will prove a liability if the main speaker intended to use this same material.
- **Don't oversell the speaker or topic.** Present the speaker in a positive light, but don't create an image that the speaker will find impossible to live up to.

JOURNAL 11.1 PUBLIC SPEAKING CHOICE POINT

The Introduction Speech

You've been assigned the pleasant task of introducing your favorite media personality to the members of your class. *In about 100 to 150 words, what are some of the things you might say?*

The Presentation or Acceptance Speech

11.2 Explain presentation and acceptance speeches and the guidelines for preparing the speeches.

We'll consider speeches of presentation and speeches of acceptance together because they're frequently paired and because the same general principles govern both types of speeches. In a **presentation speech** you seek to (1) place an award or honor in some kind of context and (2) give the award an extra air of dignity or status. A speech of presentation may focus on rewarding a colleague for an important accomplishment (being named Teacher of the Year) or on recognizing a particularly impressive performance (winning an Academy Award). It may honor an employee's service to a company or a student's outstanding grades or athletic abilities.

presentation speech
A special occasion speech in which a speaker presents an award or some sign of recognition.

The **acceptance speech** is the other side of this honoring ceremony. Here the recipient accepts the award and attempts to place the award in some kind of context. At times the presentation and the acceptance speeches are rather informal and amount to a simple "You really deserve this" and an equally simple "Thank you." At other times—for example, in the presentation and acceptance of a Nobel Prize—the speeches are formal and are prepared in great detail and with great care. Such speeches are frequently reprinted in newspapers throughout the world. Somewhere between these two extremes lie average speeches of presentation and acceptance.

acceptance speech
A special occasion speech in which the speaker accepts an award or honor of some kind and attempts to place the award in some kind of context.

In your speeches of presentation, follow these two principles:

- **State the reason for the presentation.** Make clear why this particular award is being given to this particular person.
- **State the importance of the award.** The audience (as well as the group authorizing or sponsoring the award) will no doubt want to hear something about this. You might point out the importance of the award by referring to the previous recipients (assuming they're well known to the audience), emphasizing the status of the award (assuming that it's a prestigious award), or describing the award's influence on previous recipients.

In preparing and presenting your speech of acceptance, follow these three principles:

- **Thank the people responsible for giving you the award.** Thank the academy members, the board of directors, the student body, or your teammates, for example.

- **Acknowledge those who helped you achieve the award.** Be specific without being overly detailed.
- **Put the award into personal perspective.** For example, you might tell the audience what the award means to you right now and perhaps what it will mean to you in the future.

JOURNAL 11.2 PUBLIC SPEAKING CHOICE POINT

Presenting an Award

You've been asked to present the Academy Award for best supporting actor (select your own favorite). The speech is to last no longer than 1 minute (approximately 150 words). *What are your options? What would you say to improve upon the actual speeches given at these award shows?*

In many acceptance speeches, the speaker will not only thank those who contributed to the award but also make a special plea for a cause with which the award is associated. For example, when Leonardo DiCaprio accepted the Academy Award for best actor for *The Revenant*, he also made a plea that audiences face and combat the threat of climate control.

The Speech To Secure Goodwill

11.3 Explain the speech to secure goodwill and the guidelines for preparing the speech.

goodwill speech

A special occasion speech in which the speaker seeks to make the image of a person, product, or company more positive.

The **goodwill speech** is part information and part persuasion. On the surface, the speech informs the audience about a product, company, profession, institution, or

VIEWPOINTS

Acceptance Speeches

If you were accepting a prestigious award and had an opportunity to thank those who contributed to your success but also plead the case for a special cause, what would you say?

person. Beneath this surface, however, lies a more persuasive purpose: to heighten the image of a person, product, or company—to create a more positive attitude toward this person or thing. Many speeches of goodwill have a further persuasive purpose: to get audience members ultimately to change their behavior toward the person, product, or company.

A special type of goodwill speech is the speech of self-justification, in which the speaker seeks to justify his or her actions to the audience. Political figures do this frequently. Richard Nixon's "Checkers Speech," his Cambodia-bombing speeches, and, of course, his Watergate speeches are clear examples of speeches of self-justification. Edward Kennedy's Chappaquiddick speech, in which he attempted to justify what happened when Mary Jo Kopechne drowned, is another example. In securing goodwill, whether for another person or for yourself, consider the following suggestions:

- **Demonstrate the contributions that deserve goodwill.** Show how the audience may benefit from this company, product, or person. Or at least—in the speech of self-justification—show that the listeners have not been hurt; or, if they have been hurt, that the injury was unintentional.

- **Stress uniqueness.** In a world dominated by competition, the speech to secure goodwill must stress the uniqueness of the specific company, person, profession, situation, and so on. Distinguish your subject clearly from all others; otherwise, any goodwill you secure will be spread over the entire field.

- **Establish credibility.** Speeches to secure goodwill must also establish credibility, thereby securing goodwill for the individual or commodity. To do so, concentrate on those dimensions of credibility discussed in Chapter 10. Demonstrate that the person is competent, of good intention, and of high moral character.

- **Don't be obvious.** The effective goodwill speech looks, on the surface, very much like an objective informative speech. It will not appear to ask for goodwill, except on close analysis.

JOURNAL 11.3 PUBLIC SPEAKING CHOICE POINT

Securing Goodwill

Jimmy has been asked by his catering firm—which was cited by the Board of Health for several health violations a year ago—to present to the local Board of Education the firm's case for the catering contract for the entire elementary school district. The board members agree to hear Jimmy but are generally reluctant to hire his firm because of its history of unsafe practices. *What are some of the things Jimmy could say to secure goodwill (and another chance)?*

Another type of goodwill speech is the **apology speech**, a speech in which the speaker apologizes for some transgression and tries to restore his or her credibility and the goodwill of the listeners. President Bill Clinton's speech on misleading the nation about his affair with a young intern is a good example of a speech of apology designed to secure goodwill. Another good example is reprinted here. In this speech

apology speech
A special occasion speech in which the speaker expresses regret for some transgression and asks for forgiveness.

SPEECH OF APOLOGY

Eliot Spitzer

In the past few days, I have begun to atone for my private failings with my wife Silda, my children, and my entire family. The remorse I feel will always be with me. Words cannot describe how grateful I am for the love and compassion they have shown me.

From those to whom much is given, much is expected. I have been given much—the love of my family, the faith and trust of the people of New York, and the chance to lead this state. I am deeply sorry that I did not live up to what was expected of me. To every New Yorker—and to all those who believed in what I tried to stand for—I sincerely apologize.

I look at my time as governor with a sense of what might have been. But I also know that as a public servant, I and the remarkable people with whom I worked have accomplished a great deal. There is much more to be done, and I cannot allow my private failings to disrupt the people's work.

Over the course of my public life, I have insisted—I believe correctly—that people, regardless of their position or power, take responsibility for their conduct. I can and will ask no less of myself.

For this reason, I am resigning from the office of governor. At Lt. Gov. Paterson's request, the resignation will be effective Monday, March 17, a date that he believes will permit an orderly transition.

I go forward with the belief, as others have said, that as human beings, our greatest glory consists not in never falling, but in rising every time we fall.

As I leave public life, I will first do what I need to do to help and heal myself and my family. Then I will try once again, outside of politics, to serve the common good and move toward the ideals and solutions which I believe can build a future of hope and opportunity for us and for our children.

I hope all New York will join my prayers for my friend David Paterson, as he embarks on his new mission. And I thank the public once again for the privilege of service.

VIEWPOINTS

Apologies

In crafting an apology (say, for some political wrongdoing), what should the speaker be especially careful to avoid saying? Put differently, what are some of the things you would advise a speaker making an apology not *to do?*

then Governor of New York Eliot Spitzer apologized for his transgressions—he was a client of a high-end prostitution syndicate—and resigned as governor.

The Dedication Speech

11.4 Explain the dedication speech and the guidelines for preparing the speech.

The **dedication speech** is designed to give some specific meaning to, say, a new research lab, a store opening, or the start of the building of a bridge. This speech is usually given at a rather formal occasion. In preparing a dedication speech, consider the following suggestions:

- **State the reason you're giving the dedication.** For example, you might identify the connection you have to the project.
- **Explain exactly what is being dedicated.** If it's the opening of the bridge linking Roosevelt Island to Manhattan, say so early in your dedication.
- **Note who is responsible for the project.** Tell the audience, for example, who designed the bridge, who constructed it, and who paid for it.
- **Explain why this project is significant.** What advantages will it create? For example, you might describe the relevance the bridge has to your audience; that is, what changes will occur as a result of this bridge and how the bridge will benefit your listeners.

JOURNAL 11.4 PUBLIC SPEAKING CHOICE POINT

The Dedication Speech

You won the mega-lottery and have built new computer labs for your college with some of the money. *What are some of the things you might say in a brief—2-minute—speech of dedication?*

Here is an excellent speech of dedication of the statue honoring Rosa Parks by President Barack Obama.

dedication speech

A special occasion speech in which you commemorate the opening or start of a project.

PUBLIC SPEAKING Sample Assistant

DEDICATION SPEECH

President Barack Obama

Mr. Speaker, Leader Reid, Leader McConnell, Leader Pelosi, Assistant Leader Clyburn; to the friends and family of Rosa Parks; to the distinguished guests who are gathered here today.

This morning, we celebrate a seamstress, slight in stature but mighty in courage. She defied the odds, and she defied injustice. She lived a life of activism, but also a life of dignity and grace. And in a single moment, with the simplest of gestures, she helped change America—and change the world.

Rosa Parks held no elected office. She possessed no fortune; lived her life far from the formal seats of power. And yet today, she takes her rightful place among those who've shaped this nation's course. I thank all those persons, in particular the members of the Congressional Black Caucus, both past and present, for making this moment possible.

A childhood friend once said about Mrs. Parks, "Nobody ever bossed Rosa around and got away with it." (Laughter.) That's what an Alabama driver learned on December 1, 1955. Twelve years earlier, he had kicked Mrs. Parks off his bus simply because she entered through the front door when the back door was too crowded. He grabbed her sleeve and he pushed her off the bus. It made her mad enough, she would recall, that she avoided riding his bus for a while.

And when they met again that winter evening in 1955, Rosa Parks would not be pushed. When the driver got up from his seat to insist that she give up hers, she would not be pushed. When he threatened to have her arrested, she simply replied, "You may do that." And he did.

A few days later, Rosa Parks challenged her arrest. A little-known pastor, new to town and only 26 years old, stood with her—a man named Martin Luther King, Jr. So did thousands of Montgomery, Alabama commuters. They began a boycott—teachers and laborers, clergy and domestics, through rain and cold and sweltering heat, day after day, week after week, month after month, walking miles if they had to, arranging carpools where they could, not thinking about the blisters on their feet, the weariness after a full day of work—walking for respect, walking for freedom, driven by a solemn determination to affirm their God-given dignity.

Three hundred and eighty-five days after Rosa Parks refused to give up her seat, the boycott ended. Black men and women and children re-boarded the buses of Montgomery, newly desegregated, and sat in whatever seat happen to be open. (Applause.) And with that victory, the entire edifice of segregation, like the ancient walls of Jericho, began to slowly come tumbling down.

It's been often remarked that Rosa Parks's activism didn't begin on that bus. Long before she made headlines, she had stood up for freedom, stood up for equality—fighting for voting rights, rallying against discrimination in the criminal justice system, serving in the local chapter of the NAACP. Her quiet leadership would continue long after she became an icon of the civil rights movement, working with Congressman Conyers to find homes for the homeless, preparing disadvantaged youth for a path to success, striving each day to right some wrong somewhere in this world.

And yet our minds fasten on that single moment on the bus—Ms. Parks alone in that seat, clutching her purse, staring out a window, waiting to be arrested. That moment tells us something about how change happens, or doesn't happen; the choices we make, or don't make. "For now we see through a glass, darkly," Scripture says, and it's true. Whether out of inertia or selfishness, whether out of fear or a simple lack of moral imagination, we so often spend our lives as if in a fog, accepting injustice, rationalizing inequity, tolerating the intolerable.

Like the bus driver, but also like the passengers on the bus, we see the way things are—children hungry in a land of plenty, entire neighborhoods ravaged by violence, families hobbled by job loss or illness—and we make excuses for inaction, and we say to ourselves, that's not my responsibility, there's nothing I can do.

Rosa Parks tell us there's always something we can do. She tells us that we all have responsibilities, to ourselves and to one another. She reminds us that this is how change happens—not mainly through the exploits of the famous and the powerful, but through the countless acts of often anonymous courage and kindness and fellow feeling and responsibility that continually, stubbornly, expand our conception of justice—our conception of what is possible.

Rosa Parks's singular act of disobedience launched a movement. The tired feet of those who walked the dusty roads of Montgomery helped a nation see that to which it had once been blind. It is because of these men and women that I stand here today. It is because of them that our children grow up in a land more free and more fair; a land truer to its founding creed.

And that is why this statue belongs in this hall—to remind us, no matter how humble or lofty our positions, just what it is that leadership requires; just what it is that citizenship requires. Rosa Parks would have turned 100 years old this month. We do well by placing a statue of her here. But we can do no greater honor to her memory than to carry forward the power of her principle and a courage born of conviction.

May God bless the memory of Rosa Parks, and may God bless these United States of America.

Source: https://www.whitehouse.gov/photos-and-video/video/2013/02/27/president-obama-dedicates-statue-honoring-rosa-parks#transcript

VIEWPOINTS

The Importance of Dedication Speeches

What functions do speeches of dedication serve when they are given? What functions do they serve in a more long-term historical view?

The Commencement Speech

11.5 Explain the commencement speech and the guidelines for preparing the speech.

commencement speech

A special occasion speech given to celebrate the end of some training period, often at school graduation ceremonies.

The **commencement speech** recognizes and celebrates the end of some training period, such as the listeners' school or college years. The commencement speech is designed to congratulate and inspire the recent graduates and is often intended to mark the transition from school to the next stage in life. Usually the person asked to give a commencement speech is a well-known personality. The speakers at college graduations—depending on the prestige of the institution—are often important men and women in the world: presidents, senators, religious leaders, Nobel Prize winners, famous scientists, and people of similar accomplishment. Or a commencement speech may be given by a student who has achieved some exceptional goal; for example, the student with the highest grade point average or the recipient of a prestigious award. In giving a commencement speech, consider the following:

- **Consider organizing the speech in a temporal pattern.** Beginning with the past, commenting on the present, and projecting into the future is one easy to develop and follow pattern.

- **Do your research.** Learn about the school, the student body, and the goals and ambitions of the graduates, and integrate these into your speech.
- **Be brief.** Recognize that audience members have other things on their minds—the graduation party, for example—and may become restless if your speech is too long.
- **Congratulate the graduates.** But also congratulate the parents, friends, and instructors who contributed to this day as well.
- **Motivate the graduates.** Offer the graduates some kind of motivational message, some guidance, some suggestions for taking their education and using it in their lives.
- **Offer your own good wishes to the graduates.** It often helps to end on a personal note, extending your own best wishes.

JOURNAL 11.5 PUBLIC SPEAKING CHOICE POINT

The Commencement Speech

Visualize yourself at your own graduation listening to a well-known speaker giving the commencement address. *What are some of the things you would want to hear the speaker say? What are some of the things you would not want to hear?*

The Inspirational Speech

11.6 Explain the inspirational speech and the guidelines for preparing the speech.

A great many special occasion speeches aim to inspire the audience, as you've seen in the speeches already covered. Some speeches, however, are designed *primarily* to inspire; raising the spirits of an audience is their primary objective. Many religious speeches are of this type. Similarly, speeches that corporate leaders give to stockholders when introducing a new product or a new CEO, for example, would be designed to inspire investors. A commanding officer might give a speech of inspiration to the troops before going into battle. And, of course, there are the speeches of professional motivational speakers

ETHICAL CHOICE POINT

Telling the Truth

You'll be delivering the commencement speech to a graduating class at the high school you attended. In all honesty, you thought the education you received was especially poor; the teachers were unconcerned, the science and computer labs were 30 years old, and all the money went to athletic programs. You want to criticize the poor educational training the high school provided and urge students to approach college with a new perspective. At the same time, you want to appeal to a wider audience—the school board, the community at large, the city government—and get them to provide the school with better facilities and additional staff. Given that a commencement speech is usually a positive, congratulatory exercise, you wonder if you should present this somewhat-negative picture. *What are your ethical choices for being honest and yet being consistent with the nature of the situation?*

inspirational speech

A special occasion speech designed to raise the spirits of the audience, to inspire them.

who seek to arouse the audience to feel better about themselves by organizing their lives, taking chances, giving up drugs, or doing any of a variety of things.

Before reading some suggestions for preparing and presenting an **inspirational speech**, consider the speech by Nikki Giovanni. This is a particularly impressive inspirational speech given by Virginia Tech faculty member and poet Giovanni after 32 students and faculty were killed at the college on April 16, 2007.

Here are a few suggestions for preparing and presenting an inspiration speech:

- **Demonstrate your oneness with the audience.** Try to show in some way that you and your listeners have significant similarities. Notice in this accompanying speech the repeated use of *we*: It makes listeners feel connected to the speaker.

- **Demonstrate your own intense involvement.** Display to audience members the kind of intensity you want them to show. You cannot make others feel emotions if you don't feel them yourself.

- **Stress emotional appeals.** Inspiring an audience has to do more with emotions than with logic. Use appeals that are consistent with the nature of the event. In Nikki Giovanni's speech you see appeals to pity, loyalty to friends and institution, and empathy for others.

- **Stress the positive.** Especially, end your speech on a positive note. Inspirational speeches are always positive. Note the positiveness in Giovanni's speech: "We will prevail. We will prevail. We will prevail."

JOURNAL 11.6 PUBLIC SPEAKING CHOICE POINT

An Inspiration Speech

Tonya wants to give an inspiration speech to her class on the topic of Ramadan. *What are some of Tonya's options for sharing the inspirational aspects of this holiday? What are some ways she might introduce the topic to gain attention and then conclude effectively?*

PUBLIC SPEAKING Sample Assistant

SPEECH OF INSPIRATION

Professor Nikki Giovanni*

We are Virginia Tech.

We are sad today, and we will be sad for quite a while. We are not moving on, we are embracing our mourning.

We are Virginia Tech.

We are strong enough to stand tall tearlessly, we are brave enough to bend to cry, and we are sad enough to know that we must laugh again.

We are Virginia Tech.

We do not understand this tragedy. We know we did nothing to deserve it, but neither does a child in Africa dying of AIDS, neither do the invisible children walking the night away to avoid being captured by the rogue army, neither does the baby elephant watching his community being devastated for ivory, neither does the Mexican child looking for fresh water, neither does the Appalachian infant killed in the middle of the night in his crib in the home his father built with

his own hands being run over by a boulder because the land was destabilized. No one deserves a tragedy.

We are Virginia Tech.

The Hokie Nation embraces our own and reaches out with open heart and hands to those who offer their hearts and minds. We are strong, and brave, and innocent, and unafraid. We are better than we think and not quite what we want to be. We are alive to the imaginations and the possibilities. We will continue to invent the future through our blood and tears and through all our sadness.

We are the Hokies.

We will prevail.

We will prevail.

We will prevail.

We are Virginia Tech.

*By permission of the author. © 2008.

The Eulogy

11.7 Explain the eulogy and the guidelines for preparing the speech.

The **eulogy** is a speech of tribute in which you seek to praise someone who has died. In the eulogy you attempt to put the person's life and contributions in perspective and show him or her in a positive light. This type of speech is often given at a funeral or at the anniversary of the person's birth or death. This is not the time for a balanced appraisal of the individual's life. Rather, it's a time for praise. In developing the eulogy, consider the following:

eulogy

A special occasion speech of tribute in which the speaker praises someone who died.

- **Relate the person to the audience.** Stress the connection between the life you're celebrating to yourself, to those in the audience, and, if appropriate, to the larger audience—for example, the scientific community, the world of book lovers, or those who have devoted their lives to peace.

- **Be specific.** Show that you really knew the person or know a great deal about the person. The best way to do that is to give specific examples from the person's life. Then combine the specifics with the more general so the audience can see these specifics as being a part of some larger whole—for example, after you mention the several books that an author wrote, frame the author's contribution in a more general way within the mystery genre or contemporary poetry genre.

- **Portray a deserving person.** Make the audience see that this person is deserving of the praise you are bestowing on him or her by explaining what this person accomplished and how this person influenced—for example—the world of patient care, the design of safer cars, and so on.

- **Show the audience what they can learn from this individual.** Point out the qualities of the individual that can help and guide the lives of the friends and family members. For example, the person's courage in the time of adversity or the strength of character to stand up for what he or she believed.

Here is a particularly excellent eulogy written and delivered by Bernard J. Brommel, a professor of communication and a family therapist, at the memorial service for his brother Phil.

PUBLIC SPEAKING Sample Assistant

EULOGY

Bernard J. Brommel*

Thoughts to the eight children of my brother, Phil:

Something seems unreal to be writing this seven months after your mother, Joyce's death! We hoped and thought he would long survive her. Such did not happen. Somehow saying "That's life" just seems unfair. None of you children have had enough time to say goodbye to one parent and now two! I think it must be especially hard for each of you because you had a tender relationship with your mother.

How do I speak of my brother, Phil? Phil was like Dad, both in his strengths and in his weaknesses. They both went through life "double time," two streaks of lightning blazing away. They were both "workaholics."

I grew up with Phil. I had been on this earth five years when he arrived as the sixth of the nine of us. From day one he was adored and a favorite of our mother. He had as a

baby a winsome way; he had a head of snow-white hair; he had a mind of his own. Realize that he needed that independence to find a place among his eight siblings.

Back then on the farm we had a fenced big yard with a gate at either end to help Mom corral us kids. The gates had latches but Phil never saw a latch or lock that he did not open. Mom moved on to tying the gates shut, but Phil untied them with ease. It must have been the beginning of his mechanical genius.

From the beginning Phil was a strong baby; a strong youth; a strong man. Some of you may vaguely remember when he took the Charles Atlas Body Building Course. He already was fit, but when Phil set out to do something, it happened. He became a muscled Adonis, a young Greek god. So it was with his life; he made things happen that he desired. He used that early strength to lift easily bales of hay to be followed by huge bars of steel that he could weld into tall buildings. Dad liked to tinker and fix things but by junior high Phil was the better mechanic. Phil never saw a motor that he did not want to tear apart and make work better. And he loved speed! How often did he scare you by going so fast?

We have a word for people like Phil. We call them "edge walkers." They challenge life at the edges. Phil wanted to be the most fit; the strongest, the fastest; the one to do things the rest of us did not have the guts to try.

An example of Phil as an edge walker was daily played out in his work as a welder/iron worker. He had no fear of heights. Several times I saw him, maybe 30 stories in the Des Moines sky, walking beams like they were as wide as the road. And he often was carrying tools, balancing like a gymnast. His sister, Florence, would look often out her bank office window and marvel at his agility. I do not know that Phil knew she watched, but she did watch over her younger brother!

May you now go to rest beside Joyce who was literally always by your side. You will rest as the 5th of your siblings, near your parents and the family clan. I had the joy of speaking to you a few days ago when you knew what was happening to your body. Your body may have been weak but your mind was keen. I said in the end "My best wishes to you. I will not say goodbye!" He said, "Brother, I'll see you down the road." Let's let Phillip have the last words to each of us, "I'll see you down the road."

*Reprinted by permission of the author.

JOURNAL 11.7 PUBLIC SPEAKING CHOICE POINT

The Eulogy

What are some of the things you might say in a eulogy—of one or two minutes—for a media personality that you admired?

The Farewell Speech

11.8 Explain the farewell speech and the guidelines for preparing the speech.

farewell speech
A special occasion speech designed to say goodbye to a position or to colleagues and to signal that you're moving on.

In the **farewell speech** you say goodbye to an organization or to colleagues and signal that you're moving on. In this speech you'll want to express your positive feelings to those you're leaving. Generally, the farewell speech is given after you've achieved some level of distinction within a company or other group or organization that you're now leaving. In developing a farewell speech, consider the following:

- **Thank those who contributed.** Give thanks and credit to those who made life interesting, helped you in your position, taught you essential principles, and so on.
- **Note your achievements modestly.** Put them in a positive light, but do so gently and with modesty.
- **Express your enjoyment of the experience.** This is a time for positive reflection, not for critical evaluation, so put aside the negative memories, at least for this speech.
- **State your reasons for leaving.** This isn't always appropriate, but, when it is, tell your listeners your reason for leaving and your plans for the future.
- **Express good wishes to those who remain.**
- **Offer some words of wisdom.** Tell the audience what you learned and what you now want to pass on to those remaining.

JOURNAL 11.8 PUBLIC SPEAKING CHOICE POINT

The Farewell Speech

Visualize yourself as a new hire in a large investment firm and looking forward to working there throughout your career. The manager who hired you is now leaving. *What are some of the things you would want him or her to say in the speech of farewell?*

Here is one of the classic farewell speeches of all time: Lou Gehrig's farewell to baseball. In the first column is the speech that Lou Gehrig actually gave. The second column presents the speech as delivered by Gary Cooper in the movie *Pride of the Yankees* with the camera panning the people Cooper is talking about.

Lou Gehrig's Actual Speech	Lou Gehrig's Movie Version Speech
Fans, for the past two weeks you have been reading about a bad break I got. Yet today I consider myself the luckiest man on the face of the earth.	I have been walking on ball fields for 16 years, and I've never received anything but kindness and encouragement from you fans. I have had the great honor to have played with these great veteran ballplayers on my left—Murderers Row, our championship team of 1927.
I have been in ballparks for seventeen years and have never received anything but kindness and encouragement from you fans. Look at these grand men. Which of you wouldn't consider it the highlight of his career just to associate with them for even one day?	I have had the further honor of living with and playing with these men on my right—the Bronx Bombers, the Yankees of today.
Sure I'm lucky.	I have been given fame and undeserved praise by the boys up there behind the wire in the press box—my friends, the sports writers. I have worked under the two greatest managers of all time, Miller Huggins and Joe McCarthy.
Who wouldn't consider it an honor to have known Jacob Ruppert? Also, the builder of baseball's greatest empire, Ed Barrow? To have spent six years with that wonderful little fellow, Miller Huggins? Then to have spent the next nine years with that outstanding leader, that smart student of psychology, the best manager in baseball today, Joe McCarthy?	I have a mother and father who fought to give me health and a solid background in my youth.
Sure I'm lucky.	I have a wife, a companion for life, who has shown me more courage than I ever knew.
When the New York Giants, a team you would give your right arm to beat, and vice versa, sends you a gift—that's something. When everybody down to the groundskeepers and those boys in white coats remember you with trophies—that's something.	People all say that I've had a bad break. But today—today I consider myself the luckiest man on the face of the earth.
When you have a wonderful mother-in-law who takes sides with you in squabbles with her own daughter—that's something.	
When you have a father and a mother who work all their lives so you can have an education and build your body—it's a blessing.	
When you have a wife who has been a tower of strength and shown more courage than you dreamed existed—that's the finest I know.	
So, I close in saying that I might have been given a bad break, but I've got an awful lot to live for.	

VIEWPOINTS

Saying Farewell

Examine the speeches delivered by Lou Gehrig, pictured here from a 1925 photo, as well as by Gary Cooper in the movie. *Which do you find more moving? Why?*

The Toast

11.9 Explain the toast and the guidelines for preparing the speech.

toast
A special occasion speech designed to celebrate a person or an occasion.

The **toast** is a brief speech designed to celebrate a person or an occasion. You might, for example, toast the next CEO of your company, a friend who just got admitted to a prestigious graduate program, or a colleague on the occasion of a promotion. Often toasts are given at weddings or at the start of a new venture. The toast is designed to say hello or good luck in a relatively formal sense. In developing your toast consider the following:

- **Be brief.** Realize that people want to get on with the festivities and don't want to listen to an overly long speech.
- **Focus attention on the other person(s).** Often speakers get so involved that they begin to focus on themselves instead of the person being toasted.
- **Avoid inside jokes.** Inside jokes that only you and the person you're toasting understand are out of place and will likely distance you from the audience. Remember that the toast is not only for the benefit of the person you're toasting but for the audience as well.
- **End your speech clearly.** When you raise your glass in the toast—an almost-obligatory part of toasting—make audience members realize that they should drink and that your speech is at an end.

JOURNAL 11.9 PUBLIC SPEAKING CHOICE POINT

The Toast

You're scheduled to give a toast at your best friend's wedding. *What are some of the things you might say in your brief (say, 2-minute) toast? What are some of the things you would definitely avoid saying?*

SUMMARY: SPEAKING ON SPECIAL OCCASIONS

This chapter discussed special occasion speeches, highlighting a variety of specific types.

The Introduction Speech

11.1 Explain the introduction speech and the guidelines for preparing the speech.

1. The speech of introduction introduces another speaker or series of speakers. In this speech: Establish a connection among speaker, topic, and audience; establish the speaker's credibility; be consistent in style and manner with the major speech; be brief; avoid covering what the speaker intends to discuss; and avoid overselling the speaker.

The Presentation or Acceptance Speech

11.2 Explain the presentation and acceptance speeches and the guidelines for preparing the speeches.

2. The speech of presentation explains why the presentation is being made, and the speech of acceptance expresses thanks for the award. In the speech of presentation, state the reason for the presentation and state the importance of the award. In the speech of acceptance, thank those who gave the award, thank those who helped, and state the meaning of the award to you.

The Speech to Secure Goodwill

11.3 Explain the speech to secure goodwill and the guidelines for preparing the speech.

3. The speech to secure goodwill attempts to secure or, more often, to regain the speaker's place in the listeners' good graces. In this speech: Stress benefits the audience may derive; stress uniqueness; establish your credibility and the credibility of the subject; avoid being obvious in securing goodwill; and avoid pleading for goodwill.

The Speech of Dedication

11.4 Explain the dedication speech and the guidelines for preparing the speech.

4. The speech of dedication gives specific meaning to some event or object. In this speech: Explain why you're giving the speech; explain what is being dedicated; state who is responsible for the event or object; and say why this is significant, especially to your specific listeners.

The Commencement Speech

11.5 Explain the commencement speech and the guidelines for preparing the speech.

5. The commencement speech celebrates the end of some training period. In this speech: Consider the values of a temporal organizational pattern; learn something about the training organization and demonstrate this knowledge in your speech; be brief; congratulate the larger audience, not only those who went through the training; offer some motivational message; and offer your own good wishes.

The Inspirational Speech

11.6 Explain the inspirational speech and the guidelines for preparing the speech.

6. The inspirational speech aims to inspire the audience, to lead listeners to think in a positive direction. In this speech you demonstrate your connection with the audience and your intense involvement using emotional appeals and stressing the positive.

The Eulogy

11.7 Explain the eulogy and the guidelines for preparing the speech.

7. The eulogy seeks to praise someone who has died. In this speech: Show the connection between yourself and the person you're eulogizing; be specific; combine specifics with the general; stress that the person is deserving of your praise; and show your listeners what they can learn from this person.

The Farewell Speech

11.8 Explain the farewell speech and the guidelines for preparing the speech.

8. The farewell speech signals a transition between what was and what will be. In this speech: Thank those who helped you; portray the positives of the past; explain your reasons for making the transition; and offer some words of wisdom, some motivational message.

The Toast

11.9 Explain the toast and the guidelines for preparing the speech.

9. The toast celebrates a person or an occasion. In the toast: Be brief; focus attention on the person or event you're toasting; avoid references that listeners may not understand; and make it clear that this is the end of your speech when you raise your glass.

KEY TERMS: SPEAKING ON SPECIAL OCCASIONS

acceptance speech	eulogy	introduction speech
apology speech	farewell speech	presentation speech
commencement speech	goodwill speech	toast
dedication speech	inspirational speech	

PUBLIC SPEAKING EXERCISES

11.1 Developing the Introduction Speech

Prepare an introduction speech approximately 2 minutes in length. For this experience you may assume that the speaker you introduce will speak on any topic you wish. Do, however, assume a topic appropriate to the speaker and to your audience—your class. You may wish to select your introduction from one of the following suggestions:

1. Introduce a historical figure to the class.

2. Introduce a contemporary religious, political, or social leader.

3. Prepare a speech of introduction that someone might give to introduce you to your class.

4. Introduce a famous media (film, television, radio, recording, writing) personality—alive or dead.

5. Introduce a series of speeches debating the pros and cons of a cultural emphasis in college courses.

11.2 Developing the Special Occasion Speech

Select one of the special occasion speeches discussed in this chapter, and create a scenario in which such a speech might be given—for example, you're presenting an award to the Teacher of the Year, or you're giving a eulogy at a funeral, or you're toasting the union of two people, or you're trying to secure the goodwill of high school seniors to your college. Prepare the speech, approximately 3 minutes in length should do it, and present it.

SPEAKING IN GROUPS

Public speaking skills play a significant role in groups and teams.

CHAPTER TOPICS

Small Groups and Teams

Speaking IN the Group

Speaking FOR the Group

LEARNING OBJECTIVES

12.1 Define *small group* and *team,* identify popular group formats and cultural aspects, and describe the popular types of small groups.

12.2 Explain the productive and unproductive group roles of group members, membership skills, and leadership types and skills.

12.3 Explain the general speaking guidelines when speaking for the group and some specifics of speaking in the panel, symposium, and oral and written reports.

Consider the number of groups to which you belong. Your family is the most obvious example, but you might also be a member of a team, a class, a club, an organization, a sorority or fraternity, a collection of friends on Facebook or Instagram, a work group at your job, professional groups on LinkedIn, or perhaps a band or theater group. Some of your most important and satisfying communications probably take place in small groups and teams like these.

Mastering the skills of small group communication and leadership will enable you to function more productively and creatively in groups, enjoy group interaction more, and lead groups more comfortably and effectively. Your ability to function in a group—as a member and as a leader—is an essential job skill in today's workplace (Morreale & Pearson, 2008).

This chapter offers an introduction to small group communication, especially as it relates to public speaking. Here we look at the nature of small groups and teams, the nature and skills of group membership and leadership, and some guidelines for speaking for the group.

Small Groups and Teams

12.1 Define *small group* and *team*, identify popular group formats and cultural aspects, and describe the popular types of small groups.

Let's look at a few definitions and some of the ways in which small groups and teams operate.

small group

A collection of individuals who are connected to one another by some common purpose, are interdependent, have some degree of organization among them, and see themselves as a group.

team

A particular kind of small group that is constructed for a specific task whose members have clearly defined roles, are committed to achieving the same goal, and are content focused.

A **small group** is a collection of individuals who are connected to one another by some common purpose, are interdependent, have some degree of organization among them, and see themselves as a group. A **team** is a particular kind of small group. As such it possesses all of the characteristics of the small group as well as some additional qualities. Drawing on a number of small group researchers in communication and organizational theory, *team* can be defined as a small group constructed for a specific task, whose members have clearly defined roles and are committed to achieving the same goal, and that is content focused (Beebe & Masterson, 2012; Hofstrand, 2006; Kelly, 2006).

Small groups and teams use a wide variety of channels. Often, interactions take place face-to-face; this is the channel that probably comes to mind when you think of groups. But a great deal of small group and team interaction takes place online among geographically separated members who communicate as a group via computer or phone connections, with Skype, LinkedIn, or Facebook, for example. These *virtual groups and teams* serve both relationship and social purposes on the one hand and business and professional purposes on the other.

Perhaps the best examples of virtual groups serving relationship purposes are social networking sites, where friends interact in groups but may be separated by classrooms or by oceans. And, increasingly, these social networking sites are being used to perform business tasks as well, for finding jobs, conducting business, solving organizational problems, and conducting just about any kind of function that a face-to-face group would serve.

The same principles of effective group communication apply to all kinds of groups and teams, whether social or business, face-to-face or virtual (we'll use the most inclusive term *small group* to refer to all types of groups). Whether you're working on a team project with colleagues in different countries, communicating with new friends on a social media site, or interacting face-to-face with your extended family, the principles discussed here will prove useful.

Small Group Stages

Small group interaction develops in much the same way as a conversation and may be viewed, for convenience, as consisting of five stages: opening, feedforward, business, feedback, and closing.

- **Opening** The opening period is usually a getting-acquainted time during which members introduce themselves and engage in small talk (e.g., "How was your weekend?" "Does anyone want coffee?"). Your objective here is to get comfortable with the group members.

- **Feedforward** After this preliminary get-together, there is usually some feedforward—some attempt to identify what needs to be done, who will do it, and so on. In a more formal group, the agenda (which is a perfect example of feedforward) may be reviewed and the tasks of the group identified. This is much like making a "to-do" list.

- **Business** The business portion is the actual discussion of the tasks—the problem solving, the sharing of information, or whatever else the group needs to achieve.

- **Feedback** At the feedback stage, the group may reflect on what it has done and perhaps on what remains to be done. Some groups may even evaluate their performance at this stage; for example, "We need to focus more on the financial aspects" or "We need to consider additional alternatives."

- **Closing** At the closing stage, the group members return to their focus on individuals and will perhaps exchange closing comments ("Good seeing you again," "See you next time").

Note that the group focus shifts from members to task and then back again to members. A typical pattern would look like Figure 12.1. Different groups will naturally follow different patterns. For example, a work group that has gathered to solve a problem is likely to spend a great deal more time focused on the task than on each other, whereas an informal social group, say, two or three couples who get together for

---

Figure 12.1 Small Group Stages and the Focus on Task and People

Do the groups to which you belong follow these five stages when interacting? How do these groups divide their focus between people and task?

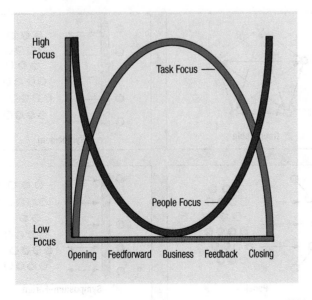

dinner, will spend most of their time focused on the concerns of individuals. Similarly, the amount of time spent on the opening or closing, for example, will vary with the type and purpose of the group.

Small Group Formats

Small groups serve their functions in a variety of formats. Among the most popular small group formats for relatively formal functions are the round table, the panel, the symposium, and the symposium–forum (Figure 12.2).

round table

A small group format in which group members arrange themselves physically (usually in chairs) in a circular or semicircular pattern.

panel

A small group format in which group members are "experts" but participate informally and without any set pattern of who speaks when, as in a round table.

symposium

A small group format where each member delivers a prepared presentation much like a public speech.

symposium–forum

A moderated group presentation with prepared speeches on various aspects of a topic, followed by a question-and-answer session with the audience.

forum

A period of questions from the audience and responses by the speakers.

- In the **round table**, group members arrange themselves physically (usually in chairs) in a circular or semicircular pattern. They share information or solve a problem without any set pattern of who speaks when. Group interaction is informal, and members contribute as they see fit. A leader or moderator may be present; he or she may, for example, try to keep the discussion on the topic or encourage more reticent members to speak up.

- In the **panel**, group members are "experts" but participate informally and without any set pattern of who speaks when, as in a round table. The difference is that they are sitting, often side by side, in front of an audience, whose members may interject comments or ask questions.

- In the **symposium**, each member delivers a prepared presentation much like a public speech. All speeches address different aspects of a single topic. A symposium leader introduces the speakers, provides transitions from one speaker to another, and may provide periodic summaries.

- The **symposium–forum** consists of two parts: a symposium with prepared speeches (as explained above) and a **forum**, a period of questions from the audience and responses by the speakers. The leader introduces the speakers and moderates the question-and-answer session.

These four formats are *general* patterns that describe a wide variety of groups. Within each type, there will naturally be variation. For example, in the symposium–forum, there is no set pattern for how much time will be spent on the symposium part and how much

Figure 12.2 Small Group Formats

With how many of these group formats have you had experience?

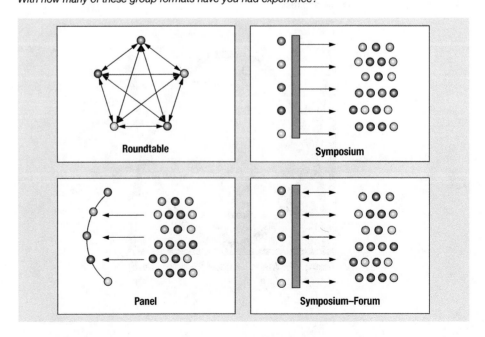

on the forum part. Combinations may also be used. Thus, for example, group members may each present a position paper (basically a symposium) and then participate in a round table discussion.

Small Group Culture

Many groups—especially those of long standing—develop cultural norms and are greatly influenced by their own high- or low-context orientation. Each of these cultural dimensions influences the group, its members, and its communication.

Group norms are rules or standards identifying which behaviors are considered appropriate (such as being willing to take on added tasks or directing conflict toward issues rather than toward people) and which are considered inappropriate (such as arriving late or failing to contribute actively). These rules for appropriate behavior are sometimes explicitly stated in a company contract or policy: *All members must attend department meetings.* Sometimes they're unstated: *Group members should be well groomed.*

Online groups vary a great deal in terms of norms, and as with all groups, it's wise to familiarize yourself with the norms of the group before actively participating. For example, social media groups will vary greatly in their tolerance for self-promotion and commercializing. LinkedIn groups and other sites frown upon self-promotion and may ostracize you for doing so. And even if you don't get thrown off Facebook, you're likely to incur considerable negative reaction. On the other hand, some groups frequently include posts in which individual members will advertise their own services or products. Sometimes, a group will tolerate self-promotion officially while individual members may look on the posts very negatively.

Norms may apply to individual members as well as to the group as a whole and, of course, will differ from one cultural group to another (Axtell, 1990, 1993). For example, although someone from the United States might prefer to get right down to business, a Japanese person might prefer rather elaborate socializing before addressing the business at hand. In the United States, men and women in business are expected to interact when making business decisions as well as when socializing. In Muslim and Buddhist societies, however, religious restrictions prevent mixing the sexes. In some cultures (e.g., those of the United States, Bangladesh, Australia, Germany, Finland, and Hong Kong), punctuality for business meetings is very important. But in others (e.g., those of Morocco, Italy, Brazil, Zambia, Ireland, and Panama), punctuality is less important; being late is no great insult and in some situations is even expected. In the United States and in much of Asia and Europe, meetings are held between two parties. In many Persian Gulf states, however, a business executive is likely to conduct meetings with several different groups—sometimes dealing with totally different issues—at the same time. In the United States very little interpersonal touching goes on during business meetings, but in Arab countries touching such as hand holding is common and is a gesture of friendship.

Small Group Types

Now that the general nature of the small group is clear, let's look at two of the more important types of small groups you'll encounter: brainstorming groups and problem-solving groups. These two groups are singled out largely because the ideas that are part of these groups' experiences will prove useful to you in a variety of communication situations. They also illustrate two very different types of small groups.

Another class of small groups are **personal growth groups**, which go in and out of favor with the times. Personal growth groups, sometimes referred to as support groups, aim to help members cope with particular difficulties—such as drug addiction, not being assertive enough, having an alcoholic parent, being an ex-convict, or having a hyperactive child or a promiscuous spouse. Other groups are more clearly therapeutic and are designed to change significant aspects of an individual's

group norms
Rules or expectations for appropriate behavior for a member of a group.

personal growth groups
A type of small group that aims to help members cope with particular difficulties—such as drug addiction, not being assertive enough, having an alcoholic parent, being an ex-convict, or having a hyperactive child or a promiscuous spouse.

TABLE 12.1 Personal Growth Groups

Group	Group Goal	Group Members
Encounter group	*Encounter groups*, also known as "sensitivity groups" or "T [training]-groups," for example, constitute a form of psychotherapy; these groups try to facilitate members' personal growth and foster their ability to deal effectively with other people (Hirsch, Kett, & Trefil, 2002; Rogers, 1970).	Members are encouraged to express their inner thoughts, fears, and doubts in the encounter group, in which interactions are always characterized by total acceptance and support.
Assertiveness training group	The *assertiveness training group* aims to increase the willingness of its members to stand up for their rights and to act more assertively in a wide variety of situations (Adler, 1977; Bishop, 2006).	The group aims to increase the assertiveness skills of its members, who are likely to be people who feel they are not assertive enough.
Consciousness-raising group	The *consciousness-raising group* aims to help people cope with the problems society confronts them with.	Members are expected to discuss an issue or problem in very personal terms and to be totally supportive of all members' comments.
Intervention group	In the *intervention group* people gather to help one of their members overcome some problem. For example, family members may gather to confront an alcoholic member.	Under the leader's guidance the group expresses its support and love for the person, explains the impact of this member's behavior on all connected others, and offers to help the person with the problem behavior.

encounter group

A type of small group in which members facilitate each other's personal growth.

assertiveness training group

A type of small group focusing on increasing assertive behavior of members.

consciousness-raising group

A small group of people who help each other to cope with the problems society confronts them with.

intervention group

A group of concerned individuals who get together to help another deal with a problem.

brainstorming

A technique for generating ideas either alone or, more usually, in a small group.

personality or behavior. Still other groups are devoted to making healthy individuals function even more effectively. Table 12.1 identifies the **encounter group**, **assertiveness training group**, **consciousness-raising group**, and the **intervention group**.

BRAINSTORMING GROUPS

Many small groups exist solely to generate ideas through **brainstorming**—a technique for analyzing a problem by presenting as many ideas as possible (Beebe & Masterson, 2012; Osborn, 1957). Although brainstorming also can be useful when you're trying to come up with ideas by yourself—ideas for speeches or term papers, ideas for a fun vacation, or ways to make money—it is more typical in small group settings. Organizations have come to embrace brainstorming because it lessens group members' inhibitions and encourages all participants to exercise their creativity. It also fosters cooperative teamwork; members soon learn that their own ideas and creativity are sparked by the contributions of others. The technique builds member pride and ownership in the final solution (or product or service) because all members contribute to it.

Brainstorming occurs in two phases: (1) the brainstorming period itself and (2) the evaluation period. The procedures are simple. First, a problem is selected. The "problem" may be almost anything that is amenable to many possible solutions or ideas—for example, how to recruit new members to the organization or how to market a new product. Before the actual session, group members are informed of the problem so they can think about the topic. When the group meets, each person contributes as many ideas as he or she can think of. Companies often use chalkboards, whiteboards, or easels to record all the ideas. A brainstorming group may appoint one person to be the scribe; that person keys the group's notes into a laptop for instant circulation via e-mail to other group members after the group has concluded its business. During the initial idea-generating session, members follow four rules:

■ **Rule 1: No evaluations are permitted at this stage.** All ideas are recorded for the group to see (or hear later). Prohibiting both verbal and nonverbal evaluation encourages group members to participate freely.

VIEWPOINTS

Chatting

In research of online messages, it was found that people were more likely to comment on a message when that message was negative than when it was positive (Rollman, Krug, & Parente, 2000). *Do you find this to be true in your social network messages? If so, why do you think this occurs? Would it be fair to say, from your own experience, that the reverse would be true in face-to-face communication?*

This first rule is perhaps the most difficult for members to follow, so you might want to practice responding to what are called "idea killers." For example, what might you say if someone were to criticize an idea with the following comments?

We tried it before and it didn't work.	It would cost too much.
No one would vote for it.	We don't have the facilities.
It's too complex.	What we have is good enough.
It's too simple.	It just doesn't fit us.
It would take too long.	It's not possible.

- **Rule 2: Quantity of ideas is the goal.** The more ideas generated, the more likely it is that a useful solution will be found.

- **Rule 3: Combinations and extensions of ideas are encouraged.** Although members may not criticize a particular idea, they may extend or combine it. The value of a particular idea may be that it stimulates another idea.

- **Rule 4: Freewheeling (i.e., developing as wild an idea as possible) is desirable.** A wild idea can be tempered easily, but it's not so easy to elaborate on a simple or conservative idea.

After all the ideas are generated—a period that lasts about 15 or 20 minutes—the group evaluates the entire list. Unworkable ideas are crossed off the list; those showing promise are retained and evaluated. During this phase, criticism is allowed.

JOURNAL 12.1 PUBLIC SPEAKING CHOICE POINT

Stimulating Contributions

You're in charge of a small group in which members will discuss what they like and dislike about the websites they visit. The problem you anticipate, based on past experience, is that a few members will do all the talking and the rest will hardly talk at all. *What are some of the ways you can confront this problem?*

problem-solving group

A group whose primary task is to solve a problem or, perhaps more often, to reach a decision.

problem-solving sequence

A logical step-by-step process for solving a problem that is frequently used by groups; consists of defining and analyzing the problem, establishing criteria for evaluating solutions, identifying possible solutions, evaluating solutions, selecting the best solution(s), and testing the selected solution(s).

A **problem-solving group** meets to solve a particular problem or to reach a decision on some issue. In a sense, this is the most demanding kind of group. It requires not only a knowledge of small group communication techniques but also a knowledge of the particular problem on the part of all group members. Also, for the most successful outcome, it usually demands faithful adherence to a set of procedural rules.

The **problem-solving sequence** identifies six steps and owes its formulation to philosopher John Dewey's insights into how people think (see Figure 12.3). These steps are designed to make problem solving more efficient and effective.

Step 1: Define and Analyze the Problem In some instances, the nature of the problem is clearly specified. For example, a work team might discuss how to package new tablets or smartphones for Valentine's Day. In other instances, however, the problem may be vague, and it may be up to the group to define it—for example, the general topic of poor campus communications. In this case, the topic has to be more clearly defined and

Figure 12.3 The Problem-Solving Sequence

Although most small group theorists would advise you to follow the problem-solving pattern as presented here, others would alter it somewhat. For example, some would advise you to reverse steps 2 and 3: to identify possible solutions first and then consider the criteria for evaluating them. The advantage of this approach is that you're likely to generate more creative solutions because you will not be restricted by standards of evaluation. The disadvantage is that you may spend a great deal of time generating impractical solutions that will never meet the standards you will eventually propose.

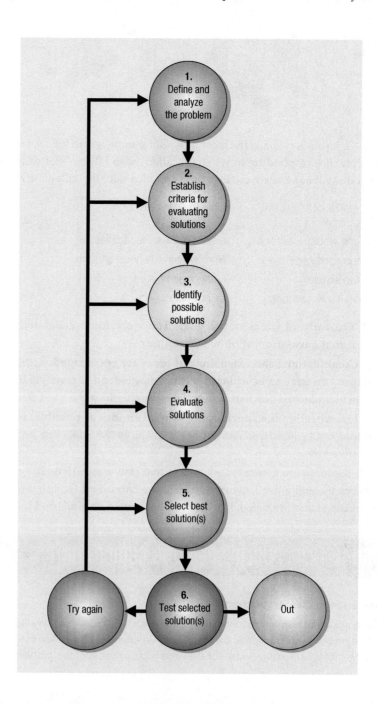

VIEWPOINTS

Developing Criteria

What type of criteria would an advertising agency use in evaluating a campaign to sell soap? A university in evaluating a new multicultural curriculum? Parents in evaluating a preschool for their children? A group of people creating a sign for protest?

limited—for example, how the college website can be improved. Define the problem as an open-ended question ("How can we improve the college website?") rather than as a statement ("The website needs to be improved") or as a *yes/no* question ("Does the website need improvement?").

Step 2: Establish Criteria for Evaluating Solutions Decide how you'll evaluate the solutions before proposing them. Identify the standards or criteria you'll use in evaluating solutions or in preferring one solution over another. For example, you might decide that a solution must lead to a 10 percent increase in website visits, that the solutions must not increase the budget, that the website information must not violate anyone's right to privacy, or that the website must provide a forum for all members of the college community. Set up criteria that are realistic and that can, in fact, be attained; otherwise, no solution is going to prove acceptable.

Step 3: Identify Possible Solutions Identify as many solutions as possible. Focus on quantity rather than quality. Brainstorming may be particularly useful at this point. Solutions to the website improvement problem might include incorporating reviews of faculty publications, student evaluations of specific courses, reviews of restaurants in the campus area, outlines for new courses, and employment information.

Step 4: Evaluate Solutions After all solutions have been proposed, evaluate each one. For example, does incorporating reviews of area restaurants meet the criteria? Would it increase the budget, for example? Would posting grades violate students' rights to privacy? Each potential solution should be matched against the evaluating criteria.

Step 5: Select the Best Solution(s) Select the best solution and put it into operation. Let's assume that reviews of faculty publications and outlines for new courses best meet the evaluating criteria for solutions. The group might then incorporate these two new items into the website.

Groups use different decision-making methods when deciding, for example, which solution to accept. The method to be used should, naturally, be stated at the outset of the group discussion. Three main decision-making methods are **authority**, **majority rule**, and **consensus**.

- **Authority:** In decision making by authority, group members voice their feelings and opinions, but the leader or boss makes the final decision. This method has the

authority

A form of decision making in which the leader or boss makes the decision, though members may offer suggestions.

majority rule
A form of decision making in which the decision is made by majority vote.

consensus
A process of reaching agreement (not necessarily unanimous) among group members.

advantages of being efficient and of giving greater importance to the suggestions of more experienced members. The disadvantage is that members may feel that their contributions have too little influence and therefore may not participate with real enthusiasm.

- **Majority rule:** The group agrees to abide by the majority decision and may vote on various issues as the group searches to solve its problem. Like decision by authority, this method is efficient. A disadvantage is that it may lead the group to limit discussion by calling for a vote once a majority has agreed. Also, members not voting with the majority may feel disenfranchised and left out.

- **Consensus:** In small group decision making, consensus means reaching agreement. The agreement does not have to be unanimous; it is, rather, something that the group members can live with; they agree that they can do whatever the group's solution requires (Kelly, 1994). It does not imply that each individual group member agrees with the solution, but only that members agree that at this time (for this situation, for this group) this solution should be adopted and followed. Consensus is the most time-consuming of the decision-making methods. However, it is also the method that best secures the cooperation and participation of all members in implementing the group's decisions. If you want members of the group to be satisfied with and committed to the decision, consensus seems to be the best way to arrive at a solution (Beebe & Masterson, 2012).

Step 6: Test Selected Solutions After putting solutions into operation, test their effectiveness. The group might, for example, poll the students or college employees about the new website. Or the group might analyze the number of visits to the website to see if the number of visits increases by the desired 10 percent. If the selected solutions prove ineffective, the group will need to return to a previous stage and repeat that part of the process. This often involves selecting other solutions to test. But it also may mean going even farther back in the process—to a reanalysis of the problem, an identification of other solutions, or a restatement of criteria, for example. If the solution proves effective, you move to "out" in Figure 12.3.

As you saw from the above discussion, you're a part of many different groups, and you serve a wide variety of roles and functions in these groups, sometimes as a member and sometimes as a leader. Here we look at speaking as a member and as a leader in small groups. By gaining insight into these roles and functions, you'll increase your own effectiveness as a group member and leader.

Speaking IN the Group

12.2 Explain the productive and unproductive group roles of group members, membership skills, and leadership types and skills.

Here we look at group membership and membership skills and leadership and leadership skills.

role
The part an individual plays in a group; an individual's function or expected behavior.

Each of us serves many **roles**, patterns of behaviors that we customarily perform and that we're expected by others to perform. Javier, for example, is a part-time college student, father, bookkeeper, bowling team captain, and sometime poet. That is, he acts as a student—attends class, reads textbooks, takes exams, and does the things we expect of college students. He also performs those behaviors associated with fathers, bookkeepers, bowling team captains, and poets. In a similar way, you develop relevant ways of behaving when participating in small groups. Before reading about these roles, consider your own group membership behavior by responding to the following statements in terms of how true or false they are of your normal group behavior:

_____ 1. I present new ideas and suggest new strategies.

_____ 2. I ask for facts and opinions.

_____ 3. I stimulate the group.

_____ 4. I give examples and try to look for positive solutions.

_____ 5. I positively reinforce group members.

_____ 6. I try to reconcile differences.

_____ 7. I go along with the other members.

_____ 8. I offer compromises as ways of resolving conflict.

_____ 9. I express negative evaluation of the actions and feelings of the group members.

_____ 10. I try to run the group.

_____ 11. I express personal perspectives and feelings.

_____ 12. I express confusion or deprecate myself.

As you read further, you'll see that these behaviors are characteristic of the three general types of group member roles. The first four statements refer to your taking on *group task roles*. The next four refer to your taking on *group building and maintenance roles*. Both of these types of roles are productive. The final four refer to your taking on *individual roles* (as opposed to group roles); these behaviors often work against the group's achieving its goals. As you read the following sections on member roles, try to relate these roles to your own behavior or to group behavior you've witnessed. Then ask yourself what worked and what didn't work, what roles were productive and what roles were unproductive.

Member Roles

Group member roles fall into three general classes—**group task roles**, **group building and maintenance roles**, and **individual roles**—a classification introduced in early research (Benne & Sheats, 1948) and still widely used today (Beebe & Masterson, 2012). These roles are frequently served by leaders as well and are applicable to both face-to-face and mediated groups.

GROUP TASK ROLES

Group task roles help the group focus on achieving its goals. Effective group members serve several roles. Some people lock into a few specific roles, but this single focus is usually counterproductive—it's better for the roles to be spread more evenly among the members and for the roles to be alternated frequently. Here are some examples of group task roles.

- **The information seeker or giver or the opinion seeker or giver** asks for or gives facts or opinions, seeks clarification of issues being discussed, and presents facts or opinions to group members: "Sales for May were up 10 percent. Do we have the sales figures for June?"

- **The initiator-contributor** presents new ideas or new perspectives on old ideas, suggests new goals, or proposes new procedures or organizational strategies. "We need to also look at the amount of time visitors spend on our new site."

- **The elaborator** gives examples and tries to work out possible solutions, trying to build on what others have said. "That three-part division worked at ABC and should work here as well."

- **The evaluator–critic** evaluates the group's decisions, questions the logic or practicality of the suggestions, and provides the group with both positive and negative feedback: "That's a great idea, but it sounds expensive."

group task roles

Member role that help the group focus on and achieve its task.

group building and maintenance roles

Group roles that focus not only on the task to be performed but also on interpersonal relationships among members.

individual roles

Behavior in groups that is usually dysfunctional and works against a sense of group cohesion.

- **The procedural technician** or recorder takes care of various mechanical duties, such as distributing group materials and arranging the seating; writing down the group's activities, suggestions, and decisions; and/or serving as the group's memory: "We have another meeting scheduled to discuss just this issue, so perhaps we can skip it for today."

GROUP BUILDING AND MAINTENANCE ROLES

No group can be task oriented at all times. Group members have varied interpersonal relationships, and these need to be nourished if the group is to function effectively. Group members need to be satisfied if they are to be productive. Group building and maintenance roles serve these relationship needs. Here are some examples of these roles.

- **The encourager or harmonizer** provides members with positive reinforcement through social approval or praise for their ideas and mediates the various differences between group members: "Pat, another great idea."
- **The compromiser** tries to resolve conflict between his or her ideas and those of others and offers compromises: "This looks like it could work if each department cut back at least 10 percent."
- **The gatekeeper-expediter** keeps the channels of communication open by reinforcing the efforts of others. "Those were really good ideas; we're on a roll."
- **The standard setter** proposes standards for the functions of the group or for its solutions. "We need to be able to increase the number of visits by several thousand a day."
- **The follower** goes along with members, passively accepts the ideas of others, and functions more as an audience than as an active member: "If you all agree, that's fine with me."

INDIVIDUAL ROLES

Whereas group task and group building and maintenance roles are productive and help the group achieve its goal, individual roles are counterproductive. They hinder the group from achieving its goal and are individual rather than group oriented. Such roles, often termed dysfunctional, hinder the group's effectiveness in terms of both productivity and personal satisfaction. Here are some examples of individual roles.

- **The aggressor** expresses negative evaluation of members and attacks the group: "That's a terrible idea. It doesn't make any sense."
- **The recognition seekers and self-confessors** try to focus attention on themselves, boast about their accomplishments rather than the task at hand, and express their own feelings rather than focus on the group: "The system I devised at B&B was a great success; everyone loved it. We should just go with that."
- **The blocker** provides negative feedback, is disagreeable, and opposes other members or suggestions regardless of their merit. "You're dreaming if you think that will work."
- **The special interest pleader** disregards the goals of the group and pleads the case of some special group. "This solution isn't adequate; it doesn't address the needs of XYZ."
- **The dominator** tries to run the group or members by pulling rank, flattering members, or acting the role of boss: "I've been here the longest; I know what works and what doesn't work."

A popular individual role born on the Internet is *trolling*, the practice of posting messages that you know are false or outrageous just so you can watch the group members correct you or get emotionally upset by your message. As in any group, behavior such as trolling or flaming wastes time and energy and diverts the group from its primary objective.

VIEWPOINTS

Membership Dos and Don'ts

You want to convince a group of students to join your pre-law study group rather than several others that are available. *What membership roles would you want to demonstrate to convince others to join your group? What membership roles would you be sure to avoid?*

Membership Skills

Here are several guidelines to help make your participation in small group communication more effective and enjoyable.

BE GROUP ORIENTED

When participating in a small group, you serve as a member of a team. You share common goals with the other group members, and your participation is valuable to the extent that it advances this shared goal. In a team situation, you need to pool your talents, knowledge, and insights to promote the best possible solution for the group. Although a group orientation calls for the participation and cooperation of all group members, this guideline does not suggest that you abandon your individuality, personal values, or beliefs for the group's sake. Individuality *with* a group orientation is most effective. And because the most effective and the most creative solutions often emerge from a combination of ideas, approach small group situations with flexibility; come to the group with ideas and information but without firmly formulated conclusions. The importance of a group orientation is also seen in one of the rules of netiquette, which holds that you should not protest the subject of, say, a mailing list or a chat group. If you don't wish to be group oriented and discuss what the group is discussing, you're expected to unsubscribe from the mailing list or withdraw from the group.

CENTER CONFLICT ON ISSUES

Conflict in small group situations is inevitable; it's a natural part of the give and take of ideas and often promotes a better outcome. To manage conflict effectively, however, center it on issues rather than on personalities. When you disagree, make it clear that your disagreement is with the ideas expressed, not with the person who expressed them. For example, if you think that a colleague's ideas to raise funds for your social service agency are impractical and short sighted, concentrate your criticisms on your colleague's proposed plan and suggest ways that the plan could be improved rather than attacking your colleague personally. Similarly, when someone disagrees with you, try not to take it personally or react emotionally. Rather, view the disagreement as an opportunity to discuss issues from an alternative point of view. In the language of the Internet, don't flame—don't attack the person. And don't contribute to flame wars by flame baiting, or saying things that will further incite the personal attacks.

BE CRITICALLY OPEN-MINDED

When members join a group with their minds already made up, the small group process degenerates into a series of debates in which each person argues for his or her position—a clear example of members' taking on individual and dysfunctional roles. Group goals are neglected, and the group process breaks down.

Let's say you have spent several hours developing what you think is the best, most effective advertising campaign to combat your company's low sales numbers. At the group meeting, however, members' reactions are extremely critical. Instead of becoming defensive, listen to their criticisms and try to think of ways that your plan could be modified to be as effective as possible for the company. To avoid this situation in the future, try to come to the group with ideas rather than conclusions; with suggestions rather than final decisions; and, of course, with information that will contribute to the discussion and the group goal. Be willing to accept other people's suggestions as well as to revise your own in light of the discussion. Listen openly but critically to comments of all members (including your own).

BEWARE OF SOCIAL LOAFING

social loafing
A theory that holds that people exert less effort when part of a group than when working individually.

Visualize yourself in a rope-pulling contest—you need to successfully pull the members of the other side into the pond or they will pull you. With this vision in mind, consider whether you would exert more effort if you were alone or if you were part of a group of five or six. The concept of **social loafing** resulted from experiments like this that measured the amount of effort people actually exerted alone versus in groups; it holds that you exert less effort when you're a part of the group than when alone (Latané, Williams, & Harkins, 1979). Being aware of this tendency is a useful first step in combating it. It's often an unproductive group tendency that leads to less productive group interactions and decisions. And it is probably noticed by others and so hurts you professionally. Table 12.2 lists a few factors that influence the likelihood of social loafing and some correctives (Kenrick, Neuberg, & Cialdini, 2010).

ENSURE UNDERSTANDING

Make sure all participants understand your ideas and information. If something is worth saying, it's worth making clear. When in doubt, ask: "Is that clear?" "Did I explain that clearly?" Make sure, too, that you fully understand other members' contributions, especially before you disagree with them. In fact, it's often wise to preface any expression of disagreement with some kind of paraphrase to ensure you really are in disagreement. For example, you might say, "If I understand you correctly, you feel that marketing should bear sole responsibility for updating the product database." After waiting for the response, you would state your thoughts.

BEWARE OF GROUPTHINK

groupthink
A tendency observed in some groups in which agreement among members becomes more important than the exploration of the issues at hand.

In **groupthink** agreement among members becomes so important that it shuts out realistic and logical analysis of a problem and of possible alternatives (Janis, 1983; Mullen, Tara, Salas, & Driskell, 1994). The term *groupthink* is meant to signal the

TABLE 12.2 Social Loafing

Social Loafing is More Likely to Occur When:	Corrective
An individual group member's contributions cannot be easily identified.	Make contributions easily identifiable and make members aware of this.
The punishment for or cost of poor performance is insignificant.	Reward excellent performance and/or punish poor performance.
The group lacks cohesion.	Stress the importance of being part of a group or team; following the suggestions for group membership and leadership will help here.
The task has little personal importance.	Stress the personal connection between the members of the group and the task.

"deterioration of mental efficiency, reality testing, and moral judgment that results from in-group pressures" (Janis, 1983, p. 9).

In groupthink, members are extremely selective about the information they consider. Members tend to ignore facts and opinions contrary to the group's position, and they readily and uncritically accept those that support the group's position. When you recognize that groupthinking is occurring, try the following:

- When too-simple solutions are offered to problems, try to illustrate (with specific examples, if possible) for the group members how the complexity of the problem is not going to yield to the solutions offered.

- When you feel that members are not expressing their doubts about the group's decisions, encourage members to voice disagreement. Ask members to play devil's advocate, to test the adequacy of the solution. If you feel there is unexpressed disagreement, ask specifically if anyone disagrees.

- To combat the group pressure toward agreement, reward members who do voice disagreement or doubt. Say, for example, "That's a good argument; we need to hear more about the potential problems of this proposal. Does anyone else see any problems?"

Approaches to Group Leadership

Leadership is defined in two very different ways in research and theory:

- Leadership is the process of influencing the thoughts, feelings, and behaviors of group members and establishing the direction that others follow; leadership and influence are parts of the same skill.

- Leadership is the process of empowering others; the leader is the person who helps others to maximize their potential and to take control of their lives.

Leadership
The ability to influence others as well as to empower others.

These two definitions are not mutually exclusive; in fact, most effective leaders do both; they influence and they empower. As you read about leadership, keep these two definitions or functions of power and empowerment in mind.

In many small groups one person serves as leader. In other groups leadership may be shared by several persons. In some cases, a person may be appointed the leader or may serve as leader because of her or his position within the company or hierarchy. In other cases, the leader may emerge as the group proceeds in fulfilling its functions or instead may be elected by the group members. Two significant factors exert considerable influence on who emerges as group leader. One is the extent of active participation: The person who talks the most is more likely to emerge as leader (Mullen, Salas, & Driskell, 1989; Shaw & Gouran, 1990). The second factor is effective listening: Members who listen effectively will emerge as leaders more often than those who don't (Bechler & Johnson, 1995; Johnson & Bechler, 1998).

Another way to understanding leadership is to dispel the myths that are common. Here are three examples of myths about leadership paraphrased from small group theorists (Bennis & Nanus, 1985, 2003):

- **Myth: The skills of leadership are rare.** Actually, all of us have the potential for leadership. There are millions of people throughout the world who are serving leadership functions in government, business, education, and countless other fields.

- **Myth: Leaders are born.** Actually, the major leadership skills can be learned by just about everyone. No specific genetic endowment is necessary. We all can improve our leadership abilities.

- **Myth: Leaders are all charismatic.** Actually, only some leaders are. According to one survey of leaders they were of all heights, varied in articulateness, and dressed both well and poorly.

JOURNAL 12.2 PUBLIC SPEAKING CHOICE POINT

Leadership Dos And Don'ts

You're running for student government president and need to be seen as a leader at various meetings. *What is the one thing you'd want to be sure to do? What is the one that you'd want to avoid doing?*

Before reading about the various approaches to leadership consider your own leadership qualities by responding to the following 12 qualities by indicating *true* if the quality is often or always true of your leadership behavior or *false* if you feel the statement often or always does not apply to your leadership behavior.

_____ 1. Popular with group members

_____ 2. Knowledgeable about the topics discussed

_____ 3. Dependable

_____ 4. Effective in establishing group goals

_____ 5. Competent in giving directions

_____ 6. Capable of energizing group members

_____ 7. Charismatic (i.e., dynamic, engaging, powerful)

_____ 8. Empowering of group members

_____ 9. Moral and honest

_____ 10. Skilled in satisfying both task and relationship needs

_____ 11. Flexible in adjusting leadership style on the basis of the situation

_____ 12. Able to delegate responsibility

This list was designed to encourage you to look at yourself in terms of the four approaches to leadership to be discussed here.

- Perceptions 1–3 refer to the *traits approach* to leadership, which defines a leader as someone who possesses certain qualities. If you answered *true* for these statements, you have the qualities normally associated with the trait theory of leadership. *False* responses would indicate that you don't see yourself possessing these traits.

- Perceptions 4–6 refer to the *functional approach*, which defines a leader as someone who performs certain functions. *True* responses indicate that you serve the functions normally viewed as the province of a leader.

- Perceptions 7–9 refer to the *transformational approach*, which defines a leader as someone who enables the group members to become the best they can be. *True* responses indicate your leadership is transformational.

- Perceptions 10–12 refer to the *situational approach*, which defines a leader as someone who can adjust his or her style to balance the needs of the specific situation. *True* responses indicate your flexibility to adjust to changing circumstances.

As you read the remainder of this chapter, try to identify specific skills and competencies you might learn that would enable you to respond with *true* to all 12 statements.

Not surprisingly, leadership has been the focus of considerable research attention. Researchers have identified several views of leadership, called *approaches*. Looking at a few of these approaches will give you a better idea of the varied ways in which leadership may be viewed and a better grasp of what leadership is and how it may be achieved.

THE TRAITS APPROACH

The **traits approach** views the leader as the one who possesses those characteristics or skills that contribute to leadership. This approach is valuable for stressing the characteristics that often (but not always) distinguish leaders from nonleaders. For example, some of the world's leading corporations seek technology project managers and leaders by looking for people who have technological skills, group building skills, and interpersonal skills (Crowley, 1999). Research has found that the traits most frequently associated with leadership include intelligence, self-confidence, determination, integrity, and sociability (Northouse, 1997).

A shortcoming of the traits approach is that these qualities often vary with the situation in which the leader functions, such as the group type, the personalities and roles of the other members, and the group's cultural context. Thus, for some groups (e.g., a new computer game company), a youthful, energetic, humorous leader might be most effective; for other groups (e.g., a medical diagnosis team), an older, more experienced, and serious leader might be most effective.

THE FUNCTIONAL APPROACH

The **functional approach** to leadership focuses on what the leader should do in a given situation. We've already encountered some of these functions in the discussion of group roles. Other functions associated with leadership are setting group goals, giving the group members direction, and summarizing the group's progress (Schultz, 1996). Additional functions are identified in the section titled "Leadership Skills" later in this chapter.

THE TRANSFORMATIONAL APPROACH

The **transformational approach** describes a "transformational" (also called visionary or charismatic) leader who elevates the group's members, enabling them not only to accomplish the group task but also to emerge as more empowered individuals (Hersey, Blanchard, & Johnson, 2001). At the center of the transformational approach is the concept of charisma, that quality of an individual that makes us believe or want to follow him or her. Gandhi, Martin Luther King Jr., and John F. Kennedy are often cited as examples of transformational leaders. These leaders were role models, were seen as extremely competent and able, and articulated moral goals (Northouse, 1997).

THE SITUATIONAL APPROACH

The **situational approach** holds that the effective leader shifts his or her emphasis between task accomplishment (i.e., identifying and focusing on the specific problem that the group must solve) and member satisfaction (i.e., providing for the psychological and interpersonal needs of the group members) on the basis of the specific group situation. This twofold function, you'll notice, rests on essentially the same distinction between relationship and task groups that we considered earlier in this chapter. Some groups call for a high focus on task issues and need little people encouragement; this might be the case, for example, with a group of experienced scientists researching a cure for AIDS. In contrast, a group of recovering alcoholics might require leadership that stresses the members' emotional needs. The general idea of situational leadership is that there is no one style of leadership that fits all situations; each situation will call for a different ratio of emphasis on task and on member satisfaction (Fielder, 1967).

Leadership Skills

Keeping the various views of leadership in mind, especially the situational theory with its concern for both task and people, we can look at some of the major functions leaders serve and their corresponding skills, the skills of leadership. These functions/skills are not exclusively the leader's; they are often shared or served wholly by group

traits approach
An approach to leadership that argues that leaders must possess certain qualities if they're to function effectively.

functional approach
An approach to leadership that focuses on what the leader should do in a given situation.

transformational approach
An approach to leadership that emphasizes elevating and empowering the group's members.

situational approach
An approach to leadership that emphasizes that the leader's style must vary on the basis of the specific situation.

members. But when there's a specific leader, she or he is expected to perform these functions and exhibit the skills for accomplishing these goals.

PREPARE MEMBERS AND START INTERACTION

Groups form gradually and often need to be eased into meaningful discussion. As the leader, you need to prepare members for the small group interaction as well as for the discussion of a specific issue or problem. Don't expect diverse members to work together cohesively to solve a problem without first becoming familiar with one another. Similarly, if members are to discuss a specific problem, a proper briefing may be necessary. If materials need to be distributed before the actual discussion, consider e-mailing them to members. Or perhaps members need to view a particular film or television show. Whatever the preparations, you need to organize and coordinate them. Once the group is assembled, you may need to stimulate the members to interact.

BUILD GROUP COHESIVENESS

cohesiveness

A quality of togetherness; in group communication situations, the mutual attraction among members and the extent to which members work together as a group.

Groups vary greatly in **cohesiveness**—the members' closeness to and liking for each other. Generally, cohesiveness is positive and cohesive groups seem to be more effective. For example, the members enjoy the interaction more and consequently come to meetings on time and stay until the end. Cohesive group members are more likely to be satisfied with the time spent in the group and to develop a "we-ness," seeing the group as a unit. Because members are comfortable with one another, they will be more willing to offer suggestions and ideas that may at first seem impossible, which may help the group eventually find a workable solution.

In a group that is excessively cohesive, however, members may be less apt to disagree with one another, which may hinder the group's critical analysis of any proposed idea. Still, a cohesive group is more likely to be successful. Cohesiveness is built by leaders who stress the positives, reward members frequently, and make the entire group experience as pleasant and personally rewarding as possible. Simple compliments and expressions of fondness will help build a cohesive group. Group accomplishments also build cohesiveness.

MAINTAIN EFFECTIVE INTERACTION

Even after the group has begun to interact, you'll need to monitor the members' effective interaction. When the discussion begins to drag, you may need to step in and motivate the group: "Do we have any additional comments on the proposal to eliminate required courses?" "What do you, as members of the college curriculum committee, think about the proposal?" You'll also want to ensure that all members have an opportunity to express themselves.

GUIDE MEMBERS THROUGH THE AGREED-ON AGENDA

As the leader, you need to keep the discussion on track by asking relevant questions, by summarizing the group discussions periodically, or by offering a transition from one issue to the next. This involves following the list of tasks to be accomplished by the group as outlined in the meeting agenda and efficiently managing the amount of time allotted for each event.

ENSURE MEMBER SATISFACTION

Members have different psychological needs and wants, and many people enter groups because of them. Even though a group may, for example, deal with political issues, members may have come together for psychological as well as for political reasons. If a group is to be effective, it must achieve the group goal (in this case, a political one) without denying the psychological purposes or goals that motivate many of the members to come together. One way to meet these needs is for you as leader to allow digressions and personal comments, assuming they are not too frequent or overly long. Another way is to be supportive and reinforcing.

EMPOWER GROUP MEMBERS

An important function of a leader is to empower others—to help group members gain increased power over themselves and their environment. Empowerment occurs when leaders:

- **Raise members' self-esteem.** Compliment, reinforce. Resist fault finding.
- **Share decision-making power.** Make use of everyone's skills and share authority among yourselves.
- **Be constructively critical.** Be willing to offer your perspective. Be willing to react honestly to suggestions from all group members, not only those in high positions.
- **Listen willingly and eagerly.** Acknowledge your understanding by appropriately nodding or using such minimal responses as *I see* or *I understand*, ask questions if something isn't clear, maintain eye contact, and lean forward as appropriate.
- **Avoid interrupting to change the topic.** When you interrupt, you say, in effect, that what the other member is saying is less important than what you're saying.
- **React supportively.** Let the person know that you appreciate what he or she is saying.

ENCOURAGE ONGOING EVALUATION AND IMPROVEMENT

All groups encounter obstacles as they try to solve a problem, reach a decision, or generate ideas. No group is totally effective. All groups have room for improvement. To improve, the group must focus on itself. Along with trying to solve some external problem, it must try to solve its own internal problems: for example, personal conflicts, failure of members to meet on time, or members who come unprepared. When you notice some serious group failing, address it, perhaps posing that very issue (say, member tardiness) as a problem to be solved.

MENTOR

Another function of leadership that is especially applicable to the small group but is used extensively in the workplace and in business and personal relationships generally is that of mentoring. A **mentoring** relationship occurs when an experienced individual helps to train a less experienced person or people. An accomplished teacher, for example, might mentor younger teachers who are newly arrived or who have never taught before. A group leader might be the group members' supervisor and may mentor those supervised. The mentor guides new people through the ropes, teaches strategies and techniques for success, and otherwise communicates his or her accumulated knowledge and experience to the "mentee" or protégé. At the same time, the mentor benefits from clarifying his or her thoughts, from seeing the job from the perspective of a newcomer, and from considering and formulating answers to a variety of questions. Just as a member learns from the leader, the leader learns from the members.

mentoring
Guidance and support given by an experienced individual to a less-experienced person.

ETHICAL CHOICE POINT

Lying

You're leading a discussion among a group of high school freshmen whom you're mentoring. The topic turns to marijuana, and the students ask you directly if you smoke pot. The truth is that you do on occasion, but you feel that it would only destroy your credibility and lead the students to experiment with or continue smoking pot if they knew you did (something you do not want to do). At the same time, you wonder if you can ethically lie to them and tell them that you do not smoke. *What is your ethical obligation in this situation? What would you do?*

Speaking FOR the Group

12.3 Explain the general speaking guidelines when speaking for the group and some specifics of speaking in the panel, symposium, and oral and written reports.

In this last section of the text, let's combine our public speaking and our small group knowledge and experience and offer some suggestions for presenting the group's thinking.

General Speaking Guidelines

If a group develops a solution to a problem, it will generally seek some way to put this solution into operation. Often it's necessary to convince others that the solution is workable and cost effective. Try these suggestions:

- **Present the solution in a nonthreatening manner.** New solutions often frighten people. For example, if your solution might lead people to feel insecure about their jobs, then alleviate these worries before you try to explain the solution in any detail. As a general rule it's best to proceed slowly, especially if you anticipate objections or hostility from your listeners.

- **Present new solutions tentatively.** In the excitement of inspiration, you may not have thought through all of the practical implications of your proposed solution. If you present your ideas tentatively and they're shown to be impractical or un-workable, you will be less hurt psychologically and—most important—more willing to present new solutions again.

- **Try to link changes to known problems in the organization.** For example, if you're going to ask employees to complete extensive surveys, then show them how this extra work will correct a long-standing problem and benefit them and the organization.

- **Say why you think the solution will work.** Give the advantages of your plan over the existing situation and explain why you think your solution should be implemented. The patterns for organizing a public speech (see Chapter 7) will help you make an effective presentation.

- **State the negatives.** There usually are some negatives with most ideas, and it may be necessary to identify these. And, of course, explain why you think the positives outweigh any potential drawbacks.

- **Relate your solution to the members' needs and interests.** Show how your solution is directly related to the needs and interests of those whom the solution will affect. Show others how your solution will benefit them.

Speaking in the Panel Group

Here are a few suggestions for making the panel format more effective:

- As moderator, always treat panel members and their questions with respect. You'll notice this on the popular talk shows: No matter how stupid the question may be, the moderator treats it as serious, though often restructuring it just a bit so that it makes more sense. Treat questions objectively; don't try to bias either a question or its answer through your verbal or nonverbal responses.

- As a panel member, speak in short turns. The group's interaction should resemble a conversation rather than individual public speeches. Resist the temptation to tell long stories or go into too much detail.

- Try to spread the conversation around the group. Generally, try to give each member the same opportunity to speak.

JOURNAL 12.3 PUBLIC SPEAKING CHOICE POINT

Adjustments

You're the third of four speakers on a panel. The problem is that the first two speakers covered just about everything you intended to cover. *What are some of your choices in this situation? What would you do?*

Speaking in the Symposium and Team Presentations

Here are a few suggestions for making symposia and team presentations more effective:

- **Coordinate your presentations very carefully.** Team presentations and symposia are extremely difficult to synchronize. Make sure that everyone knows exactly what he or she is responsible for. Make sure there's no (or very little) overlap among the presentations.
- **Rehearse the speech and envision the proceedings.** Much as you would rehearse a public speech, try to rehearse these presentations and their coordination. This is rarely possible to do in actual practice, but it is very helpful to "rehearse" mentally or imaginatively, going through the proceedings in your mind in advance.
- **Adhere carefully to time limits.** If you speak for more time than allotted, that time will be deducted from the minutes available to a later speaker. As you can appreciate, violating time limits will severely damage the entire group's presentation.
- **Provide clear transitions between the presentations.** Internal summaries work especially well as connectives between one speech and the next: "Now that Judy has explained the general proposal, Peter and Margarita will explain some of the advantages and disadvantages of the proposal. First, we'll hear from Peter with the advantages and then from Margarita with the disadvantages."

Oral and Written Reports

In many cases, the small group leader will make a presentation of the group's findings, recommendations, or decisions to some larger group—for example, to the class as a whole, the entire student body, the board of directors, the union membership, or the heads of departments.

Depending on the specific situation, these reports may be similar to speeches of information or speeches of persuasion. For example, if you are the group leader, your task may be simply to inform the wider group of the findings or recommendations of your committee—the proposed ways to increase morale, the new pension scheme, the new developments in competing organizations. In other cases, your report will be largely persuasive; for example, you may need to convince the larger group to provide increased funding so that your group's recommendations can be implemented.

In some situations, both a brief oral report and a more extensive written report are required. A good example is the press conference. At a press conference you deliver an oral report to members of the press, who also receive a written report. The press will then question you for further details. In some cases, you may want to use a computer-assisted presentation and prepare handouts of your slides, your speaker's notes, or selected slides with space for your listeners to write notes. Here are a few suggestions for more effective oral and written reports.

VIEWPOINTS

Oral and Written

How would you characterize the differences between the oral and written report, as these might be used at a press conference?

- Write the written report as you would a term paper, and from that develop a summary of the report in the form of a public speech, following the 10 steps explained throughout this text.

- Don't read the written report. Even though the oral and the written report may cover essentially the same content, they're totally different in development and presentation. The written report is meant to be read; the oral report is meant to be listened to.

- In some instances it's helpful to distribute the written report and to use your oral presentation to highlight the most essential aspects of the report. Listeners may then refer to the report as you speak—a situation not recommended for most public speeches.

- In some instances you might distribute the written report only after you have completed your oral report. Generally, however, people don't like this procedure; they prefer the option of thumbing through the report as they listen or reserving reading until after they've heard the oral report.

SUMMARY: SPEAKING IN GROUPS

This chapter provided an overview of the small group's nature, the ways in which some major types of small groups (brainstorming and problem-solving) work, the roles and styles of group membership and group leadership, and some suggestions for presenting the group's thinking.

Small Groups and Teams

12.1 Define *small group* and *team*, identify popular group formats and cultural aspects, and describe the popular types of small groups.

1. A small group is a collection of individuals who share a common purpose, are interdependent, operate with organizing rules, and see themselves as a group. A team is also a small group but usually established for a specific task in which the members' roles are specifically defined; members are committed to accomplishing the task, and their messages are largely content focused.

2. Virtual groups and teams are increasing dramatically in businesses and social networking.

3. Small group interactions generally follow the five stages of conversation: opening, feedforward, business, feedback, closing.

4. Four popular small group formats are the roundtable, the panel, the symposium, and the symposium–forum.

5. The brainstorming group attempts to generate as many ideas as possible by avoiding critical evaluation and encouraging quantity, combinations and extensions, and freewheeling.

6. The personal growth group helps members to deal with personal problems and to function more effectively. Popular types of personal growth groups are the encounter group, the assertiveness training group, the consciousness-raising group, and the intervention.

7. The problem-solving group attempts to solve a particular problem, or at least to reach a decision that may be a preface to solving the problem, and may do so through decision by authority, majority rule, or consensus.

8. The steps in the problem-solving approach are (1) define and analyze the problem, (2) establish criteria for evaluating solutions, (3) identify possible solutions, (4) evaluate solutions, (5) select best solution(s), and (6) test solution(s).

Speaking IN the Group

12.2 Explain the productive and unproductive group roles of group members, membership skills, and leadership types and skills.

9. A popular classification of small group member roles divides them into three types: group task roles, group building and maintenance roles, and individual roles.

10. Among the group task roles are those of information seeker or giver, opinion seeker or giver, evaluator–critic, and procedural technician or recorder. Among the group building and maintenance roles are encourager/harmonizer, compromiser, and follower. Among the individual (dysfunctional) roles are aggressor/blocker, recognition seeker/self-confessor, and dominator.

11. Group members should be group oriented, center conflict on issues, be critically open-minded, and ensure understanding.

12. Groupthink is an excessive concern with securing agreement that discourages critical thinking and the exploration of alternative ways of doing things.

13. Several theories of leadership help to clarify aspects of leadership. The traits approach identifies characteristics, such as intelligence and self-confidence, which contribute to leadership. The functional approach focuses on what the leaders should do. The transformational approach focuses on leaders as people who raise the performance of group members and empower them. The situational approach views leadership as varying its focus between accomplishing the task and serving the members' social and emotional needs, depending on the specific group and the unique situation.

14. Among the leader's functions and requisite skills are to prepare members for and start the group interaction, maintain effective interaction, guide members through the agreed-on agenda, ensure member satisfaction, empower members, encourage ongoing evaluation and improvement, manage conflict, and mentor the less-experienced.

Speaking FOR the Group

12.3 Explain the general speaking guidelines when speaking for the group and some specifics of speaking in the panel, symposium, and oral and written reports.

15. Public speaking skills will prove invaluable in general group speaking, speaking in the panel group, speaking in the symposium or team, and presenting oral and written reports.

KEY TERMS: SPEAKING IN GROUPS

assertiveness training group	group norms	problem-solving sequence
authority	group task roles	role
brainstorming	groupthink	round table
cohesiveness	individual roles	situational approach
consciousness-raising group	intervention group	small group
consensus	leadership	social loafing
encounter group	majority rule	symposium
forum	mentoring	symposium–forum
functional approach	panel	team
group building and	personal growth groups	traits approach
maintenance roles	problem-solving group	transformational approach

PUBLIC SPEAKING/GROUP EXERCISES

12.1 Using Brainstorming Techniques

Together with a small group or with the class as a whole, sit in a circle and brainstorm on one of the topics identified in the Public Speaking/Group exercise "Solving Problems in Groups," which follows. Be sure to appoint someone to write down all the contributions, or record the discussion. (Of course, brainstorming is useful even if you do it by yourself. Follow the same rules.) After this brainstorming session, consider these questions:

1. Did any members give negative criticism (even nonverbally)?
2. Did any members hesitate to contribute really wild ideas? Why?
3. Was it necessary to re-stimulate the group members at any point? Did this help?
4. Did possible solutions emerge that would not have been thought of without the group stimulation?

12.2 Solving Problems in Groups

Together with four, five, or six others—online or face-to-face—problem-solve one of the following questions: (a) *What should we do about homelessness?* (b) *What should we do to improve the college's website?* (c) *What should we do to better prepare ourselves for the job market?* (d) *How can social networking sites be used more effectively?* or (e) *How can we improve student–faculty communication?* Before beginning discussion of the topic, prepare a discussion outline, answering the following questions:

1. What is the problem? What are its causes? What are its effects?
2. What criteria should a solution have to satisfy?
3. What are some possible solutions?
4. What are the advantages and disadvantages of each of these solutions?
5. What solution seems best (in light of the advantages and disadvantages)?
6. How might this solution be tested?

12.3 Responding to Individual Roles

One major value of small group interaction is that everyone profits from the insights of everyone else; individual roles can get in the way. For each of the five individual roles, compose a response or two that you as a leader might make in order to deal with this dysfunctional role playing. Be careful that your responses don't alienate the individual or the group.

Individual, Dysfunctional Roles	Responding to Individual Roles
The aggressor:	_____
The recognition seeker or self-confessor:	_____
The blocker:	_____
The special interest pleader:	_____
The dominator:	_____

12.4 Empowering Group Members

Power is not a zero-sum game; empowering others often adds to, rather than subtracts from, your own power. For each situation, indicate what you might say to help empower the other person, using such strategies as (a) raising the other person's self-esteem; (b) listening actively and supportively; (c) being open, positive, and empathic; and (d) avoiding verbal aggressiveness or any unfair conflict strategies.

1. A team member is having lots of difficulties: He recently lost his job, received poor grades in a night class, and is gaining a lot of weight. At the same time, you're doing extremely well. You want to give your team member back his confidence.

2. You're managing four college interns, three men and one woman, who are working on redesigning your company's website. The men are extremely supportive of one another and regularly contribute ideas. Although equally competent, the woman doesn't contribute; she seems to lack confidence. Because the objective of this redesign is to increase the number of female visitors, you really need the woman intern's input and want to empower her.

3. You're a third-grade teacher. Most of the students are from the same ethnic–religious group; three, however, are from a different group. The problem is that these three have not been included in the social groupings of the students; they're treated as outsiders. As a result, these children stumble when they have to read in front of the class and make a lot of mistakes at the chalkboard (though they consistently do well in private). You want to empower these students.

Appendix of Speeches

Public Speaking Sample Assistants

The speeches in this appendix will help you to see the public speech as a whole and to ask critical questions about structure, support, language, and numerous other public speaking factors we consider throughout the book. The annotations will help you explore important principles that you'll find helpful in your own speeches.

Two of the speeches, one informative ("Biases") and one persuasive ("Prenups"), are purposely designed to illustrate ineffective speeches (no one really gives speeches this bad). Not surprisingly, research shows that we learn a great deal from negative examples (Goldstein, Martin, & Cialdini, 2008; Hesketh & Neal, 2006). All other speeches included here as well as the outlines integrated into the chapters are presented as models of effectiveness.

PUBLIC SPEAKING Sample Assistant

A POORLY CONSTRUCTED INFORMATIVE SPEECH

Here is an example of a poorly constructed informative speech. As you'll see, no one really gives a speech this bad. It was constructed to illustrate clearly and briefly some of the major faults that can occur in such speeches. The Public Speaking Sample Assistant,

"A Lot of Heart," presented later in this Appendix offers an example of a truly excellent speech. Together, the negative and the positive speech examples will offer you a variety of guidelines for errors you'll want to avoid and principles you'll want to follow in your own speeches.

SPEECH		PROBLEMS/CORRECTIVES
Title:	Biases	The title is likely to lead listeners to think of racial or religious bias—which the speech is not about. Select a title that is interesting, attention-getting, and relevant to the speech. After reading the speech, give the speech an interesting, attention-grabbing title.
Thesis:	What are confirmation, disconfirmation, in-group, and belief biases?	Stating the thesis as a question will prove confusing. Instead state the thesis as a declarative sentence, for example: Types of biases include confirmation, disconfirmation, in-group, and belief.
General Purpose:	To inform	The general purpose is fine although when you read the speech, you'll see the speaker moves beyond informing.
Specific Purpose:	To inform you about biases	The specific purpose is too general. It needs to be more specific: to define confirmation, disconfirmation, in-group, and belief biases.

Introduction

Whew! I'm here. This public speaking is all new to me. My major requires public speaking so I may be a bit nervous—I mean, a lot nervous.

These kinds of introductory comments are best avoided. They merely focus the listeners' attention on your weaknesses. Instead encourage listeners to focus on your strengths.

Let's see [shuffles through notes, arranging them and mumbling, "page 1, page 2"—OK, it's all here.]

Things like this reveal a decided lack of preparation. Instead, have your notes arranged and in order before getting up to speak.

I want to talk with you about bias and biases—confirmation, disconfirmation, in-group, and belief. I read an interesting article on this on the Internet and I thought, you know, since I have to give an informative speech this would be really good. It's interesting; really it is.

Getting right into the topic is not necessarily a bad idea. But, some more attention-grabbing way of gaining attention might have worked better. Perhaps a question or a dramatic illustration.

I have a lot of biases so I'm really concerned with this topic and I know you all have lots of biases so this might help you. So you should listen, like our textbook says.

Confessing to having biases—which are almost universally considered negative—is probably not a very good way to establish a connection with the audience. And, saying the audience has biases, will likely prove insulting to many listeners. Again, stress strengths rather than weaknesses.
The "So you should listen..." sentence was intended to get a laugh but is likely to fall on its face. Pretest your humor; it may not be as funny to others as it is to you.

So, like I said, I mean, that I'm going to talk about biases.

This statement functions as a transition—a sentence or phrase that guides the listeners from one part of the speech to another but it is too brief. A more elaborate transition here might have identified the four biases and the reason why these are being discussed.

Body

Confirmation bias—this means, like, you know, that you seek the kinds of information that will confirm your beliefs. And, not only this, but you also would give more importance to information that confirms your beliefs that to information that would not confirm your beliefs. I guess this could be about anything—religion or politics, maybe. I can give you a good example of this. My sister thinks that Chevrolet is the best car and only reads advertisements for Chevys.

Another example is if you want to persuade an audience to believe X, then you're going to do your research to find information that makes you believe X. But, that may be because you just want to get the speech prepared and don't want to waste time looking at information you won't use.

Disconfirmation bias—this means that people will reject information that goes against their beliefs—So, my sister would reject advertisements that claim that BMW is a better car. It's crazy but she does that. BMW is definitely the better car. That's what I want to get when I get a permanent job and make the big bucks.

Let's say, for example, that you believe X and someone gives you the information in favor of X and against X. You would believe the information in favor of your belief about X and that you will also reject information that goes against what you believe about X. This was actually shown in a research study on capital punishment.

In-group bias—this is also called intergroup bias—this means that people like people who are in the same groups as they are. So, if you're in the photography club and you hear that someone else is in the club, you'll probably have positive feelings for this person. I don't know about this, though; I'm in the photography club and I don't like a lot of the people. And I think some of them don't like me— actually a lot of them. This is supposed to work but I'm not sure.

Wikipedia says that there are two theories about in-group bias: realistic conflict theory and social identity theory. I'm not sure that helps but that's what Wikipedia says.

Belief bias—this means that people will accept a conclusion if it fits in with the beliefs they have. And, at the same time, people will reject a conclusion if it doesn't fit in with the beliefs they have. So, what happens here is that people don't look at the evidence; they only look at the conclusion. Like my sister doesn't examine the research on BMW; she just goes with the conclusion that Chevys are the best.

The speaker begins here with the first bias but doesn't define bias. It needs to be defined first and then the other four biases could be introduced as types of bias. Further, you would want to answer the audience's inevitable question, Why these four biases? Some reason for selecting these biases or some unifying thread would be effective in answering the audience's question.

This X example doesn't work; it says that the speaker didn't think hard enough about this topic. It tells listeners that the speaker hasn't thought about this sufficiently to come up with a good specific example. Generally, specific examples work better than the unidentified "X."

The sister example is trite. And the personal asides about BMW and the car the speaker wants to get just detract from the speech and, again, make you think the speaker didn't think this out clearly. Examples are extremely important; think them out and rehearse them carefully.

Again, the X adds little to clarity. But, the research study cited on capital punishment would have made an excellent example and could have easily explained how those who were for capital punishment believed the studies that supported capital published more than the studies that did not support capital punishment.

Also, the study on capital punishment requires an oral citation, a more specific identification of the study cited.

Notice that the speaker is evaluating the concept rather than simply explaining it. If the speech were on evaluating these bias theories, then this personal example would not have been so inappropriate. In a speech of definition, stick to defining.

Introducing these two theories without any explanation will confuse rather than clarify, unless the audience was very sophisticated in their knowledge of this topic. Further, some instructors may frown upon using Wikipedia as a source. So, know your audience.

By this time, the sister example is likely to seem silly to the audience. Avoid examples that might be considered silly; one laugh at the wrong time is likely to prove upsetting even to a seasoned speaker.

This is really confusing and has to do with the validity of arguments. It seems if you have belief bias you don't care about the validity of the argument. That's because you just look at the conclusion.

The term validity might have been defined though it's a complex term and would likely take up too much time. It may have been easier to not use the term and say something like "the strength or truthfulness of the arguments."

Conclusion

There are four biases—confirmation bias (like my sister and her car), disconfirmation bias (my sister and her car again), in-group bias (the photography club), and belief bias (my sister again).

This summary does little to help listeners remember what was discussed; they're likely to remember the example of the speaker's sister and not the four types of biases. It might also have helped to use a transitional sentence to guide the listener from the body of the speech to the conclusion, for example, "As we've seen there are four biases …"or even "In summary, we've seen there are four biases that …"

By the way, I got most of my information from a website which I can't remember.

This type of source credit is woefully inadequate. As we'll see, in the discussion of the oral citation (pp. 000-000), citing sources is an essential component of the speech. And, of course, one or two sources are hardly sufficient for such a complex topic.

If you want to read more about these, they are on the Internet.

This is much too general and more of a throw-away line. Something more specific might have helped, for example, a handout on the terms and where listeners can get more information.

Further the speaker seems almost without concern about whether or not listeners will want to learn more about these biases. Express enthusiasm about your topic, from the start of the speech to the very end. Listeners prefer speakers who are enthusiastic about their topic and really want to share their knowledge.

PUBLIC SPEAKING Sample Assistant

A POORLY CONSTRUCTED PERSUASIVE SPEECH

This speech illustrates some really broad as well as some more subtle errors that a beginning speaker might make when constructing a persuasive speech. First, read the entire speech without reading any of the "Problems/Correctives." As you read the speech, consider what errors are being demonstrated and how you might correct them. Then, after you've read the entire speech, reread each paragraph and combine your own analysis with the "Problems/Correctives" annotations.

SPEECH	PROBLEMS/CORRECTIVES
Title: Prenups **Topic:** Prenuptial agreements **Purpose:** Prenuptials are bad. **Thesis:** Why do we need prenuptial agreements?	This title sounds like an informative speech title and doesn't give the idea that a position will be argued. In addition, the topic, purpose, and thesis are not clearly focused or appropriately worded. A more appropriate title might be something like "Prenups Have Got to Go" or "The Dangers of Prenups." The topic would need to be narrowed by some qualification such as *The negative aspects of prenuptial agreements*. The purpose should be stated as an infinitive phrase: *To persuade my audience that prenuptial agreements should be declared illegal*. The thesis needs to be stated as a declarative sentence: *Prenuptial agreements should be declared illegal*.
Introduction You're probably not worried about prenuptial agreements yet. But maybe you will be. At any rate, that's what my speech is on. I mean that prenuptial agreements should be made illegal.	This opening is weak and can easily turn off the audience. After all, if they're not worried about it now, why listen? The speaker could have made a case for the importance of this topic in the near future, however. It appears as if the speaker knows the topic's not important but will speak on it anyway. A more effective introduction would have (1) captured the audience's attention—perhaps by citing some widely reported celebrity prenup; (2) provided a connection among the speaker-audience-topic—perhaps by noting the consequences individuals might suffer with or without a prenup; and (3) oriented the audience as to what is to follow.
Body	Here, a transition would help. In fact, transitions should be inserted between the introduction and the body and between the body and the conclusion. Using transitions between the main points and signposts when introducing each main point would help. The speaker might have said something like: "There are three main reasons why prenups should be banned."
Prenuptial agreements make marriage a temporary arrangement. If you have a prenuptial agreement, you can get out of a marriage real fast—and we know that's not a good thing. So if we didn't have prenups—that's short for prenuptial agreements—marriages would last longer.	This is the speaker's first argument but it isn't introduced in a way the audience will find easy to understand. Abbreviations should be introduced more smoothly. A simple signpost like, "My first argument against prenups is …." would make the audience see where the speaker is and get a visual of the outline. To introduce the abbreviation that will be used throughout the speech, the speaker might have incorporated it into the first sentence—"Prenuptial agreements—for short, prenups—make a marriage. …"

Right now, most people don't have prenups and yet somewhere around 50 percent of marriages last. That would be equivalent to a baseball player batting 500. If we had prenups that number would go up—I mean down—I mean the number of marriages that last will go up if we had prenups, I mean if we didn't.

The fact that 50 percent of the marriages fail seems to be the more telling statistic, yet the speaker treats a 50 percent success rate as good—something the audience is likely to see very differently. And the baseball analogy seems weak at best. The speaker also betrays a lack of preparation in confusing *up* with *down*.

Poor people are going to be discriminated against. Poor people won't be able to marry rich people because rich people will want a prenup and if a poor person doesn't want a prenup they wouldn't get married.

This argument just doesn't seem logical and the speaker would have been better served by omitting this entirely. For this argument to be useful in advancing the speaker's purpose, the speaker would have had to show that in fact poor people suffer in, say, divorce proceedings *because of* prenups.

These agreements are difficult to discuss. I mean, how do you tell someone you've told you love that you now want a prenup just in case the marriage gets screwed up? I guess you can say something like, "By the way, how about signing a prenup?"

This argument too doesn't seem important or logical. The fact that something is difficult to discuss doesn't mean you shouldn't discuss it; it merely means it's difficult to discuss. The speaker seems to be implying that if something is difficult to discuss, it should be abandoned—clearly a poor communication strategy.

And they're expensive. I mean you need a lawyer and all. I don't know what a lawyer charges but I'd guess it's a lot. So it's expensive and a young couple could use the money on other things.

This argument also seems weak simply because if there is enough money involved to warrant a prenup, there's probably enough money to hire a lawyer. If the speaker wanted to make this argument, specific costs should have been cited.

I had a prenup two years ago. And when we got divorced, I got nothing. If we didn't have a prenup, I'd be rich and I'd be at some private college instead of here.

Here the audience is likely thinking that there was a personal and emotional reason for arguing against prenups and not any logical reasons. And yet, the audience is probably asking itself, what were the specifics of the prenup and how much money was involved. The speaker probably should have disclosed this earlier in the speech and assured the audience that this personal experience led to a thorough study of the subject. And if a personal experience is going to be used—and there's no reason it shouldn't—then it needs to be discussed more fully and, at the least, answer the audience's obvious questions.

Conclusion

My conclusions. So you can see that prenups are not a good thing. Like they're unfair to poor people. And it creates a lot of stress for the couple, especially for the one who didn't want the prenup in the first place, like myself.

Using the word "conclusion" is not a bad idea but it stands out like a heading in a textbook. This speech also needed a more detailed conclusion, reiterating the main points in the speech. This speaker also commits one of the common faults of conclusions—that is, to introduce new material. Notice that we hadn't heard of the stress factor before. The speaker might have said something like: "In conclusion, we can see there are three main arguments against prenups. First, …"

Any questions?

This seems too abrupt. A good pause should preface this request for questions and perhaps a more inviting request could be offered—something like, "If anyone has any questions, I'd be happy to respond."

PUBLIC SPEAKING Sample Assistant

AN EXCELLENT INFORMATIVE SPEECH

This excellent informative speech was constructed and delivered by Blake Joseph Bergeron, a student from the University of Texas at Austin. Blake explains his interest in the topic: "I have worked in healthcare for a couple of years now. So, health topics tend to interest me. I heard about decellularizing hearts, my second sub-point in my second point, and upon further research, the topic really interested me." Blake's biggest challenge "was to inform the audience, yet still keep things fun and interesting."

SPEECH	COMMENTS
Title: A Lot of Heart	What do you think of this title? Does it make you want to listen to this speech? What expectations does this title set up?

Introduction

Art can be a feast for the eyes and apparently, the mouth. At the New York Parsons School of Design, students have decided to move away from the paint brush and to the beaker where they are taking used plant and animal tissues, soaking them in solutions, and creating something like this—it's a piece of steak. Tasty. The students, using a process known as decellularization, intended to explore humanities relationship between biology and technology.

The topic of decellularization is one that is both significant and current. It's likely that a good number of listeners would not have heard of or at least not know much about the topic. So, the speaker's task is to gain attention and make the subject relevant to his audience. This specific example not only gains attention but makes it clear that listeners will learn something new.

However, *Nature* on May 9, 2014 explains outside the art realm, this easy to use process can do so much more.

This is a neat transition from the art class example to the rest of the speech and to the topic generally.

The May 2014 *Harvard Science Journal* defines decellularization as the process of taking an organ or tissue and oxidizing it, removing all of its personalized blood cells. The January 2015 *American Journal of Transplantation* emphasizes this whole process can be done for about 50 dollars. By turning organs into blank slates, *Science Daily* on May 11, 2014 outlines, scientists can create personalized organs using a patient's stem cells, making them a perfect match for transplants.

Here the speaker defines this "new" term of decellularization (using a reputable and recent source) and shows its great potential, thus establishing the importance of the topic. It's something we feel we should know.

This technology could not only expedite the process for the over 122,000 patients on donor waiting lists but considering that the July 2014 *Greater Louisville Medical Society* reports, 28 percent of organ transplants end in rejection, decellularization could be the cure the medical community has been waiting for.

122,000 patients is surely a lot and again helps to establish the importance of the topic. Public speaking textbooks would generally advise making this number more meaningful to the audience. Saying something like: 122,000 patients—that's more than 10 times the number of students at my college—might have helped listeners appreciate how large a number this is.

Body

To better understand the process that went from the lab to the studio, let's first examine how decellularization works, its impact on the medical community, and finally discuss some implications. *LiveScience* on July 31, 2014 explains every day 18 patients die waiting for the transplants they desperately need. Decellularization could save the 90 lives that will be lost before this tournament even ends.

Here the speaker explains the purpose of the speech: to inform his audience about the process of decellularization. The thesis of the speech might be stated as We can understand decellularization. From this we might ask, How can we understand decellularization? We'd then get answers very similar to those of the speaker: We can understand it by examining (1) how it works, (2) its impact, and (3) its implications.

The Greeks kind of had their own form of decellularization except instead of organs, they used parchment. Because parchment was more durable than paper, fifth-century Greeks developed a process where they would essentially wash the parchment using milk and oat bran. I guess breakfast really is the most important meal of the day.

Let's explore decellularization in two key ways: how it's done in the lab and at home.

Decellularization is the process of removing existing cells from an organ. As Dr. Doris Taylor explains in the 2014 documentary *Stem Cell Universe*, each of the cells in our body have unique chemical makeup. It's kind of like a fingerprint, but in our cells. This unique chemical makeup is what causes organ rejection because no two organs are ever the same.

Decellularization wipes away all of those personalized cells by soaking the organ in chemicals and leaving the extracellular matrix; basically the skeleton of the organ. Scientists have recently perfected the process and as the February 2014 book *Biocoder* explains, the main chemicals needed are sodium dodecyl sulfate, nucleic acids, and soluble cytoplasmic inclusions. With these three things, scientists can remove all of the personalized cells of an organ, leaving only a blank slate.

But scientists aren't the only ones doing this anymore. As Michelle Quint explains in her February 14, 2014 Ted Talk, modern science has made this process simple and it can be done using water, OxyClean, salt, and Everclear because who said science can't be fun. I've even done it. Using Oxy-Clean, I decellularized a sheep heart. As Nina Tandon describes in her 2014 book *Super Cells*, the chemical similar to that in OxyClean, peracetic acid, washes away all of the cells in the organ, leaving only the matrix. It's like bleaching a white shirt that got washed with the reds. The OxyClean acts like the bleach, removing all of the blood cells and leaving only the product in its most basic state.

Once the importance of the topic is established, the speaker provides a clear orientation as to what the speech will cover. The speech clearly follows a topical organization pattern with three main points: how decellularization works, its impact on the medical community, and some implications of this process.

In outline the body of the speech would look something like this:

I. Workings of decellularization
II. Impact of decellularization
III. Implications of decellularization

The speaker cleverly emphasizes the importance of this process by connecting it to the lives that will be lost before this speaking tournament is over. Referring to the speaking tournament also encourages the audience to feel at one with the speaker—we're all in this together.

As a preface to the discussion of how decellularization works, the speaker explains with a simple example its general workings.

Here we learn that the first main point will have two subdivisions: how it's done in the lab and how it's done in the home. In outline, it would look something like this:

I. Workings of decellularization
    A. In the lab
    B. In the home

Here a general description of the process is provided before explaining how it's done in the lab and then how it's done in the home.

Here an extremely complex process is described to provide an initial or basic understanding.

With terms like these it's important that the speaker pronounce them without hesitation or stumbling. Some significant rehearsal was obviously needed.

Here we learn that the speaker has actually worked with the process, which is an effective way of establishing credibility.

The speaker makes use of a wide variety of research sources that convinces us that he knows the topic and has done more than adequate research on the topic.

Now, I have no clue what someone could do with a decellularized steak. I mean, I know they definitely can't eat it.

Thankfully, there are two clear uses for the process that got that steak there: research and transplants.

Here is an excellent transition connecting the first major point with the second.

Here is an orientation to the second major point, which we learn will be divided into two parts: research and transplants. In outline, it would look something like this:

II. Impact of decellularization
  A. On research
  B. On transplants

Here the speaker explains how decellularization can be used in research.

Initially, decellularized organs can be used to study the human body, without needing the human. As it stands, scientists have a hard time understanding how certain chemicals and conditions affect our organs directly. This is because, as the January 5, 2015 journal *Cell* points out, the government thankfully forbids testing dangerous products on humans. The National Center on Biomedical Technology on August 19, 2014, highlights that scientists are currently using decellularized human lungs in order to figure out how smoking directly affects their structure. While we know that smoking covers our lungs in tar, little is known concerning how chemicals affect our body on a cellular level. Decellularization allows researchers to look beyond just the surface and see something more.

Second, decellularized organs could be transplanted into human bodies. At the head of this application is the Texas Heart Institute. As the Texas Heart Institute outlines in July 2014, after a heart has been decellularized, the next step is to take somatic stem cells from the person in need—these are the stem cells that are found all over our body—and attach those stem cells to the organ. Once these cells are placed on the heart, as *Transformational Technologies* details on August 8, 2014, they instantaneously take hold. After about 48 hours, the organ is covered in a layer of cells that exactly match the patient in need, meaning decellularization allows for organ transplants free from the worries of rejection.

Here is the second use of decellularization: transplants. Again, the speaker succeeds in making an extremely complex process understandable by explaining the several steps involved in the process.

In 2006, the FDA decided to step into the stem cell debate, when they classified any type of stem cell as a drug; thus, putting them under FDA regulation. Yet, discourse over these laws was only inside the scientific community. Outside the field of science, decellularization could have lasting implications. Let's look at two.

Here is the speaker's third main point: the implications of decellularization. Again the speaker divides this into 2 parts. In outline, this point would look something like this:

III. Implications of decellularization
  A. Government regulation
  B. Commercialization of organs

The first implication is the government's classification of decellularization as a drug.

Initially, decellularization challenges our perceptions of stem cell regulations. When the government decided to regulate stem cells in 2006, the limited scope of the debate caused us to misunderstand what exactly was and was not regulated. This is because NPR on October 14, 2014, explains the debate focused solely on embryonic stem cells, leaving other types behind.

Decellularization challenges our perception of those laws because it uses the very stem cells that were left out of the conversation—causing us to not only question the regulations but the government's initial classification of stem cells as a drug. When the government has its hands on something our body naturally produces, it sets a dangerous legal precedent for future regulatory policies, urging us to ask: where is the line between protecting people and turning our bodies into government-regulated drug factories?

This classification as a drug, argues the speaker, can create a dangerous legal precedent.

Next, decellularization could lead to the complete commercialization of organs. Currently, it is illegal to pay for an organ in any way, whether it be placing yourself higher on a waiting list or to paying someone for their organ. However, *ScienceDirect* points out on January 15, 2015, nine companies are already manufacturing decellularized organs and selling them. While most are for research, once the transplant application is fully developed, it is feasible that a major pharmaceutical company could create a system, where with the right amount of money, an individual could purchase a complete organ transplant. These types of procedures could question the technical legality of purchasing an organ. Further, insurance companies are forced to define whether these procedures cosmetic or medically necessary, subsequently allowing them to have complete control over who lives and who doesn't.

The second implication is the potential commercialization of organs which we might have thought of negatively may actually be a positive.

Conclusion

Today we have examined the background, applications, and implications to the next big wave in modern science.

Here the speaker brief summarizes the three main points.

Turns out artists and scientists have more in common than we thought. Artists like Michelangelo and Caravaggio were praised for their works depicting human life; turns out the next generation of artists might be creating life itself.

In this final sentence the speaker reconnects this summary with the opening about the artists and scientists working together and thus brings the speech to a crisp close.

Works Cited

Your instructor or college may have a specific reference style that is preferred. So, it's best to find out the format used early in your speech preparation process so you can record all the information you'll need.

"The 3D Bioprinting Revolution." *Harvard Science Review*. N.p., 01 May 2014. Web. 09 Apr. 2015.

"About Regenerative Medicine Research at the Texas Heart Institute." *About Regenerative Medicine Research at the Texas Heart Institute*. Texas Heart Institute, 1 July 2014. Web. 09 Apr. 2015.

"American Journal of Transplantation." *Volume 15, Issue 1*. N.p., 1 Jan. 2015. Web. 09 Apr. 2015.

"Better Tissue Healing with Disappearing Hydrogels." *ScienceDaily*. ScienceDaily, 11 May 2014. Web. 09 Apr. 2015.

Cell | Vol. 160, Iss. 1–2, Pgs 1–354 (15 January 2015) | "ScienceDirect.com." *Cell* | *Vol. 160, Iss. 1–2, Pgs. 1–354, (15 January 2015) | ScienceDirect.com*. Science Direct, 5 Jan. 2015. Web. 09 Apr. 2015.

"Chapter 10. Mission Possible: Ghost Heart Protocol." *BioCoder: Issue 2*. N.p., 15 Feb. 2014. Web. 09 Apr. 2015.

"Download PDFs." *An Overview of Tissue and Whole Organ Decellularization Processes*. Cell, 5 Jan. 2015. Web. 09 Apr. 2015.

"Embryonic Stem Cells Restore Vision in Preliminary Human Test." NPR. NPR, 14 Oct. 2014. Web. 09 Apr. 2015.

"Ghost Heart: Miracle in Medicine." *Guardian Liberty Voice*. Transformational Technologies, 8 Aug. 2014. Web. 09 Apr. 2015.

"Perfusion Decellularization of Whole Organs." *Nature.com*. Nature Publishing Group, 9 May 2014. Web. 09 Apr. 2015.

Price, Andrew P., Kristen A. England, Amy M. Matson, Bruce R. Blazar, and Angela Panoskaltsis-Mortari. "Development of a Decellularized Lung Bioreactor System for Bioengineering the Lung: The Matrix Reloaded." *Tissue Engineering. Part A*. Mary Ann Liebert, Inc., 28 Aug. 2014. Web. 09 Apr. 2015.

Quint, Michelle. "A Ghost Heart?" *Ideastedcom*. N.p., 13 Feb. 2015. Web. 09 Apr. 2015.

Society, Greater Louisville Medical. "Organs." *In Kentucky There's One* (n.d.): N.p. *Greater Louisville Medical Society*. Greater Louisville Medical Society, 1 July 2014. Web. 09 Apr. 2015.

Staff, By Live Science. "Transparent Organs: Images Reveal See-Through Mouse." *LiveScience*. TechMedia Network, 31 July 2014. Web. 09 Apr. 2015.

Tadon, Nina. "'Super Cells — Building with Biology' — The Hope (And Hype) of Bio-Design [Book Review]." *PlanetSave*. Np., 15 Apr. 2014. Web. 09 Apr. 2015.

Taylor, Doris. "Stem Cell Universe." *Youtube*. Youtube, 1 June 2014. Web. 9 Apr. 2015.

PUBLIC SPEAKING Sample Assistant

AN EXCELLENT PERSUASIVE SPEECH

This excellent persuasive speech was constructed and delivered by Farrah Bara from the University of Texas at Austin. In explaining her interest in the topic, Farrah said "Growing up a Muslim in a post-9/11 American has certainly provided me with a very different outlook on the racism and hatred faced by many Muslims today. After reading a Human Rights Watch report on the FBI Entrapment Program, I felt that the issue was very important to talk about because awareness and activism are key to true justice for the millions of Muslims that live in this country." Farrah's biggest challenge was "convincing people that FBI Entrapment is more than just a conspiracy theory. I think people want to believe that the systems that are designed to protect us *are* protecting us. We want to believe that our law enforcement is good, that racial and religious injustice is something people do, not something a massive institution like the FBI engages in. So having to shatter that image of "justice" did create quite a challenge in the construction of this speech."

SPEECH	COMMENTS
Title: The FBI Entrapment Program	What do you think of this title? Does it make you want to listen to this speech? What expectations does this title set up?
Introduction	
	As you'll see, this speech, like the informative speech presented earlier, has a fairly long introduction and a short conclusion.
On the tenth anniversary of 9/11, 26-year-old Rezwan Ferdaus aimed an explosive drone at the U.S. capitol. *The Guardian* of September 29, 2011, reports, moments before the attack, the FBI flooded the scene, arrested their culprit, and released a statement calling his capture a success. This, they said, is exactly how counterterrorism is supposed to work. This is what American taxpayers pay $3.3 billion for the FBI to do.	This speech deals with a pretty powerful and potentially explosive subject or topic and is sure to be one with which some will agree and some will disagree. The speaker dives directly into the topic with a particularly effective attention getter—a single dramatic example.
But the April 23, 2013, *Florida Center for Investigative Reporting* reveals, Rezwan lives with his parents in Boston, has no source of income, and suffers from mental disabilities so severe, he couldn't have planned this crime; constructed a military-like drone; or even figured out how to buy a plane ticket to Washington. No, the real mastermind was a man named Khalil, who should be facing the 17-year prison sentence, except for one small technicality—Khalil works for the FBI.	Here the speaker builds her case for dismantling the entrapment program by detailing some major abuses committed under this program. The information presented here is likely to be new to most listeners and some listeners are likely to take objection to this. But, the speaker effectively cites two powerful sources—and more later—to give what she's saying credibility.
The July 20, 2014, *New York Post* reveals Rezwan's story is part of the FBI Entrapment Program, which frames innocent Muslims, as terrorists. In fact, of the 500 US terrorism prosecutions since 9/11, the July 21, 2014, Human Rights Watch reports half were planned by the FBI, funded by the FBI, to be miraculously stopped by the FBI moments before the crime takes place. The FBI Entrapment Program—our leading counterterror strategy—is blatantly unconstitutional and terrorizes Americans, while we pay the FBI for what we think is security.	Here the speaker connects the specific example with the general issue of FBI entrapment. Often, beginning speakers fail to make the connection between the example and the idea the example is designed to support.
This program needs to end.	This is the thesis of the speech: The FBI entrapment program must be stopped. The specific purpose of the speech is also clear: to persuade listeners to actively support the ending of the FBI Entrapment program. The speaker offers specific suggestions later in the speech.

Let's first determine why it exists, next uncover the consequences, and finally develop solutions so that we can stop a program that willingly turns the law-abiding citizens into terrorists.

Here is a detailed orientation that identifies the three major parts of the speech (why it exists, the consequences of the program, and solutions to stop the program). The speech follows a problem solution pattern where the first main point explains the reasons for the program, the second establishes the problem, and the third point addresses the solutions.

In outline the speech would look something like this:
   I. Reasons for program
   II. Consequences of the program
   III. Solutions to the problem

Body

Entrapment follows this routine: The FBI targets a person, sends an informant to befriend them, then watches as the informant pressures the target and orchestrates their arrest. This happens for two reasons: the illusion of counterterror and the presumption of guilt.

Here the speaker clarifies how entrapment works as a preface to explaining why it exists.

This part of the speech in outline might look like this.
   I. Reasons for the program
      A. Illusion of counterterrorism
      B. Presumption of guilt

The FBI website notes, 67% of FBI agents are devoted to counterterror—it's literally their job—which is why the first reason entrapment happens is because the FBI wants to look like it's doing its job. Back in 2004, the 9/11 *Commission Report* detailed, after 9/11, we were thinking about dismantling the FBI completely. Instead, we gave them a second chance. And with it, as a June 2013 FBI report reveals, an 84% budget increase. So if the FBI needs anything, it's results. That's where entrapment comes in. A September 2013 report by the ACLU explains it's hard to tell the difference between a real terror plot and a fake one, which is the point—give the illusion that our counterterror program is fine. And for the FBI, entrapment becomes synonymous to a job well done.

This is the speaker first main point and explains why the entrapment program is in effect. The first reason given here is that the FBI needs to make it seem they're effective and doing their job.

It seems like entrapment should just be taken to court. And it has. In fact, in 1915, the federal judiciary recognized entrapment defense, which requires proof of FBI involvement and proof the defendant wouldn't naturally commit the crime.

The speaker answers a question many listeners might be asking themselves.

The next reason entrapment happens is because we think Muslim Americans would naturally commit terrorism, failing the second criteria of entrapment defense. As the May 2014 *National Coalition to Protect Civil Freedoms* explains, 94% arbitrarily profile. And so to date, every person filing for entrapment, under terrorism, has failed. Additionally, entrapment is an affirmative defense, the 2014 *Washington University Law Review* explains this means if you're accused of terrorism, you are guilty, unless you can prove yourself innocent.

Here is the second reason why this program continues in operation—people assume that Muslim Americans would normally commit acts of terrorism.

In 2007, the FBI approached Shahwar Siraj with a request—to place these bombs at the 34th Street Subway Station. The July 21, 2014, *Guardian* explains, Siraj, a middle-aged man with autism, replied "I need to ask my mom's permission first." He never got his mom's permission and never took the bombs, but the FBI arrested him anyway, embodying entrapment's effects: cyclical rights violations and unstable national security.

This is a particularly dramatic example of entrapment and especially of its injustice and ineffectiveness. It offers a specific example in support of the assumption the FBI makes about Muslims. In addition, the example leads directly into the second major point: the consequences of this program.

In outline the speech would look like this.

   II. Consequences of the program
      A. Abuse of power
      B. Unstable national security

First, the FBI routinely abuses its power. The December 27, 2013, *Huffington Post* details in 2012, FBI informants committed 5,939 crimes, an increase of 5% from the year before. Former informant Craig Monteilh tells the March 4, 2015, *Daily Mail* as part of the entrapment program, Monteilh's "patriotic duty" included having sex with whatever Muslim woman he wanted, yet as Monteilh himself noted, "They were not espousing terrorist rhetoric, but I was still spying on them." We are so afraid of another 9/11, we continue to empower the very organization that abuses Americans. This past December, the ACLU reported, when President Obama approved guidelines to reduce racial profiling, he included a loophole that exempts the FBI.

Here the speaker addresses the first of the consequences: the abuse of power and of Americans.

Second, entrapment hurts national security because it disengages Muslim communities and wastes resources. The March 9, 2012, New York *Daily News* explains, since 2001, Muslims have become less cooperative with law enforcement. And so the people most capable of stopping terrorism, stopped trying. In a December 13, 2014, personal interview, investigative journalist Trevor Aaronson explained the idea of national security is a joke. Back in 2011, Russia warned Boston FBI agents of a man they thought was a terrorist. And Boston told them they were too busy. Too busy entrapping the mentally disabled Rezwan Ferdaus. Too busy and the FBI completely missed the lead up to the Boston Marathon bombing.

The second consequence is that it hurts national security by disengaging the Muslim community and wastes resources that could be deployed elsewhere. The news article and the personal interview with an investigative journalist support the speaker's assertion that this discourages Muslims from stopping terrorism and that the FBI is in fact wasting resources.

The FBI does not make stopping entrapment easy. Take Tarek Mehanna's 2012 trial. The previously cited *Human Rights Watch* explains, prosecutors showed 28 images of the World Trade Center burning, which had nothing to do with the trial. In an age where the FBI's words are taken for granted, we've got to take some precautions: legal aid and awareness.

Here the speaker introduces her third main point—the solution, which has two parts: legal aid and awareness. In outline this part of the speech would look like this.

III. Solutions to the problem
    A. Legal aid
    B. Awareness

First, we must fix a legal system that presumes Muslims guilty. Thankfully, the Constitutional Law Center for Muslims in America wants to do exactly that. When I asked Charles Swift, founder of the Center, on March 10, 2015 what we can do to help, he reminded me, the collegiate community is where revolutions ignite. As a mass group of people, we should help fund this Law Center, committed to legally combat the presumption of guilt. After the round, pick up a pledge card, fill it out, and hand it right back. Also, after talking to Muslim leaders in my community, they told me they'd double any amount of money we raise right now because as impossible as it seems to stop the FBI, our collective effort is the only thing standing in the FBI's way.

Here the speaker details how the legal system must be fixed and offers the listeners a specific way to help. Notice too the speaker's personal involvement she talked with a key person.

Second, the FBI wants to create the illusion of effective counterterror. To demystify that illusion, we've got to start spreading awareness. So pick up a folder. Think of it as your education toolbox, because it includes op-eds, case studies, articles, lists of books, and even a guide to write letters to the entrapped. Fifty years from now, those who remember 9/11 will remember it by the phrase "Never Forget." But those who remember entrapment will recall how a government replaced basic decency with fear. How thousands have been lashed out against for attacks they did not commit. How we forgot Muslims died on 9/11 too—victims who should not be forgotten because their skin is a different color or because their god has a different name.

Here is the second part of the solution—awareness—and again asks the listeners to do something specific. The folder offers substantial evidence that the speaker obviously prepared this speech very carefully.

Conclusion

This conclusion is rather short for a speech of this length. Though most contest speeches follow this pattern of long introductions and short conclusions, the general advice from public speaking theorists is to keep them about the same length. There are times, however, when the audience needs to be given background information—as in these two speeches—which justifies breaking the general rule of equal time for both introductions and conclusions.

The FBI built entrapment from desperation.

This first sentence of the conclusion summarizes one of the main assumptions made by the speaker and crystallizes the speaker's analysis of why this program exists.

After looking at its causes, effects, and solutions, it's clear what they forgot is genuine security.

Here the speaker summarizes the three main points and links them back to the argument that this program does not bring security.

In 1908, President Roosevelt created the FBI to serve one purpose—law enforcement. It's about time the FBI fulfills its actual purpose.

The speaker closes crisply on a positive note—let the FBI fulfill its real purpose.

Works Cited

Your instructor or college may have a specific reference style that is preferred. So, it's best to find out early in the process so you can record all the information you'll need.

Aaronson, Trevor. "How the FBI in Boston May Have Pursued the Wrong 'Terrorist'" *Florida Center for Investigative Reporting*. N.p., 23 Apr. 2013. Web. 10 Apr. 2015.

Ackerman, Spencer. "Shahawar Matin Siraj: 'impressionable' Young Man Caught in an NYPD Sting." *The Guardian. The Guardian*, 21 July 2014. Web. 12 Apr. 2015.

"Boston Marathon Bombing." Personal interview. 13 Dec. 2014.

"Cyber Security: Preparing for and Responding to the Enduring Threat." FBI. FBI, 12 June 2013. Web. 10 Apr. 2015.

Dailymail.com, Joel Christie For. "Former FBI Mole Who Was Paid to Go Undercover and Infiltrate California Mosques Says He Was 'encouraged' to Sleep with Muslim Women to Obtain Better Intel." *The Daily Mail Online*. Associated Newspapers, 05 Mar. 2015. Web. 10 Apr. 2015.

Downs, Stephen. "INVENTING TERRORISTS The Lawfare of Preemptive Prosecution." *Project SALAM*. National Coalition to Protect Civil Freedoms, May 2014. Web. 10 Apr. 2015.

"Ending Entrapment." Telephone interview. 10 Mar. 2015.

Harris, Paul. "FBI Faces Entrapment Questions over Rezwan Ferdaus Bomb Plot Arrest." *The Guardian*. N.p., 29 Sept. 2011. Web. 10 Apr. 2015.

"Illusion of Justice: Human Rights Abuses in U.S. Terrorism Prosecutions." *Human Rights Watch* (2014): N.p., 21 July 2014. Web. 10 Apr. 2015.

Murphy, Laura. "Time for Obama and Holder to Truly End Racial Profiling by Law Enforcement." *American Civil Liberties Union*. ACLU, 21 Dec. 2012. Web. 10 Apr. 2015.

Pagones, Stephanie. "'Newburgh Four' Terrorism Case Was FBI Entrapment: HBO Film." *New York Post*. N.p., 20 July 2014. Web. 10 Apr. 2015.

Reilly, Ryan J. "FBI Allowed Informants To Commit More Crimes In 2012 Than Year Before." The Huffington Post. TheHuffingtonPost .com, 27 Dec. 2013. Web. 12 Apr. 2015.

Roth, Jessica. "The Anomaly of Entrapment." *Washington University Law Review*. N.p., 22 Oct. 2014. Web. 10 Apr. 2015.

"UNLEASHED AND UNACCOUNTABLE The FBI's Unchecked Abuse of Authority." ACLU (N.D.): N.p., American Civil Liberties Union, Sept. 2013. Web. 10 Apr. 2015.

"The U.S. 9/11 Commission on Border Control." *Population and Development Review* 30.3 (2004): 569–74. 2004. Web. 10 Apr. 2015.

PUBLIC SPEAKING Sample Assistant

AN EXCELLENT PERSUASIVE SPEECH

This speech was constructed and delivered by Kevin King from the University of Texas at Austin. When asked why he became interested in the topic, Kevin said: "I've watched a number of relatives and family friends battle Alzheimer's. After doing some basic research, I uncovered a truly frustrating problem—we simply aren't doing enough to find a cure for this disease." Kevin's biggest challenge was "to construct the tightest possible structure, and one that offered my audience members very tangible solutions."

SPEECH	COMMENTS
Title: Funding Alzheimer's Research	What do you think of this title? Does it make you want to listen to this speech? What expectations does this title set up?

Introduction

Last Spring, comedian Seth Rogen set aside his joint and headed to the halls of Congress to testify before the Senate Committee on Appropriations. For the past 9 years, Rogen has watched his mother-in-law's health spiral out of control at the hands of Alzheimer's disease. In his February 26, 2014 testimony, Rogen called on Congress to prioritize Alzheimer's research. And his plea was heard—by 2 of the committee's 30 members.

Here the speaker introduces the topic with a specific instance that gains attention. The audience can easily visualize and identify with Rogan, and it clearly identifies the subject of the speech—prioritizing Alzheimer's research.

While death from major diseases like HIV and cancer continue to decrease, an Alzheimer's Association March 2015 report laments Alzheimer's remains the only cause of death in the top 10 that continues to rise—over 70% in the last decade. A March 13, 2015 CNN article warns that by 2050, more than 14 million baby boomers will develop the disease, tripling the current number of cases and costing taxpayers more than $1.2 trillion in cost of care, which the April 4, 2014 Stanford Medicine Journal alerts will bankrupt Medicare and Medicaid. These numbers don't yell problem, they scream epidemic, which is why thankfully, in 2011, President Obama signed the National Alzheimer's Project Act, or NAPA, with the goal of curing the disease by 2025.

Here the speaker establishes the importance of Alzheimer's by noting that it's a disease that is increasing, that some 14 million boomers will develop Alzheimer's, and that, because of this, it can bankrupt Medicare and Medicaid.
Note too the use of research throughout the speech: (1) The qualifications of the researchers cited are clear and from respected sources. (2) The research is current; the speech was given in 2015. (3) It seems fair, given the sources cited. (4) It is definitely sufficient. (5) It seems accurate; we don't get the feeling that the speaker is omitting contradictory evidence.

But despite the administration's ambitious plan, U.S. News of February 15, 2015—more than four years after NAPA's passing—notes the National Institute of Health's budget devoted to Alzheimer's research is exactly the same as it was twenty years ago. In fact, for every $27,000 Medicare and Medicaid spend on Alzheimer's care, the NIH spends only $100 on research. We have to end our collective silence about this disease and make Alzheimer's research a financial priority—before it's too late.

With the importance of the disease well established, the speaker here notes the lack of adequate funding.
Here is a clear statement of the thesis of the speech: Funding for Alzheimer's must be increased.

To do so, let's discuss three causes of insufficient Alzheimer's research funding—stigma, practical challenges, and lack of advocacy—and follow each directly with a solution. As Rogen puts it, Americans whisper the word Alzheimer's because their government whispers the word Alzheimer's. I say, let's make some noise.

Here the speaker provides an orientation to the rest of the speech. From this we learn that the speech will have three parts corresponding to the three causes of insufficient research funding: stigma, practical challenges, and lack of advocacy. And we further learn that each of these three points will contain two parts: explanation of the cause and a solution to the cause. From this brief introduction you can easily picture the structure of the speech; it would probably look something like this:

I. Stigma
   A. Stigma as cause
   B. Stigma solutions

II. Practical challenges [last of research subjects]
   A. Practical challenges as cause
   B. Practical challenges solutions

III. Advocacy
   A. Lack of advocacy as cause
   B. Lack of advocacy solutions

Notice that the three main points are organized into a topical pattern and each of these main points is organized in a problem–solution pattern.

Note too the neat image created by the use of the word *whisper*.

Body

The March 4, 2014 Washington Post asserts many people still think of Alzheimer's as just a memory problem—you forgot where you left your keys or to turn off the stove—not the universally fatal brain disease that it is. This is the first cause of the research funding shortage: ignorance and social stigma, so let's explore this cause and then discuss some ways to combat it.

Here the speaker identifies the first major proposition—the stigma that many feel because of the disease.

Initially, our conversations about Alzheimer's disease are ill-informed, or worse, because of stigma, nonexistent. The February 5, 2015 Houston Chronicle reveals many patients are so embarrassed by their diagnosis, they work to conceal the disease. That's because as a September 4, 2014 Medical Daily article notes, sixty percent of patients feared people would trivialize the disease or begin to exclude them socially.

Here the speaker provides evidence that stigma is a major problem—that large numbers of people with Alzheimer's hide it because of embarrassment.

The reality is this disease is a brutal thief that will steal your memory, speech, bladder control, and ability to feed yourself. When one patient described the silence he experienced, he noted: "Friends [and] family are uncomfortable, they don't know how to behave normally around me anymore." When we can't even talk about this disease with our loved ones, how can we expect Congress to hold an informed conversation of their own?

Here the speaker shows that far from being trivial the disease is horrendous.

To begin addressing the inadequacy of research funding, we must start engaging in informed dialogues. First, learn how to communicate about the disease by listening to the Banner Alzheimer's Institute's free webinar series "Dementia Dialogues." Follow the QR code on this card for information about how to tune in.

Here is the solution to this stigma problem, cued by the words "to begin addressing the inadequacy of research funding." And we learn that there are two parts to this, cued by "First" and "Second."

Second, once we do learn how, we have a responsibility to honestly talk about Alzheimer's with other people. Watch a film like *Still Alice* with friends, reach out to a loved one that's been diagnosed and offer a supportive ear, or read and share stories of parents or grandparents who suffer from Alzheimer's on the tumblr I created, alzstories.tumblr.com. If we ever hope to sufficiently fund this disease, we have to make the harsh reality of its symptoms part of our collective consciousness.

Carol Harrison told the Philadelphia Inquirer on March 18, 2015, she thought she had seen the worst of both her mother and aunt's Alzheimer's until she visited one morning to find the two sisters sitting next to each other, neither with any sense the other was there. To help families like the Harrisons, let's examine the next cause of this funding disparity—practical research challenges—and then see how we can help.

First, Alzheimer's is underfunded because it lacks a crucial resource money can't buy—test subjects. UPI on February 10, 2015 states after a medical breakthrough, researchers at Boston University were ready to take their drug T-817MA to phase 2: testing on human patients. But The Alzheimer's Disease Center, explains in an article from that same day that progress into phase 2 is at a standstill because there simply is not enough patients to pool for the drug trial. While the benefits of a drug trial could be tremendous, fear and shame outweigh the benefits of participation for many patients who have just been diagnosed. Moreover, patients who are far along in their battle with the disease don't have the cognitive function to consent to experimental medication, and caregivers are understandably reluctant to consent for them. This practical challenge makes Alzheimer's research a risky investment for investors.

Fortunately, we can all play a role in helping the research community. The Alzheimer's Association just launched a program called TrialMatch, a free service that matches Alzheimer's patients to clinical studies. If you care for a loved one suffering from this disease, follow this QR code for more information about TrialMatch and consider talking to them about the benefits of participating. But from a long term perspective, the onus is on our generation to fix this shortage. So my fellow millennials in the room, when you sit down to write your living will, inform your family that, in the event of a diagnosis, you give consent for participation in trials, and after death, eventual donation of your brain to Alzheimer's research. When funding is finally met, participation from patients will be essential for putting that money to use and finding a cure.

Last year, President Obama finally cashed in and raised the federal Alzheimer's research budget to $500 million. But as a February 2, 2014 Alzheimer's Association report points out, if we have any hope of curing this disease, the research community doesn't need $500 million, it needs $2 billion. Let's examine the last cause—ineffective advocacy fundraising—and then, how we can make a difference right here, right now.

Note that the speaker gives very specific suggestions as to what the listener can do to become a part of the solution. Note too how informed the speaker is and how exceptionally well prepared he is.

His knowledge of the topic and his citations to research clearly establish the speaker's credibility.

Here the speaker introduces the second cause (practical challenges) with a specific example—again, stressing how horrible such a disease is.

Here the speaker establishes that the lack of test subjects is a major cause of the lack of adequate funding.

Here the speaker offers some solutions to this problem of lack of test subjects by providing a variety of things you can do.

Here the speaker introduces the third cause by saying simply: "Let's examine the last cause—ineffective advocacy fundraising."

Simply, there isn't enough advocacy surrounding this disease. The NIH's Annual funding report reveals last year, $3 billion dollars was spent on research for the 1 million Americans battling HIV/AIDS, but just $480 million for the over 5 million Americans suffering from Alzheimer's. This is by no means a competition among diseases, but frequently, when it comes to medical research—the louder the campaign, the bigger the check. There is no BroadwayCares or pink ribbons for Alzheimer's because, as the February 2015 edition of AARP emphasizes, it lacks social presence and high profile survivors that could help personify a campaign for more federal funding. Alzheimer's needs more active, grassroots campaigns and advocates who recognize the generational implications if this disease is left unfunded.

Here the speaker shows that there is in fact a lack of advocacy for Alzheimer's funding.

The reality is, I don't have the power to shift the funding conversation at the federal level, but we can each do our part to cure this disease today. I've launched the 1for33 campaign within the speech community and my university campus. If left underfunded, by 2050, 1 patient will be diagnosed every 33 seconds, and so I'm asking all of you to donate however much you're able—from $3, $33, or even 33 cents. Find me after the round to donate directly to the 1for33 gofundme page using my square device. The funds will be donated directly to the Alzheimer's Association's New Investigators Research Grants. Last year, the NIH had to deny 700 promising research projects funding simply because they ran out of money. With every dollar we give, we are one step closer to funding a project and one step closer to finding a cure.

Here the speaker offers some solutions to the third cause of inadequate funding: lack of advocacy.

Conclusion

How would you have organized this speech using the motivated sequence pattern? How did the speaker gain attention, establish the need, satisfy the need, visualize the need satisfied, and call for action?

Today we explored three independent causes to the lack of research funding for Alzheimer's and provided tangible solutions for each. Last spring, my grandfather failed the clock test, an early tool for detecting Alzheimer's. He has not been fully diagnosed, but when he is I want to know I have done everything I can to help end this brutal disease. I encourage each of you, in your own circumstances, to join me.

In this brief conclusion the speaker summarizes the speech in the first sentence. The speaker then provides a final motivation to do everything we can in the second sentence. And the third sentence brings the speech to a crisp close.

Works Cited

Your instructor or college may have a specific reference style that is preferred. Find out which style is required and carefully record your source information.

http://www.alz.org/documents_custom/hearing_statement_022614.pdf

http://www.alz.org/facts/overview.asp

http://www.cnn.com/2015/03/13/opinions/shriver-wipe-out-alzheimers/

http://med.stanford.edu/news/all-news/2014/04/gene-variant-puts-women-at-higher-risk-of-alzheimers-than-it-does-men-study-finds.html

http://www.usnews.com/news/articles/2015/02/05/advocates-say-more-money-needed-to-fend-off-alzheimers-epidemic

http://www.washingtonpost.com/local/new-study-ranks-alzheimers-as-third-leading-cause-of-death-after-heart-disease-and-cancer/2014/03/05/8097a452-a48a-11e3-8466-d34c451760b9_story.html

http://www.chron.com/entertainment/movies/article/Moore-shines-with-eloquent-portrayal-of-6064497.php
http://www.medicaldaily.com/alzheimers-social-stigma-begins-diagnosis-they-treat-me-child-301318
http://articles.philly.com/2015-03-19/news/60254484_1_alzheimer-nursing-home-care-mother
http://www.upi.com/Health_News/2015/02/10/Promising-Alzheimers-research-stalled-by-lack-of-volunteers-for-studies/
    2311422945413/
http://www.bu.edu/news/2015/02/10/promising-alzheimers-research-stalled-by-lack-of-volunteers-for-studies/
http://www.alz.org/research/clinical_trials/find_clinical_trials_trialmatch.asp
http://www.alz.org/news_and_events_unchecked_threat.asp
http://report.nih.gov/categorical_spending.aspx
http://www.aarp.org/health/brain-health/info-2015/alzheimers-research.html

Glossary

acceptance speech   A special occasion speech in which the speaker accepts an award or honor of some kind and attempts to place the award in some kind of context.

active listening   A process of putting together into some meaningful whole the listener's understanding of the speaker's total message—the verbal and the nonverbal, the content and the feelings.

agenda-setting   A fallacy or pseudo-argument in which a speaker contends that only certain issues are important and others are not—in an attempt, for example, to focus attention on the strong points of a plan and divert attention from the weak points.

alliteration   A figure of speech in which the initial sound in two or more words is repeated.

analogy   Comparison of two things; analogies may be literal (in which items from the same class are compared) or figurative (in which items from different classes are compared).

anecdotal evidence   A fallacious persuasive tactic in which the speaker offers specific examples or illustrations as "proof."

antithesis   A figure of speech in which contrary ideas are presented in parallel form, as in Charles Dickens's opening lines in *A Tale of Two Cities*: "It was the best of times, it was the worst of times."

apology speech   A special occasion speech in which the speaker expresses regret for some transgression and asks for forgiveness.

appeal to tradition   A fallacy often used as an argument against change, as when a speaker claims that a proposed plan should not be adopted because it was never done before.

articulation   The movements of the speech organs as they modify and interrupt the air stream from the lungs, forming sounds.

assertiveness training group   A type of small group focusing on increasing assertive behavior of members.

assimilation   A process of message distortion in which messages are reworked to conform to our own attitudes, prejudices, needs, and values.

attention   The process of responding to a stimulus or stimuli; usually some consciousness of responding is implied.

attitude   A predisposition to respond for or against an object, person, or position.

audience analysis   The process of analyzing a speaker's intended listeners.

audience   A group of people listening to or reading a speech.

authority   A form of decision making in which the leader or boss makes the decision, though members may offer suggestions.

backchanneling cues   Verbal and nonverbal signals that tell the speaker you're listening.

bar graph   A type of diagram in which numerical values are represented in the height or size of the column.

belief   Confidence in the existence or truth of something; conviction.

bias   Preconceived ideas that predispose you to interpret meaning on the basis of these ideas rather than on the basis of the evidence and argument.

body   The main part of your speech; the speech minus the introduction and conclusion.

brainstorming   A technique for generating ideas either alone or, more usually, in a small group.

cause–effect pattern   An organizational system in which the speech is divided into causes and effects.

channel   The vehicle or medium through which signals are sent.

character   One of the qualities of credibility; an individual's honesty and basic nature; moral qualities.

charisma   One of the qualities of credibility; an individual's dynamism or forcefulness.

chart boards   Large semi-rigid boards that come in a variety of colors and sizes and are useful when you have one or two relatively simple graphs, a few word charts, or diagrams that you want to display during your speech.

claim-and-proof pattern   An organizational pattern in which the thesis is the claim and each main point offers proof in support of this claim.

clarity   A quality of speaking style that makes a message easily intelligible.

cognitive restructuring   A theory for substituting logical and realistic beliefs for unrealistic ones; used in reducing communication apprehension and in raising self-esteem.

cohesiveness   A quality of togetherness; in group communication situations, the mutual attraction among members and the extent to which members work together as a group.

collectivist culture   A culture in which the group's goals rather than the individual's are given primary importance and where, for example, benevolence, tradition, and conformity are given special emphasis. Opposed to *individualist cultures.*

commencement speech   A special occasion speech given to celebrate the end of some training period, often at school graduation ceremonies.

communication apprehension   Fear or anxiety over communicating.

comparison and contrast pattern A pattern for organizing a speech in which you compare and contrast two different items.

competence One of the qualities that undergirds personal credibility; encompasses a person's ability and knowledge.

consciousness-raising group A small group of people who help each other to cope with the problems society confronts them with.

consensus A process of reaching agreement (not necessarily unanimous) among group members.

context The physical, social-psychological, temporal, and cultural setting in which communication takes place.

context factors Those characteristics of the place in which the speech will be given, for example, the physical environment in which the speech will be presented.

credibility proof The presentation of an individual's qualifications (competence, character, and charisma) to support the individual's arguments.

critical listening A style of listening that includes analyzing and evaluating the message rather than simply receiving it.

criticism The reasoned judgment of some work; although often equated with faultfinding, criticism can involve both positive and negative evaluations.

cultural context The cultural beliefs and customs of those communicating.

cultural sensitivity An awareness of and sensitivity to the rules for communicating in varied cultural settings.

dedication speech A special occasion speech in which you commemorate the opening or start of a project.

definition A statement explaining the meaning of a term, phrase, or concept.

definition by authority A type of definition advanced by an expert.

definition by etymology A type of definition that refers to the origin and development of the word's meaning.

definition by negation A type of definition in which a word is defined by what it's not.

definition by specific example A type of definition in which the word's meaning is suggested by examples.

delivery outline A brief outline of a speech that the speaker uses during the actual speech presentation.

diagrams Simplified drawings often in outline form that are often useful for explaining complex structures.

display rules Cultural norms for what is and what is not appropriate to display in public.

emotional proof The presentation of appeals to the feelings, needs, desires, and wants of others in order to persuade them.

empathy The feeling of another person's feeling; feeling or perceiving something as another person does.

encounter group A type of small group in which members facilitate each other's personal growth.

ethics The rightness or wrongness of actions; the branch of philosophy that studies moral values.

ethos From the Greek, another term for *credibility proof.*

ethnocentrism The tendency to see others and their behaviors through our own cultural filters, often as distortions of our own behaviors; the tendency to evaluate the values and beliefs of our own culture more positively than those of another culture.

eulogy A special occasion speech of tribute in which the speaker praises someone who died.

evaluating A stage in the listening process in which you judge the messages you hear.

example A form of supporting material in which a specific instance is used to explain a concept.

expert testimony The testimony of an authority.

extemporaneous speech A speech that is thoroughly prepared and organized in detail and in which certain aspects of style are predetermined.

eyewitness testimony The testimony of someone who has witnessed an event.

farewell speech A special occasion speech designed to say goodbye to a position or to colleagues and to signal that you're moving on.

feminine cultures Cultures that encourage both men and women to be modest, oriented to maintaining the quality of life, and tender. Feminine cultures emphasize the quality of life. Opposed to *masculine cultures.*

fiction–fact pattern An organizational pattern in which the fictions or untruths are identified and disputed by the facts.

figurative analogy An expressed comparison of two items of different types.

figure of speech Stylistic device and way of expressing ideas that is used to achieve special effects.

filled pauses Interruptions in speech that are filled with such vocalizations as *er* or *um.*

flip chart A presentation aid consisting of sheets of paper for writing key terms or numbers while presenting a speech.

flow diagram Drawings that show a sequence of events or processes.

forum A period of questions from the audience and responses by the speakers.

functional approach An approach to leadership that focuses on what the leader should do in a given situation.

general purpose The overall aim of your speech, for example, to inform or to persuade.

goodwill speech A special occasion speech in which the speaker seeks to make the image of a person, product, or company more positive.

graphs Diagrams showing relationships that are useful for clarifying how a whole is divided into parts, showing differences over time, and comparing different amounts or sizes.

group building and maintenance roles Group roles that focus not only on the task to be performed but also on interpersonal relationships among members.

group norms Rules or expectations for appropriate behavior for a member of a group.

group task roles Member role that helps the group focus on and achieve its task.

groupthink A tendency observed in some groups in which agreement among members becomes more important than the exploration of the issues at hand.

handouts Printed materials distributed to the audience.

high-ambiguity-tolerant cultures Cultures that are accepting of ambiguity and do not feel threatened by unknown situations; uncertainty is a normal part of life, and people accept it as it comes.

high-context culture A culture in which much of the information in communication is in the context or in the person rather than explicitly coded in the verbal message. Opposed to *low-context cultures.*

high-power-distance cultures Cultures in which power is concentrated in the hands of a few: there's a great difference between the power held by these people and the power of the ordinary citizen. Opposed to *low-power-distance cultures.*

hyperbole A figure of speech in which something is exaggerated for effect but is not intended to be taken literally.

idioms Expressions that are unique to a specific language and whose meaning cannot be deduced simply from an analysis of the individual words.

illustration A specific instance drawn in greater detail than a brief example.

immediacy A quality of interpersonal effectiveness; a sense of contact and togetherness; a feeling of interest in and liking for the other person.

immediate audience The audience that hears the speech as it is presented.

impromptu speech A speech given without any explicit prior preparation.

inclusive language Language that includes all people and all cultures rather than terms that are specific to any one specific cultural group.

individual roles Behavior in groups that is usually dysfunctional and works against a sense of group cohesion.

individualist culture A culture in which the individual's rather than the group's goals and preferences are given primary importance. Opposed to *collectivist cultures.*

indulgent cultures Cultures that emphasize the gratification of desires and a focus on having fun and enjoying life. Opposed to *restrained cultures.*

infographic Visual representation of information.

informative speaking Speaking to convey information, something that is not already known.

informative speech A speech designed to communicate information to an audience rather than to persuade.

inspirational speech A special occasion speech designed to raise the spirits of the audience, to inspire them.

intervention group A group of concerned individuals who get together to help another deal with a problem.

introduction speech A special occasion speech designed to introduce the speaker himself or herself to an audience or a speech designed to introduce another speaker or group of speakers.

irony A figure of speech employed for special emphasis in which a speaker uses words whose literal meaning is the opposite of the speaker's actual message or intent.

leadership The ability to influence others as well as to empower others.

levels of abstraction The different levels of specificity ranging from the highly abstract to the very concrete.

line graph A diagram in which numerical values are connected with lines and that is especially useful for showing changes over a period of time and comparing the relative changes of two or more groups.

listening The process of receiving, understanding, remembering, evaluating, and responding to verbal and/or nonverbal messages.

literal analogy An expressed comparison of two items from the same class or type.

I-messages A type of message in which the speaker takes responsibility for the message.

logical proof The presentation of evidence and reasoned argument to support an assertion.

logos From the Greek, another term for *logical proof.*

long-term-oriented cultures Cultures that promote the importance of future rewards and so, for example, members of these cultures are more apt to save for the future and to prepare for the future academically. Opposed to *short-term-oriented cultures.*

low-ambiguity-tolerant cultures Cultures that are uncomfortable with ambiguity, do much to avoid uncertainty, and have a great deal of anxiety about not knowing what will happen next.

low-context culture A culture in which most of the information in communication is explicitly stated in the verbal messages. Individualist cultures are usually low-context cultures. Opposed to *high-context cultures.*

low-power-distance cultures Cultures in which power is relatively evenly distributed throughout the citizenry. Opposed to *high-power-distance cultures.*

main points The major assertions or propositions of a speech.

majority rule A form of decision making in which the decision is made by majority vote.

manuscript speech A speech designed to be read verbatim from a script.

masculine cultures Cultures that view men as assertive, oriented to material success, and strong and view women, on the other hand, as modest, focused on the quality of life, and tender. Masculine cultures emphasize success and so socialize their people to be assertive, ambitious, and competitive. Opposed to *feminine cultures.*

mean The arithmetic average.

measures of central tendency Typical values, for example, the mean, median, and mode.

measures of correlation A measure of the degree to which two items are related; the extent to which one item can be predicted from the other item.

measures of difference   A measure of disparity or difference, for example, the difference between the highest score and the lowest score.

median   The middle score in an array of scores.

memorized speech   A method of oral presentation in which the entire speech is committed to memory and then recited.

mentoring   Guidance and support given by an experienced individual to a less-experienced person.

message   Any signal or combination of signals transmitted to a receiver.

metaphor   A figure of speech in which there is an implied comparison between two unlike things; for example, "That CEO is a jackal."

metonymy   A figure of speech in which some particular thing is referred to by something with which it is closely associated, for example, *Rome* for the *Catholic Church* or the *White House* for the *U.S. government*.

mode   The most frequent score in an array.

models   Replicas of actual objects.

motivated sequence   A persuasive strategy consisting of five steps: attention, need, satisfaction, visualization, and action.

multiple-definition pattern   An organizational structure for a public speech in which each of your main points consists of a different type of definition.

narrative   An illustration told in story form.

negative correlation   A relationship is which two items move in opposite directions, for example, as one becomes higher the other becomes lower.

noise   Anything that interferes with a person receiving a message as the source intended the message to be received. Noise is present in a communication system to the extent that the message received is not the message sent.

oral citation   The source citation in the speech itself.

oral style   The style of spoken discourse that, when compared with written style, consists of shorter, simpler, and more familiar words; more qualification, self-reference terms, allness terms, verbs, and adverbs; and more concrete terms and terms indicative of consciousness of projection—for example, "as I see it."

organization   In public speaking, the pattern of the speech.

orientation   In public speaking, a preview of what is to follow in the speech.

outline   A blueprint or pattern for a speech.

owning criticism   Taking responsibility for your comments and evaluations.

oxymoron   A term or phrase that combines two normally opposite qualities as in *bittersweet*.

panel   A small group format in which group members are "experts" but participate informally and without any set pattern of who speaks when, as in a round table.

percentages   The portion of a total, expressed as a portion of 100.

performance visualization   A method for reducing communication apprehension in which you visualize yourself performing effectively and confidently.

personal growth groups   A type of small group that aims to help members cope with particular difficulties—such as drug addiction, not being assertive enough, having an alcoholic parent, being an ex-convict, or having a hyperactive child or a promiscuous spouse.

personification   A figure of speech in which human characteristics are attributed to inanimate objects for special effect; for example, "After the painting, the room looked cheerful and energetic."

persuasive speech   A speech designed to strengthen or change the attitudes or beliefs of audience members or to move them to take some kind of action.

physical context   The tangible environment in which communication takes place.

picture graphs   Diagrams that use images (icons, symbols, or photos) to represent numerical values.

pie graph   A type of presentation aid that divides a whole into pieces and represents these as pieces of a pie.

pitch   The highness or lowness of the vocal tone.

plagiarism   The act or process of passing off the work (ideas, words, illustrations) of others as your own.

positive correlation   A relationship in which two items move in the same direction, for example, as one becomes higher so does the other.

pathos   From the Greek, another term for *emotional proof*.

power priming   Verbal and nonverbal movements that make one feel powerful.

prejudice   Preconceived and unreasonable negative evaluations, usually used in reference to race.

preparation outline   A thorough outline (or blueprint) of the speech.

presentation aid   A visual or auditory form of supporting material.

presentation speech   A special occasion speech in which a speaker presents an award or some sign of recognition.

primary sources   Firsthand, contemporary accounts written or spoken by someone who has had direct experience with or witnessed a particular event. Distinguished from *secondary sources* and *tertiary sources*.

pro-and-con pattern   A pattern for organizing a speech in which the arguments for the thesis are advanced and the arguments against the thesis are noted and attacked; also referred to as the advantages-disadvantages pattern or the comparative advantage pattern.

problem–solution pattern   An organizational structure for a public speech divided into the problem and the solution, a structure that's especially useful in persuasive speeches in which you want to convince the audience that a problem exists and that your solution would solve or lessen the problem.

problem-solving group   A group whose primary task is to solve a problem or, perhaps more often, to reach a decision.

problem-solving sequence   A logical step-by-step process for solving a problem that is frequently used by groups;

consists of defining and analyzing the problem, establishing criteria for evaluating solutions, identifying possible solutions, evaluating solutions, selecting the best solution(s), and testing the selected solution(s).

pronunciation   The production of syllables or words according to some accepted standard as presented, for example, in a dictionary.

proof   Evidence for a proposition.

proxemics   The study of the communicative function of space; the study of how people unconsciously structure their space—the distance between people in their interactions, the organization of space in homes and offices, and even the design of cities.

psychological audience analysis   An analysis of such audience characteristics as the willingness to listen and the degree to which audience members favor your position.

public speaking   Communication in which a speaker presents a relatively continuous message to a relatively large audience in a unique context.

questions of fact   Issues revolving around potentially answerable questions.

questions of policy   Issues focused on what should or should not be done, what is and what is not a valuable policy.

questions of value   Issues focused on what is good or bad, just or unjust.

range   The difference between the highest and the lowest score.

rate   The speed at which you speak, generally measured in words per minute.

raw numbers   Numbers that have not be subjected to manipulation.

reasoning from causes and effects   A form of reasoning in which you reason that certain effects are due to specific causes or that specific causes produce certain effects.

reasoning from sign   A form of reasoning in which the presence of certain signs (clues) are interpreted as leading to a particular conclusion.

reasoning from specific instances   A form of reasoning in which several specific instances are examined and then a conclusion about the whole is formed.

receiving   In receiving messages, focus your attention on both the verbal and the nonverbal messages because both communicate meaning.

rehearsal   The process of practicing the delivery of your public speech.

remembering   To enhance your ability to remember messages, identify the central ideas, summarize the message in an easy-to-retain form, and repeat (aloud or to yourself) key terms and names.

remote audience   The audience that receives the speech from those who heard/read it or heard/read about it.

research   The systematic search for information; an investigation of the relevant information on a topic; an inquiry into what is known or thought about a subject.

responding   A stage in the listening process in which you react to the messages.

restrained cultures   Cultures that foster the curbing of immediate gratification and regulate it by social norms. Opposed to *indulgent cultures.*

rhetorical question   A question that is used to make a statement or to produce a desired effect rather than secure an answer.

role   The part an individual plays in a group; an individual's function or expected behavior.

round table   A small group format in which group members arrange themselves physically (usually in chairs) in a circular or semicircular pattern.

secondary sources   Materials that interpret, comment on, analyze, or summarize primary source material. Distinguished from *primary sources* and *tertiary sources.*

selective exposure   A principle of persuasion that argues that listeners actively seek out information that supports their opinions, beliefs, and values while actively avoiding information that would contradict these opinions, beliefs, and values.

self-affirmation   A positive statement about oneself.

short-term-oriented cultures   Cultures in which people look more to the past and the present; these cultural members spend their resources for the present and want quick results from their efforts. Opposed to *long-term-oriented cultures.*

simile   A figure of speech in which a speaker compares two unlike things using the words *like* or *as.*

situational approach   An approach to leadership that emphasizes that the leader's style must vary on the basis of the specific situation.

small group   A collection of individuals who are connected to one another by some common purpose, are interdependent, have some degree of organization among them, and see themselves as a group.

social loafing   A theory that holds that people exert less effort when part of a group than when working individually.

social proof   Examples of other people who do or don't do as you want the audience to do.

social-psychological context   The status relationships among speakers, the formality of the situation, the norms of a group or organization; you don't talk the same way in the cafeteria as you would at a formal dinner at your boss's house.

sociological audience analysis   An analysis of such audience characteristics as age, gender, and educational levels.

spatial pattern   An organizational scheme in which the main topics of a speech are arranged in spatial terms, for example, high to low or east to west.

speaker   The one who presents the speech.

special occasion speech   A speech designed for and presented at some specific occasion such as a commencement speech at a graduation or a toast at a wedding.

specific purpose   The information you want to communicate (in an informative speech) or the attitude or behavior you want to change (in a persuasive speech).

speeches of definition   Informative speeches devoted to explaining the meaning of a concept.

speeches of demonstration Informative speeches in which the speaker shows the audience how to do something or how something operates.

speeches of description Informative speeches in which you explain an object, person, event, or process.

state apprehension A fear that is specific to a given communication situation. Opposed to *trait apprehension*.

statistics Summary numbers such as the mean (or average) or the mode (or most common score).

stereotyping Using a generalized designation for a group of people that fails to acknowledge individual differences; using language that implies that all people of a group are the same.

structure-function pattern An organizational pattern in which the speech is divided into two parts, one dealing with structure and one with function.

supporting materials Usually used in reference to public speaking; enlarging a concept or principle through the use of examples, illustrations, narratives, testimony, definitions, statistics, and visual aids.

symposium–forum A moderated group presentation with prepared speeches on various aspects of a topic, followed by a question-and-answer session with the audience.

symposium A small group format where each member delivers a prepared presentation much like a public speech.

synecdoche A figure of speech in which a part of an object is used to stand for the entire object as in *green thumb* for *gardener*.

systematic desensitization A theory and technique for dealing with fears (such as *communication apprehension*) in which you gradually expose yourself to and develop a comfort level with the fear-causing stimulus.

taboo topics Subjects that violate a culture's principles of appropriateness and that are best avoided in public speeches.

team A particular kind of small group that is constructed for a specific task whose members have clearly defined roles, are committed to achieving the same goal, and are content focused.

template outline An outline in which the essential parts of the speech are identified with spaces for these essential parts to be filled in; a learning device for developing speeches.

temporal context A message's position within a sequence of events; the time in history in which the communication takes place.

temporal pattern An organizational scheme, often referred to as chronological, in which the main points of a speech are arranged chronologically, for example, from past to present.

tertiary sources A combination of primary and secondary source materials. Distinguished from *primary sources* and *secondary sources*.

testimonial A persuasive and often fallacious technique in which the speaker uses the authority or image of some positively evaluated person to gain your approval or of some negatively evaluated person to gain your rejection.

testimony A form of supporting material consisting of the opinions or eyewitness report of another person.

thesis The main assertion of a message—for example, the theme or central idea of a public speech.

thin entering wedge A persuasive fallacy in which a speaker argues against a position on the grounds that it is a thin entering wedge that will open the floodgates to all sorts of catastrophes, though there is no evidence to support such results.

time management The efficient use of the available time.

toast A special occasion speech designed to celebrate a person or an occasion.

topic generators Computer programs that generate a variety of subject matter topics, often useful for finding ideas for speeches and compositions.

topic The subject matter of the speech.

topical pattern An organizational pattern in which a topic is divided into its component parts.

topoi A system for analyzing a topic according to a preestablished set of categories.

trait apprehension A general fear of communication, regardless of the specific situation. Opposed to *state apprehension*.

traits approach An approach to leadership that argues that leaders must possess certain qualities if they're to function effectively.

transfer A persuasive technique in which a speaker associates an idea with something you respect to gain your approval or with something you dislike to gain your rejection.

transformational approach An approach to leadership that emphasizes elevating and empowering the group's members.

transitions Words, phrases, or sentences that help your listeners follow the development of your thoughts and arguments and get an idea of where you are in your speech.

understanding A stage in the listening process in which you decode the speaker's signals and grasp their meaning.

unfilled pauses Silences of unusually long duration.

value Relative worth of an object; a quality that makes something desirable or undesirable; ideals or customs about which we have emotional responses, whether positive or negative.

volume The relative intensity of the voice.

"what if" questions Questions of anticipation, useful in considering and preparing for the unexpected.

Who? What? Why? Where? When? pattern An organizational pattern dividing the speech into sections that answer the questions *who, what, why, where,* and *when*.

you-messages A type of message in which the speaker avoids personal responsibility for the message and blames the other person.

References

Akinnaso, F. N. (1982). On the differences between spoken and written language. *Language and Speech, 25* (Part 2), 97–125.

Albright, M. K. (1998, June 15). North Atlantic Treaty Organization. *Vital Speeches of the Day, 64*, 518–520.

Alessandra, T. (1986). How to listen effectively. *Speaking of success* [videotape series]. San Diego, CA: Levitz Sommer Productions.

Allan, K., & Burridge, K. (2007). *Forbidden words: Taboo and the censoring of language.* Cambridge, UK: Cambridge University Press.

Allen, R. L. (1997, October 6). People—the single point of difference—listening to them. *Nation's Restaurant News, 31*, 130.

Annan, K. (2006). *General Assembly Sixty-first Session 10th plenary meeting.* Retrieved from http://unbisnet.un.org

Anthony, C. (2012). Put an end to convenience devocalization. In L. G. Schnoor (Ed.), *Winning orations* (pp. 63–66). Mankato, MN: Interstate Oratorical Association.

Associated Press. (2013, January 10). New York Gov. Cuomo proposed gun, ammo magazine limits in fiery speech. Retrieved from foxnews.com/politics/2013/01/10

Axtell, R. E. (1990). *Do's and taboos of hosting international visitors.* New York, NY: Wiley.

Axtell, R. E. (1993). *Do's and taboos around the world* (3rd ed.). New York, NY: Wiley.

Axtell, R. E. (2007). *Essential do's and taboos. The complete guide to international business and leisure travel.* Hoboken, NJ: Wiley.

Ayres, J. (2005, April). Performance visualization and behavioral disruption: A clarification. *Communication Reports, 18*, 55–63.

Ayres, J., & Hopf, T. S. (1992). Visualization: Reducing speech anxiety and enhancing performance. *Communication Reports, 5*, 1–10.

Ayres, J., & Hopf, T. S. (1993). *Coping with speech anxiety.* Norwood, NJ: Ablex.

Ayres, J., Hopf, T., & Ayres, D. M. (1994, July). An examination of whether imaging ability enhances the effectiveness of an intervention designed to reduce speech anxiety. *Communication Education, 43*, 252–258.

Barker, L. L. (1990). *Communication* (5th ed.). Englewood Cliffs, NJ: Prentice-Hall.

Barker, L. L., Edwards, R., Gaines, C., Gladney, K., & Holley, F. (1980). An investigation of proportional time spent in various communication activities by college students. *Journal of Applied Communication Research, 8*, 101–109.

Beatty, M. J. (1988). Situational and predispositional correlates of public speaking anxiety. *Communication Education, 37*, 28–39.

Bechler, C., & Johnson, S. D. (1995). Leadership and listening: A study of member perceptions. *Small Group Research, 26*, 77–85.

Beck, A. T. (1988). *Love is never enough.* New York, NY: Harper & Row.

Beebe, S. A., & Masterson, J. T. (2012). *Communicating in small groups: Principles and practices* (10th ed.). Boston, MA: Allyn & Bacon.

Bellafiore, D. (2005). *Interpersonal conflict and effective communication.* Retrieved from http://www.drbalternatives.com/articles/cc2.html

Benne, K. D., & Sheats, P. (1948). Functional roles of group members. *Journal of Social Issues, 4*, 41–49.

Bennis, W., & Nanus, B. (1985). *Leaders: The strategies for taking charge.* New York, NY: Harper & Row.

Bennis, W., & Nanus, B. (2003). *Leaders: Strategies for taking charge.* New York, NY: Harpercollins.

Benson, S. G., & Dundis, S. P. (2003, September). Understanding and motivating health care employees: Integrating Maslow's hierarchy of needs, training and technology. *Journal of Nursing Management, 11*, 315–320.

Bishop, S. (2006). *Develop your assertiveness.* London, UK: Kogan Page.

Bodie, G. D. (2010). A racing heart, rattling knees, and ruminative thoughts: Defining, explaining, and treating public speaking anxiety. *Communication Education, 59*, 70–105.

Bok, S. (1978). *Lying: Moral choice in public and private life.* New York, NY: Pantheon.

Boyle, J. (2015). Spyware stalking: Time to take back the technology. In L. G. Schnoor (Ed.), *Winning orations* (pp. 32–34). Mankato, MN: Interstate Oratorical Association.

Brownell, J. (2013). *Listening: Attitudes, principles, and skills* (5th ed.). New York: Routledge.

Brownell, J. (2015). *Listening: Attitudes, principles, and skills* (4th ed.). Boston, MA: Allyn & Bacon.

Burgoon, J., Guerrero, L., & Floyd, K. (2010). *Nonverbal communication.* Boston, MA: Allyn & Bacon.

Burke, K. (1950). *A rhetoric of motives.* New York, NY: Prentice-Hall.

Butler, M. M. (2005). Communication apprehension and its impact on individuals in the work place. Howard University. *Dissertation Abstracts International: A. The Humanities and Social Sciences, 65*(9-A), 3215.

Cahill, T. (2012). Law school: A degree, a debt, and unemployment. In L. G. Schnoor (Ed.), *Winning orations* (pp. 67–70). Mankato, MN: Interstate Oratorical Association.

Chase, S. (1956). *Guides to straight thinking, with 13 common fallacies.* New York, NY: HarperCollins.

Cialdini, R. (2013). The uses (and abuses) of influence. *Harvard Business Review, 91*(7–8), 76–81.

Cialdini, R. T. (1984). *Influence: How and why people agree to things.* New York, NY: Morrow.

Clark, H. (1974). The power of positive speaking. *Psychology Today, 8*(102), 108–111.

Colpean, M. (2012). Silencing the vote: Legislative disenfranchisement. In L. G. Schnoor (Ed.), *Winning orations* (pp. 46–48). Mankato, MN: Interstate Oratorical Association.

Crawford, L. (2005). *Speech before World Pharma IT Congress.* Retrieved from http://www.fda.gov

Crowley, A. (1999, August 30). Project leaders wanted. *PC Week,* 76.

Cuddy, A. (2015). *Presence: Bringing your boldest self to your biggest challenges.* New York: Little, Brown and Company.

Davidson, J. (2014). Nature's bounty: The psychobiotic revolution. *Psychology Today.* Retrieved from https://www.psychologytoday.com/articles/201403/natures-bounty-the-psychobiotic-revolution

deBono, E. (1967). *Lateral thinking.* New York, NY: Harper Paperbacks.

deBono, E. (1976). *Teaching thinking.* New York, NY: Penguin.

Decenteceo, N. (2015). Life on the farm: Poultry factors farm abuse. In L. G. Schnoor (Ed.), *Winning orations* (pp. 17–19). Mankato, MN: Interstate Oratorical Association.

Dejong, W. (1979). An examination of self-perception mediation of the foot in the door effect. *Journal of Personality and Social Psychology, 37,* 2221–2239.

DePino, D. (2012). Lost to silence. In L. G. Schnoor (Ed.), *Winning orations* (pp. 43–45). Mankato, MN: Interstate Oratorical Association.

DeVito, J. A. (1974). *General semantics: Guide and workbook* (Rev. ed.). DeLand, FL: Everett/Edwards.

DeVito, J. A. (1976). Relative ease in comprehending yes/no questions. In J. Blankenship & H. G. Stelzner (Eds.), *Rhetoric and communication* (pp. 143–154). Urbana, IL: University of Illinois Press.

DeVito, J. A. (1981). *The psychology of speech and language: An introduction to psycholinguistics.* Washington, DC: University Press of America.

DeVito, J. A. (1996). *Brainstorms: How to think more creatively about communication (or about anything else).* Boston, MA: Allyn & Bacon.

DeVito, J. A. (2010). *The interviewing guidebook,* 2nd ed. Boston, MA: Pearson.

DeVito, J. A. (2014). *The nonverbal communication book.* Dubuque, IA: Kendall-Hunt.

Dillard, J. P., & Marshall, L. J. (2003). Persuasion as a social skill. In J. O. Greene & B. R. Burleson (Eds.), *Handbook of communication and social interaction skills* (pp. 479–514). Mahwah, NJ: Erlbaum.

Djietror, J. (2013). But aren't they starving. In L. G. Schnoor (Ed.), *Winning orations* (pp. 124–126). Mankato, MN: Interstate Oratorical Association.

Dodd, C. (2007). Senator Dodd speaks at Rev. Jesse Jackson's Wall Street Summit. *Chris Dodd United States Senator for Connecticut.* Retrieved from http://dodd.senate.gov

Dwyer, K. K. (2005). *Conquer your speech anxiety* (2nd ed.). Belmont, CA: Wadsworth.

Eilola, A. (2012). Better serving those who served. In L. G. Schnoor (Ed.), *Winning orations* (pp. 80–83). Mankato, MN: Interstate Oratorical Association.

Eisenberg, N., & Strayer, J. (1987). *Empathy and its development.* New York, NY: Cambridge University Press.

Ekman, P., Friesen, W. V., & Ellsworth, P. (1972). *Emotion in the human face: Guidelines for research and an integration of findings.* New York, NY: Pergamon Press.

Ellis, A. (1988). *How to stubbornly refuse to make yourself miserable about anything, yes anything.* Secaucus, NJ: Lyle Stuart.

Emmert, P. (1994). A definition of listening. *Listening Post, 51,* 6.

Erber, R., & Erber, M. W. (2011). *Intimate relationships: Issues, theories, and research* (2nd ed.). Boston, MA: Allyn & Bacon.

Feinstein, D. (2006, October 23). *Gang violence: An environment of fear.* Speech delivered at the Gang Summit hosted by the U.S. Department of Justice. Retrieved from http://feinstein.seate.gov/public

Fensholt, M. (2003, June). There's nothing wrong with taking written notes to the podium. *Presentations, 17,* 66.

Fielder, F. E. (1967). *A theory of leadership effectiveness.* New York, NY: McGraw-Hill.

Floyd, J. J. (1985). *Listening: A practical approach.* Boston, MA: Allyn & Bacon.

Forbes, A. (2012). Prioritize children. In L. G. Schnoor (Ed.), *Winning orations* (pp. 103–106). Mankato, MN: Interstate Oratorical Association.

Fraser, B. (1990, April). Perspectives on politeness. *Journal of Pragmatics, 14,* 219–236.

Freedman, J., & Fraser, S. (1966). Compliance without pressure: The foot-in-the-door technique. *Journal of Personality and Social Psychology, 4,* 195–202.

Frey, K. J., & Eagly, A. H. (1993, July). Vividness can undermine the persuasiveness of messages. *Journal of Personality and Social Psychology, 65,* 32–44.

Fukushima, S. (2000). *Requests and culture: Politeness in British English and Japanese.* New York, NY: Peter Lang.

Galinsky, A. D., & Kilduff, G. J. (2013). Be seen as a leader. *Harvard Business Review 91,* 127–130.

Gamble, T. K., & Gamble, M. W. (2003). *The gender communication connection.* Boston, MA: Houghton Mifflin.

Gates, B. (2004). *Bill Gates—United Nations Media Leaders Summit on HIV/AIDS.* Retrieved from http://www.gatesfoundation.org/speeches-commentary/Pages/bill-gates-un-media-summit-hiv.aspx

German, K. M., Gronbeck, B. E., Ehninger, D., & Monroe, A. H. (2013). *Principles of public speaking* (18th ed.). Boston, MA: Pearson.

Giuliani, R. (1995, September 19). *Address Before the United Nations General Assembly.* Retrieved from http://home2.nyc.gov/html/records/rwg/html/96/united.html

Glucksberg, S., & Danks, J. H. (1975). *Experimental psycholinguistics: An introduction*. Hillsdale, NJ: Erlbaum.

Goldstein, N. J., Martin, S. J., & Cialdini, R. B. (2008). *Yes! 50 scientifically proven ways to be persuasive*. New York, NY: Free Press.

Grant, A. (2016). Three quick tips for speaking with presence and power. *Fast Company*. Retrieved from http://www.fastcompany.com/3056760/how-to-be-a-success-at-everything/three-quick-tips-for-speaking-with-presence-and-power

Groves, J. (2014). Fifty years later: Revisiting Gideon. In L. G. Schnoor (Ed.), *Winning orations* (pp. 135–137). Mankato, MN: Interstate Oratorical Association.

Gudykunst, W. B., & Kim, Y. Y. (Eds.). (1992). *Readings on communication with strangers: An approach to intercultural communication*. New York, NY: McGraw-Hill.

Gudykunst, W., & Nishida, T. (1984). Individual and cultural influence on uncertainty reduction. *Communication Monographs, 51*, 23–36.

Gudykunst, W., Yang, S., & Nishida, T. (1985). A cross-cultural test of uncertainty reduction theory: Comparisons of acquaintance, friend, and dating relationships in Japan, Korea, and the United States. *Human Communication Research, 11*, 407–454.

Hager, A. (2015). Improper repositioning of Native American children. In L. G. Schnoor (Ed.), *Winning orations* (pp. 119–121). Mankato, MN: Interstate Oratorical Association.

Hall, E. T. (1976). *Beyond culture*. Garden City, NY: Doubleday.

Hall, E. T., & Hall, M. R. (1987). *Hidden differences: Doing business with the Japanese*. New York, NY: Doubleday.

Hall, J. A. (2006). Women's and men's nonverbal communication: Similarities, differences, stereotypes and origins. In V. Manusov & M. L. Patterson (Eds.), *The Sage handbook of nonverbal communication* (pp. 201–218). Thousand Oaks, CA: Sage.

Han, S. P., & Shavitt, S. (1994). Persuasion and culture: Advertising appeals in individualistic and collectivist societies. *Journal of Experimental Social Psychology, 30*, 326–350.

Hayakawa, S. I., & Hayakawa, A. R. (1990). *Language in thought and action* (5th ed.). New York, NY: Harcourt Brace Jovanovich.

Hendry, J. (1995). *Wrapping culture: Politeness, presentation, and power in Japan and other societies*. New York, NY: Oxford University Press.

Herrick, J. A. (2004). *Argumentation: Understanding and shaping arguments*. State College, PA: Strata Publishing.

Hersey, P., Blanchard, K. H., & Johnson, D. E. (2001). *Management of organizational behavior: Leading human resources* (8th ed.). Upper Saddle River, NJ: Prentice-Hall.

Hesketh, B., & Neal, A. (2006). Using "war stories" to train for adaptive performance: Is it better to learn from error or success? *Applied Psychology: An International Review, 55*, 282–302.

Higgins, J. M. (1994). *101 creative problem solving techniques*. New York, NY: New Management Publishing.

Hill, T. (2015). To seize and profit: Civil forfeiture and the end of altruistic justice. In L. G. Schnoor (Ed.), *Winning orations* (pp. 110–112). Mankato, MN: Interstate Oratorical Association.

Himle, J. A., Abelson, J. L., & Haghightgou, H. (1999, August). Effect of alcohol on social phobic anxiety. *American Journal of Psychiatry, 156*, 1237–1243.

Hinderliter, D. (2013). Eating better through reducing food waste. In L. G. Schnoor (Ed.), *Winning Orations* (pp. 109–111). Mankato, MN: Interstate Oratorical Association.

Hofstede, G., Hofstede, G., & Minkov, M. (2010). *Cultures and organizations: Software of the mind* (3rd ed.). New York, NY: McGraw-Hill.

Hofstrand, D. (2006). Retrieved from http://www.extension.iastate.edu

Holmes, J. (1995). *Women, men and politeness*. New York, NY: Longman.

Jaksa, J. A., & Pritchard, M. S. (1994). *Communication ethics: Methods of analysis* (2nd ed.). Belmont, CA: Wadsworth.

Janis, I. (1983). *Victims of group thinking: A psychological study of foreign policy decisions and fiascoes* (2nd ed.). Boston, MA: Houghton Mifflin.

Joel, B. (1993). *Commencement address Billy Joel*. Retrieved from http://www.berklee.edu/commencement/past/bjoel.html

Johannesen, R. L. (1996). *Ethics in human communication* (5th ed.). Prospect Heights, IL: Waveland Press.

Johnson, C. E. (1987). An introduction to powerful and powerless talk in the classroom. *Communication Education, 36*, 167–172.

Johnson, S. D., & Bechler, C. (1998). Examining the relationships between listening effectiveness and leadership emergence: Perceptions, behaviors, and recall. *Small Group Research, 29* (August), 452-471.

Kelly, M. S. (2006). *Communication@work: Ethical, effective, and expressive communication in the workplace*. Boston, MA: Allyn & Bacon.

Kelly, P. K. (1994). *Team decision-making techniques*. Irvine, CA: Richard Chang Associates.

Kenrick, D. T., Neuberg, S. L., & Cialdini, R. B. (2010). *Social psychology: Goals in interaction* (4th ed.). Boston, MA: Allyn & Bacon.

Kiel, J. M. (1999, September). Reshaping Maslow's hierarchy of needs to reflect today's educational and managerial philosophies. *Journal of Instructional Psychology, 26*, 167–168.

King, P. E., Schrodt, P., & Weisel, J. J. (2009). The instructional feedback orientation scale: Conceptualizing and validating a new measure for assessing perceptions of instructional feedback. *Communication Education, 58*, 235–261.

Kleinke, C. L. (1986). *Meeting and understanding people*. New York, NY: W. H. Freeman.

Kluger, A. N., & DeNisi, A. (1996). The effects of feedback interventions on performance: A historical review, a meta-analysis, and a preliminary feedback intervention theory. *Psychological Bulletin, 119*, 254–284.

Korzybski, A. (1933). *Science and sanity: An introduction to non-Aristotelian systems and general semantics*. Concord, CA: International Society for General Semantics.

Kramarae, C. (1981). *Women and men speaking*. Rowley, MA: Newbury House.

Kucinich, D. J. (2007, January 8). *Rep. Dennis Kucinich: Out of Iraq and back to the American city*. Retrieved from http://www.politicalaffairs.net/article/articleview/4666/

Lakoff, R. (1975). *Language and women's place*. New York, NY: Harper & Row.

Latané, B., Williams, K., & Harkins, S. (1979). Many hands make light the work: The causes and consequences of social loafing. *Journal of Personality and Social Psychology, 37*, 822–832.

Lee, A. M., & Lee, E. B. (1972). *The fine art of propaganda*. San Francisco, CA: International Society for General Semantics.

Lee, A. M., & Lee, E. B. (1995, Spring). The iconography of propaganda analysis. *ETC.: A Review of General Semantics, 52*, 13–17.

Lindsay, B. D. (2015). Caught between the redlines. In L. G. Schnoor (Ed.), *Winning orations* (pp. 64–66). Mankato, MN: Interstate Oratorical Association.

Lustig, M. W., & Koester, J. (2013). *Intercultural competence: Interpersonal communication across cultures* (7th ed.). New York, NY: Allyn & Bacon.

Mahoney, B. (2015). They're not a burden: The inhumanity of anti-homelessness legislation. In L. G. Schnoor (Ed.), *Winning orations* (pp. 20–22). Mankato, MN: Interstate Oratorical Association.

Marano, H. E. (2003). Procrastination: Ten things to know. *Psychology Today*. Retrieved from http://www.psychologytoday.com/articles/200308/procrastination-ten-things-know

Marien, M. (1992, March 15). Education and learning in the 21st century. *Vital Speeches of the Day, 58*, 340–344.

Martin, M. M., & Rubin, R. B. (1994, Winter). Development of a communication flexibility measure. *The Southern Communication Journal, 59*, 171–178.

Martin, M. M., & Rubin, R. B. (1995). A new measure of cognitive flexibility. *Psychological Reports, 76*, 623–626.

Martz, B. (2012). Just do something. In L. G. Schnoor (Ed.), *Winning orations* (pp. 120–122). Mankato, MN: Interstate Oratorical Association.

Maslow, A. (1970). *Motivation and personality*. New York, NY: HarperCollins.

Matsumoto, D. (2006). Culture and nonverbal communication. In V. Manusov & M. L. Patterson (Eds.), *The Sage handbook of nonverbal communication* (pp. 219–235). Thousand Oaks, CA: Sage.

McCroskey, J. C. (1970). Measures of communication-bound anxiety. *Communication Monographs 37*, 269–273

McCroskey, J. C. (2006). *An introduction to rhetorical communication* (9th ed.). Boston, MA: Allyn & Bacon.

Midooka, K. (1990, October). Characteristics of Japanese style communication. *Media, Culture and Society, 12*, 477–489.

Molloy, J. (1981). *Molloy's live for success*. New York, NY: Bantam.

Mora, A. (2006). *Acceptance Speech by Alberto Mora*. Retrieved from http://www.jfklibrary.org/Education+and+Public+Programs/Profile+in+Courage+Award/Award+Recipients/Alberto+Mora/Acceptance+Speech+by+Alberto+Mora.htm

Morreale, S. P., & Pearson, J. C. (2008). Why communication education is important: The centrality of the discipline in the 21st century. *Communication Education, 57* (April), 224–240.

Mullen, B., Salas, E., & Driskell, J. (1989). Salience, motivation, and artifact as contributions to the relation between participation rate and leadership. *Journal of Experimental Social Psychology, 25*, 545–559.

Mullen, B., Tara, A., Salas, E., & Driskell, J. E. (1994). Group cohesiveness and quality of decision making: An interaction of tests of the groupthink hypothesis. *Small Group Research, 25*, 189–204.

Neher, W. W., & Sandin, P. (2007). *Communicating ethically*. Boston, MA: Allyn & Bacon.

Neuliep, J. W., Chaudoir, M., & McCroskey, J. C. (2001). A cross-cultural comparison of ethnocentrism among Japanese and United States college students. *Communication Research Reports, 18*, 137–146.

Nordahl, H. M., & Wells, A. (2007). *Changing beliefs in cognitive therapy*. New York, NY: Wiley.

Northouse, P. G. (1997). *Leadership: Theory and practice*. Thousand Oaks, CA: Sage.

Obama, B. (2006). *Dr. Martin Luther King Memorial dedication speech*. Retrieved from http://obama.senate.gov

Obama, B. (2015). "We Are Not Cured: Obama Discusses Racism in America With Marc Maron." *NPR*. June, 2015. http://www.npr.org/sections/thetwo-way/2015/06/22/416476377/we-are-not-cured-obama-discusses-racism-in-america-with-marc-maron. March, 2016.

Osborn, A. (1957). *Applied imagination* (Rev. ed.). New York, NY: Scribner's.

Pearson, J. C., West, R., & Turner, L. H. (1995). *Gender and communication* (3rd ed.). Dubuque, IA: William C. Brown.

Perkins, D. F., & Fogarty, K. (2006). Active listening: A communication tool. Retrieved from http://edis.ifas.ufl.edu

Petty, R. E., & Wegener, D. T. (1998). Attitude change: Multiple roles for persuasion variables. In D. T. Gilbert, S. T. Fiske, & G. Lindzey (Eds.), *The handbook of social psychology* (4th ed., Vol. 1, pp. 323–390). New York, NY: McGraw-Hill.

Pratkanis, A., & Aronson, E. (1991). *Age of propaganda: The everyday use and abuse of persuasion*. New York, NY: W. H. Freeman.

Reynolds, C. L., & Schnoor, L. G. (Eds.). (1991). *1989 championship debates and speeches*. Normal, IL: American Forensic Association.

Richmond, V. P., & McCroskey, J. C. (1998). *Communication: Apprehension, avoidance, and effectiveness* (5th ed.). Boston, MA: Allyn & Bacon.

Richmond, V. P., Wrench, J. S., & McCroskey, J. C. (2013). *Communication apprehension, avoidance, and effectiveness* (6th ed.). Boston, MA: Pearson.

Riggio, R. E. (1987). *The charisma quotient.* New York, NY: Dodd, Mead.

Rogers, C. (1970). *Carl Rogers on encounter groups.* New York, NY: Harrow Books.

Ryland, K. (2012). Needed: Vaccines against exemptions. In L. G. Schnoor (Ed.), *Winning orations* (pp. 59–62). Mankato, MN: Interstate Oratorical Association.

Salopek, J. (1999, September). Is anyone listening? *Training and Development, 53,* 58.

Schnoor, L. G. (Ed.). (1994). *1991 and 1992 championship debates and speeches.* River Falls, WI: American Forensic Association.

Schnoor, L. G. (Ed.). (2000). *Winning orations of the Interstate Oratorical Association.* Mankato, MN: Interstate Oratorical Association.

Schnoor, L. G. (Ed.). (2008). *Winning orations of the Interstate Oratorical Association.* Mankato, MN: Interstate Oratorical Association.

Schnoor, L. G. (Ed.). (2013). *Winning orations.* Mankato, MN: Interstate Oratorical Association.

Schnoor, L. G. (Ed.). (2014). *Winning orations.* Mankato, MN: Interstate Oratorical Association.

Schnoor, L. G. (Ed.). (2015). *Winning orations.* Mankato, MN: Interstate Oratorical Association.

Schultz, B. G. (1996). *Communicating in the small group: Theory and practice* (2nd ed.). New York, NY: HarperCollins.

Schwartz, B. (2004). *The paradox of choice.* New York, NY: Ecco.

Schwartz, M., & the Task Force on Bias-Free Language of the Association of American University Presses. (1995). *Guidelines for bias-free writing.* Bloomington, IN: Indiana University Press.

Schwartz, S. H., & Rubel, T. (2005). Sex differences in value priorities: Cross-cultural and multi-method studies. *Journal of Personality and Social Psychology, 89,* 1010–1028.

Schwarzenegger, A. (2007). *Prepared text of Gov. Schwarzenegger's remarks to tackle California's broken health care system.* Retrieved from http://gov.ca.gov/index.php?/print-version/speech/5066/

Shaw, M. E., & Gouran, D. S. (1990). Group dynamics and communication. In G. Dahnke & G. W. Clatterbuck (Eds.), *Human communication: Theory and research.* Belmont, CA: Wadsworth.

Singh, N., & Pereira, A. (2005). *The culturally customized web site.* Oxford, UK: Elsevier Butterworth-Heinemann.

Smith, T. E., & Frymier, A. B. (2006, February). Get "real": Does practicing speeches before an audience improve performance? *Communication Quarterly, 54,* 111–125.

Sprague, J., & Stuart, D. (2008). *The speaker's handbook* (8th ed.). Belmont, CA: Wadsworth.

Steil, L. K., Barker, L. L., & Watson, K. W. (1983). *Effective listening: Key to your success.* Reading, MA: Addison-Wesley.

Stephan, W. G., & Stephan, C. W. (1992). *Improving intergroup relations.* Thousand Oaks, CA: Sage.

Surowiecki, J. (2005). *The wisdom of crowds.* New York, NY: Doubleday.

Tannen, D. (1990). *You just don't understand: Women and men in conversation.* New York, NY: Morrow.

The Pew Research Center for the People & the Press. (2006, August 24). Many Americans uneasy with mix of religion and politics. Retrieved from http://people-press.org/reports/pdf/287.pdf

Timmerman, L. J. (2002). Comparing the production of power in language on the basis of sex. In M. Allen & R. W. Preiss (Eds.), *Interpersonal communication research: Advances through meta-analysis* (pp. 73–88). Mahwah, NJ: Erlbaum.

Tompkins, P. S. (2011). *Practicing communication ethics: Development, discernment, and decision-making.* Boston: Allyn & Bacon.

von Oech, R. (1990). *A whack on the side of the head: How you can be more creative* (Rev. ed.). New York, NY: Warner.

Walsh, S. (2012). Re-thinking drug re-importation. In L. G. Schnoor (Ed.), *Winning orations* (pp. 18–20). Mankato, MN: Interstate Oratorical Association.

Watts, R. J. (2004). *Politeness.* Cambridge, UK: Cambridge University Press.

Watzlawick, P. (1978). *The language of change: Elements of therapeutic communication.* New York, NY: Basic Books.

Watzlawick, P., Beavin, J., & Jackson, D. D. (1967). *Pragmatics of human communication: A study of interactional patterns, pathologies, and paradoxes.* New York, NY: Norton.

Withers, L. A., & Vernon, L. L. (2006, January). To err is human: Embarrassment, attachment, and communication apprehension. *Personality and Individual Differences 40,* 99–110.

Wolking, G. (2015). Panhandling bans. In L. G. Schnoor (Ed.), *Winning orations* (pp. 116–118). Mankato, MN: Interstate Oratorical Association.

Wolpe, J. (1957). *Psychotherapy by reciprocal inhibition.* Stanford, CA: Stanford University Press.

Wolvin, A. D., & Coakley, C. G. (1996). *Listening.* Dubuque, IA: William C. Brown.

Wood, W. (2000). Attitude change: Persuasion and social influence. *Annual Review of Psychology, 51,* 539–570.

Worthington, D. L., & Fitch-Hauser, M. E. (2012). *Listening: Processes, functions and competency.* Boston, MA: Pearson.

https://yougov.co.uk/news/YouGov (2013). *YouGov UK.* Retrieved from https://yougov.co.uk/news/

Index

Page numbers with f and t indicate figures and tables.

Credits

Text Credits

Chapter 1

Page 10: McCroskey, James, "Measures of Communication-Bound Anxiety," *Speech Monographs* 37 (1970): 269-277.; **p. 13**: McCroskey, J. (2000). How Apprehensive Are You in Public Speaking in An Introduction To Rhetorical Communication. Boston, MA: Allyn & Bacon.; **p. 20**: Santa Clara University website on Ethical Decision Making: www.scu.edu/ethics/ethics-resources/ethical-decision-making/.

Chapter 2

Page 23: Alessandra, T. (1986). How to listen effectively. Speaking of success [videotape series]. San Diego, CA: Levitz Sommer Productions; Barker, L. L. (1990). *Communication* (5th ed.). Upper Saddle River, NJ: Prentice-Hall; Brownell, J. (2010). Listening: Attitudes, principles, and skills (4th ed.). Boston, MA: Allyn & Bacon.; **p. 30**: Holmes, O. W. (1891) *The Poet at the Breakfast-table: He Talks with His Fellow-boarders and the Reader*. Riverside Press.

Chapter 3

Page 30: Asch, S. (1946). Forming impressions of personality. *Journal of Abnormal and Social Psychology*, 41, 258–290.

Chapter 5

Page 92: Kyle Akerman, a student from the University of Texas at Austin (2010).; **p. 92**: Jillian Collum, a student from the University of Texas at Austin (2008).; **p. 93**: Giuliani, R. September 19, 1995. Address Before the United Nations General Assembly. New York: United Nations.; **p. 94**: Cuomo, A. (2013). State of the State Speech; **p. 96**: Dennis Kucinich (then Representative from Ohio) (2007).; **p. 96**: Greta Wolking, a student of James Madison University (2015).; **p. 97**: Branden DaVon Lindsay, a student of William Carey University.; **p. 98**: John Groves (2014) of the University of Texas at Austin; **p. 101**: Brianna Mahoney, a student of the University of Florida (2015).; **p. 102**: Daniel Handerliter, a student of West Chester University, Pennsylvania (2015).; **p. 102**: Obama, B. (2006). World AIDS Day Speech. The White House.; **p. 102**: Meagan Hagensick, a student of Wartburg College.

Chapter 6

Page 111: Hasset, J. *Psychology in Perspective*, 2nd ed. Copyright © by James Hasset. Reprinted by permission of Addison Wesley Educational Publishers, Inc.; **p. 111**: Data from DeSilver, D. (2015) Growth from Asia drives surge in in U.S. foreign students. Pew Research Center, (www.pewresearch.org). Accessed January 9, 2016.; **p. 112**: Data from the U.S. Census Bureau; **p. 113**: Federal Bureau of Investigation; **p. 113**: Infoplease.com; **p. 114**: National Geographic Creative.

Chapter 7

Page 128: Julius Caesar, in a letter to the Roman Senate; **p. 131**: Djietror, J. (2013). But aren't they starving. *Winning orations*, 124–126, (Ed.) L. Schnoor. Mankato, MN: Interstate Oratorical Association.; **p. 131**: Boyle, J. (2015). Spyware stalking: Time to take back the technology. *Winning orations*, 32–34, (Ed.) L. Schnoor. Mankato, MN: Interstate Oratorical Association.; **p. 136**: Caleb Graves, a student at the University of Texas at Austin (2010).; **p. 136**: Cahill, T. (2012). Law school: A degree, a debt, and unemployment. In L. G. Schnoor (Ed.), *Winning orations*, 67–70, Mankato, MN: Interstate Oratorical Association.; **p. 137**: Dennis Kucinich (then Representative from Ohio) (2007).; **p. 137**: Christopher Dodd (then Senator from Connecticut) (2007).; **p. 138**: Lester M. Crawford (then Acting Commissioner of Food and Drugs) (2005).; **p. 138**: Joel, B. 1995. *Comencement Speech at Berkeley*.; **p. 139**: Barack Obama (then Senator from Illinois) (2006).; **p. 139**: Walsh, S. (2012). Re-thinking drug re-importation. In L. G. Schnoor (Ed.), *Winning orations*, 18–20, Mankato, MN: Interstate Oratorical Association.; **p. 139**: Anthony, C. (2012). *Put an end to convenience devocalization*. In L. G. Schnoor (Ed.), *Winning orations*, 63–66, Mankato, MN: Interstate Oratorical Association.; **p. 139**: Arnold Schwarzenegger (then California Governor) (2007).; **p. 140**: Aviva Pinchas, a student from the University of Texas at Austin.; **p. 141**: Mora, A. (2006). *Acceptance Speech by Alberto Mora*. Retrieved from www.jfklibrary.org/Education+and+Public+Programs/Profile+in+Courage+Award/Award+Recipients/Alberto+Mora/Acceptance+Speech+by+Alberto+Mora.htm; **p. 141**: Sarah Hoppes, a student from Ohio University.; **p. 141**: Christi Liu, a student from the University of Texas at Austin.; **p. 141**: Linse Christensen, a student from Northern State University; **p. 141–142**: Martz, B. (2012). *Just do something*. In L. G. Schnoor (Ed.), *Winning* *orations*, 120–122, Mankato, MN: Interstate Oratorical Association.; **p. 142:** Colpean, M. (2012). Silencing the vote: Legislative disenfranchisement. In L. G. Schnoor (Ed.), *Winning orations*, 46–48, Mankato, MN: Interstate Oratorical Association.; **p. 142:** DePino, D. (2012). Lost to silence. In L. G. Schnoor (Ed.), *Winning orations*, 43–45, Mankato, MN: Interstate Oratorical Association.; **p. 142:** Madeleine K. Albright (then U.S. Secretary of State) (1998); **p. 143:** Forbes, A. (2012). Prioritize children. In L. G. Schnoor (Ed.), *Winning orations*, 103–106, Mankato, MN: Interstate Oratorical Association.; **p. 144:** Eilola, A. (2012). Better serving those who served. In L. G. Schnoor (Ed.), *Winning orations* (80–83). Mankato, MN: Interstate Oratorical Association.

Chapter 8

Page 159: Dickens, C. (1859). *A Tale of Two Cities*. London: Chapman & Hall.

Chapter 9

Page 183: Betsy Heffernan, a student from the University of Wisconsin.

Chapter 10

Page 201: German, Gronbeck, Ehninger, & Monroe. (2013). *Principles of Public Speaking*. New York: Routledge.; **p. 208:** Based on Maslow, A. (1970). *Motivation and Personality*. New York: HarperCollins.; **p. 212:** Anan, K. September (September 16, 2006). *Pushing Rocks to the Top of the Mountain*. United Nations Publications Board.

Chapter 11

Page 226: Reprinted by permission of The Elizabeth Taylor Trust; **p. 228:** Copyright ©2015 TheHuffingtonPost.com, Inc.; **p. 229–230:** Barack. B. (February 27, 2013). President Obama Dedicates a Statue Honoring Rosa Parks. www.whitehouse.gov/photos-and-video/video/2013/02/27/president-obama-dedicates-statue-honoring-rosa-parks#transcript; **p. 234:** Eulogy by Bernard J. Brommel; **p. 235:** Gehrig, L. (1939). Farewell Speech to Baseball.

Chapter 12

Page 253: Janis, I. (1983). *Victims of group thinking: A psychological study of foreign policy decisions and fiascoes* (2nd ed.). Boston, MA: Houghton Mifflin.

Appendix

Page 265–267: Courtesy of Joseph DeVito.; **p. 268–269:** Courtesy of Joseph DeVito.; **p. 270–273:** Blake Joseph Bergeron, a student from the University of Texas at Austin; **p. 274–277:** Farrah Bara, a student from the University of Texas at Austin; **p. 278–282:** Kevin King, a student from from the University of Texas at Austin.

Photo Credits

Chapter 9

Page 180: Shutterstock/michaeljung; **p. 185:** Shutterstock/Peter Bernik; **p. 186:** Shutterstock/Monkey Business Images; **p. 190:** Shutterstock/Andrey Popov; **p. 191:** Shutterstock/Pressmaster.

Chapter 10

Page 195: Digital Vision/Photodisc/Getty Images; **p. 200:** Andrey Popov/Shutterstock; **p. 212:** Michael Mardo; **p. 217:** Blend Images/Alamy Stock Photo.

Chapter 11

Page 223: Darren Lehane/Alamy; **p. 226:** Matt Sayles/Invision/AP; **p. 226:** Matt Sayles/Invision/AP; **p. 228:** Everett Collection Inc/Alamy; **p. 230:** Olivier Douliery/Pool via CNP/Alamy Live News; **p. 235:** Mark Rucker/Transcendental Graphics/Getty Images.

Chapter 12

Page 239: Maskot/Getty Images; **p. 245:** John Lund/Alamy; **p. 247:** Wavebreak Media LTD/123RF.com; **p. 251:** Stock Connection Blue/Alamy; **p. 260:** Hero Images Inc./Alamy.